THE

Perceptive

MUSIC LISTENER

by *Hans Tischler*

Chicago Musical College
of Roosevelt University

PRENTICE-HALL, INC.

Englewood Cliffs   *1955*

TO MY WIFE

ACKNOWLEDGMENTS

I wish to thank several people whose help has been essential to the completion of this book.

Professor Howard Murphy of Columbia Teachers College in New York has earned my special gratitude for his final revision of the entire manuscript, which he accomplished with wisdom, scholarliness, and an uncommon depth of understanding. His advice has been invaluable, and he has contributed in hundreds of small and big ways to the completion of this volume.

Mr. David Bush of Chicago has not only aided in refining the style, but has also given many valuable suggestions and, with his excellent gift, rendered the translations of foreign lyrics in a truly poetic English without straying from the literal and musical sense.

Some additional advice concerning the translations has come from Mr. Francis Nipp of Chicago, and the Chicago artist, Mr. Robert Donald Erickson, has helped in the selection of illustrations.

[v]

First and foremost, however, thanks to my wife, Louise, whose many suggestions have been incorporated in the text. Without her patient and ubiquitous help the writing of this book would have been impossible.

The following publishers have graciously permitted quotations from their publications:

Arrow Music Press: Walter Piston, *Symphony No. 2*

Boosey & Hawkes: Béla Bartók, *Concerto for Orchestra*
Ernest Bloch, *String Quartet No. 2*
Aaron Copland, *Billy the Kid*
Gustav Mahler, *The Song of the Earth*
Igor Stravinsky, *Le sacre du printemps*

Elkan-Vogel: Claude Debussy, *L'après-midi d'un faune*
Claude Debussy, *Minstrels*
Maurice Ravel, *Daphnis et Chloé*
Maurice Ravel, *Bolero*

Mercury Music Co.:   Francis Poulenc, *Toccata*

New World Music Co.:   George Gershwin, *Prelude No. 3*

G. Schirmer, Inc.:   Samuel Barber, *Piano Sonata, op. 26*

TABLE OF CONTENTS

[vii]

PART II

COMPOSITE WORKS

PART **III**

LARGE SINGLE PIECES

VI ADDITIVE FORMS, 203

IX ENSEMBLE WORKS, 283

X ORCHESTRAL MUSIC, 315

APPENDICES

LIST OF MUSICAL EXAMPLES

[xv]

LIST OF PLATES

THE APPROACH

Music is a universal companion of man. Today we usually think of it as the product of a highly skilled composer who puts on his work the stamp of his own ingenuity and personality. But music is not merely the result of conscious effort. Its primitive manifestations, such as shouting, thumping, or clapping, are immediate reactions to basic stimuli: They help dispel the primeval fear of loneliness, relax nervous tensions, calm emotions, and give expression to moods. In addition, imitation of sounds of nature—of beasts, birds, insects, rivers, or wind—aids primitive man in self-defense and in stalking game.

In response to the needs of organized society, man developed music beyond this role of filling basic individual needs, and it became a means by which the community could share emotions and moods, and even information (as in the singing of epics and ballads). The war cry—the spontaneous shout of the individual fighter

—was turned into formal sword dances and march music; the sharp command of the overseer and the anguished response of the laborer evolved into work songs, such as the "Heave-ho!" of the sea-chantey; the shrieks and murmurs accompanying worship and exorcism took the form of chants, hymns, and ritual dances.

A further step was taken: As tools and machines gave man some leisure from the task of meeting the needs of the body, music, too, gradually lost its connection with these needs. It became an art satisfying spiritual and aesthetic cravings, enriching men emotionally, and stimulating their imagination and thought. Music came to be valued for the continuity, the logic, the finesse of texture and design it revealed. Thus, attentive, appreciative listening, based on some technical knowledge, began to play an important role in daily social living.

So did historical information, which enables one to understand the relations of music to the other arts and to society in general, and which gives insight into the attitudes of the composers and the periods that produced the various musical styles. Equipped with this information, we are better able to judge and compare different works and styles, and to recognize their significance with respect not only to ourselves but to society at large.

The humanistic implications of music then become clear. Intellectual, technical, ethical, historical, and aesthetic backgrounds illuminate its personal and social values and relationships. The correlation of all these elements produces the highest level of musical experience—a level which, like all ideals, is not so much attained as constantly sought throughout our lives.

This volume is designed to help the reader reach this level of musical experience. To acquire knowledge about music is only part of his task; to apply it, so that genuine aesthetic experience results, is the real goal. Therefore, nearly all ideas expressed in this book are illustrated by examples or derived from them. Some analyses are quite detailed, but the reader who has limited time and wishes to omit these, may do so. (The analyses are set in smaller type. Passages in which technical concepts and listening procedures are explained are set off by a heavy black dot at the beginning and end of such sections.) On the other hand, additional information about composers and their works that does not contribute directly to an understanding of their music has been omitted, and the reader is urged to use the bibliographies for the various sections, given in Appendix II, to achieve a closer acquaintance with these interesting matters.

Learning is aided by understanding how the material to be learned is organized. The reader will find it helpful, therefore, to refer constantly to the Table of Contents, a brief explanation of which follows.

There are several logical classifications of music, but in practice none can be applied with complete accuracy, since transitional and combined types are frequent in any living art, a spiritual organism as difficult to analyze as mankind itself. Nevertheless each of the following five classifications may serve as a basis of discussion.

As a convenient overall arrangement for the book we shall employ a general classification chiefly based on the length and complexity of works. It differentiates (a) short single pieces (Part I); (b) works composed of several short pieces (Part II); (c) large single pieces (Part III); and (d) works composed of several large pieces (Part IV). As we have already said, these headings do not mean to set up a completely rigid classification that would exclude intermediate types.

Each of the four Parts will be further subdivided according to a different principle of classification.

The principle used in Part I relates to the place of music in society. It leads us to distinguish between functional and aesthetic or art music, though this distinction should not be interpreted to mean that the latter is useless. Functional music may serve man in work, war, maintenance of the group (e.g. through ballads and epics), social life (e.g. through the dance), and religious rites. Art music, on the other hand, finds a place in the home, in the concert hall, and in the theatre. Theatre music, however, will be treated in Part II.

Part II follows a historical sequence. According to this method the material presented is divided into medieval, Gothic, Renaissance, Baroque, Classic-Romantic, and contemporary music. Within these classes, study is especially directed toward the emergence of new species of music, such as instrumental music or opera, and toward the recognition and distinction of styles and stylistic trends, such as impressionism and expressionism.

Another classification may be based on the types of musical organization. Because vocal and instrumental music follow different lines of organization, they are usually considered in turn. Vocal music is then subdivided according to the literary species involved, such as dramatic, religious, or lyric, and in each of these categories the various standard types are discussed: opera, mass, song, and the like. Instrumental music, on the other hand, is subdivided according to the pattern of the musical material—the subject matter of Part III. It should be noted that these patterns apply to vocal music also, but they are greatly affected by the organization of the text. The merging of literature and music necessarily creates some problems whose solutions are discussed in other contexts.

The last principle of classification is based on the types of musical performance, leading to a first division into vocal and instrumental music. Subdivided according to the number of participants, vocal music falls into (a) solo; (b) ensemble (several soloists); and (c) choral divisions; and instrumental music into (d) solo; (e) ensemble; and (f) orchestral types. Again we shall be concerned only with instrumental music in Part IV.

This arrangement assures the reader some familiarity with basic musical materials before he studies the evolution of styles and their historical significance in Part II. The subsequent consideration of patterns and instrumentation will not merely add important technical information, but will also deepen the understanding of styles and their social implications, and open the way to a practical application of these studies.

PART I

SHORT SINGLE PIECES

I FUNCTIONAL TYPES

WORK SONGS

Primitive Music

Long before concert and dance halls were built, men and women at work, in love, or at worship sang, clapped, stamped—made music. Many daily activities were connected with music, and their successful accomplishment was deemed impossible without it. Music was an integral part of action and was believed to possess magical powers. Modern research, in fact, reaffirms the power of music, though on psychological rather than on magical grounds.

Much interesting music of the type termed primitive exists and functions today, e.g. among American Indians, Eskimos, and certain African, Malayan, and Australian tribes. Folklorists, social scientists, anthropologists, and musicologists have studied portions of it. These studies have contributed to a better understanding of various peoples and their history and social organization. For example, music often furnishes the only clue to relationships among various tribes.

Basic Activities and Functional Types

Human living involves five basic processes: work, defense, social
organization, propagation, and death. For each of these a specific
type of music evolves in most primitive societies: work songs, war
dances, ballads, ritual dances, and chants. It is easily seen that
much of the music we hear around us today stems from these five
types, which are called FUNCTIONAL MUSIC.[1] They will therefore be
discussed in the five sections of this chapter.

Work Songs

We begin by turning our attention to music that accompanies
the first of the five life processes: work. Semi-civilized and civilized
men alike, as long as their vital interest in each task is as yet un-
dulled by the machine, create songs for every situation in their
working day. They sing when sowing and threshing, at the spinning wheel and at the cradle, while felling trees and rowing boats.
In a society composed of guilds, like that of feudal days, songs arise
among the various crafts: Tailors, weavers, carpenters, smiths, all
have songs appropriate to their work. Men working in groups sing
to unify their efforts as they heave a towline, guide a caisson, or
quarry stone.

Industrial man has almost lost such direct touch with music. He
often employs it merely for relaxation after work or as a soothing
background during work in factories and offices. Nevertheless, in
certain work situations music still assumes significance for him. The
regular alternation of tension and relaxation in singing makes labor
easier and more efficient. Where only a combined effort of many
can accomplish a task, regularity of effort and rest is especially
necessary. Music creates such regularity.

Repetition

In the following examples we note the persistent accentuation,
expressing regular motion. These songs are inspired by repetitious
activity, each act requiring little time and few motions; hence the

---

[1] Technical terms appear in small capitals when they are used for the first
time. For purposes of later reference all terms are listed in the Index.

tunes are short and simple, and are repeated as long as the task continues. When such songs are taken from their original context to yield pleasure to a listener, these repetitions are naturally curtailed.

• The following simple but fundamental listening procedure is suggested:

(1) Read in the record album whatever information or comment is offered regarding the music.
(2) Listen to the music.
(3) Listen again and tap out the musical accents that would regulate the implied work.
(4) Play the record once more and sing or hum with it while continuing to tap. •

EXAMPLE 1: *Lake Bunyoni Boat Song* [2]

This song from the eastern Belgian Congo in Central Africa is in all respects typical of the work song: It has many repetitions; a short "verse" by a soloist (the helmsman), sung with slight variations; and a choral response (by the oarsmen) of but one syllable and tone, which suggests, through its recurrence, the regular fall of the oars.

EXAMPLE 2: *Batwa Lullaby*

This song comes from the northeastern Belgian Congo. Repetition, regularity, and the ebb and flow of the voices joining in the choral verse suggest its purpose: to quiet children, overwrought at bedtime. The psychology is interesting: The song invites the children to go to bed; it does not serve to put them to sleep.

In our civilization, too, ballads and chanteys have been continually created to serve as work songs. Two specimens are the following ballads of Southern Negroes:

EXAMPLE 3a: *She done got ugly*

EXAMPLE 3b: *Now your man done gone*

Such work songs may accompany any kind of repetitive work, such as harvesting cotton, and may deal with many themes—dramatic adven-

---

[2] Some recordings not readily found in catalogues are listed in Appendix II under "Recordings Used as Examples."

ture, personal ridicule, the status of the Negro which must be borne with patience and irony, a love affair, or the work the men perform.

From Work Song to Art Song

In other work songs the tunes are longer, approaching in length those of art songs. Such songs are usually created by folk musicians in whom awareness of functional music still lingers. They form a bridge between primitive and art music and often have a particularly broad appeal. A famous instance is:

EXAMPLE 4:   *Song of the Volga Boatmen*

In length and variety the chorus of this song resembles the combined tunes of leader and chorus in the primitive songs. This chorus, *a,* is a full REFRAIN, i.e. a complete, brief tune, repeated in every stanza. It is balanced by a solo verse, *b,* of similar length, sung to a new tune that uses the same ending as the refrain. The heavy accents of the music strongly suggest the action: men leaning against a towline as they haul a heavily loaded scow upstream.

Work songs have inspired many art songs, but usually few of their basic characteristics are retained. In art songs the length of the tune increases, repetitions decrease; accentuation, although often prominent, no longer spurns all change. Some such songs are listed in Appendix II under "Additional Recordings." (Cf. also Example 27, p. 45.)

---

[3] The signs ‖: and :‖ indicate repetition of the music between them, but they are also used throughout this book for text repetitions. The first, ‖: , means the beginning of a repeated passage (but is omitted at the very beginning of a piece), and the second, :‖ , the end. They may be combined in one sign: :‖: .

Meter and Measure

• The measured pace of accents, which in work songs reflects regulated motion, is appropriately called METER in music. The time that elapses between two equally strong accents of the music is known as a MEASURE. Comparable to the inch on the ruler, the measure is the common, regular unit of time (not of music!) in most pieces of our music.[4] •

CONCEPTS AND TOPICS DISCUSSED IN THIS SECTION

accentuation—p. 4
functional music—p. 4
measure—p. 7
meter—p. 7

refrain—p. 6
repetition—p. 4f
work song—p. 4

---

[4] See Appendix I, p. 375, for an explanation of notational symbols connected with the measure.

Section B

WAR DANCES AND MARCHES

Group Defense and Music

Men discovered very early that by banding together against animal or human enemies they could defend themselves better than by fighting alone. Indeed, the individual fights better as a member of a group. One is not only encouraged by the physical and moral support of others but is stimulated by the desire to emulate those battling with him.

The stimulation is considerably increased by a preparation for the fighting, undertaken by the group with the aid of music. Thus, semi-civilized peoples have their war dances which, in higher civilizations, are refined to sword dances, lance drills, and similar activities. These preparatory rituals have been further standardized in the march and the march song, which often assume the function of ceremonial processionals. All such music serves to train muscles and invigorate bodies through exercise; to co-ordinate the activities of many men and concentrate their minds on the task ahead; and finally to parade the men's prowess before the women.

• The suggestions as to procedure given on p. 5 should be applied to the examples below. •

EXAMPLE 5: *Acholi Royal Dance*

This dance from Uganda in central Africa is used as a means to display the prowess of a King and his retinue. Characteristically it employs many varied percussion instruments, against which a recurring, brief tune is intoned. The sway of the music, half march, half dance, is sustained throughout. The excitement increases by a cumulative effect of the repetitions.

The March

Among semi-civilized tribes the accents that help co-ordinate and stimulate physiological reactions are marked by shouting, clapping, stamping, or beating of drums. Drumbeats and strong accentuation, derived from the bands of the Turkish armies that invaded

Europe during the sixteenth and seventeenth centuries, are still characteristic of our military marches, as are repetition and loudness. Like art songs, discussed on p. 6, modern marches have much longer tunes than their primitive ancestors.

Therefore, marches display two features: (1) They usually start with a drumbeat or a fanfare pattern that is heard throughout, and (2) they include several repeated sections. In fact, most modern marches consist of two contrasting marches, each with two repeated sections, whereafter the first march is played again, but without sectional repetitions. One march alone would be too brief. The second march, usually somewhat lyrical, not only doubles the length of the composition, but also provides the contrast in theme and spirit needed to make the return of the first march and the resulting rounded pattern pleasurable.

This second march is known as a TRIO (meaning "three"), a term that is employed by musicians in several contexts. In this instance its application derives from the early use, especially in certain dances, of only three instruments in the second dance, whereas the complete ensemble was employed in the first dance. This tradition lapsed in the eighteenth century, but the name "trio" for a second march has continued in use.

Typical in all respects is:

EXAMPLE 6:   JOHN PHILIP SOUSA [1854–1932]

Washington Post March

Trio

When marches occur as single concert pieces or as parts of larger works, their association with power or war is attenuated but not ignored. The main features discussed above reappear, with modifications, in the following examples.

EXAMPLE 7:   HECTOR BERLIOZ [1803–69]

Hungarian March from "The Damnation of Faust" [1846] [1]

This is a setting of one of Hungary's outstanding national melodies, known as the "Rákóczy March," named after a national hero of Hungary. Composed early in the nineteenth century, possibly after an old folk tune, the Rákóczy March has since been arranged by several serious composers, including Liszt and Kodály, both Hungarians. As arranged here by the French composer, Berlioz, it forms an interlude in a large dramatic work and is handled somewhat freely.

March

Trio

---

[1] The analysis of this example as well as all subsequent analyses are designed to be read not as reading matter but only in conjunction with listening to the music, to which they are meant to be guides.

The *March* starts with a fanfare figure. Both the *March* and the *Trio* have their two repeated sections, but thereafter the *March* is freely expanded: Instead of melodies with a recognizable beginning and end, small musical fragments follow each other restlessly with ever new turns. The only moment of relaxation occurs when, in the middle of this expansion or DEVELOPMENT, the first section of the *March* reappears. The development gives the piece the needed length and dramatic urgency to fit it into the context of the large work. A special attribute of this composition is its brilliancy, clarity, and sharpness without bombast. Berlioz was one of the outstanding orchestrators of the nineteenth century.

The next example departs even further from the usual, simple pattern of marches.

EXAMPLE 8: EDWARD ELGAR [1857–1934]

Pomp and Circumstance, March No. 1

This *March* is introduced by a drumbeat pattern. The two repeated sections of the *March*

are followed by a further passage, called CODA (Italian—tail, end), which rounds off the section. All this is then repeated as a whole and crowned by a second, longer coda, which concludes with the drumbeat pattern of the introduction. The *Trio*

consists of only one long, repeated section. The entire *March* then returns, but without its overall repetition, followed by the *Trio*, also unrepeated, and the work ends with a brief, rousing coda.

Many other types of march music accompany various kinds of ceremony: festival processional marches, wedding and funeral marches, and march songs of youth organizations. Despite some differences, especially with respect to speed or TEMPO, they all share most major characteristics discussed in this section. A few such works are included among the "Additional Recordings" in Appendix II.

Beats and Duple Meter

• Note that all marches and march songs must make possible a regular footfall: left, right, left, right. For this reason there must always be one secondary accent exactly midway between any two main accents. Such equal time values carrying primary or secondary accents are called BEATS in music. Marches always have two or twice two beats in each measure to allow for the regular footfall. Music in which each measure has two beats is said to be in DUPLE METER.

The reader may now turn again to the examples in Section A to determine which are in duple meter: We must be able to march to music in duple meter, or to count ONE, two, ONE, two, allowing an equal time to elapse between any two counts. •

CONCEPTS AND TOPICS DISCUSSED IN THIS SECTION

beat—p. 12   march—p. 8f
coda—p. 11   sectional repetition—p. 9
development—p. 11   trio—p. 9
duple meter—p. 12

SECTION C

BALLADS

Social Memory and Ballads

Man has always felt a need to preserve the memory of important happenings and of the deeds of heroes in war and in peace. He has also felt a need to articulate the aspirations and the traditional values of his society. Several means of recording these things were employed before the art of writing was invented. Among them were the ballads—narrative or lyric poems that are easily remembered because of their meter and rhymes.

As these poems are passed on by word of mouth, music plays a major role in keeping them alive. It furnishes a simple melody, which is co-ordinated, one tone to each syllable, with a line or stanza of the poetry and is repeated over and over in performance. With the aid of these tunes, poems may withstand decay and oblivion for centuries, as they are sung by bards and folk singers at village fairs and carnivals, by grandfathers at the hearth, by hunters around the campfire, and by villagers in front of their doors on summer evenings.

Here are two folk ballads, American and English respectively, which have become part of the concert repertory. They well exemplify the two major types of such works, one describing a socially approved attitude, the other recounting an event.

EXAMPLE 9: *Down in the Valley*

In our society courtship is still carried on in almost the same forms as those evolved by medieval chivalry. *Down in the Valley* exemplifies one of its typical ingredients—the longing for the distant beloved. In its quaint, partially expressed way, the text gives a highly imaginative description of the nostalgia felt by a lover. As is true of all folk ballads, the simple melody serves without change the various lines of the poem, whatever their individual meaning. The poem, in turn, may well be extended through additional stanzas, improvised to suit new occasions.

EXAMPLE 10: *Lord Randall*

The narrative ballad relies on direct, vivid speech and deals with dynamic action rather than with passive narration. The music to this dramatic story of the fiancé who has been poisoned recalls in many respects that of Example 9. The poignancy of the poem is brought home to us both by the simple sing-song rendition of the folk singer and by the highly dramatized performance of the concert singer.

The Art Ballad

Since the music in folk ballads does not change for the different stanzas, varied expression can be imparted only by the singer. It is here that the art ballad makes its contribution. Subtle changes in the tune or in the accompaniment underscore the word meanings. Each of the various speakers in the ballad is sometimes given a characteristic tune, leading to a more complex composition (cf. Example 13). Here are examples of this kind of ballad.

EXAMPLE 11:   HUGO WOLF [1860–1903]

Der Rattenfänger (The Pied Piper, 1888)

Wolf was almost exclusively a song composer. He wrote over two hundred and fifty songs, whose artistic value places him among the four or five greatest masters of the German song or *lied* (plural: *lieder*). When a poet captured his imagination, Wolf would set a large number of his poems to music, all in one creative wave. This is one of his forty-eight songs to words by Johann Wolfgang Goethe (1749–1832).

An explanation regarding the translation of poetic texts is in order before we consider the *Song*. All the translations have been worked out to conform not merely to the words but to the syllables and accents in their original association with the music, so that the student may be enabled to recite the texts while listening to the music. Whereas there may be some better translations in a purely literary sense, none will serve the student's purpose as well. The foreign language is used only where musical examples are given. The musical examples are correlated with single lines of text and have nothing to do with succeeding text lines.

> the man that this distinguished town
>   is much in need of now, at once.
> All rats and mice, however many,
>   and weasels also, if they're present,
> from ev'ry hole I charm them forth,
>   they have to leave and go with me.

2. Also this good and merry singer
       may now and then some children capture,
   even the strongest does he hold,
       when he his magic legends sings.
   And boys, though they may be quite stubborn,
       and girls, however they seem bashful—
   I pluck the strings and make them sound,
       and all must follow after me.

3. Also the many-gifted singer
       sometimes becomes a maid enticer;
   in ev'ry small town where he stops,
       many a girl is lured by him.
   And maidens, though demure they may be,
       and women, though as coy as can be—
   yet all succumb, bewitched with love
       and spell-bound by my magic song.

The three stanzas and the repetition of the first at the end are set to the same music with only minor changes. But note how well Wolf characterizes the sense of "when he his magic legends sings" and "yet all succumb, bewitched with love." With the lengthening of a few tones the eerie lure of the singer is vividly suggested. To understand the artistic effectiveness of these passages we need only think how an actor would slow down in speaking these lines. These are RHYTHMIC changes. They are, moreover, supported by further musical means of characterization, discussed under the following example.

EXAMPLE 12:   ROBERT SCHUMANN [1810–56]

Die beiden Grenadiere (The Two Grenadiers, 1840)

Heinrich Heine's (1797–1856) stirring poem runs as follows:

> *Nach   Frank - reich   zo - gen zwei   Gre - na - dier',*
> 1. Tow'rd France   came   march-ing two   gren - a - diers,
>
> re - turn - ing from bon - dage   in   Rus - sia;

and when they sighted Germany's camps,
   they lowered their faces, anguished.
For then did the two hear the heartbreaking news:
   that France had been thoroughly beaten,
the army of conquerors routed and lost,
   and Napoleon, the emperor, captured!

2. Together they wept, the two grenadiers,
       to hear such desperate tidings.
    One of them cried: "Ah woe is me,
       my old wound again is bleeding!"
    The other said: "The song is done,
       now death alone awaits us;
    but I have wife and child at home,
       who will be lost without me."

3. "What of my wife! What of my child!
       I have much stronger allegiance:
    Let them beg for food when their hunger calls—
       Napoleon, the emperor, captured!
    Now comrade pledge me only this:
       When my last breath has left me,
    then carry my body to France with you,
       and lay me at rest in French soil.

4. The cross of honor with its band
       lay on my heart for ever;
    the musket place within my hand
       and on me gird my sabre.

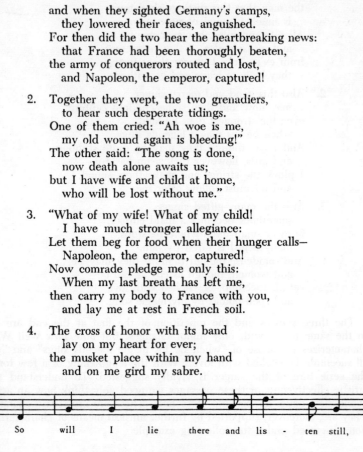

So   will   I   lie   there and   lis - ten still,

a   watch - ful   sen - try, though bur - ied,

till once I hear roar of cannon again
   and neighing of horses at gallop.
Then charges the emperor over my grave,
   ‖:and swords are clanging and flashing;:‖
then full-armed I rise and come out of my grave,
   Napoleon, Napoleon to follow!"

The first three stanzas of this famous *Song* are written to similar
music, but with significant changes to accommodate the words. The

final, longer stanza is set to new music, appropriately involving the
French national anthem, "*La Marseillaise.*"

Note the changes in MELODIC character with the progress from the
initial bitterness and despair to the final triumph of illusory hope. At
first the melodic line breaks, stumbles, descends. At the end of the
second stanza despair, in a rising line, nearly culminates in sobs. When
the resolution to be buried in home soil forms in the first soldier's mind,
however, the music steadies. The hope expressed at the beginning of the
final stanza is mirrored by a fluent, almost winged strain, leading into
the triumphant hymn. Yet the last few measures of the piano postlude
sharply contrast with what has preceded. At the sound of these slow
tones one can almost see the man, erect and with eyes aflame the instant
before, as he tragically collapses.

Our last example is, fittingly, one of the greatest of all art ballads
of the nineteenth century—written though it was by a boy of
eighteen:

EXAMPLE 13:   FRANZ SCHUBERT [1797–1828]

Der Erlkönig (The Elfin King, 1815)

From the beginning, the repeated tones in the accompaniment induce
a tense, expectant atmosphere and suggest the sound of galloping hoofs.
These reiterations set a pattern for many other art ballads throughout
the century. The poem includes, besides brief narrations at beginning
and end, the words of three speakers, for each of whom Schubert found
a characteristic expression. The phantom of the elfin king three times
interrupts the harried dialogue of the father and his delirious son, and
each time the mood changes significantly. The music is thus more complex than in the previous examples.

These are Goethe's (1749–1832) lines:

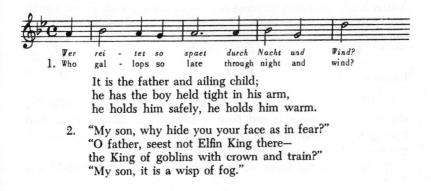

    Wer   rei - tet so   spaet   durch Nacht und   Wind?
1. Who   gal - lops so   late   through night and   wind?

    It is the father and ailing child;
    he has the boy held tight in his arm,
    he holds him safely, he holds him warm.

  2. "My son, why hide you your face as in fear?"
     "O father, seest not Elfin King there—
     the King of goblins with crown and train?"
     "My son, it is a wisp of fog."

"Du   lie - bes   Kind,   komm',   geh   mit   mir!"
"My   love - ly   child,   come   you   with me!"

The finest games, I'll play them with you;
the brightest flowers grow on the beach;
and my mother has fine garments of gold.

4. "My father, my father, now surely you hear
   what Elfin King softly whispers to me?"
   "Be quiet, hush, be quiet, my child;
   through drying leaves there rustles the wind."

5. *Come, darling boy, won't you come with me?*
   All my daughters will your companions be;
   and my daughters dance all night at the stream,
   ‖: *and rock you and dance you and sing you to sleep."*:‖

6. "My father, my father, and do you not see
   his pretty daughters in darkness there?"
   "My son, my son, I see very well,
   old willows are shining yonder so gray."

7. *I love you, child, your beautiful body I ask;*
   if you are not willing, then must I use force!
   "My father, my father, he reaches for me!
   Elf King has wounded me grievously!"

8. The father shudders. He gallops apace,
   in both arms pressing his suffering child.
   The inn he gains with his last strength;
   within his arms his young son was dead.

It is hardly necessary to point out the excitement engendered by the
rapid tone repetitions in the accompaniment or the effect of the last few,
half spoken words, separated from those preceding by a REST, i.e. by
silence. These again are rhythmic effects.

Rhythm

• Rhythm is fundamental in all arts. In music specifically,
rhythm means the ebb and flow of longer and shorter tones and
tone groups. It may be observed in isolation when one taps out all
the tones of a tune without singing its melody.

We have met the term "meter" before, and we have studied several pieces in duple meter. Yet obviously these pieces differed as to the disposition of long and short tones. In each case we counted two or four equal beats, but the number of tones per beat ranged from zero to two or more, as for example in the *Song of the Volga Boatmen* (see p. 6; also Appendix I, p. 377). Consequently these tones did not always coincide with the beat (when we counted), but often occurred afterwards (between counts), on subdivisions of the beat. We refer to such differences in length or time value under the general term "rhythm." •

Meter and Rhythm

• We may now define "meter" as a certain regularity in rhythmic or temporal patterns, a regularity marked by accents. The meter is easily apprehended by tapping out, not the tones of a melody, but only the beats or accents (comparable to every first beat of the short-long pattern of the pulse). By tapping all the tones we become aware of the differences in their duration (rhythm); by tapping only the beats, the regularity of the music (meter) becomes apparent.

This regularity, i.e. meter, may be present in various degrees in certain types of music (cf. p. 67) or may even be entirely absent (cf. Examples 21, 22, pp. 31ff), but varied length of tones and tone groups, i.e. rhythm, is absolutely essential, for rhythm is the primary ingredient in most musical patterns. And in turn, patterns and their recurrence are fundamental elements of art, as they are of intelligence and of life itself. The seasons, day and night, the heartbeat, breathing, sleeping and waking, and growth and decay furnish us with examples of recurrent patterns in life.[1] •

CONCEPTS AND TOPICS DISCUSSED IN THIS SECTION

art ballad—p. 14   melodic character—p. 17
folk ballad—p. 13   rhythm—pp. 15, 19

---

[1] See Appendix I, pp. 375ff for an explanation of rhythmic symbols: notes and rests.

SECTION D

DANCES

Dance, Music, and Social Intercourse

Birth, growth, and marriage are among the most obvious and important facts of human life. (Cf. the discussion of the five basic life processes, p. 4.) They inspire some of the greatest expressions in literature, poetry, philosophy, art, and music. Music, especially in connection with dances, is employed at the ceremony that marks the beginning of maturity (confirmation) and at the celebrations of engagements and weddings. Again, dance and music play an important role when at sowing and harvesting time agrarian peoples solicit the fertility of the earth in ceremonies that identify its fruitfulness with human fertility (cf. Example 62, p. 179ff). Instruments, too, take a prominent part in such rituals. Indeed, in most cultures certain of them are identified with one of the sexes, and frequently it is a capital offense for members of one sex to play, hear, or see the instruments symbolically associated with the other.

On another level of culture these various ceremonies lose their pristine magical meanings and, without in the least diminishing their social value, are employed to facilitate social relationships. In this section our attention is directed to a type of music which has, in many periods and many cultures, served this purpose. One such type is light or dinner music; another, much more important in this respect, is the dance. Unless completely ceremonial, it has always promoted the participants' knowledge of each other. It is music that guides the dance and interprets its spirit.

Origins and Musical Differences of Dances

Dances function on various levels. Some serve the social entertainment of urban people and are accompanied by "popular" music. Then there are folk dances, with music played by small bands that usually improvise their own tunes and accompaniments. Others are adopted by the aristocracy and become court and ballroom dances, with their music often written by composers of art music. Still others are invented by ballet masters or fashionable dancers to satisfy the craving for novelty.

The variety of dances is consequently so great that we must limit our discussion to the dance as it has existed during the past few centuries in Europe and America. As noted in previous sections, the functional types have had a great influence on art music. Therefore, in order to make this section most profitable, the examples are taken from art compositions which, although reflecting actual dances faithfully, are also interesting as music.

Most dances can be easily distinguished by their choreography, i.e. by the patterns of steps, turns, bows, leaps, and other motions, which are combined in many ways. The accompanying music, on the other hand, may serve several types of dances, if they do not differ in meter and tempo. Sometimes a characteristic rhythm or accentuation helps to distinguish the music for various dances, but meter and tempo are the primary elements that do so.

We start with two idealized contemporary dances, that is, pieces intended only to be heard, not danced. Both dances are in duple meter, but they differ in rhythm and tempo.

EXAMPLE 14: GEORGE GERSHWIN [1899–1937]

Prelude No. 3

Copyright 1927 by New World Music Corporation. Copyright Renewed. Reproduced by Permission.

"Fox trot" has become a general term for popular dances of the United States as contrasted with those of Latin America. *Prelude No. 3* by Gershwin, who began as a composer of popular music, clearly suggests the typical fox trot with its rather fast tempo and its simple, straightforward accents on the beats.

In order to accommodate the steps, most dances proceed in groups of two measures. This holds for this *Prelude* also; but being a piano piece rather than a dance, it deviates slightly from the complete regularity of actual dances. There is a brief introduction. Then we hear a brisk tune of eight measures,

followed by a second, equally long,

after which *a* is repeated with slight variants. A third tune of eight
measures,

is heard twice in succession, whereupon a few measures of rapid passage
work outside the regular pattern bring back *a* in a further variant to
round off the *Prelude*.

• The listener should determine the entrance of each new tune;
he should also ascertain, by counting and tapping, the two-measure
groups, and try to acquire a feeling for the entire eight-measure
length of each tune. If one hand is used to tap the first or strong
beat of each measure, and the other to tap the second or weak beat,
the duple meter of the dance will be clearly apparent. •

The second dance in duple meter is by the Spanish composer
and pianist, Albeniz.

EXAMPLE 15: ISAAC ALBENIZ [1860–1909]

Tango in D (Major)

With respect to the regularity of the two-measure dance pattern, this
piece is still freer than the preceding example. It has two ingratiating
tunes that alternate; each, as is typical of the art and folk music of
Spain and South America, appears in several variants:

Albeniz was the first serious composer to use the novel tango of Argentina. In his time it was musically still identical with its parent, the Cuban *habañera;* the characteristic change, made subsequently in Central and North America, consisted in the omission in each measure of the third tone of the accompaniment thus:

habañera rhythm: 𝄆 𝅘𝅥𝅭𝅘𝅥𝅮𝅘𝅥𝅮𝅘𝅥𝅮 𝄇 —tango rhythm 𝄆 𝅘𝅥𝅭𝅘𝅥𝅮, 𝅘𝅥𝅮 𝄇 or 𝄆 𝅘𝅥𝅭𝅘𝅥𝅮𝅘𝅥𝅮𝅘𝅥𝅮 𝄇 .

Syncopation and Triplet

● Although in the accompaniment of the North-American tango no tone commences on the second, presumably accented beat, the listener nevertheless feels the accent that he does not hear. Such an omission of felt accents is called SYNCOPATION. Actually the accent is withdrawn to the preceding tone, introducing the well-known lilt of many Latin-American dances.

The second outstanding characteristic of the tango is the alternate splitting of the beat in the melodic line into either two or three equal subdivisions. When a normal note value [2] is split into three rather than two subdivisions, the resulting group is called a triplet, meaning "three notes instead of two," and is indicated in writing by an oblique "3" above or below the group thus:

$$\text{♩} = \overset{3}{\text{♫♪}}$$

Similarly we speak of a number of other irregular groupings as duols, quradruplets, quintuplets, and the like, but the triplet is by far the most frequently used. ●

---

[1] The notes in small print indicate a brief ornament. These, called GRACE NOTES, are taken so fast that no value is assigned to them. Single grace notes usually have their stems crossed.

[2] See Appendix I, p. 376, for an explanation of note symbols.

Dance Through the Ages

The fox trot, together with its relatives, is probably the most characteristic dance of our time, which may in this respect be called the "age of the fox trot." Indeed, every period of Western civilization can be named according to the dominance of some social dance. This dance makes its appearance during the decline of the previously dominant dance, assumes the lead, and then in its turn declines in prominence. When a new dance age has emerged, the older dances often become art music, no longer danced but listened to, as indicated by the dots in the diagram below. Thus the time from 1650 to the present has been marked by a succession of dominance from minuet through waltz to fox trot, approximately as follows:

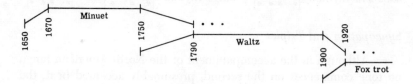

We turn to illustrations of the minuet and the waltz.

EXAMPLE 16:   JEAN-BAPTISTE LULLY [1632–87]

Minuet from "Amadis de Gaule" or
Minuet from "The Temple of Peace"

Lully, though born in Italy, was the leading French composer of his time. Rising rapidly from the status of a kitchen helper to that of royal confidant and ballet master, he finally became the dictator of seventeenth-century French music. If he did not create the minuet, he certainly made it the dance of his era throughout Europe. Its popularity was spread by the armies and the political influence of his patron, Louis XIV (1642–1715).

Any minuet is in two repeated sections, the second often twice as long as the first. Sometimes a second minuet, or trio, is added, after which the first is heard again without repetitions (cf. the organization of the march and trio on p. 9). Both these *Minuets* were composed to accompany actual dancing; they are therefore completely regular.

The waltz, like the minuet, evolved from a peasant dance, the

south-German *ländler* (see *Trio 2*, p. 294). Our example is one of
the best of the hundreds of ballroom dances written by the Viennese
waltz king, Johann Strauss, and his family—his father, Johann, his
brothers, Joseph and Eduard, and Eduard's son, Johann. Its tunefulness bears the mark of genius. Because of their melodic charm
many of Strauss's compositions have become concert favorites.

EXAMPLE 17:   JOHANN STRAUSS [1825–99]

Roses from the South

Like most waltzes, this one consists of a series of single dances, each
itself a waltz. There are four of them, each with its own two tunes. The
series is preceded by an *Introduction* where snatches of tunes from
Dances No. 2 and *1*, are tentatively put forward, and followed by a *Coda*.
Though starting with a new tune, this *Coda* is otherwise a free repetition of tunes previously heard in *Dances No. 3, 1*, and *4*. Here the tran-
quil sequence of complete melodies is abandoned; the object is to find
a satisfactory conclusion, and the tunes intermingle and rush on to the
final climax. (Both *Introduction* and *Coda* are omitted when the music
serves actual dancing.)

No. 3, a

b

No. 4, a

b

Coda

• It is suggested that the listener proceed as follows: Determine where the second section and the repetitions start in the *Minuet*. Note the beginning of the various *Waltzes* and the *Coda* in *Roses from the South*. Try to whistle or sing the various tunes involved. •

Triple Meter

• Tap the meter of these two dances. In both waltz and minuet one hears two equally long secondary beats between any two main accents. In other words, one has to count ONE, two, three, ONE, two, three. Again use one hand for tapping the first beat, the other hand for the others. Obviously one cannot march to this music, for it is not in duple but in TRIPLE METER.

Waltz and minuet are, however, rhythmically different. In the waltz a secondary stress in a measure, when it occurs, is introduced always on the third beat, whereas in the minuet such secondary stresses occur alternately on the second' and third beats and thus produce a characteristic lilt.[3]

The reader may now turn to the examples in Sections A to C and determine which ones were in triple meter.   •

National Dances

Every nation has its own dances. Whereas many of them are still confined to their particular localities, others have become internationally known and have influenced art music. We shall now consider three such dances of various nations. Their national character is revealed both in the costumes worn and in the rhythms employed, though the latter often transcend national limitations. Nevertheless such rhythms are frequently used in art music to evoke associations with particular locales.

EXAMPLE 18:   BEDŘICH (FREDERICK) SMETANA [1824–84]

Polka from "The Bartered Bride" (1866)

The polka was popular throughout Europe between 1830 and 1900. Today it still is the national dance of Czechoslovakia, where it is danced in colorful folk costumes; but it has also remained popular in America and elsewhere. This gay dance is characterized by a vigorous tempo, duple meter, and the frequent rhythm

Smetana is looked upon as the founder of Czech music, and *The Bartered Bride* as Czechoslovakia's national opera. Like the *Waltz* in the preceding example, this *Polka* has an *Introduction*, composed of snatches anticipating the main idea. The first dance, *a*, is followed by two further polkas, *b* and *c*, by partial repetitions of *a* and *b*, and by a faster *Coda*, based on *a*.

----

[3] See Appendix I, p. 378, for an explanation of simple time signatures.

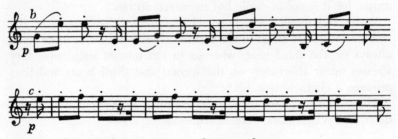

EXAMPLE 19:   FRÉDÉRIC CHOPIN [1810–49]

Mazurka No. 21, op. 30, 4 [4] (in *C*-sharp Minor)

Although Polish by descent only through his mother, and although an emigré from Poland at the age of nineteen, Chopin is justly claimed as Poland's outstanding composer. With his thirteen *Polonaises,* over fifty *Mazurkas,* and several other works, he paid homage to his native country and contributed much to its artistic prestige.

The *mazurka* is one of Poland's national dances; sometimes fiery, sometimes languid, it often contains certain sections to accompany steps for the men only, marked by a vigorous accompaniment. The tempo of *mazurkas* varies; the meter is always triple, the rhythm often

Our example is not, of course, meant to serve dancers, but it does preserve the essential regularity of dances. A brief prelude ushers in an energetic tune, *a,* which is repeated and somewhat spun out:

---

[4] The designation *"opus,"* abbreviated *op.,* was used by music publishers as early as the seventeenth century to keep account of a composer's works. But its regular employment dates from about 1790, when composers began to arrange their works roughly, but not always reliably, in chronological order with the aid of *opus* numbers. (Latin: *opus*—work; plural: *opera.* From the term *"opera in musica"* derives the designation of musico-dramatic works as operas.)

Two further repeated tunes are heard, *b*

and *c*

and then the entire *a* again. An interesting coda, in which a fragment of tune glides gradually downward, brings the piece to a charming, somewhat melancholy close.

EXAMPLE 20:   ARCANGELO CORELLI [1653–1713]

Pastorale from "Concerto No. 8" (Christmas Concerto)

Corelli, one of the foremost organists and violinists of his time, was in the employ of the Catholic Church at Rome. The *pastorale* or *siciliano* *(sicilienne)* is a quietly flowing Italian dance, originating, as its two names imply, with Sicilian peasantry. Between 1680 and 1750 a *pastorale* was frequently included in larger works of art music. Because of its peasant connotation and its general flavor it became associated with the adoration of the shepherds at Christmas. Later in the eighteenth century its vogue declined, but the *pastorale* still lives in such Christmas carols as "Silent Night."

Our example, too, was used to beautify the Christmas season, though without dramatic implications; it gave to the whole work—of which it is an optional last (sixth) portion—the name "Christmas Concerto." The gentle flow is interrupted briefly at the end of the first section,

a slightly different middle section based on *a* follows, after which the first returns.[5]

---

[5] See Appendix I, p. 378f, for an explanation of further meters and time signatures.

Tempo

● Strangely enough, until the sixteenth century composers paid little attention to tempo. Only in the seventeenth century, when Italian music dominated that of all other nations, were names for the various tempos standardized. Since then tempo marks and many other musical terms have remained Italian. Here is a list of the more important tempo markings from the slowest to the fastest:

> *largo, largamente*—broad, very slow
> *lento, grave, adagio* (lit. "at ease"), *larghetto*—slow
> *andante* (lit. "walking"), *andantino*—moderately slow
> *moderato, allegretto*—moderately fast
> *allegro* (lit. "cheerful"), *vivace*—fast
> *presto*—very fast (but before 1750 merely "fast")
> *prestissimo*—as fast as possible

The tempos of the examples discussed in this section were as follows:

> Example 14, Gershwin's *Prelude*—*allegro*
> Example 15, Albeniz's *Tango*—*allegretto*
> Example 18, Smetana's *Polka*—*moderato*
> Example 19, Chopin's *Mazurka*—*allegretto*
> Example 20, Corelli's *Pastorale*—*largo* (but after 1750
> it would have been marked "*larghetto*")

Minuets usually had no tempo mark; sometimes they were played *andante,* and at other times *allegro.* The waltz also, as an active ballroom dance, is not specifically marked, but understood to be *allegro.*[6] ●

---

[6] See Appendix I, p. 404ff, for a list of dances, each with its origin, time of vogue, tempo, and meter.

SECTION E

CHANT AND HYMN

Music and Rite

The contemplation of death is the well-spring of religion. At all stages of civilization religious ritual involves much music. The music may be intended to help drive away demons or attract good spirits, to propitiate gods or invoke their favorable attention. It may be used as a personal confession or as an expression of belief and fervor. In any case, the emotional tone of music enriches and deepens the experience of religious mystery.

There are many types of religious music: the songs of the medicine man, the dances of the boy and girl admitted to adult society, the greetings of solstices, birth and death rituals, magic incantations against enemies. In our society most religious music, though by no means all, is connected with the services (or liturgy) of the various churches. Portions of such music that are used in many services tend to form large works (to be discussed in Part II). The essential features are, however, clearly present also in the independent short pieces discussed in this section.

The oldest liturgy in use in the Occident is the Jewish, from which the first example is taken.

EXAMPLE 21: *Aharei Mot* (After the Death)

The text is *Leviticus* (Third Book of Moses), chapter xvi, verses 1-2. It begins the account of the ritual for the Day of Atonement *(Yom Kippur)* and is chanted on that day:

And the Lord spoke unto Moses after the death of the two sons of Aaron on their (sacrilegious) approach before the Lord (in the tabernacle), when they perished. And the Lord said unto Moses: "Speak unto your brother Aaron, that he come not into the Holy of Holies, within the veil, before the cover which is upon the ark, so that he should not die; for I shall appear in the cloud above the cover. . . ."

This *Chant*—a term applied to unaccompanied liturgical singing in general—sounds like free improvisation; for rhythm in Hebrew chants is not fixed but left to the finesse of the cantor (Latin—singer); and meter is absent. On the other hand, the melodies of all sections are fixed by tradition. Each consists of a group of tones, known as a "trop" or

"mode," [1] which may not be altered, except that the cantor may inter-
polate further, ornamental tones. Thus the beginning of this *Chant* is
based on the following tone groups or MOTIFS:

Va - je - da - ber a - do - nai el Mo - she a - ha - rei mot

Everything else is interpolated by the cantor.

For every festival and for the various needs of prosody (punctuation,
stress on words, and versification) these motifs have been fixed for well
over two thousand years. In early times each probably had a definite
symbolic meaning (such as morning, autumn, sun, glory, death, or love),
transcending the demands of prosody, as have to this day the motifs of
Near-Eastern and Hindoo music. (A Hindoo, for example, would not
use in a morning song a motif that traditionally connotes evening. This
would seem just as nonsensical to him as to use the word "evening" for
"morning.")

Scale and Tone Names

The chants of the Catholic Church were derived in great part
from those of the Synagogue. But the idea of motifs having fixed
symbolic meanings slowly faded during the first thousand years of
Christianity, until around the year 1000 a new, Western idea crystallized. Theorists were then bringing order into the multiplicity of
melodies. Their major discovery was that all the motifs then in use
shared a small number of single tones. This observation or abstrac-
tion, which in various ways had been independently made before
by such other peoples as the Greeks, Chinese, and Hindoos, is
similar in scope to the one by which all the sounds constituting
language were found to be capable of representation with the aid
of a relatively few letters.

In fact, when for the purpose of instruction the single tones had
been put into a ladder-like, ascending order, called SCALE (Latin:
scala–ladder), the letters of the alphabet were applied to them.[2]
The tones of this scale were identical with those produced by the

---

[1] These terms must not be confused with "trope", a type of Catholic chant,
or with "mode" in the sense explained on p. 43 and in Appendix I, pp. 381f,
383f.

[2] This general meaning of the term "scale" must not be mistaken for its
more limited use, as explained in Appendix I, p. 383; for an explanation of
modes see Appendix I, p. 381f.

white keys of our pianos; and soon it was found that only seven consecutive tones needed names, as the next seven sounded relatively the same. Thus the tones were called A, B, C, D, E, F, and G, and every eighth tone above or below any one of them received the same name. The distance from one to the next of such similar-sounding and identically named tones is called an octave (Latin: *octavus*—eighth).[3]

Gregorian Chant; Monophony

Catholic chants are also called GREGORIAN CHANTS, because Pope Gregory I (Pope 590–604) initiated the codification and systematic employment of the various melodies. Western regard for order eliminated all improvisation from the chants. Every tone was fixed by Church rule and changes were not permitted. Over a period of centuries many new chants were added, however, until about 1300.

In our example we shall observe the use of a soloist (often replaced by a half-choir) and choir as a means of artistic variety. However, this is done in strict alternation, since there is only one line of music and no accompaniment. (In other words, only one tone is heard at any moment.) Such music is called MONOPHONIC (Greek: *monos*—single, *phoné*—voice). A further characteristic is that many tones are often sung to a single syllable, a usage known as florid or MELISMATIC singing—involving MELISMAS. (Example 21 was, of course, both monophonic and melismatic.)

EXAMPLE 22:   *Alleluya, Assumpta est Maria* (Upraised is Mary)

This *Alleluya* is part of the services of Assumption Day, August 15th. The text is:

> *Alleluya* (Praise ye the Lord)
> (Verse:) Upraised is Mary into heaven; joyful th'angels' host.
> *Alleluya*

Separate melodies are sung to the *alleluya*, to the melisma which occupies the "ya" of *alleluya*, and to the verse. Designating these melodies as *a, b,* and *c,* we perceive the arrangement of this *Chant* to be well rounded, as follows:

---

[3] See Appendix I, p. 379f, for an explanation of clefs and of staff notation.

PLATE I: Anonymous Italian master—Miniature from a church
            book written and illustrated for Matthias Corvinus,
            King of Hungary 1458–90.

Ten men are singing from a single tome. The one nearest the
book beats time for all, while others do so for themselves, one even
tapping his foot. The picture well illustrates size and customs of
church choirs in the fourteenth and fifteenth centuries, except that,
as other pictures show, instruments, especially an organ and trombones, often joined in the performance.

alleluya	—*a*—solo (half choir)
alleluya	—*a*—choir
melisma	—*b*—choir
verse, 1st section	—*c*—solo (half choir)
verse, 2nd section	—*a*—solo (half choir)
verse, 3rd section	—*b*—choir
alleluya	—*a*—solo (half choir)
melisma	—*b*—choir

Hymns; Phrase and Melody

Since earliest times the Church has responded to popular influences by introducing a more regular, easily performed type of religious song—the hymn. With the gradual abandonment of much other vocal music in the Protestant services after 1600, the hymn, or CHORALE as the Lutherans came to call it because it was sung by the entire congregation, *choraliter*, became the most prominent feature of their church music. In hymns, derived originally from Judaeo-Syrian and Roman folksongs, each tone usually belongs to a separate syllable: Their style is SYLLABIC, not melismatic (cf. Example 23 below).

There is, moreover, no trace of the Hebrew idea of fixed motifs. Instead, the melody closely parallels the poetry: Metric PHRASES—short sections of music that can be sung in one breath and have definite beginnings and endings—correspond to the metric lines in the poems; partial repetitions and allusions to earlier phrases are the equivalents of rhyme and alliteration, and faithful or varied repetitions of the complete melody answer to the stanzaic organization of the poetry. Such melodies, organized in a few simple phrases, are commonly called TUNES. Though most music has a melody or melodic line, tunes occur only in certain types of music (cf. Example 4, p. 6; Example 9, p. 13; Example 11, p. 14f).

One of the great achievements of the director of Lutheran church music, still called cantor, though he never sings, has been the setting of chorales to ever new accompaniments—for choir, solo singers, organ, orchestra, or combinations of these. The following example is typical, and one of the most beautiful.

EXAMPLE 23: JOHANN SEBASTIAN BACH [1685–1750]

O Haupt voll Blut und Wunden
(O Head with Wounds Becrimsoned)

The melody of this *Chorale* is that of a famous love song composed by
the German master, Hans Leo Hasler (or Hassler) in 1601. Many others
set this melody to different words, as a song, as funeral music, and as
a chorale—a usage known as PARODY (without any implication of ridicule); Bach reset it at least eleven times in various works and under
varying titles. The first stanza of the particular text used here follows.
The first and second lines are sung to the same music, and the entire
melody is repeated with every stanza.

	O	Haupt	voll	Blut und Wun	den, voll Schmerz und	vol - ler Hohn!
1.0	head,	with	wounds be -crim - soned, be - set	by	pain and scorn,
	O	Haupt,	zu	Spott ge - bun - den mit	ei - ner	Dor - nen - kron'!
2.0	head,	by	scof - fers wreath - ed with	cru - el	crown of thorns,

	O	Haupt, sonst schoen ge - zie - ret mit	hoech - ster Ehr' und Zier,
3.0	head,	where once dwelt beau - ty, a	brow se - rene, re - vered,

	jetzt	a - ber hoch schim - pfi - ret:	ge - grues - set seist du	mir!
4.	now,	though thou art be - smirch - ed, my	love goes out to	thee.

Chromatic Scale and Half-Tones

• In addition to the seven tones within the octave used in Gregorian chant, those represented by the white keys on the piano, several more are frequently heard here, namely those corresponding to
the black keys on the piano. There are five such tones in every
octave. Their combination with the others brings about a scale
of twelve tones per octave, called CHROMATIC (Greek: *chroma—*

---

⁴ The sign ⌒ or ⌣ , called *fermata*, hold, or pause, usually indicates a considerable lengthening of the note above or below which it appears. In hymns it is traditionally used, without necessarily implying an extension of duration, to indicate the last note of each phrase.

color [5]), as distinguished from the DIATONIC scale of seven tones per octave. The distances, or INTERVALS, between any two neighbors among the twelve tones, whether represented by white or black keys on the piano, are identical. These intervals are called HALF-TONES, and there are, of course, twelve half-tones in every octave, or six whole-tones: [6]

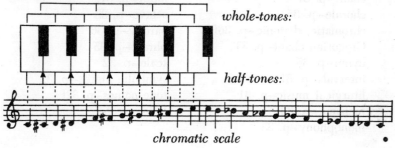

whole-tones:

half-tones:

chromatic scale

Summary

The three examples given in this section represent the most usual approaches to religious music on a small scale: (1) the symbolic and prosodic meaning of motifs and their free, imaginative combination in new melodies (Example 21); (2) the creation of an accepted tradition about such melodies and about the manner and occasion of their performance (Example 22); and (3) the folk and art song used for religious purposes by giving it an appropriate new text known as a parody (Example 23). These approaches remain the same in all types of ceremonies, except in the most elaborate ones, which demand larger compositions. Some of these will be discussed in Part II.

The fact emerges clearly from the study of these five sections that music may serve well-defined functions in connection with the five chief aspects of human life—work, defense, social organization, propagation, and death. These aspects are reflected in numerous activities, and in semi-civilized societies many of them would be

---

[5] One reason for this name is that on keyboard instruments keys of different color have always been used for the five additional tones in the octave.

[6] See Appendix I, p. 380f, for an explanation of accidentals. Be sure not to confuse the terms "half-note" and "whole-note" with "half-tone" and "whole-tone". The former are note values, the latter intervals, distances between tones, sometimes also called "half-steps" and "whole-steps."

deemed impossible without music. Even much art music is, as we have seen, but refined functional music. Let us keep this in mind, as we turn to art music in its basic manifestations.

CONCEPTS AND TOPICS DISCUSSED IN THIS SECTION

II AESTHETIC TYPES

Section F

SHORT SINGLE PIECES FOR THE HOME

Functions of Art Music

The types of music that we have been discussing thus far arose in answer to some practical needs. Such music is said to be functional. We have also referred to another type of music, which we call aesthetic or art music. It also has a function, but one less easily understood; for art music does not directly answer a primary drive of physical existence, but rather fills those human needs that are often called spiritual (without the implication of "religious").

Art music stimulates the imagination and rouses the emotions in a manner radically different from physical stimuli. It may be said to fulfill three chief purposes: (1) relaxation, escape from everyday chores and worries; (2) intellectual satisfaction at the composer's finesse, his seriousness of purpose, and his broad humanity—a satisfaction more easily sensed than expressed in words; and (3) the inspiring and uniting of people during a performance. Art music

[39]

fulfills this last function even when a person plays or sings for himself alone, for he feels a sense of kinship with humanity at large.

Art music, therefore, cannot be looked upon as a useless game, or the pastime of a few. It is an important and typically human activity. Though one of the finest and proudest achievements of the human mind, it can be enjoyed by almost all people.

Types of Art Music

Functional music is superseded by art music (and by music for entertainment only, which lacks the intellectual and social components mentioned above) in the same measure as advanced civilization furnishes people with leisure time. Art music is used to vitalize leisure in three chief ways: as a means of private edification through potential or actual participation in the performance, as a vehicle of virtuosity, or as the interpreter of ideas. It may therefore be said to belong in one of three settings—the home, the concert platform, or the dramatic stage. Some art music, to be sure, may be performed at various times in two or all three of these places; but basically every composition is intended primarily for one of them.

We turn first to short pieces of chamber music—music originally intended for performance in the home. We shall study short concert pieces in the next section, leaving dramatic music and longer works for groups of performers or ensembles for later.[1]

The Art Song

The nineteenth century, a great era of chamber music, cultivated the art song for a solo singer with piano accompaniment. The most eminent song composer was the Viennese, Franz Schubert (cf. his *Erlkönig*, p. 17f). Although Schubert did not, as is often said, create the type, he did set its style for the ensuing century. He also set the record for the greatest number of such compositions with over six hundred *lieder* (German songs). The following famous example well represents the poetic expressiveness of most of them.

---

[1] Though in recent times the term "chamber music" has been used in a limited sense, to designate music for instrumental ensembles only (see Part IV, Section B), it has also retained its more general meaning as employed here.

EXAMPLE 24: FRANZ SCHUBERT [1797–1828]

Ständchen (Serenade) from "Swan Song" (1828)

These are Ludwig Rellstab's (1799–1860) words in translation:

Lei - se fle - hen   mei - ne Lie - der   durch   die Nacht zu dir;
1. Soft - ly plead - ing   float my songs now   through   the Night to thee;
to the quiet grove below here, darling, come to me!

2. Whis - p'ring, slen - der   tree - tops rus - tle ‖:in ___ the moon's mild light,:‖
and the evil, hostile listener ‖: do not fear, my love.:‖
3. Hear the nightingales' clear warblings! O, they plead to thee,
with the tones of sweet complaint they plead to thee for me.
4. Well they know the heart's deep longing, ‖:know of love's sweet pain,:‖
pleading with their silv'ry voices ‖: to no heart in vain.:‖
5. Let their song thy heart awaken, hearken, love, to me,
trembling do I wait for thee, love, ‖:bliss lies all in thee,:‖
lies all in thee.

The simplest type of song is that in which an easy-flowing melody, combined with a simple accompaniment, is repeated to several stanzas of poetry, much as in folksongs. Many of Schubert's songs are of this type, but rarely does he miss the opportunity of changing the melody here and there in the various stanzas, in order to bring about better expression of the words. Here *stanzas 1* and *2*, and *stanzas 3* and *4*, are gathered into two identical musical stanzas, followed by a coda derived from the same material set to *stanza 5*. This is a very frequent arrangement, not alone of Schubert songs.

A more typically Schubertian feature is the echo in the accompaniment that follows text *stanzas 1* and *3*. In addition, the composer has employed text repetitions to underscore the meaning. It is interesting to note how much the triplet at the start of the melody contributes to the expression: It seems to indicate the serenader's urging, the welling-up of emotion in him as he beseeches his beloved.

Schumann was the next great German song composer (cf. his *The Two Grenadiers*, p. 15ff). The third was Brahms, whom Schumann launched on his career. There were, of course, many others who composed lovely songs, but none so productive of excellent

lieder as these three and Hugo Wolf (cf. his *The Pied Piper,* p. 14f).
One of Brahms's many deeply serious songs is the following:

EXAMPLE 25:   JOHANNES BRAHMS [1833–97]

Auf dem Kirchhofe (In the Graveyard, 1888)

The words are by Detlev von Liliencron (1844–1909):

1.
Der Tag ging   re - gen-schwer   und   sturm - be-wegt,
The day hung   rain - op-pressed   and   storm - y gray;

I passed by graves where now no mourner kneeleth,

'mid weath-ered stone and cross   and with - - ered wreath,

where crowding, crawling vine man's name concealeth.

2.   The day hung stormy-gray and rain-oppressed;
     on ev'ry grave the freezing words: "Death stealeth!"

—While,   deaf   to   storm, bleak   cof -fins   slum - bered   there,

there came the thaw, and I could read: "Death healeth!"

The music set to the first two lines of each *stanza* is, like these lines
of the poem, similar, interpreting the stormy weather. But, as the last
two lines of each *stanza* differ, so does the corresponding music; broken,
half-spoken phrases at the end of the *first stanza,* expressing desolation,
contrast with the even, melodious pace of the hopeful conclusion of the
Song.

The listener will note the quiet lyricism of these songs, and the
introspective attitude, especially of the second. Softness prevails
overall, without a trace of display, marking them as genuine music

for the home. Both songs are composed to poetry organized in stanzas; the music is therefore also stanzaic or strophic. But it should be mentioned that there are other songs whose music differs for each line of the poem. They are usually called "through-composed" songs (though "non-stanzaic" is probably a better term).

Major and Minor Modes

• The great difference between the endings of the musical stanzas of Brahms's *In the Graveyard* is based not only on the use of longer and more even note values in the *second stanza*—a rhythmic change—but also on a change that makes the second ending sound brighter and more hopeful—a change in MODE. This term requires some explanation.

A mode organizes or relates tones by investing one tone of a diatonic scale with pre-eminence and by making all other tones subsidiary to it and gravitating toward it. The two standard modes used during the past three hundred years are those in which, when employing only the white keys of the keyboard, the composer makes the *C* and the *A* respectively the chief tones or TONICS. These modes are called MAJOR and MINOR. Either may use any of the other eleven tones as a tonic, but this will necessitate the employment of some or all black-key tones. The resulting KEYS are named after the tonics, for example, *D* Major, *F*-sharp Minor, and so forth.[2]

The effect of brightening in the Brahms *Song* was due to a change from Minor to Major. The *first stanza* and part of the *second* are in a minor key (*C* Minor), whereas the end is in Major (*C* Major). In other words, in either section of the song the melody employs mostly tones belonging to the particular key or TONALITY (*C* Minor or *C* Major), and it possesses a certain gravitation toward the tonics of these tonalities (*C*).

The accompaniment is similarly organized; but here several tones of the key are usually heard at once. Any such combination of three or more different tones is called a CHORD; and chords that recognizably belong to a certain key are called HARMONIES.[3] •

---

[2] See Appendix I, p. 381ff, for explanations of Major and Minor, of intervals, keys, and key signatures.

[3] See Appendix I, p. 384f, for an explanation of triads.

Eras of Song

Combining poetry and music, the song is one of the best vehicles for expressing individual as well as collective moods and feelings. It is perhaps the oldest type of art music, which had passed through several periods of brilliant flowering before the nineteenth century. Such a period was, for example, the twelfth and thirteenth centuries, the time of the troubadours. Mostly of noble birth, and active in northern Spain, southern France, and northwestern Italy from the late eleventh to the early thirteenth centuries, these men may be regarded as the first genuinely Western lyric poets and singers. Their art and that of their instrumental accompanists, the minstrels, spread through Europe and inspired both the northern French trouvères, active from the middle of the twelfth century through the thirteenth, and the German minnesingers, active in the thirteenth and fourteenth centuries, and succeeded in the fifteenth and sixteenth by the meistersingers. Other cultures, too, had their great song ages, as testified to, for example, by the biblical Book of Psalms (cf. p. 68) or by the classic Chinese poetry of the eighth century (cf. p. 165ff).

Character Pieces

Having discussed the small piece in vocal chamber music, we now turn to comparable instrumental pieces. There are innumerable small pieces for piano that may be called chamber music. One type, especially popular since about 1830 and testifying to the literary leanings of nineteenth-century composers, is the CHARACTER PIECE, which usually bears a title illustrated by the music.

The illustrative character of the pieces is produced by three main factors:

(1) a judicious use of melody and chords for achieving contrast and tension;

(2) rhythm, a prime agent of characterizing motion and behavior; and

(3) expression with its three main elements:

(a) tempo;

(b) loudness or VOLUME and its variations, i.e. DYNAMICS; and

(c) TONE PRODUCTION or attack, such as smooth connection of
tones or their interrupted enunciation, and various other
effects.

These factors apply, of course, to all other music as well, but they
are most easily studied in this connection. This is especially true
of the third. We turn to examples.

EXAMPLE 26:   ROBERT SCHUMANN [1810–56]

Träumerei (Dreaming), No. 7 of "Scenes from Childhood,"
op. 15 (1838)

The outstanding master of such illustrative small pieces, the man who
virtually founded or re-established [4] this type in the nineteenth century,
was Schumann. He formulated such pieces simply. Here a melody of
two phrases is stated and repeated; then it is varied, and finally repeated
with a slight change at the close.

The initial phrase:

seems to express a desire that ebbs away in wavelets, a sensation typical
of many day dreams. In all its brevity the piece perfectly illustrates its
title, suggesting languor and a certain lazy abandon. The tempo is slow
but flexible, the volume, though varied continuously, is nevertheless
rather subdued, and all tones are smoothly connected or LEGATO. This is
indicated by the bows or SLURS above or below the groups of notes in
the example.

Songs Without Words

Another composer who excelled in small pieces was Schumann's
close friend, Mendelssohn. This brilliant conductor, pianist, and
composer rebelled against the mediocre piano music played in his
time. For his own use and that of amateurs he therefore wrote
many small piano pieces, whose refined lyricism called forth thousands of imitations. He called them *Songs Without Words,* because
his idea was to transfer the song with piano accompaniment to the

---

[4] Cf. p. 222ff; Appendix I, p. 403.

piano alone, making the music expressive enough to carry its effect without words. Whereas some of these "piano songs" are generally lyrical, others have definite connotations, and the result is character pieces, such as the following.

EXAMPLE 27:   FELIX MENDELSSOHN [1809–47]

Spinning Song, "Song Without Words" No. 34, *op.* 67, 4 (1845)

This is one of the few pieces whose titles originate with Mendelssohn or his circle, the others being inventions of publishers. The *Spinning Song* has three stanzas separated by brief interludes. The second stanza varies the first and is itself varied in the last. The unceasing hum of the spinning wheel, represented by a continuous and rapid flow of tones, accompanies this gay and at times excited ditty:

The tempo is fast, the volume rather low, though rising to some climaxes, allowing the lightly interrupted or STACCATO melody to breathe playfulness. The *staccato* is indicated by a dot above or below each note.

Another master of small pieces was Debussy, the undisputed leader of French music in the early years of this century. His imaginative compositions for piano and for orchestra set a style that has had a lasting influence both on art music and the popular field. Debussy's subtlety and humor are manifest in our final example.

EXAMPLE 28:   CLAUDE DEBUSSY [1862–1918]

Minstrels, No. 12 of "Preludes", Book I (1910)

Permission for reprint granted by Durand et Cie, Paris, France. Copyright owners: Elkan-Vogel Company, Inc., Philadelphia, Pennsylvania.

Minstrels describes a troupe of carnival clowns, jugglers, and musicians with their capers, trumpets, and drums, and their comic sentimentality. The "capers" of the first phrase:

are succeeded by "trumpets" in the next section:

Then the "performance" starts, represented by an ominous silence punctuated by the "bass drum" only, and ended by a bit of lyricism:

The dots and slurs together, as used here, indicate PORTATO, a manner of performance in which tones are neither connected as in *legato* nor short as in *staccato,* but are disconnected and yet have substantial length. After an interruption by further "fanfares" the "drums" prepare for the end of the "act," indicated by the resumption of sentimental lyricism (but with a new tune). Clowning and playing their instruments, the troupe then departs.

The tempo and the volume are highly variable, whimsical and erratic. Especially charming is the dry *staccato* of the "trumpets" and "drums," as opposed to the sentimental *legato* of the lyric phrases.

Tempo Changes

• As has been said, there are three avenues toward artistic presentation, interpretation, or expression, namely tempo, dynamics, and tone production. On p. 29 the tempo marks were given; we may now add indications of changes of tempo. The most usual are:

> *accelerando, accel.*—increase speed gradually (cf. end of Example 28)
> *ritardando, ritenuto, rit., ritard., riten.*—decrease speed gradually
> *tempo rubato* (lit. "robbed speed")—somewhat free (cf. Examples 26, 28) •

Volume

• Volume and volume changes are indicated by the following signs on the music page—in the musical score:

---

⁵ The small horizontal line above the note indicates that the tone is held rather than played *staccato.*

f, forte—loud
ff, fortissimo—very loud
fff, forte-fortissimo—extremely loud
mf, mezzo-forte—medium loud
p, piano—soft
pp, pianissimo—very soft
ppp, piano-pianissimo—extremely soft
mp, mezzo-piano—medium soft
sf, sforzato, sforzando—momentary accent
fp, forte-piano—momentarily loud
pf, poco forte—somewhat loud
> (above or below a note)—accent
crescendo, cresc., or ![crescendo hairpin] —increase loudness gradually
diminuendo, dim., decrescendo, decresc., or ![diminuendo hairpin] —decrease loudness gradually •

Tone Production

• The basic types of tone production are the following:

legato, indicated by a slur above or below note groups—smoothly
  connected, without interruption (cf. Example 26)
staccato, indicated by dots above or below (not following!)
  notes—as short as possible, interrupted (cf. Example 27)
portato, indicated by both dots and slurs—half short, interrupted, but each tone receiving substantial length

There are many further markings referring to tone production.
We mention only a few of the most frequent: On stringed instruments usually played with a bow, such as the violin, the plucking
of strings with the finger is called *pizzicato, pizz.;* the light bounc-
ing of the elastic bow on the strings, producing a light *staccato,* is
known as *spiccato.* On the same instruments, as also in human
voices and on the trombone, the effect of connecting two tones by
sliding quickly through all intermediate pitches is called *porta-
mento.* On keyboard instruments and on the harp this amounts to
ultra-rapid scales and is called *glissando, gliss.* If not all tones but
only some of them, selected in a chordal manner, are thus rapidly
presented, the term *arpeggio* ("in the manner of a harp") is used,
a term employed also for many kinds of other BROKEN-CHORD pas-

sages, i.e. passages in which the tones of chords are presented separately in succession. •

Phrasing

Tempo, dynamics, and tone production are the means of good PHRASING, which, in turn, is essential to good interpretation or expression in the artistic performance.[6] Minute variations of these ingredients are all that is needed to make clear where phrases start and end, reach their climax, or relax. The attentive listener will derive great satisfaction from observing how these factors influence the performance in the examples considered in this section and in all other music.

Other Small Pieces in Chamber Music

There are innumerable types of small pieces in chamber music. Some are derived from dances (cf. Section D), others from ballads, marches, or hymns; still others are stylized improvisations—lyrical, excited, sad, or otherwise. All of them are originally intended for the relaxation or recreation of the individual, the family, or groups of friends, mainly through the participation in the performance of all those present. In our time many of them, in addition, have found a wide listening public, and despite their basic intimacy and simplicity have a large share in our recital programs. Here the character piece has been singled out because its literary quality provides a clear insight into the use and meaning of the various elements of musical expression.

CONCEPTS AND TOPICS DISCUSSED IN THIS SECTION

---

[6] To apply these means at the right places the performer must, of course, first understand the construction of the music; cf. Part III.

Section G

SHORT SINGLE PIECES FOR THE CONCERT HALL

Music for Display

Concert music is performed by virtuosi for an audience and serves to exhibit the prowess of the performers. These must successfully overcome great technical difficulties and display great physical endurance. Usually, therefore, concert music is difficult and lengthy. In fact, several examples in this section approach the large single pieces discussed in Part III. However difficult, many concert pieces are intrinsically expressive, demanding fine artistry in performance, which is more satisfying than mere technical prowess. Concert pieces that give scope to expressive presentation beyond mere firework displays of skill are therefore accorded greater esteem.

We shall here examine only solo concert pieces, more appropriately called virtuoso or recital pieces. Many such compositions are cast as studies or ETUDES, but they may bear other titles, such as CAPRICE or CAPRICCIO (for a fanciful content), SCHERZO (lit. "joke," nearly identical with *caprice*), prelude (usually very brief), and TOCCATA (lit. "touch piece," a keyboard etude of large dimensions). However, some compositions so titled may be chamber music—intimate and without stress on brilliance—whereas others, truly *bravura* concert music, are not designated as such in the title.

Violin Technic

Our first example is a display piece for violin alone. Because of its construction the violin is best suited to play only one tone at a time rather than several, i.e. chords; it is, in other words, very difficult for the player to supply both melody and accompaniment, and the composer for this instrument usually provides for a piano accompaniment. The mere fact that the present composition is written for one violin alone points to its purpose: to tax the skill of the performer. Indeed, great difficulties are created by the many skips (evoking the impression of more or less simultaneous melody and accompaniment) and by chords or MULTIPLE STOPS.

The last term derives from the fact that the violin player achieves the tones by STOPPING the strings with his fingers, i.e. by pressing the strings to the FINGERBOARD. This is difficult enough to do for one tone at a time, especially in a fast tempo; to stop two or more strings simultaneously and in rapid succession—to play DOUBLE or multiple STOPS—is very hard. So are large skips, because the bow has to travel across the strings and the fingers have to stretch and change their positions rapidly.

EXAMPLE 29:   NICCOLO PAGANINI [1782–1840]

Caprice No. 24, in A Minor (1797)

This is the last in the famous book of *Caprices* which Paganini, perhaps the greatest of all violinists, wrote for himself. He dazzled audiences with them in his day, and their influence on concert music has persisted. In fact, several composers, among them Liszt, Brahms, and Rachmaninoff, employed this particular *Caprice*, all in compositions for the piano.

Our example is skilfully arranged. There is a brief, characteristic melody, called *Theme:*

and a succession of repetitions of this *Theme*, each varying it so as to allow for the exhibition of ever new difficulties. In addition to large skips and multiple stops, the virtuoso must meet such technical challenges as the fast alternation of plucked *(pizzicato)* and bowed tones; the use of the highest REGISTER (region of pitches) of the violin, where accurate pitch, or INTONATION, becomes difficult; and extremely fast tempo.

Aria and Bel Canto

A vocal display piece is called an "aria." Many arias are parts of large works, such as operas or oratorios (cf. Part II). Yet, although included in an opera, our next example is neither dramatic nor narrative but rather a typical recital piece. Just as Example 29 showed off the violin, this one exhibits the voice and demands the utmost mobility and flexibility of the performer. This type of singing is known as COLORATURA singing. It is part of the Italian tradition of BEL CANTO (lit. "beautiful singing"), which flourished from about 1650 to 1850 and which, in addition to mobility and flexibility, aimed at the display of an unforced, free-flowing voice of large RANGE (or distance between high and low tones).

EXAMPLE 30:   GIOACCHINO ROSSINI [1792–1868]

Una voce poco fà from "The Barber of Seville" (1816)

Rossini was one of the last and greatest composers of the *bel canto*. The text of this *Aria*,[1] one of his most famous, functions merely as a vehicle for the spirited music. The music makes no attempt at interpreting the words, except in setting a general mood. Lines of the text are repeated not for emphasis, but wherever the music is repeated. Intended to exhibit the voice, the piece might equally well have been written for violin or flute and accompaniment. In fact, many such *coloratura* arias introduce a solo flute with which the voice competes in the display of agility.

The present *Aria* falls into two sections, each with an orchestral introduction. The vocal portion of the slow first section has four phrases, the second and fourth of which are identical. Using letters to designate the phrases, we may describe this section as *a-b-c-b*. The fast second section is formulated *d-e-f-e-f*, and the first phrase is also heard in the orchestral introduction to this section. The *coloratura* passages are rather evenly distributed, except in *a* and *c*. The words follow:

---

[1] Rossini calls it a *cavatina,* a term used about 1750–1850 to denote rather vaguely a subtype of aria, usually lyrical in character.

a 'Twas a voice, a while a - go, that struck
deep in - to my heart,

gave my heart so sweet a wound, 'twas Lindoro's ringing voice.

b ‖:Yes, Lin - do - ro shall be mine, I have

sworn it, I shall win him!:‖

c Though my guardian will object, I shall bend him to my will;
in the end he will submit, and I shall be well content.
b ‖: Yes, Lindoro shall be mine, I have sworn it, I shall win him!:‖

Allegro moderato

d Do - - cile and tame am I,

son ri - spet - to - - sa,
yes and re - spect - - ful;

I am obedient, and sweet, and gentle.
‖: I let myself be ruled and do obey. :‖

e But if they dare wound me where I feel ten - - der - est,

---

² See Appendix I, p. 376, for an explanation of double-dotted notes.

they'll have a viper on their hands.
A hundred traps I'll spring, ere I submit to them,
and tricks contrive, and tricks contrive.
f A hundred traps I'll spring, ere I submit to them,
and tricks contrive, and tricks contrive.
A hundred traps I'll spring, ere I submit to them,
a hundred traps I'll spring, and tricks, and tricks contrive.
f 1 Docile and tame am I, meek and obedient,
I let myself be ruled and do obey.
e (as before)
f (as before)
f 2 ‖: A hundred traps I'll spring, and tricks contrive,:‖
‖: and tricks contrive,:‖ and tricks contrive.

Display or virtuoso pieces composed during the past century-and-
a-half have been written mainly for the piano. Most nineteenth-
century composers were pianists themselves and therefore wrote
such pieces prolifically under the most varied titles, such as prelude,
etude, waltz, ballade, nocturne, and so forth. A case in point is
Chopin, one of the most remarkable pianists of his time and one
of the most influential composers for his instrument (cf. his *Mazurka*, p. 28f).

EXAMPLE 31: FRÉDÉRIC CHOPIN [1810–49]

Prelude No. 24, in D Minor, op. 28

This impassioned piece concludes Chopin's famous volume of *Preludes*.
It is an endurance test and a study in stretching for the left hand, shown
in the lower staff of the musical example, and for the right hand a challenge in difficult runs. However, it far transcends the usual etude in
melodic interest and in its exciting drive. We easily observe how the
wide range of the melody, run through rapidly and often, contributes to
the agitation; so does the repeated left-hand figure, which has an effect
similar to that of the tone repetitions in Schubert's *Erlkönig* (cf. p. 17f).

Allegro appassionato 3)

---

3 Fast and impassioned.

Chopin's friend, Liszt, was another important composer for the piano. Liszt is generally regarded as the leading nineteenth-century pianist—the counterpart of Paganini among violinists. The following *Etude* is typical of his virtuosic style.

EXAMPLE 32:   FRANZ LISZT [1811–86]

La Campanella (Chimes, 1833)

La Campanella is a concert etude, based on a section of Paganini's *Second Violin Concerto*. Etudes usually try to create opportunity for the study of certain problems of performance. In this, an unusually long one, the player must utilize a wide span of hand: He must practice long and fast skips of changing width, accelerate them to allow for added tones between skips, perform simultaneous span and passage work in the same hand, and finally manage difficult runs of consecutive octaves in the same hand. The music is arranged as in Example 29: a theme and its varied repetitions:

Toccatas are very similar to etudes, but are generally longer. They are normally brilliant and fast, and often follow the idea of perpetual motion; *perpetuum mobile* is, indeed, found as a title. A fresh recent composition may serve as an example:

---

[4] The sign *8* -------- or *8va* -------- indicates that a passage is to be played an octave higher than written. Similarly *8*------- or *8va* ---------- indicates playing an octave lower. These signs avoid the reading difficulties connected with the use of too many auxiliary or LEDGER lines (also "leger" lines) above or below the staff.

EXAMPLE 33: FRANCIS POULENC [b.1899]

Toccata (1931)

*Musical examples reproduced by special authorization from the publishers,
Heugel and Cie, Paris, France. Mercury Music Co., New York.*

This contemporary composer has a facile talent and has written many
rather light and enjoyable works of which this nonchalant, sparkling
Toccata is representative. It moves from one idea to another with hardly
a backward glance. A brisk introduction precedes the first melodic
idea:

Very Animated

After its repetition two new ideas are heard successively and then repeated:

and

A fourth:

also presented twice, adds a touch of lyricism, which is dispelled by the
few brilliant closing measures.

Among the greatest of all toccatas is the following one for organ
by Bach, who excelled in this as well as in many other types of
composition. Besides this *Toccata*, Bach wrote two others for organ
and seven mighty specimens for harpsichord, today usually played
on the piano.[5] Our example is one of the shortest of these ten
works.

---

[5] See Appendix I, p. 388ff, for an explanation of the keyboard instruments:
clavichord, harpsichord, piano, and organ.

EXAMPLE 34: JOHANN SEBASTIAN BACH [1685–1750]

Toccata in D Minor

The *Toccata* starts haltingly, with startling changes of tempo. Several short ideas succeed each other, incidentally displaying the richness and versatility of the organ. The main section is akin to the *perpetuum mobile:* Here the motion is never interrupted or accelerated until the mighty close. Then another turbulent section, corresponding to the beginning, rounds out the powerful and inspiring work.

This *Toccata* gives us a superb opportunity to study the notions of "motif" and "motif development." The main section opens with the statement of the chief idea by itself, which is then taken up at various pitch levels: [6]

The entire section evolves from the opening motif (*m*). This motif actually combines two motifs: a steady alternation of high and low tones and the stepwise descent of the lower tones. From these two ideas five further motifs are developed. The alternation of tones occurs at half speed (here against itself at its original speed):

and at a quarter speed:

as well as at a quarter speed with the interval filled in by other tones:

---

[6] This section is a fugue; the work is therefore often called *Toccata and Fugue in D Minor.* A full discussion of fugues follows on p. 99ff. Many toccatas typically include one or more sections of fugue.

The stepwise descent, on the other hand, appears at double speed:

and with its direction reversed as in (m^1). The interrelations among these various figures give the main section compactness, cohesion, and sustained interest. It is as if we were following the fate of a person, the motif, through a drama or story, as his character reveals itself in various circumstances and contexts.

From this discussion a definition of "motif" may be derived. It is the smallest configuration of musical entities—intervals, rhythms, chords, and so forth—which is understood as a unit. It is comparable to the word in language.

Summary

The reader has now briefly scanned the various ways in which both functional and art music serve us in our lives. The sector of human activities in which music is important is smaller in urban society than in societies less highly organized. Music still functions all around us in dance, march, hymn, and work song, but its direct connection with human needs, especially in the last three of these categories, has shrunk considerably. Actually, however, much more music is created in urban society—music for entertainment and art music, which yields relaxation and mental balance, so important in our hurried lives. During the past several centuries art music has evolved into many species and subspecies. Our next task is to trace in broad outline this evolution.

CONCEPTS AND TOPICS DISCUSSED IN THIS SECTION

PART II
COMPOSITE WORKS

III

MUSIC IN THE GOTHIC AND RENAISSANCE ERAS

SECTION A

MADRIGAL, MOTET, AND MASS

Composite Pieces

In Part I we discussed mostly short single pieces. Whereas these satisfy the needs of functional music, art music reaches beyond such simple formulations. On the road to greater complexity and diversity, musicians turned to additive procedures. Out of several small pieces, connected or disconnected, they began to fashion larger, composite works, such as those discussed in Part I, Section G. The few basic types of music—songs, chants, dance pieces—were thus found to yield many new species and subspecies. This evolution was primarily European, for it was made possible by a discovery that is unique in Western music.

Chief Characteristic of Western Music

The music of Western civilization differs considerably from that favored by the other three-quarters of mankind. The chief difference, which gives rise to many others, is due to the discovery that

[61]

more than one tone may be heard at a time, and that chains of such combinations may be felt as orderly and pleasant. Most non-Westerners, unless they have learned through contact with the West to appreciate such passages, still hear them as disorderly and ugly. They are used to hearing tones only consecutively, in MELODIC INTERVALS, whereas to us the simultaneous combinations of tones, or HARMONIC INTERVALS, have become second nature.

Peoples outside Western civilization that have chanced on the interesting sound of a particular harmonic interval, have proceeded to apply it continuously, without ever searching for the many further combinations that offer themselves. The investigation into the systematic use of simultaneous tones is unique with the West. Its start some time before the year 1000 (the time when our system of tones and scales was established, cf. p. 32f) may be taken as an indication of the birth of Western civilization, and is similar in import to the emergence of distinct European nations and languages in France, England, Germany, and elsewhere, the first literary and original philosophic achievements of the Occident (Beowulf, the Roland's Song, the Eddas, and so forth, and scholasticism), and, soon thereafter, the creation of the new Gothic style in architecture.

Gothic Music: Intervals and Counterpoint

The exploration of the various harmonic intervals extended over a long period. It was especially the work of musicians in the Gothic era (about 1140–1440), but it began earlier. The simplest approach was to add a second PART or VOICE to an established melody, something very similar to what our folk singers still do today when they "harmonize," for example:

| *Rex* | *coe* | - | *li,* | *Do* | - | *mi* | - | *ne* | *ma* | - | *ris* | *un* | - | *di* | - | *so* | - | *ni* |
| King | of | | Heav | - | en, | Lord | of | the | o | - | cean's | thund' | - | ring | waves |

This rendition of a chant enriched by a lower, accompanying voice comes from an anonymous manuscript of around 900. After about 1000 the new voice in such liturgical pieces, known as *órgana* (singular: *órganum*), was added above the chant and given melodic and rhythmic independence.

Musicians and music lovers were captivated. Even after four centuries of evolution in art music, when people had learned to appreciate combinations of three, four, and more parts, they still clung to the intervals as their basic materials.

With certain exceptions, such as Gregorian chant or the songs of the troubadours, trouvères, and minnesingers, Gothic music was devoted to the combination of different parts, adjusted to each other according to pleasant and harsh intervals called CONSONANCES and DISSONANCES respectively. These terms are often misinterpreted. What people in one part of the world or at one time find dissonant, those living in a different culture or period may find otherwise. Thus consonance and dissonance are relative terms, like heat and cold: What is felt to have tension, or to need relaxation or resolution, is called dissonant, whereas a point of relative repose is called consonant.

Three time-honored terms derive from the procedure of the Gothic musician: COMPOSITION, i.e. putting together (Latin: *compónere*); POLYPHONY, or many voices (Greek: *poly + phoné*); and COUNTERPOINT, i.e. writing in each part one note, or several notes, against a note (Latin: *punctus contra punctum*) in another part (see the examples immediately preceding and following). Today we use the term "polyphony" as synonymous with "applied counterpoint"; we speak of counterpoint as a technic that may be studied as part of music "theory" and leads to polyphony in actual composition. The respective adjectives, however, are used without such a distinction; the terms "polyphonic music" and "contrapuntal music" are roughly equivalent in meaning.

Renaissance Music: Chords and Imitation

About 1400 the English brought to the continent a practice which they had already accepted for well over a century: hearing three tones as a unit. The result was such passages as this:[1]

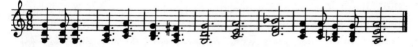

---

[1] Quoted from *The Old Hall Manuscript*, edited by Alexander Ramsbotham, The Plainsong & Mediaeval Music Society, London, 1933, vol. 1, p. 9f.

By 1500 a few such combinations, or chords, were well established, and heard as pleasant in themselves. No longer merely chance niceties of a polyphonic setting, they rather served as the basic medium within which polyphony could unfold. Another century passed, however, before chords, independent of melody, were generally considered an important element of music.

This chordal concept began to take root during a period known as the Renaissance (about 1440–1600). It is the period in which Western artists first applied perspective (see Pl. II, facing this page), when the first Western secular drama emerged, when doctors turned to the study of anatomy, when geographers began to describe the Earth as spherical rather than flat, and when Leonardo da Vinci devised flying machines. These developments reveal that a change was occurring—the displacement of two-dimensional thinking by three-dimensional ideas, to which the chordal concept furnishes the musical analogy.

The newly discovered three-dimensional world led people to become aware of more complex relationships. This awakening is vividly reflected in Renaissance music when, after some time of experimentation, all parts of a composition were related to each other by melodic IMITATION. In other words, in this music one usually hears the same motif taken up by all voices at various times and tossed back and forth among them. For the performers— and the music was mainly written for performers rather than listeners—this technic evokes an uncommon degree of intellectual interest and aesthetic satisfaction.

The Madrigal

The outstanding type of Renaissance chamber music using imitation was the MADRIGAL. This originated in Italy, where it was the most favored court entertainment between 1535 and 1615. Other nations soon learned to enjoy the madrigal. It was welcomed throughout Europe and especially in England, where it struck new roots and had a second flowering between 1590 and 1630.[2]

Most often madrigals were rather formal love poems, set for several voices. Usually each idea or each line of the poem received

---

[2] See Appendix I, p. 399f, for additional information about Renaissance chamber music.

PLATE II: Raphael (1483–1520), Italian painter — St. Cecilia (from an altar in a church dedicated to this Saint).

The picture vividly, if incidentally, symbolizes the attitude of the sixteenth century toward vocal and instrumental music. A broken gamba (cf. Appendix I, p. 392) on the ground together with discarded pipes, drums, cymbals, triangle, and tambourine, and a portative organ with its pipes falling loosely while the instrument is slipping from St. Cecilia's hands are in sharp contrast to her rapt listening to the voices of the angels singing from a book and symbolize the inferiority of instrumental music to vocal music. In its symmetry, unity, and stillness, this painting is typical of the Renaissance.

its own individual music, its particular tune and well-defined motif, interpreting the word content. These sections are contrasted in TEXTURE, i.e. they alternate between imitational polyphony and chordal writing—the two major musical discoveries of the age. Thus a madrigal may be regarded, in a sense, as a chain of small pieces, although complete breaks between them are usually avoided.

The stringing together of several different small sections is one of the first solutions of the problem of writing long pieces. The result is satisfactory when used with a text. Without a text, however, such series of small sections, especially when extended, easily become tiresome, because they lack a unifying pattern. A short and charming example by one of the minor Elizabethan composers follows:

EXAMPLE 35:   JOHN FARMER [1565?–1605?]

Fair Phyllis I Saw

This pastoral piece for four voices is truly music for friends gathered around a dinner table after a meal. It shows all the essentials of the English madrigal: simple rhythm and melody, use of contrasting textures, and musical expression of words. Each line of the short poem has an individual setting and a melodic idea all its own as shown below:

4. but af - ter her lov - er Amyntas hied.

c 5. Up and down he wan - dered,

6. Whilst she was miss - ing.   7. When he found her,

8. O then they fell a - kiss - ing!

Listening will disclose the following differences in setting:

Line 1 is sung by the highest voice alone.

Line 2 is sung by the highest voice to the chordal accompaniment of the three others.

In *line 3* all voices take up the tune, but at different times, imitating each other.

Line 4 follows the same procedure with yet another tune.

Line 5 pursues the same technic; the words "up and down" are expressed by an appropriate motif, whose many repetitions charmingly suggest "search," while the lowest voice has long, repeated tones as an effective contrast.

In *line 6* the two low voices in a short, simple setting are followed by the two high voices.

In the brief *line 7* the setting again becomes more chordal, and it remains so throughout the repetitions in *line 8*.

The first two and the last four lines are repeated to give the piece added length and balance *(a-a-b-c-c)*.

Rhythm and Performance in Renaissance Music

In the preceding piece duple meter is plainly felt, except in the last line, which is in triple meter. But no measure bars were written in Renaissance scores; commas above the staff therefore indicate the "measures" in our examples. Indeed, most Renaissance music has no meter or regular pattern of accentuation. The free flow of even beats in such music often exhibits to us an unearthly, emotionless quality, particularly suited to liturgical music (cf. Example 37,

p. 75f), though it did not necessarily impress its original audiences thus, since they found the same style in secular compositions.

The Renaissance is often referred to as the "golden age of vocal polyphony," but instrumental music was also quite common in the period (cf. Pl. IV, p. 71). In church the sound of the organ was conspicuous, and solo performance on the lute [3] and on keyboard instruments as well as ready accompaniments to songs and dances were regarded as essential accomplishments of a cultured lady or gentleman. Also, while most Renaissance music was written for from three to eight vocal parts, instrumental playing usually combined with the singing. (In later periods composition in four parts remained standard for certain types of religious music, conservatively composed in the Renaissance manner, as for example for hymns.)

In secular music such as madrigals, today often heard in choral performance, each part was usually sung by one person only, and various stringed instruments normally participated, either doubling on the voices' parts or playing those parts for which there was no singer in the company. Church music, on the other hand, was sung by choirs, often supported by the organ. In our choirs, composed of both men and women, the voices are divided into high and low ranges. The female voices are called respectively SOPRANO and ALTO (or contralto), and the male, TENOR and BASS (abbreviated S, A, T, B). Before 1600 (and in strictly orthodox churches thereafter) women were not permitted to sing in church; the higher parts were therefore performed by boys, whose voice ranges are nearly the same as those of women.

The Motet

The Renaissance composer reserved his ultimate achievement for the Church, which was frequently his employer. Much of the finest music of the period was therefore religious music,[4] whose two outstanding species were the MOTET and the MASS. Renaissance motets normally are settings of Psalms (from the one hundred and fifty contained in the biblical *Book of Psalms*) or of other Latin liturgical poetry inspired by Psalms. Musically these motets are the counterparts of the madrigals, but usually they are more serious

---

[3] For the lute cf. Appendix I, p. 391.

[4] For a somewhat earlier performance of church music see Pl. I, p. 34.

PLATE III: Abraham Bossé (1602–76), French engraver and painter—Musical Company.

This is a scene from everyday bourgeois life in the sixteenth and seventeenth centuries. Family and friends gather with their music books around the table. The man at the right plays a gamba (cf. Appendix I, p. 392), the girl in the center a lute (cf. p. 68, Appendix I, p. 391), and the others sing, probably a *chanson* (cf. Appendix I, p. 399) or a madrigal.

and longer. The following example by one of the greatest masters of the period is unusually short since it treats only a few verses of a Psalm. In keeping with the words the music is full of vigor and joy.

EXAMPLE 36:   ORLANDUS LASSUS [1532?–94]

Iubilate Deo

The text of this *Motet,* used for several liturgical occasions every year, is *Psalm 100* (99 in the Vulgate, the Latin translation of the Bible accepted by the Roman Catholic Church), verses 1-3. It is divided into five sections, each of which has its own melodic idea, as shown below, but the end of one section generally overlaps the beginning of the next.

Verse 1 is presented as a duet, heard first in the upper parts, repeated by the lower ones (while the others continue to sing), and then once more by the upper parts.

Verse 2: During the last presentation of *a* the tenor re-enters after a rest with the repeated tones of *b*. Soon the other three parts take up this idea, which is handed back and forth among all voices. *Intrate* opens a new section in which all voices conclude simultaneously.

Verse 3: The hopeful, rising line of *d* well expresses the words.

By courtesy of the Sibley Library, Eastman School of Music.

PLATE IV: Johannes Nel (?) (15??–??), German engraver and
            painter—Orlandus Lassus and His Instrumentalists.

This section of the title page from a volume of Lassus's motets
printed during his time shows the master seated at the portable
harpsichord surrounded by two boy and three men singers and
eight musicians, including a tenor viol or gamba, a lute, and an
alto viol, as well as two zinks, one transverse flute, and two trombones. It exemplifies the type of ensemble used for the performance
of motets during the period.

Rhythmically modified it is also used for *e*, which pauses jubilantly on the highest tone for *Deus* and rises triumphantly higher and higher with every repetition to reach the glorious final chords.

In contrast with the duets of *a* and the imitational polyphony of *b* and *c*, *d* and *e* are chordal.

The Mass and Cantus Firmus

The mass is the solemn service of the Roman Catholic and some other Christian churches. Over a long period its various portions developed until, during the thirteenth century, they became stable. The most momentous change thenceforward was the use of polyphonic music at solemn occasions instead of the monophonic Gregorian chants.

The text for the liturgical action—the preparatory prayers and the re-enactment of the Last Supper with the ceremony of Communion—remains unchanged on all occasions. That of additional portions changes with the season and with the holiday on which the mass is celebrated. The musical rendition of major portions of the basic, unchanging action, or ORDINARY, of the mass (so called because these portions are part of the regular order of the ceremony) is what is spoken of in music as a mass; and among the additional pieces, or PROPER, of the mass (so called because they are employed at appropriate occasions only) motets are most important.

In general style and character the music of the Renaissance mass is similar to that of the motet. It consists of five portions, however, each composed like a motet and as long as an average motet or longer, making the mass a much longer work. Therefore in the mass, even more than in motets, a need for musical unification was felt.

As noted, the original idea of "composition" was the adding of parts to an established tune. This principle governed much music before and during the Renaissance. It gave the composer a welcome opportunity not only to establish a relationship between a mass or a motet and the feast to which it belonged, but also to unify a mass. He had merely to choose one of the Gregorian-chant melodies that by Church rule were employed in the particular service and make it the basis of his composition, the CANTUS FIRMUS (Latin—fixed melody). By using the same *cantus firmus*, abbreviated c.f., for all five portions of a mass, the composer could unify them into a larger unit or CYCLE. (This practice was frequent in the Renaissance, though not before and rarely thereafter.) He would present this tune in one part throughout and add other parts contrapuntally to it; or he could derive from the c.f. all the motifs used in the various sections of the work. These procedures satisfied the Renaissance musician and music lover whose approach to music was quite intellectual, but for us they hardly suffice to establish unity in a mass or in a motet. Nevertheless, it helps us considerably to appreciate such works if we know the c.f. and can follow it through its rhythmic and melodic derivatives. This the listener may be able to do, at least partially, in the following example.

- The listener may proceed as follows:

(1) Listen to each major portion and note where the subsections start.
(2) Try to identify the elements of contrast used in and among these subsections.
(3) Try to identify the motif with which each subsection starts, and then follow it in the various voice parts. (This, of course, applies only to imitative passages.) Often also a subsection is further divided into phrases, each derived from a different motif. •

The five portions of the ordinary that form the musical mass are known by their text beginnings as:

(1) *Kyrie*   (2) *Gloria*   (3) *Credo*
(4) *Sanctus–Benedictus*   (5) *Agnus Dei*

Each is further subdivided as follows:

(1) *Kyrie*

(a) *Kyrie eleison* (Lord have mercy)
(b) *Christe eleison*
(c) *Kyrie eleison*—each sung three times

(2) *Gloria*

(a) *Gloria in excelsis Deo* (Glory be to God on high)—intoned by the priest, not sung by the choir

(b) *Et in terra pax* (and on Earth be peace to men of good will. We laud Thee, praise Thee, adore Thee, glorify Thee.)

(c) *Gratias agimus* (We give Thee thanks because of Thy great glory,)

(d) *Domine Deus* (Lord God, King of Heaven, omnipotent Father; Lord, only-begotten Son, Jesus Christ, highest Lord God, Lamb of God, Son of the Father,)

(e) *Qui tollis* (Who takest away the sins of the world, take pity on us; for Thou alone art holy, Thou alone the Lord, Thou alone the highest, Jesus Christ; with the Holy Ghost in the glory of God the Father. Amen.)

(3) *Credo*

(a) *Credo in unum Deum* (I believe in one God,)—intoned by the priest, not sung by the choir.

(b) *Patrem* (the omnipotent Father, creator of Heaven and Earth, of all visible and invisible things; and in our Lord, Jesus Christ, the only-begotten Son of God, begotten by the Father before all time, a God from God, a light from the light, a true God from the true God, begotten, not made, from the same substance as His Father, by Whom all was created, Who for us men and for our salvation descended from Heaven,)

(c) *Et incarnatus est* (and was made flesh through the Holy Ghost out of the Virgin Mary, and became a man.)

(d) *Crucifixus* (He was also crucified for us under Pontius Pilate, suffered, and was buried. And he rose again on the third day according to the Scriptures, and ascended to Heaven, sits at the right of the Father, and will come again in glory to judge the quick and the dead; His reign will have no end.)

(e) *Et in spiritum sanctum* (And I believe in the Holy Ghost, Lord and life-giver, Who proceeds from the Father and the Son, Who is adored and glorified together with the Father and the Son, Who has spoken through the prophets.)

(f) *Et unam sanctam* (And I believe in one holy, catholic, and apostolic Church. I profess one baptism for the remission of sins, and expect the resurrection of the dead and eternal life. Amen.)

(4) *Sanctus—Benedictus*

(a) *Sanctus* (Holy, holy, holy)
(b) *Dominus Deus* (Lord, God Sabaoth,)
(c) *Pleni sunt coeli* (full are the Heavens and the Earth of Thy glory.)
(d) *Osanna* (Hosanna on high!)
(e) *Benedictus* (Praised be, Who comest in the name of God.)
(f) *Osanna*—sections (e) and (f) are sometimes counted as a separate portion of the mass; and sections (d) and (f) may have the same music.

(5) *Agnus Dei*

(a) *Agnus Dei* (Lamb of God, Who carriest the sins of the world, take pity on us,)—sung three times
(b) *Dona nobis pacem* (give us peace.)

EXAMPLE 37:   GIOVANNI PIERLUIGI DA PALESTRINA [1525–94]
Missa [5] *Assumpta est Maria* (1585)

This *Mass* was composed for the feast of Assumption, August 15, and is therefore based on Gregorian chants for that feast (cf. Example 22, p. 33f), especially on the following:

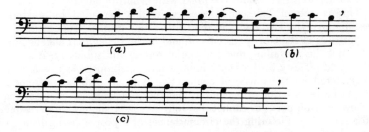

From the chants Palestrina derived the motifs that are worked into the web of voices. In fact, these motifs had earlier served him as material for a motet, and the *Mass* draws on portions of this motet throughout.

Most of this *Mass* is composed in imitative polyphony. The main motif, for instance, derived from the c.f. [see (a) in the above example], is heard, each time in a different setting, at the beginning of each of the five major portions:

---

[5] The name "mass" derives from the final words of the ceremony: *Ite, missa est, Deo gratias*—Go, the congregation is dismissed; thanks to the Lord.

Other motifs derived from the c.f. [see (*b*) and (*c*) above] appear first at the end of the second *Kyrie* and at the end of the *Christe* respectively:

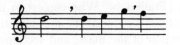

and

In the *Gloria* and in the *Credo,* which have long texts, polyphony is often abandoned for chordal setting to avoid consuming too much time in the service. Although these sections thus provide contrasts, they employ the same motifs as the polyphonic sections. Another source of contrast is employed by Palestrina in the *Christe,* the *Crucifixus,* and the *Benedictus:* They are all written for only four voices as against the fuller six-voice setting of the other sections of the *Mass.* Moreover, in the *Christe* only the lowest voices are heard, in the other two sections only the highest four. Such contrasts between partial and full choir and contrasts between higher and lower voices also give pattern to many phrases and subsections throughout the *Mass* with beautiful effect.

This is one of Palestrina's greatest works, pervaded by a kind of ecstatic joy. The low voices in the *Christe* may intimate supplication, the high voices in the *Crucifixus* lament, and in the *Benedictus* angelic adoration; but the prevailing mood is one of repose and sublimity. A sense of glory and majesty of the Deity imbues the worshipper. As this feeling is engendered by the music in conjunction with an elaborate ceremonial, the beautiful interior of a church, and the psychological effect of many fellow worshippers, it cannot be fully realized merely from listening to a recording. Picturing the circumstances of a proper performance will considerably enhance one's response to the music.

Summary

Renaissance music covers a wide range: dances, religious music, chamber music, and virtuoso pieces.[6] It includes instrumental solo

---

[6] Dramatic music was yet to be developed; and the remaining types of functional music have left few traces, for those who practiced them did not know how to notate music. See Appendix I, p. 407f, for a list of the most eminent Renaissance composers.

and ensemble music, especially settings of dances and of vocal numbers such as motets and madrigals, and many types of accompanied solo songs. Much of this music still awaits a hearing in our day, but what we know of it already proves it to be very enjoyable and often inspiring. Music lovers everywhere are discovering the beauties of many scores that until recently were gathering dust in archives.

The chief characteristics of Renaissance music are related to the concept of space, in that era a central concept. Chords replaced the intervallic writing of the Gothic era, and imitations unified the various voices that had previously been merely juxtaposed, just as in painting perspective replaced two-dimensional design and provided spatial unity where before there had been a multiplicity of scene and action. Likewise a preference for unified sound quality, as in ensembles of human voices or of similar instruments, succeeded a Gothic predilection for disparate sound qualities. The principle of the *cantus firmus*, which played a prominent rôle in the music of both eras, was during the Renaissance pressed into the service of yet another unity, namely that of the mass cycle.

Two other important ideas generally accepted in the period were dignity, or noble restraint, and simplicity. The Renaissance composer usually expressed himself in an even flow of unaccented beats, simple rhythm, and gently undulating lines, as opposed to the regular metric accents, highly complex rhythms, and erratic melodic lines favored by Gothic musicians.

Spread of Art Music and Music Printing

The audience for art music expanded considerably during the Renaissance. In the Middle Ages only small circles within the highest strata of society enjoyed it. With the spread of education during the Renaissance more people discovered the beauties of the various arts. As in other fields of endeavor, the invention of the printing press tremendously accelerated this process. 1501, the year in which Ottaviano Petrucci published in Venice the first book of printed polyphonic music, remains one of the important dates in the history of music.

Endurance of Concepts

The historical importance of the concepts we have discussed is evident. Their import is not, however, merely historical; as with cultural discoveries generally, they have enduring relevance. The reader will find the ideas that were conceived by the composers of the Gothic and Renaissance eras reflected in the music he hears today. Notation of pitch and rhythm, meter, polyphony, chords, imitation—all these we, too, employ. The search for cohesion and unity in large compositions, which led to the cyclic employment of a c.f., of imitational polyphony, and of contrast, has never ended; and the rediscovery of the motif, so important in non-Western music (cf. Example 21, p. 31f), as a primary element of artistic formulation has continued to be a major factor in the evolution of music.

CONCEPTS AND TOPICS DISCUSSED IN THIS SECTION

IV MUSIC IN THE BAROQUE ERA

CONCERT MASS, CANTATA, AND ORATORIO

The Baroque and the Concept of Motion

Late in the sixteenth century many concepts that had long been widely accepted began to be displaced. In the representative arts geometric, static perspective (cf. Pl. II, p. 65) yielded to motion in space (cf. Pl. V, following this page). The Ptolemaic world-picture, in which the Earth was the stationary center of the universe, gave way to the Copernican view, which showed the Earth like other planets hurtling about the sun through space. The ideal of restful balance in Renaissance architecture was abandoned for dynamic force, with motion in space expressed by powerful curves directing the onlooker's eye along turbulent paths (cf. Pl. V, following this page), and in landscaping by mile-long vistas through artfully cut parks toward central edifices. Space was no longer a thing to be filled by stationary objects, but rather a medium for motion.

This turbulence, this urge toward movement drew upon its followers the censure of the conservatives, who clung to their aristocratic taste for balance. They called this new craze of the younger

[79]

By courtesy of Wolfrum Art Publishers, Vienna, Austria.

PLATE V: Peter Paul Rubens (1577–1640), Flemish painter—The
           Death of Decius Mus (a hero of Roman history, about
           340 B.C.E.).

This early Baroque canvas is in style typical of the era—in size,
violence, turbulence of motion, use of powerful curves, and the
implication of vast space.

generation "baroque," that is, grotesque, in corrupt taste; and the term stuck. Today it is applied to a period roughly from 1600 to 1715, yet its tendencies evolved several decades before 1600, and its force was not spent until several decades after 1715.

Harmony and Emotion

In Baroque music, chords, which are the musical equivalent of three-dimensionality, were no longer treated as the end product of the arrangement of three or more parts. They became a basic means for creating and revealing musical motion. Such motion can be generated in two ways:

(a) Tensions can be set up within a consonant chord by introducing tones which do not belong to it, i.e. by creating dissonances. Such tensions then need to be relaxed or resolved. In this process the part that executes the motion easily swings like a pendulum across the position of repose to a new point of tension, occasioning further motion, for example:

(b) Tensions can be set up between one particular chord, which is established as the center or home base, and all others. The latter then tend back toward the center of repose either directly or through a series of further chords, for example:

This second method introduces us to the field of HARMONY,[1] which may be defined as the study of coherent chord progressions.

Broadly generalizing, we may say, with respect to these two ways of creating motion, that the history of music since 1600 has

---

[1] Harmony, like rhythm, melody, and counterpoint, is one of the elements of music. A harmony, on the other hand, is a chord that belongs to a certain key (cf. p. 43).

been a search for ever greater tensions and ever longer routes of detour before the final relaxation. Now motion is, in human affairs, associated with emotion; indeed, motion is the most frequent clue to personal tensions labeled emotional. The search for tensions, therefore, means that since 1600 music, along with drama, poetry, and painting, has, on the whole, tended toward ever greater emotionalism.[2] It is easy to understand, then, why, with emotion in the focus of their interest, Baroque composers began to stress different tempos and dynamics (cf. pp. 29, 46f) as well as dramatic music.

Homophony

With the change from part-writing to chord-writing and the increasing use of instruments, composers began to abandon vocal polyphony as their chief concern and turned to the accompanied solo—either vocal or instrumental. The resulting texture, a melody with a chordal accompaniment, has been called HOMOPHONY (Greek: *homós*—same, *phoné*—voice; all voices in the chord move essentially at the same time) or MONODY (Greek: *mónos*—single, *odé*—melody). Moreover, since emotion could now be expressed by purely musical means, without the aid of words, instrumental music took its place as an equal beside vocal composition.

Classes of Baroque Music

After 1600 there existed therefore three major classes of music: (1) conservative church music, continuing sixteenth-century choral polyphony, although much church music followed current trends; (2) instrumental music, mostly homophonic but also including many polyphonic works; and (3) the accompanied vocal solo, above all in dramatic music both secular and religious. Among these classes there existed many transitional types, compromises, and combinations.

Concert and A-Cappella Mass

This section is devoted to one of the compromise types—vocal-

---

[2] Motion as described under (a) above served emotional expression during the Renaissance, and other forms of motion were known to previous eras. But the tensions made possible by the advent of harmony far surpass earlier means of musical motion in force and variability.

instrumental church music, which points up the differences between Renaissance and Baroque music. To this type belong, for example, the Roman Catholic CONCERT MASSES, which combine choral polyphony with orchestral accompaniment and vocal solo, and abandon the *cantus-firmus* idea. Sung in churches until the early nineteenth century, when a papal encyclical declared concert masses too distracting for the worshippers, they are today heard in concert only.[3]

As a reaction against the trend toward employing instruments in church, the notion of *a cappella* (Italian—for chapel choir only) arose in the seventeenth century. This notion was then also applied to earlier music, such as that of Palestrina and Lassus, which had originally not been exclusively choral (cf. p. 68). Both *a-cappella* and concert masses are, of course, written to the unchanging Latin text already given (see p. 73ff). One example, drawn from what is probably the greatest of all concert masses, may suffice to show the depths of emotion plumbed by Baroque music.

EXAMPLE 38:   JOHANN SEBASTIAN BACH [1685–1750]

Crucifixus and *Et resurrexit* from the "High Mass in *B* Minor" (1733)

The greatness of the *High Mass* has been recognized only in this century. Much too long for liturgical use, it is nevertheless one of the most sublime expressions of the religious spirit. Bach, a Protestant, composed much of this *Mass* for the Catholic Duke of Saxony in order to receive the honorary title of Court Conductor.

The fourth section of the *Credo* is here subdivided into two contrasting sections. The depth of sadness of the *Crucifixus* is hardly surpassable. This section employs in the lowest part, or bass, a melodic idea that is repeated over and over again without interruption:

The other parts add ever new configurations of various motifs. Like the first one:

---

[3] Music that supports ritual action has the purpose of inducing a mood favorable to a religious experience. It is usually not meant to be listened to for aesthetic pleasure, as preoccupation with aesthetic quality may distract the listener from serious worship.

each is taken up in turn by all voices.

The small accompanying ensemble of flutes and strings, the slow tempo, the low range of the voices, the prevailing *legato* and *portato*, and the steady softness that mark the *Crucifixus* meet a vehement contrast in the full orchestra, the fast pace, the high range of the voices, the *staccato*, and the prevailing *forte* of the *Et resurrexit*. Here we encounter ecstatic jubilation, which also emanates from the *coloraturas* that pervade this section. The four main thoughts of the text are given separate settings, of which the fourth is a rather close restatement of the first:

Orchestral interludes precede the second and third subsections, the latter being for bass solo, and set them off as a contrasting middle portion, though both are melodically derived from the main idea.

The Cantata

The Protestants gradually eliminated Latin from their services, and by about 1750 had replaced it with the vernacular—German, English, Dutch, Swedish, and so forth. The outline of their services, however, remained substantially the same as that of the Catholic Church. The unchanging portions (ordinary) of the mass were translated and set in simple hymn style; the motet, on the other hand, was replaced by the church CANTATA, a work for one to three solo voices, often also choir, and instrumental ensemble or orchestra, based, like the motet, on the text of the gospel-reading for the particular service; the remaining changeable portions (proper) were supplied by chorales (cf. p. 35).

Usually a cantata has an instrumental opening or OVERTURE (often called *sinfonia*), or it begins with a choral number. Then there follow two or three arias, contrasting in mood and tempo, and a final duet or *terzetto* (an aria for two or three singers), all numbers expressing varied contemplations upon the central thought connected with the occasion; but there is no fixed order. Often a chorale closes a church cantata.

Every German cantor wrote many such works. The peak of achievement in this regard was reached in Bach.

EXAMPLE 39: JOHANN SEBASTIAN BACH [1685–1750]

Cantata No. 140, Wachet auf, ruft uns die Stimme
(Wake Ye, Wake! Rings Forth the Warning, 1742)

This is one of the about three hundred cantatas Bach wrote during his busy life. Only about two hundred of them have been preserved, and these contain some of the finest music of all time. In orchestration, number and types of sections, voices employed, and compositional approach each is individually conceived; the variety among these works is truly astonishing.

Cantata No. 140 is written for three solo voices (soprano, tenor, and bass), choir, and an orchestra of two oboes, English horn (a low or alto oboe), French horn, solo violin, string orchestra, and organ or harpsichord. The text is based on *Matthew*, chapter xxv, verses 1-13, the parable of the wise and the foolish virgins.

This is what is called a CHORALE CANTATA, i.e. it not only concludes with a chorale, as do most of Bach's cantatas, but also uses the chorale elsewhere in the work. Indeed, the chorale organizes the entire *Cantata*. Its first stanza is heard in clarion tones of the sopranos during the mighty opening chorus. A short RECITATIVE (for an explanation of this term see *No. 2*, p. 86f) and a duet follow, the latter embellished by the solo violin, and then the second stanza of the chorale is sung by the tenors. Another recitative and duet are presented—and this time the duet includes an oboe solo—before the third stanza of the chorale is sung in simple hymn fashion.

The seven numbers of this *Cantata* are thus symmetrically arranged. Such rational order in composite works is a characteristic trait of Bach and the Baroque era in general.

No. 1, Chorus

> "Wake ye, wake!" rings forth the warning
> of guardians high up on the watchtow'rs.
> "Wake thou, O wake, Jerusalem!"
>
> 'Tis the very dead of midnight.
> They summon us with clarion voices:
> "Where bide ye then, ye virgins wise?

"See! There the bridegroom comes!
Arise! Your lanterns take!
Alleluya!

"Prepare yourselves
for wedding rites!
Haste! Greet the bridegroom on the way!"

The orchestral prelude exhibits two rhythmic motifs:

which accompany the entire first number. Throughout, the lower voices oppose their own imitative passages to the unadorned phrases of the chorale melody, triumphantly presented in the soprano. (The melody is given under *No. 7*, p. 91.) This is one of the many ways in which Bach and other cantors set chorale melodies. The practice of presenting a pre-existing melody or *cantus firmus* in new polyphonic contexts goes back, as we have seen, to the very beginnings of Western music (cf. pp. 62f, 72).

Each of the four sections of the chorale stanza contains three lines. Each of these lines is presented as a new phrase, separated from the others by orchestral interludes. As is usual in chorales, the first two sections of the stanza are musically identical (cf. Example 23, p. 36). The third section (lines 7-9) is treated somewhat more elaborately than the others, the brief ninth line being preceded by a long *alleluya* in the lower choir voices. After the fourth section the orchestral prelude is repeated, DA CAPO (Italian—from the beginning). Such a repetition of an introduction was a favorite device of Baroque composers to round off a composition.

No. 2, Recitative for Tenor

Er kommt, er kommt, der Braeut'-gam kommt! Ihr Toech-ter
He comes! He comes! The bride - groom comes! Go forth, ye

---

[4] The tenor is usually written in treble clef, but sung an octave lower.

Zi - ons, kommt her - aus, sein Aus - gang ei - let aus der
daught - ers of Zi - on! His way leads from the lof - ty

Hoe - he in eu - er Mut - ter Haus.
pla - ces: He nears your ver - y door!

The bridegroom comes, and light as roebuck or fallow fawn
he springs from ledge to rocky ledge
and brings to you the wedding meal.
Awake: Stir ye from sleep! The bridegroom welcome meetly!
There! See there! It is He that cometh!

During the Baroque the combination of recitative and aria (or duet)
became standard. The former derived from the solemn recitation of scrip-
ture in the service and evolved into two types—one highly melodic and
richly accompanied, sometimes called ARIOSO (aria-like) and more often
ACCOMPAGNATO RECITATIVE (Italian—accompanied; see *No. 5*, p. 89f);
the other less melodic, more in the manner of speaking, accompanied only
by the organ or by the harpsichord supported by a 'cello, known as
SECCO RECITATIVE (Italian—dry).

The music that the performer of the keyboard instrument played was
written as a single bass line, beneath which figures were added to indicate intervals to be played along with the bass notes; "2" would indicate
a second, or an octave and a second, above the bass note; "4" a fourth,
or an octave and a fourth; and so forth. From this FIGURED BASS the ac-
companist would improvise the desired harmonies.

This *Recitative* is a *secco* recitative. Its complete score, like that of
many other Baroque compositions, consists of two parts only, the vocal
line and the figured bass.

No. 3, Duet for Soprano and Bass

a Phrases 1, 2, and 5

| Wenn | kommst | du, | mein | Heil? |
| My | Sav - | ior, | how | long? |

Soprano: My Savior, . . .
Bass: I come with thy bliss.
Soprano: I wait Thee, with oil blazing brightly.

b Phrases 3 and 4

I   ö - - pen the hall.

Bass: I open . . .
Soprano: Ah, open the hall!
Both: Celestial the fare!
Soprano: Come, Jesus!
Bass: Come greet me, O my love-laden soul!

All phrases employ the same motif, but through a reversal of its direction the third and fourth phrases contrast with the first, second, and fifth. Instrumental interludes follow the second, third, and fourth phrases, and the prelude is repeated at the end.

A garland of solo-violin passages adorns the highly expressive, lyric duet, representing the bride (conventional symbol of the Church) and the bridegroom (Jesus), whose words, according to Baroque custom, are almost endlessly repeated (cf. *No. 6*, p. 90). In addition to these three lines of music, only a very active melodic line of the bass instruments is heard.

Such a continuous bass line is one of the outstanding marks of Baroque music. It is appropriately called BASSO CONTINUO or THOROUGHBASS, and is played by all bass instruments—'cello, bassoon, double bass, and harpsichord or organ. These were therefore referred to as *continuo* instruments, playing *continuo* parts, terms also applied to recitatives. With the help of figures the player of the keyboard instrument, here as in a recitative, improvised chords, much as our guitar or accordion players do today.

Musicians therefore often call the Baroque era the "period of the *basso continuo*" or the "period of figured bass." Both these related technics were gradually abandoned in the succeeding era.

The beauty of this *Duet*, like that of the second one, lies in the ever-new variants of the motifs: the changes of mode and pitch and the new figurations of the violin. The answering and rhythmic complementation of the two singers adds much charm.

No. 4 Chorus

> Zion hears her guardians singing.
> Her heart leaps high in bliss ecstatic.
> She wakens and springs swiftly forth:
>
> Her friend comes from heav'n in splendor,
> Though gracious, firm; in truth his power.
> Her light grows bright—her sun mounts high.
>
> Now come, Thou priceless crown,
> Lord Jesus, Son of God!
> Hosianna!
>
> All follow Thee
> To festive hall,
> Companions at the evening meal.

A second type of CHORALE SETTING constitutes the center piece of the *Cantata*. Above the *basso continuo* there is a single melodic line, played by the combined strings, developing out of the following motif:

To this duet is added one line after another of the second stanza of the chorale, sung by the choir tenors. (For the melody see *No. 7*, p. 91.) This piece is also well known as a chorale setting for organ alone, and such organ chorales belong to the outstanding contributions of Bach and his fellow cantors (cf. Example 44, p. 106).

No. 5, Recitative for Bass

> Now enter unto me, O thou, my chosen bride!
> This troth I have with thee made for eternity.
> Thee shall I at my heart and on my arm bear as a holy signet,
> and thy beclouded eye make brighter.

Forget, O Zion, now thy fears, the pangs that thou in durance
suffer'dst!
On my left arm shalt thou recline;
caressingly my right will shield thee.

As often in works of Baroque composers, the singer who represents
Jesus is a bass, and his recitative is accompanied by full string chords.
The music is also more melodious, more dignified than the declamation in
No. 2. Here we have an *accompagnato* recitative. (An *arioso* usually has
a more elaborate accompaniment than this; see Example 40, *No. 2*,
p. 93.)

No. 6, Duet for Soprano and Bass

a Sections 1 and 3

Soprano: I know my friend!
Bass: I am thy friend.
Both: Eternal love doth bind us.

b Section 2

Soprano: I shall with Thee—
Bass: Thou shalt with me—
Both: 'mid heaven's roses wander,
            there joy in its fulness, there ecstasy know!

Here a solo oboe joins the two singers. The *Duet* is organized in two
distinct sections, and the first is repeated at the end: *A-B-A.* This type of
organization is known as that of the DA-CAPO ARIA, then in great vogue.
The first section is framed by instrumental passages; the only other
such passage occurs after the first vocal phrase, which is then repeated.
This feature, a brief initial vocal phrase, stating the main motif, followed
by an instrumental passage, and then repeated in the presentation of the
entire melody, is another trait typical of eighteenth-century arias, called
DEVISE. The main motif of the *Duet* is:

No. 7, Chorale

The third stanza of the chorale, sung by the choir and supported by
the full orchestra, provides a solemn and effective conclusion to the
Cantata:

1. Glo - ri - a to Thee be chant - ed
4. Twelve pure pearls a - dorn the port - als
2. by all the tongues of men and an - gels,
5. of ho - ly Zi - on! We are fel - lows
3. with harp and cym - bal join - ing in!
6. to an - gels stand - ing by Thy throne.
7. No eye has yet dis - cerned, 8 no ear has
ev - er heard 9. So deep a joy.
10. Thus in our bliss, 11. be - - hold! be - hold!
12. in sweet re - joic - ing e'er we live.

The text of this *Cantata* may strike us today as quaint, even in translation. It is rather typical of works produced by the strong religious current that swept Leipzig during the time when Bach lived there (1723–
50). The music, however, is exquisite—grand, joyful, lyrical, and edifying
in turn, highly inspiring both as art and as church music.[5]

---

[5] In England a slightly different type of work arose to replace the motet in
the service—the ANTHEM. (This term is used today in a completely different
sense to denote a nation's flag-song or national hymn.) In the anthem the
choir is always prominent, either employed throughout ("full anthem") or alternating with soloists ("verse anthem"). First composed by Elizabethan composers, especially by William Byrd, it reached its peak in the works of Henry
Purcell and George Frederick Handel. Today church musicians employ the
term "anthem" also for simple hymns sung in lieu of true anthems.

The Oratorio

In a drive for popular education and participation in religion on the basis of understanding rather than custom, both Catholic and Protestant Churches developed a further type of religious music, the ORATORIO. This was an outgrowth of dramatizations of biblical and gospel scenes, presented during several decades before and after 1600 in the prayer room (Italian: *oratorio*) of a Roman church. In the 1630's the simple four-part polyphony and the conservative *a-cappella* singing of these presentations were displaced by the new dramatic style for solos and instrumental accompaniment. This was accomplished by the Roman master, Giacomo Carissimi (1605–74), often called the "father of the oratorio."

The greatest masters of the oratorio, however, were German Protestants, especially Handel. This composer established it as a large work in several "parts" or "acts" (two or three), typically but not always based on biblical material, often highly dramatic but without stage action, and with prominent use of the choir. The oratorio usually involves from four to seven soloists and a large orchestra with organ. Though often religious, it is not liturgical and is frequently performed in concert halls.

EXAMPLE 40: GEORGE FREDERICK HANDEL [Georg Friedrich Händel, 1685–1759]

Nos. 2-4 from "The Messiah" (1741)

Handel was German by birth and upbringing. But in his early twenties he studied in Italy and became one of the eminent followers of the *bel-canto* tradition. The major portion of his life—from 1711 onward— he spent in England, whose music he influenced profoundly. Among Handel's twenty-odd oratorios *The Messiah* is the most popular, though several others are equally excellent. This work has three *Parts;* the first deals with prophecies about the Messiah and the birth of Jesus; the second, with his death; and the third, with the meaning of the whole event.

Except for the orchestral *Overture,* the example presents the opening three numbers of the work. Within this brief excerpt we meet all the typical ingredients of such works: recitatives, arias, and choruses.

No. 2, Recitative for Tenor

‖: Comfort ye, comfort ye, my people! :‖: saith your God. :‖
‖: Speak ye comfortably to Jerusalem :‖
and cry unto her that her warfare, her warfare is accomplished,
‖: that her iniquity is pardoned. :‖
The voice of him that crieth in the wilderness,
prepare ye the way of the Lord,
make straight in the desert a highway for our God!

An *arioso* occupies the major portion of *No. 2* (lines 1-4), whereas its last portion is a *secco* recitative. The words are taken from *Isaiah*, chapter xl, verses 1-3, and with many repetitions Handel emphasizes their meaning.

No. 3, Aria for Tenor

In *No. 3*, an aria, the repetitions follow the custom of the period (a custom which survived long thereafter) and serve chiefly as a vehicle for vocal display (cf. the *Aria* from Rossini's *Barber of Seville*, p. 52ff; also Example 39, *Nos. 3* and *6*, pp. 88f, 90):

and ev'ry mountain and hill made low,
the crooked straight,
and the rough places plain.

The exaltation expressed in the words of *Isaiah* xl, 4, is paralleled by the generally rising melody. Of the two large sections of this *Aria*, the second repeats the words of the first and varies its music. Both are subdivided into two subsections, one characterized by long *coloraturas* on the word "exalted," the other by long-held tones and gently undulating figures, symbolizing the word "plain." The employment of such musical symbols was very common in Handel's time. It added an intellectual side to the beauty of the melody and the brilliance of the vocal display.

No. 4, Chorus

and all flesh ____ shall see it together,

for the mouth of the Lord hath spok-en it.

The text is *Isaiah* xl, 5. The first phrase, *a*, is spun out to over four times its length by slightly varied repetitions to make up the opening section. A second section is entirely derived from one small motif of the first, *b*, which is sung against the long, repeated tones of *c*. This second section balances the first through repetitions of *b* and *c* in an effective use of the various ranges of the voices. A third section then combines all three ideas in a variety of repetitions. These three sections are clearly separated by the only instrumental interludes in this *Chorus*. A final fourth section, starting with *a* in the sopranos, reviews all ideas once more.

This *Chorus* is an excellent example of Handel's grand choral writing, which perhaps constitutes the main force of his oratorios. Melodic ideas and contrapuntal lines are secondary and often, as here, somewhat slight. Handel's majestic sweep depends on vigorous and steady tempo, the repetition of simple but characteristic rhythmic patterns, and full volume. The magnificent impact of his large works is also due to a careful disposition of vocal and instrumental resources: Starting out with strings alone in the *Recitative (No. 2)*, the scoring is enriched in the *Aria (No. 3)*, and reaches its greatest fullness in this *Chorus*.

The Passion Oratorio

An important subtype of the oratorio is the PASSION ORATORIO, for short also "passion" (from Latin: *passus*—having suffered; "patient" has the same root). Such works describe the sufferings of Jesus as recounted in the gospels and are named according to the one of the Evangelists from whom the text is derived: Matthew, Mark, Luke, or John, the authors of the four gospels in the *New Testament*. They are performed in Protestant churches (today also in concert halls) during Holy Week, preceding Easter.

Outstanding among early composers of passion music was Heinrich Schütz (1585–1672), the greatest German composer of his century. His passions were still *a cappella*, following the sixteenth-century tradition. Immediately after Schütz's death, however, the passion oratorio rose to vogue. Like the oratorio it employs an or-

chestra and consists of recitatives, arias, and choruses. It reached
its apogee in two of Bach's *five Passions,* those according to St.
John and according to St. Matthew. Bach gave increased solemnity
to these solemn works by including many chorales, one of which
has already been considered (see Example 23, p. 36).

EXAMPLE 41:   JOHANN SEBASTIAN BACH [1685–1750]

Nos. 42-47 from the "Passion According to St. Matthew" (1729)

This work uses the entire Chapters xxvi and xxvii of *Matthew.* The
First Part recounts the events up to Jesus' capture, and the *Second* his
trial and death. Additional reflections—the aria texts—are the work of
Christian Friedrich Henrici (pseudonym: Picander, 1700–64). The passages here chosen are from the *Second Part,* dealing with *Matthew,*
chapter xxvi, verses 63-75.

The narrative portions of the text are sung by the Evangelist, by tradition a tenor, while all direct speeches are sung by soloists, basses being
used for the High Priest, Jesus, and Peter, and sopranos for the two
maids. As in the *Cantata* (Example 39), Jesus' lines are always accompanied more solemnly by all the stringed instruments, whereas the lines
of the other speakers are set in *secco* recitatives. We may observe how
much more detailed attention Bach gives to each word than does Handel.
For this reason his melodic line is often more jagged.

Excitement and realism are added to the drama in the frequent interruptions of the recitatives by choral passages: the direct speeches of the
crowd or of the disciples, vividly presented by a double choir. In the
first such insertion (end of *No. 42*) the eight voices enter in rapid succession with telling effect; it is as though the excitement were fast spread-
ing through the council chamber, for one group after another of the
onlookers breaks into the cry: "His guilt by death be purgéd!" And later
(end of *No. 43*), as with mounting fury they belabor the accused, their
mocking queries: "Soothsayer! Messiah! Who struck thee this blow?"
re-echo in the two choirs.

These are the words of this dramatic scene:

No. 42, Recitative

Ev.:   And the High Priest thus gave answer to him and said to
        him:
H.P.:   Now I charge thee by the living, all-judging God, that
        thou tell plainly if thou be Messiah, yea, e'en God's son.
Ev.:   Jesus said to him:
Jes.:   'Tis thy word. Yet I say to you: Hereafter it will happen
        that ye see with wonder the Son of Man placed at the
        right hand of pow'r and coming in the clouds of high
        heaven.

Ev.:   Then in anguish did the High Priest rend his garments
        and said:
H.P.:   He is God's blasphemer! What need now of further wit-
        ness? Look ye, now have ye heard no hearsay, but his
        lips blaspheming. How judge ye him?
Ev.:   They answered to him and shouted:
Choir: His guilt by death be purgéd!

No. 43, Recitative

Ev.:   The elders and the scribes then spat in his face and struck
        him with their clenched fists. Some in the multitude did
        smite his very face, reviling:
Choir: Soothsayer! Messiah! Who struck thee this blow?

No. 44, Chorale

At this point the drama is interrupted by a *Chorale,* reflecting upon
the situation. The melody of the first three lines is repeated for the last
three with only a minor change at the end; but Bach harmonizes the
repetition very differently.[6]

Wer   hat dich   so   ge - schla - gen,
1. Who was it, Lord, did smite Thee, 2. Thy good with ill re -
4. For Thou wert no   of - fen - der, 5. nor didst to sin sur -

quite Thee, 3. so foul - ly treat - ed Thee?
ren - der; 6. from ev - il   Thou wert ev - er free.

No. 45, Recitative

Then the scene shifts to Peter outside, as he is asked first by two maids
and then by a crowd of bystanders and thrice denies knowing Jesus. The
end of this scene, describing the crowing of the rooster and Peter's bitter
tears, is one of the famous passages in this score. The words are as
follows:

6 The translation is by Henry S. Drinker.
7 For passages that, when repeated, deviate toward the end, the device here
shown is employed: the repetition with "first" and "second ending" or *prima*
and *seconda volta.*

Ev.:   Peter meanwhile sat near the palace gates; there approached him one of the maids and said:

M.1:   And thou, wast thou not with that Jesus from Galilea?

Ev.:   But Peter denied it before those present and said:

Pet.:   I know not what thou sayest.

Ev.:   When he stepped to the door to leave her, yet a second one saw him there and spoke to those that were around her:

M.2:   This is one of those with Jesus of Nazareth.

Ev.:   He denied it a second time and swore to it:

Pet.:   Of this man I know not aught!

Ev.:   And after but a little while there came before him those there present and said unto Peter:

Choir: Surely thou art one of his disciples; the way thou speakest betrays thee.

No. 46, Recitative

Ev.:   Then in his wrath he started cursing and swore loudly:

Pet.:   Of this man I know not aught!

Ev.:   And soon there crowed the distant cock. Then came to Peter's mind the word of Jesus as he had forewarned him: "Ere thou the cock's crow hearest, thou shalt have three times denied me." And he went forth and wept, crying bitterly.

No. 47, Aria for Alto

The *Aria* that concludes our selection from this work is one of the most heart-rending supplications for mercy. These are its much repeated words:

> Be merciful!
> Be merciful, my God; look on my tears so bitter;
>   ‖: be merciful, :‖   my God,   ‖: be merciful, :‖
> look on my tears, O look on my tears so bitter;
> be merciful, my God, look on my tears,
> O look on my tears so bitter!
>   ‖: Look Thou here; :‖
>   heart and eye now weep to Thee,
>   weep to Thee bitterly.
> ‖: Be merciful! :‖   (repetition of lines 2-6)

The *Aria* is actually a duet of the alto voice and a solo violin, accompanied by the strings and the *continuo*. The solo violin introduces the main idea:

which is then heard twice with lovely contrapuntal variants and frequent exchanges between the violin and the voice. This constitutes the first section (lines 1-6). The middle section (lines 7-9), starting instrumentally, expands the melody somewhat. The next brief pause in the voice marks the beginning of the varied recapitulation of the first section, which is concluded with the orchestral prelude, *da capo.*

Bach and Handel

Vocal display is clearly much less important to Bach than it is to Handel and other *bel-canto* composers. Bach seeks apt expression of idea rather than beautiful vocalization. Even when he uses *coloratura,* he uses it as a means of expression of idea, not as display.

A comparison between the grand line and sweep of Handel and the minutely detailed, highly expressive craftsmanship of Bach affords deep insight into the social meaning of art music. Whereas the one wrote for large halls and sizable choirs and orchestras, the other wrote for small groups performing in the intimacy of a middle-sized church. Both achieved their several goals admirably—Handel as a grand seigneur, and Bach as a craftsman in the service of God.

CONCEPTS AND TOPICS DISCUSSED IN THIS SECTION

PRELUDE AND FUGUE

Vocal music flourished during the Baroque era, but instrumental music did not lag behind. During the Renaissance it had already become an independent category, springing from three roots, namely (a) imitation of vocal music, (b) improvisation and display, and (c) dance music. Instrumental music developed rapidly, and at the close of the Baroque comprised a rich repertory, including many works of superb quality. Those deriving from the first two roots are the subject of this section; the next one will deal with music growing from the third root.

First Root of Instrumental Music: Imitation of Vocal Types

Among the most characteristic types of Baroque instrumental music are those that grew from the first root. The motet, the madrigal, and the mass of the sixteenth century had two features in common: the imitation of motifs by all voices, and the construction of the whole composition from chains of such imitative sections. The playing of vocal music by instrumental ensembles is reported as early as the thirteenth century. It increased rapidly in vogue during the Renaissance; but the more the meaning of the words in such pieces became lost in purely instrumental performance, the more it became clear that these chains of imitative phrases without pattern and unity were musically unsatisfactory.

The Fugue

A long search started therefore in the sixteenth century to meet the demands of purely musical coherence in these instrumental counterparts of motets, known as RICERCARI (singular: *ricercar* or *ricercare*). Composers gradually reduced the number of imitative sections while increasing their length, until early in the seventeenth century the Dutch organist, Jan Pieterszon Sweelinck (1562–1621), produced a well unified type: an extended piece in imitative polyphony, based on a single motif or on a musical idea of some length termed a SUBJECT. This is the kind of piece we heard in the central portion of Bach's *Toccata* (see p. 57f).

Such a work is called a FUGUE (from Latin: *fuga*—flight, referring to the feature of imitation, as one voice appears to flee from another). This type of composition reached its apogee with Bach in the early eighteenth century; but it is still with us. Hindemith, Shostakovich, and Barber, to name but a few contemporary composers, have contributed excellent examples. Whereas a fugue is normally based on a single subject, composers at times introduce two or three subjects in a fugue in such a fashion that they react upon each other. These subjects may be introduced and developed separately and then combined, or they may be introduced simultaneously at the outset. Such fugues are called DOUBLE and TRIPLE FUGUES.

Second Root of Instrumental Music: Improvisation and Display

A second root of instrumental music is found in the preludes, interludes, and postludes performed with songs as far back as the songs of the troubadours in the twelfth century. The desire of instrumentalists to exhibit both their technic and their instruments is reflected in virtuoso pieces such as toccatas. During the sixteenth century full chords and rapid passages were favored for this purpose. They are heard, for example, in the improvisational opening and closing sections of Bach's *Toccata*.

Prelude and Fugue

Many early toccatas include, besides such portions, one or two fugues, thus combining the fruit of both evolutions. Later in the Baroque a new type of composition developed from this combination, the PRELUDE AND FUGUE. Here the improvisational sections are combined into a single unified portion, the prelude, which can stand by itself. It often preserves the character of an etude, but frequently exhibits lyricism (imitating the contemporary aria) or derives from a dance of the period (as discussed in the next section). Sometimes such a prelude is given larger proportions; in such cases the title "fantasy" often appears. The fugues in such composite works similarly present a variety of expressions, ranging from profound gravity to ethereal lightness.

Our first example of such composite works is for organ, which offers many possibilities for contrasting sound qualities (cf. Appendix I, p. 390f). Organ works of this type, while of varied length, are therefore usually quite long. This one opens with a fantasy.

EXAMPLE 42:   JOHANN SEBASTIAN BACH [1685–1750]

Fantasy and Fugue in G Minor for Organ

Fantasy

The *Fantasy* starts with majestic chords and a quasi-improvised, ornate melody, each played on a different MANUAL (hand keyboard), all above a repeated and then sustained bass tone played on the PEDALS (foot keyboard). Such a tone is called a PEDAL POINT or ORGAN POINT ("point" being used here in the same sense as in "counterpoint," meaning "note"):

¹ The sign ⌵ indicates a mordent:

² The signs ⌁ , ⌁⌁ , or tr (⌁⌁⌁)

indicate a TRILL:

A quiet, melodious, contrapuntal section furnishes a beautiful contrast. It is, in turn, succeeded by a dramatic quasi-recitative. Once more the quiet section is heard, varied, followed by truly improvisational chords. The concluding section is derived from the beginning.

Fugue

This magnificent *Fantasy,* fanciful yet well rounded, ushers in a vigorous *Fugue.* Jauntily skipping through a wide pitch range, the subject enters:

The four voices enter with the subject from the soprano downward. (The terms "soprano," "alto," "tenor," and "bass," as well as "voices," used for the parts in polyphonic instrumental music, reflect its root— imitation of vocal music.) As is typical, the subject is first heard by itself, based on the tonic, *G.* Its second entrance, on a level other than the tonic and usually, as here, on the fifth step of the scale (here *D*), is called the ANSWER. Brief interludes appear before the next two entrances of the subject, which, in this four-voiced *Fugue,* complete the EXPOSITION or first POINT OF IMITATIONS, i.e. the first cycle of presentations of the subject in all or most voices.

From the subject derives the figuration that brings the first section of the *Fugue* to a close; such an interlude, in which the subject itself is not heard, is called an EPISODE. After this episode the exposition is almost faithfully repeated though somewhat elaborated and without the tenor entrance, forming what is sometimes called a COUNTEREXPOSITION, a feature not present in all fugues.

The second episode even brightens the music by leading to Major as the third section opens. Three of the four subject entrances (in the order T, S, A, B) are followed by long episodes, of which the second entrance and episode, because they are in only two parts, are especially conspicuous. The brightness of the music is enhanced by a long silence of the pedals, which only with the fourth entrance rejoin the manuals.

A partial entrance of the subject in the soprano anticipates the fourth section, which returns to the main key, G Minor. Here each of the three entrances (T, S, A) is spun out into a long episode, the first and last of which derive from the episode that closes the third section.

The final section opens with a variant of the two-part entrance from the third section. The subject enters four times (S,T,A,B); its last entrance, using the pedals, previously silent for a long time, gives the work a ringing, triumphant conclusion.

In resumé: This *Fugue* has five sections—exposition and counterexposition in Minor, a central section stressing Major, and two sections in Minor which act as a "return." In sections two and four there are only three complete entrances of the subject. On the other hand, the episodes relate section three to each of the succeeding sections. The interesting plan of the *Fugue* is clear from this diagram:

$$\text{Tonalities:} \quad \text{I} - \text{I} - \quad \text{II} - \quad \text{I} - \text{I}$$
$$\text{Number of entrances:} \quad 4 - 3 - \quad 4 - \quad 3 - 4$$
$$\text{Episodes:} \quad E_1 - E_2 - E_{3-4-5} - E_{5-6-5} - E_{4-7}$$

There is no stereotyped, overall pattern for fugues; each is an individual solution of the problem of deriving from one subject several melodic lines in an interplay of voices. The art of the fugue composer is only partly revealed in the way in which he combines the various parts. His true gift is primarily that of inventing a characteristic subject that both sets a definite mood and provides opportunities to derive from it further material, so that the entire composition grows from it. The whole subject, as we have seen, reappears throughout at various intervals and pitch levels in all parts, virtually unchanged, while the other voices form ever new counterpoints.

Our next example, a deeply serious work, includes a fugue of much greater complexity. It is one of the *Forty-Eight Preludes and Fugues* that make up Bach's famous collection called *The Well-Tempered Clavier*—The Well-Tuned Keyboard Instrument, i.e. in this case, probably the harpsichord.[3]

EXAMPLE 43:   JOHANN SEBASTIAN BACH [1685–1750]

Prelude and Fugue No. 8, in E-flat Minor
from "The Well-Tempered Clavier," vol. 1 (1722)

Prelude

The *Prelude* has the character of an aria and is in the rhythm of a slow, triple-meter dance of Spanish origin, called *sarabande* (cf. Example 45, p. 109):

---

[3] See Appendix I, p. 385f, for an explanation of "equal temperament."

The first and third sections correspond: In each there is only one melodic line, alternating in the right and left hands, to the accompaniment of full chords. In the middle section both hands play the melody in imitation, and chords are for the most part absent. Intensity increases with this increase of activity.

Fugal Devices

For the *Fugue* some preliminary explanations are needed. In each section of a fugue it is usual for every part to enter once with the subject. The subject may, however, be presented in various guises (see the examples below), namely in

INVERSION, i.e. reversing the direction of all intervals, those originally descending rendered ascending, and *vice versa;*

RETROGRESSION (also known as CRAB or as CANCRIZANS, from Latin: *cancer*—crab), or reading the subject backwards, last note first and first note last;

a new rhythmic version;

AUGMENTATION, with each note value of the subject doubled;

DIMINUTION, with each note value half as long as originally;

STRETTO, an entrance of the subject in any shape in one voice while another is in the process of presenting it.

In addition, several of these FUGAL DEVICES may be applied simultaneously. However, in a given fugue none or only a few of these devices may be employed. The following appear in this *Fugue:*

"s" is the subject itself:

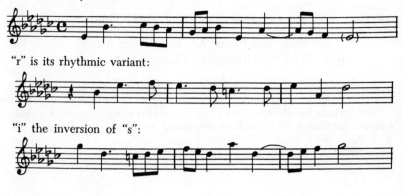

"r" is its rhythmic variant:

"i" the inversion of "s":

"ir" the inversion of "r":

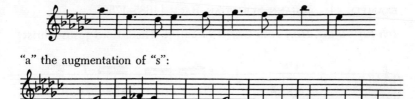

"a" the augmentation of "s":

Fugue

As in the preceding example, the *Fugue* starts typically with the subject—a deeply contemplative one—in a single voice (A). The other two voices gradually enter with the subject (S, B), from which flows all the melodic invention that follows. The fourth entrance of the subject in the exposition (B) leads the listener to expect a four-part fugue. However, this is a "redundant" entrance—a mere exuberance; Bach needs only three voices to create an astonishing variety of combinations.

The second section proceeds to new keys, but remains in Minor. It has three entrances, all in *stretto* (between S and A), the second of which involves "r." The central section, in Major, introduces "i" (S, A, B). Continuing chiefly with "i," the fourth section also involves "r," "ir," and "s." Harmonically it is a "return"; in addition, because of its three *stretto* entrances (plus one "redundant" single entrance), it corresponds to the second section. The fifth and final section is a second return; it has three entrances of "a" (B, A, S), all in *stretto* with "s," "i," or "r," and one additional unaugmented entrance.

The ingenious relationships of the sections can be best made clear by the following diagram:

Sections:	I	—	II	—	III —	IV	—	V
Tonalities:	E♭ Minor	—	new Minors	—	Major —	E♭ Minor	—	E♭ Minor,
Types of								some Major
entrances:	single	—	*stretto*	—	single —	*stretto*	—	*stretto*
Versions of								
subject:	s	—	s	—	i —	i	—	a

Chorale Settings

The fugue was derived, through the *ricercar*, from the motet. Yet another important type of instrumental music was derived from vocal music: settings of songs and especially of chorales for organ.[4] One of the finest and simplest chorale settings is this one by Bach:

[4] See Appendix I, p. 400, for information on the various types of chorale settings.

EXAMPLE 44:   JOHANN SEBASTIAN BACH [1685–1750]

Ich ruf zu dir, Herr Jesu Christ (I call to Thee, Lord Jesus Christ)

Here the chorale melody is heard throughout in the soprano, while the calm, supplicating accompaniment establishes perfectly the mood of prayer.

Baroque Tempo and Rhythm

In all these pieces the rhythm is steady, unflagging; whether fast or slow, once the tempo is set, it is hardly ever altered, except in some toccatas and fantasies and in expressive, slow arias. This illustrates the Baroque ideal, pursued by all the arts in their particular ways, of consistency of mood in a given work. The emotion expressed appears as a generalized, pervasive attitude. The contrast, in this respect, with other styles—e.g. the Romantic—is apparent and serves to identify Baroque music.

CONCEPTS AND TOPICS DISCUSSED IN THIS SECTION

chorale settings—p. 105f
fugal devices—p. 104f
fugue—pp. 99f, 102f
pedal point—p. 101

prelude-and-fugue—p. 100
subject—p. 99
two roots of instrumental music
—pp. 99, 100

Section D

THE DANCE SUITE

Third Root of Instrumental Music: Dances

The third main source of instrumental music, in addition to imitation of vocal music and instrumental improvisation, is the dance. Dances were discussed in Part I as single pieces; but even there we found that minuets often have trios, and that waltzes and polkas come in series. A single dance seems too short to satisfy dancers and provides no variety. Very early, therefore, a custom of playing groups of dances was begun.

The Suite

From the sixteenth century we can follow the development of ever longer chains of various dances, contrasting in meter and tempo, which we call SUITES. At first they were played on the lute and later also on keyboard instruments, by wind bands, string ensembles and orchestras. With the evolution of musical style and the changing vogue of certain dances the suites also changed. Those played today are mostly the product of the later Baroque, the "age of the minuet," sired by Lully (cf. p. 24).[1]

Suites served increasingly as dinner and chamber music. In the eighteenth century they were therefore often enlarged by non-dance numbers such as marches, instrumental arias, and preludes of various types. Even the dances became idealized and lost all practical connection with actual dancing.[2] Thus suites are essentially art rather than functional music.

Doubtless Bach is today considered the greatest of suite composers. Our first example is one of his *Six 'Cello Suites*. This particular work was written for an instrument of Bach's day, a 'cello whose range was extended upward by a fifth string added to the usual four.[3]

---

[1] The Baroque suite went under several names: *ordre* or *partie* in France, *partita* or *sonata da camera* in Italy, and lesson in England.

[2] See Appendix I, p. 403, for information on suite composers.

[3] See Appendix I, p. 392f, for information on the violin family.

EXAMPLE 45:   JOHANN SEBASTIAN BACH [1685–1750]

Suite No. 6 in D Major, for 'Cello Alone

This work contains the four customary dances in the order favored by German suite composers: an *Allemande*, a *Courante*, a *Sarabande*, and a *Gigue*.[4] (Suites favored in France and elsewhere were, by contrast, fancifully varied; cf. Example 46, p. 110ff.) These dances are preceded by a *Prelude*, and after the *Sarabande* an "optional" dance is inserted, i.e., a dance other than the four customary ones, namely a *Gavotte* with *Trio* (*Gavotte II*), which is one of Bach's best known compositions.

Prelude

The *Prelude* could be called a toccata, were it intended for a keyboard instrument. Several times it reverts to the figure of the beginning:

thus marking out several sections.

Allemande

The stately, slow, duple-meter *Allemande*, like all the subsequent dances, is in two repeated sections, the second about twice as long as the first. The *Allemande* is expressive, *legato*, and in a complicated rhythm:

Courante

In sharp contrast we now hear the fast, triple-meter *Courante, staccato* and incisive in rhythm:

---

[4] See Appendix I, p. 403f, for a list of dances of the suite.

Sarabande

The *Sarabande* is likewise in triple meter. This dance is usually, as here, grave, highly expressive, and has in many measures a stress on the second beat. It furnishes the frame for many slow arias in the Baroque (cf. Bach's *E-flat-Minor Prelude*, p. 103f):

Gavottes

The pace changes. The *Gavottes*, in duple meter, move brightly. Whereas the first three pieces display the 'cello in fast passage work, the *Sarabande* and the *Gavottes* exhibit it in chordal playing, or multiple stops:

I:

II:

Gigue

Runs and multiple stops combine in the fast, brilliant *Gigue*. As usual in this dance, the second section starts with an inversion (here a partial one) of the beginning of the first: section 1:

section 2:

The only unifying factor in suites is the key, which remains unchanged throughout, though occasionally one dance changes from the prevailing Major to the Minor with the same tonic—the TONIC MINOR—or *vice versa* from Minor to the TONIC MAJOR. The principle of organization of the suite as a work of art appears to lie in contrasts and cross-relations in tempo, meter, and texture. These may be briefly tabulated for this *Suite* as follows:

	Prelude	Alle-mande	Cou-rante	Sara-bande	Gavottes	Gigue
tempo:	fast	slow	fast	slow	fast	fast
meter:	compound [5]	duple	triple	triple	duple	compound
technic:	p	p	p	ch	ch	p+ch

(p = passage work; ch = chordal texture)

Of the three items—tempo, meter, and technic—we note that two change from number to number.

Our second example is the shortest of Bach's *Four Orchestral Suites.*

EXAMPLE 46:   JOHANN SEBASTIAN BACH [1685–1750]

Overture (Orchestral Suite) No. 3, in D Major

The sequence of dances in this *Suite* is typically French: individual, without regard for the "regular" dances. It opens with an *Overture,* and since this is by far the longest and most elaborate number, the entire work takes its name from it. The second piece also is of non-dance character—an *Air* (aria). The last three pieces—the *Gavotte, Bourrée,* and *Gigue*—include only one of the staple dances of the suite, namely the *Gigue.*

---

[5] See Appendix I, p. 378f, for an explanation of compound and combination meters.

Overture

The opening piece is what is known as a FRENCH OVERTURE. This type, developed by Lully, usually has two sections—the one slow and majestic, involving, as here, certain characteristic rhythms, especially and

; the other bright, fast, and fugal. As in this example, an-

other slow section often concludes a French overture.

section 1

section 2

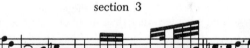

section 3

In this *Overture* the music unrolls for long passages without stop. The phrases seldom come to a definite end. The slow sections, based on the same rhythmic motifs but otherwise different, can hardly be subdivided at all.

The rapid tempo of the main section introduces a sharp contrast. This is a fugue in three large sections set for full orchestra—two oboes, three trumpets, timpani, and strings. These three sections are separated by two soft episodes in which the strings predominate. Except for the first few measures, the *perpetuum-mobile* idea is carried through the entire section.

Air

The long and exciting *Overture* is followed by an *Air* or instrumental aria.[6] Its melody, one of Bach's loveliest lyric ideas, is accompanied by another one in the low range:

Such writing in two voices, a typical feature of much music of the later Baroque (cf. p. 87), is found frequently in arias. It can be observed through most of this *Suite*. The bass melody of the Air exhibits a further characteristic of much Baroque music: It has the steady rhythmic tread of what has been called a "walking bass." This steady rhythm is one of the means of conferring individuality upon a secondary voice. The steady pace of a walking bass gives the composition an aspect of security and strength.

This *Air* contrasts with the *Overture* in many ways: (a) It has a *legato* melody with long tones as against *staccato* and *non-legato* in the *Overture;* (b) its tempo is slow throughout; (c) it employs only the strings; (d) it is organized in phrases that begin and end distinctly, not in unbroken continuity; and (e) it presents a single melody with an accompaniment, in a homophonic rather than a polyphonic texture.

The Dances

The last two comments about the *Air* apply also to the three dances, which, as noted above, are idealized and not actual dance music. In all of them the second section is about twice as long as the first one (cf. Example 45). In each second section the opening motif is heard both at the beginning and in the middle, as the point of departure for variants of the first section or for new material. The only exception is *Gavotte II,* which has equally long sections. Being rather rustic, it contrasts with the delicate *Gavotte I,* which easily evokes a picture of lace-collared and bewigged gentlemen in an atmosphere of perfume and Baroque magnificence, bowing around hoop-skirted, coiffured, and fan-fluttering ladies.

---

[6] This *Air,* transcribed in 1871 by the famous violinist August Wilhelmj to be played exclusively on the lowest string of the violin, has since become known as the "Air on the G-String." The fashion of playing only on the G-string was introduced by Paganini.

Gavotte I

Gavotte II

Bourrée

Gigue

Moderate in tempo, the *Gavottes* differ from both the slow *Air* and the much faster *Bourrée*. Usually the *Gigue* is the fastest of the dances; here, however, its tempo is moderate. It happens also that, though most *gigues* are written fugally, in the present one there is a straightforward melody and accompaniment.

CONCEPTS AND TOPICS DISCUSSED IN THIS SECTION

SECTION E

OPERA I

The Opera and Its Libretto

One of the most prominent, and certainly the most spectacular of all musical types is the opera. Our operatic repertory today is almost exclusively devoted to works of the past two hundred years or less, but opera was actually created earlier, around 1600, and was the representative type of music in the Baroque era. The most extreme of the novel types of music then emerging, it surpassed all others in volume of production and in general interest, and exerted the greatest impact of them all on standards of taste and manners. Some ideas and traditions of Baroque opera have never been completely abandoned. Indeed, they have seen periodic revivals even in the different operatic repertory of the Classic-Romantic era. For this reason a brief discussion of early opera will not only round out our ideas about Baroque music, but aid us in our approach to the opera more familiar to us.

Opera is an extraordinary creation. In it all the major and some minor arts—drama and poetry, vocal and instrumental music, dance and dramatic acting, painting, design, sculpture, and architecture—fuse in a most complex work whose presentation demands a larger and more varied body of cooperating individuals than any other work of art. The opera cannot therefore be fully treated without a consideration of its several constituent arts. This is not the place for such treatment; nevertheless we must give special attention to the libretto, the play which underlies an opera, and which can cause its success or failure.

Often derived from an already existing play or story, the libretto presents several special problems differing from those of a spoken play. For example, words sung take more time than words spoken, and they are harder to understand; a libretto must therefore be less verbose and more concise than a play. Verbal wit and finesse, philosophic discussion, and psychological problems must be restrained, and overt action stressed throughout. On the other hand, moods and emotional situations are especially adaptable to musical setting, and hence lyric passages may occur frequently. In addition, the introduction of large groups, such as a choir or a ballet, require consideration in the making of a libretto. Likewise important are the sequence and the prominence of the different solo voices used.

Therefore the writing of a libretto requires the collaboration between an author of special gifts and a composer of some experience. Nearly all the masters whose music we shall study in this section and the next collaborated to a greater or lesser degree with their librettists; some even wrote their own librettos.

The Beginnings of Opera

Opera began as MUSIC DRAMA, that is, as a dramatic play whose action is interpreted by music. Through the music the psychological situations in the drama are reinforced and the emotional response of the audience is greatly deepened. The idea of using music for these purposes sprang from a wide-spread enthusiasm for the Greek tragedy and the desire to revive it. Chief among the means of musical interpretation, created in emulation of the Greek drama, was the recitative of the kind heard in Examples 39-41, p. 85ff. The year in which such a recitative first replaced the spoken word in a dramatic play, probably 1597, is therefore usually taken as that of the birth of opera.

Greek drama was not the only source of inspiration for the new art form. From the tenth century onward, through most of the Gothic era, the LITURGICAL DRAMA had flourished in the West. Built around various scriptural incidents and interspersed with much music of the Gregorian-chant type, liturgical dramas were performed by the clergy for public edification and instruction, as a special feature of church festivals.

In the fourteenth century these dramas were succeeded by the MYSTERY PLAYS. Here the scriptural scenes were nearly lost among secular additions. The performances, in which music was only incidental, were enacted by townspeople, and often continued for ten to twenty days. PASSION PLAYS today are descendants of this type.

Mystery plays became the chief inspiration of the oratorio in the Baroque. (Cf. p. 92 for a related root of the oratorio.) From them also sprang, during the Renaissance, the secular drama, which usually involved some music of the madrigal type as well as some instrumental pieces. The rise of the secular drama was paralleled by a growing vogue of instrumental music and of soloistic singing.

These three, merging at the beginning of the Baroque and reinforced by dramatic recitative, produced the new art form—opera.

Monteverdi, Creator of Opera

The genius of early opera, and virtually its founder, was the
Italian, Claudio Monteverdi, one of the greatest composers of all
time. Boldly progressive, he has often been called the creator of
"modern" music, in the sense of music of the past three centuries.
Monteverdi recognized that recitative, which at the time was all
of the type later known as *accompagnato* (cf. Example 39, *No. 5*,
p. 89f), lacked the musical organization necessary in large works
to sustain interest. He therefore distinguished between a more narrative, conversational type and the more dramatic, emotional *arioso*
(cf. Example 40, *No. 2*, p. 93), and for lyric moments he introduced the aria, or fully organized song. In these and in other ways
the master set the operatic style for the entire seventeenth century.
His ideas were carried on not only by the disciples he gathered at
Venice, but also by composers in France, England, and Germany.

Our first example is the sole existing fragment of Monteverdi's
music drama, *Arianna*.[1]

EXAMPLE 47:   CLAUDIO MONTEVERDI [1567–1643]

Lamento d'Arianna (Ariadne's Lament, 1608)

Created as a result of admiration for Greek tragedy, early opera usually
turned to subjects of Greek mythology. Here Ariadne, forsaken on an
uninhabited island by her lover, Theseus, mythical king of Athens, whose
life she had saved when he went forth to battle the Cretan monster,
Minotaur, pours out her grief:

Recitative:

Is this how thou restor'st me
    queen, to my throne ancestral?
Is this the promised circlet,
    thy gift, my brow adorning,
these then the promised sceptre
    and gold-encrusted jewels?

---

[1] The reader will find that his enjoyment and understanding of the operas
discussed will be furthered by a study of the librettos or at least the plots (see
"Bibliography for Librettos," Appendix II, p. 428). It is also suggested that he
memorize the names and voice types of the important characters.

> Thou leav'st me here, abandoned,
>   that beasts may fell me, rend me, and devour me!
> Ah Theseus! Ah Theseus, sweet one!
>   Wouldst thou leave me to perish—
> in vain lamenting,
>   in vain imploring, quite helpless—
> me, desperate Ariadne,
>   who in thee trusted,
>   and gave thee glory—yes, thy life?

Arioso:

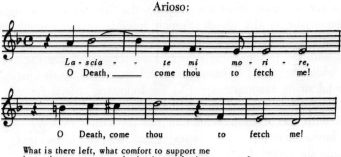

What is there left, what comfort to support me
in my desperate sorrow, in the deep pain that tears me?
‖:O Death, come thou to fetch me! :‖

Such laments near the end of operas, at the height of tragedy, remained a staple feature for over a century, and in altered form they still appear in many later works (cf. Examples 53, 54, pp. 140f, 142ff). Our example starts with a long recitative and ends with an *arioso* whose main phrase is heard twice, at its beginning and conclusion. This is one of the earliest attempts at dramatic expression in music, yet the forcefulness of the recitative and the beauty of the *arioso* are undimmed. Indeed, the beginning of the latter is hardly surpassable in its haunting quality.

Court Opera and Lully

Opera has always been surrounded by glamor and wealth. For centuries the rise and fall of operatic stars was nearly as important to the masses as was the rise and fall of royalty, or as is the fate of moving-picture stars today. Early operas, like *Arianna*, were composed for the lavish private entertainment of rich noblemen on specific occasions. To be sure, in 1637 the first public opera house opened its doors in Venice, rapidly followed by others throughout Italy where opera became an art of the people, and it was for the public stage that Monteverdi's later music dramas were written.

Elsewhere, however, especially outside Italy, opera long continued as the display of private splendor and power.

Thus the French TRAGÉDIES LYRIQUES of Lully were composed for the private royal stage of Louis XIV, and public performance was a secondary consideration. Such sponsorship accounts for the dignified, slow melody, expressive but always restrained, for the emphasis on sumptuous ballets, for the rather stilted heroics of the subject matter derived from Greek myths or medieval romances, and for the ostentatious stagecraft (for which Louis squeezed enormous special taxes from his people)—the last features being also characteristic of the classic French tragedy of the contemporary dramatists, Corneille and Racine.

In addition to the French opera Lully created the string orchestra, which has been the nucleus of all orchestral music since. The chordal string accompaniment in the following *Aria* is typical: full and completely worked out by the composer. This is in sharp contrast with the accompaniment of the preceding example, written for *basso continuo* only, requiring no specific instruments, and lacking the color of the violin family.

EXAMPLE 48:   JEAN BAPTISTE LULLY [1632–87]

Bois épais from "Amadis de Gaule" (1684)

Amadis, Welsh hero of a large cycle of medieval romances, popular from the fourteenth to the seventeenth centuries, sings of his lady, princess Oriana:

Bois   é - pais   re - dou - ble   ton om - bre,
‖:For - est dense,   thy   dark - ness re - doub - le!
Though deep thy shadows, they suffice not
to hide my bitter grief, the sorrow of my love.:‖

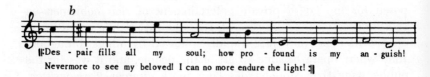

‖:Des - pair fills all   my   soul; how pro - found is my an - guish!
Nevermore to see my beloved! I can no more endure the light! :‖

Together with the text the music is repeated to form a simple *a-a-b-b* arrangement, preceded by an orchestral introduction that anticipates *a*. The dramatic situation here is very similar to that in Example 47, but following court decorum the music is more restrained in the expression of emotion.

Purcell and English Opera

The third great operatic composer of the seventeenth century was Henry Purcell, virtually the only English writer of serious operas until the twentieth century. He was influenced by both Italian and French composers: From the former he adopted the employment of deeply expressive singing and from the latter the employment of a full orchestra.

EXAMPLE 49:   HENRY PURCELL [1658–95]

Dido's Lament from "Dido and Aeneas" (1689)

Here we have a lament in the Monteverdi tradition: Like Ariadne lamenting the Athenian hero Theseus, Queen Dido of Carthage is mourning the departure of her lover, Aeneas, ancestral hero of Rome, as she dies:

Recitative:

Thy hand, Belinda; darkness shades me:
On thy bosom let me rest:
More I would, but Death invades me:
Death is now a welcome guest.

Aria:

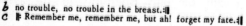

b no trouble, no trouble in the breast.:‖
c ‖: Remember me, remember me, but ah! *forget my fate.*:‖

This *Aria* is one of the noblest and most touching expressions of grief ever composed. In construction and mood as well as through its chromatic subject "S," which reappears in many similar Baroque compositions, it is closely related to the *Crucifixus* from Bach's *High Mass* (see p. 83f). First stated by itself, this subject is heard eight more times in the bass, while the other orchestral parts vary each time, except that the music set to the fourth and fifth presentations of the subject repeats that set to the second and third. Above six statements of the subject the singer intones a highly expressive melody, phrased   *a—b —c, a* and *b* each spanning one statement and *c* two. The last two repetitions of the subject are interpreted by the orchestra alone.

Summary

Let us summarize this chapter on Baroque music. Most types of compositions created during the period are still with us. We have discussed the oratorio and the passion oratorio, the cantata, the concert mass, the prelude-and-fugue, the chorale setting, and the dance suite—all typical Baroque types that have not undergone much change. The opera, on the other hand, has been significantly transformed and is known to us mostly in its more recent shapes. We shall therefore discuss it further in the next section. Similarly the discussion of the concerto will be deferred until later, when large instrumental works will be discussed in Part IV.[2]

Baroque artists tended to build large composite works with sharp contrasts among the sections. Most single pieces of the period are

---

[2] For comment on other types of Baroque music see the discussions of: *concerto grosso*—Example 20, p. 29, Example 88, p. 317ff; minuet—Example 16, p. 24; *passacaglia*—Example 66, p. 211f; toccata—Example 34, p. 57f; trio sonata—Example 79, p. 264f.

elaborations of one basic motif or subject, with beginning and end of units or phrases often artfully obscured by overlapping. A steady, driving tempo and rhythm, often expressed in a walking bass, characterize most pieces. They reflect the Baroque ideal of consistency of mood in a composition.

Three tendencies, partly opposed to each other, influence the style: elaborate polyphony (fugue), dramatic expression (oratorio, opera), and soloistic display (*coloratura* aria, toccata, concerto). Three types of texture correspond to these tendencies: polyphony, the recitative accompanied by scattered chords, and homophony with an harmonic accompaniment based on a two-part concept, with chords filling in between bass and soprano.

In contrast to the vocal music of the Renaissance, that of the Baroque is very dramatic. It explores the heights and depths of emotion, possesses at times brilliance and power, and at times great delicacy. In that era the art of singing as well as that of vocal composition attained an excellence that has never been surpassed. Opera singers reaped honors that nearly equaled those given to royalty.

Instruments and Orchestra

On the other hand, the Baroque witnessed the first large-scale use of instrumental music. Various solo instruments were employed, and, for the first time also, the orchestra—chiefly a group of strings reinforced by woodwinds. Except for setting off certain phrases, the woodwinds in the orchestra would be heard by themselves only where the music contained more parts than the usual four for strings, and even then they would be heard without regard to their particular qualities—their TIMBRES or TONE COLORS. The harpsichord or the organ, or both, were always part of the orchestra. Baroque orchestration did not lack variety of sound qualities, but this was a secondary consideration.[3]

CONCEPTS AND TOPICS DISCUSSED IN THIS SECTION

---

[3] See Appendix I, p 408f, for a list of Baroque composers.

V MUSIC OF THE CLASSIC-ROMANTIC ERA

SECTION F

OPERA II

The Rococo Style

Although the spirit and the methods of the Baroque lingered on in some countries until well after the mid-eighteenth century, a new era, beginning in Italy and France as early as 1715, was heralded by parallel changes in the arts and manners. In architecture large curves and long vistas were abandoned in favor of filigree lacework and intricate line arrangements in the style called Rococo (from French: *rocaille*—artificial ornamental rock and shell work). The ideal of grand symmetry among architectural sections with unending variety in each yielded to that of clarity of details grouped in small units and abundantly repeated. (Cf. Plate VI, facing this page.) In painting, the bold, deep reds and blues of a Rubens and the saturated browns of a Rembrandt gave way to the pale hues of a Boucher; enormous canvasses to miniatures. Contrast among large sections of pictures was replaced by finely worked-out contrast in details; portrayal of grand emotions by delineation of subtle nuances of expression. In manners the grandiose diction and the

PLATE VI: Interior of the Castle Schönbrunn at Vienna (1774).

An example of the exquisite filigree ornamentation and the delicate, curved lines of rococo art.

passionate, robust, even heroic behavior of Baroque man was super-seded by polished restraint of language and grace in motion. In dress the huge, curled periwig was discarded for the sleek pigtail.

All this was reflected in corresponding changes of musical style. The grand sweep of the Baroque offended the new taste for delicate finesse. Unchanging volume and tempo over long sections were abandoned for fine shadings and sudden contrasts. Long sections, unrolling continuously and derived from one subject or motif, were displaced by clearly divided, repeated phrases involving con-trasting ideas, for example, in a phrase arrangement like *a-a-b-b-a*. Indeed, the musical subject itself changed to become a theme which, although it often includes contrasting motifs, is presented in one or two well rounded PERIODS. This term is used to signify a unit of several phrases, usually two or three, a unit that normally presents a complete musical thought (cf. the *Theme* in two periods of Paganini's *Caprice*, p. 51). Phrase, period, and theme are anal-ogous to clause, sentence, and paragraph in language.

The vigorous interaction between bass and soprano was dissolved, and polyphony rejected; simple, standard chord sequences, called CADENCES (see below, p. 132) now served to articulate the often whimsical, delicately carved melody in a strictly homophonic tex-ture, i.e. without any secondary melodic lines anywhere. Wind instruments, which were rapidly being added to the orchestra, permitted new, finer shadings and tone colors. At the end of the eighteenth century this Rococo music culminated in the Classic style, which, in turn, served as the basis of the subsequent develop-ment of Romanticism throughout the nineteenth century and well into the twentieth.

Classics and Classicists

These two terms, "classic" and "romantic," used so often and so glibly, demand some explanation. The first, "classic," refers his-torically to the most eminent creators of Greco-Roman antiquity (and by transfer also to their works). In using the term, we may emphasize either the idea of "eminence" or the idea of "Greco-Roman antiquity," implying a highly developed sensitivity to bal-ance and clarity. In order to avoid confusion of these two meanings, we shall use the term "classic" to refer to individual eminence and the term "classicist" to refer to a reverence for antiquity, established patterns, balance, and clarity. Thus, men like Thomas Aquinas, Leonardo da Vinci, Goethe, or Beethoven we shall call classics, because they were eminent and set standards for others. On the other hand, the Renaissance, because it harked back to antiquity and venerated balance and clarity, is a classicist period.

To state it differently: A classic artist creates models, a classicist accepts them. The fact of this acceptance of models is crucial to an understanding of the classicist attitude; for it is basically an expression of satisfaction with one's surroundings. From this satisfaction flow a fundamental optimism and rationalism together with a deliberate shutting-out from consciousness of what is undefinable or unaccountable—mystical doctrines, emotions, poverty, sickness, and the like—attitudes that affect every classicist to a varying degree.

Classic Eras and the Viennese Classic Composers

In addition to the emergence of single classics and of classicist trends there is a third phenomenon: classic eras, i.e. generations in which classicism prevails and which also produce many outstanding geniuses. Such classic eras seem to follow two or three generations of artists who afterwards are looked upon as pioneers or precursors; they are, in turn, followed by several generations which accept their standards. A classic generation, because of its peculiar midway position, is able to strike a balance among all elements of an art. No longer engrossed in pioneering, it seizes upon models furnished by the "precursors" or by other periods, and with their aid creates an order and harmony to which later generations turn in the quest for fresh inspiration.

Classic eras in the various arts need not coincide, however, since they depend on two circumstances—a favorable historical situation and the genius to translate it into great art. One such classic generation occurred around 440 B.C.E. in Greece (excelling in drama, philosophy, sculpture, painting, and architecture); others around 1250 in France (philosophy, architecture), 1500 in Italy (painting, sculpture, architecture), and 1590 in England (literature, music), to mention a few.

Similarly there arose during the classicist period in the latter part of the eighteenth century and at the beginning of the nineteenth, but especially during the brief span between 1781 and 1803, a group of eminent masters in music and literature in Germany, specifically called "the Classics" there. The musical Classics had their center at Vienna, Austria, the home of Haydn, Mozart, and Beethoven. Only with them did German music, for the first time in history, acquire pre-eminence in Europe. This supremacy it maintained, though certainly not unchallenged, almost until the First World War. The Classic German poets, on the other hand, gathered at Weimar, Germany, around Goethe (1749–1832) and Friedrich Schiller (1759–1805), who in their creative works during those years were guided by the Hellenic idea of balance and repose.

The Classic Style in Music

The Classic musical style, as stated above, was the outgrowth of the Rococo style. To the latter's features, however, it added a certain repose, an untroubled spirit of rest, a bright but mellow color. There is neither excessive seriousness nor boisterous hilarity: Neither tragedy nor comedy go to extremes. A fine balance is brought about between melody and significant accompaniment, between expressive leading voice and inconspicuous but masterly polyphony, between even tempo and meter and ever new rhythmic-melodic variants, or development.

To be sure, this Classic balance was reached only rarely, and predominantly in Mozart's works. Frequently Rococo elements, such as surprise and strict homophony, affect the works even of the greatest Classic composers, and they dominate those of lesser masters. Often also there are Romantic traits in Classic music—a leaning toward exciting contrasts, especially of volume, tempo, and instrumentation, a predilection for emotional outbursts, a penchant for fairy tales in operas. All these features emerged about fifty years before Mozart during the Rococo, and they became central in the music of the succeeding century. The Viennese Classics may thus well be called the central generation of the "Classic-Romantic" era, about 1740–1910 (for Italy and France about 1715–1910); what is usually termed the Romantic era—roughly the nineteenth century —is truly but the second half of that period.

Romanticism

How then may romanticism be differentiated from classicism? Perhaps the most fruitful point of departure for an explanation is that, whereas classicism tends to reflect a feeling of satisfaction with one's environment, romanticism is imbued with discontent. While the former is therefore characterized by quiet self-assurance, the latter is marked by unrest, search, and extremes of expression. Periods that are characterized by such dissatisfaction we may call "romanticistic," whereas we shall call artists of the nineteenth century more specifically "Romantics"—men of "the Romantic era."

Dissatisfaction with one's surroundings can express itself in three principal ways, namely (1) in attempts at improvement, (2) in surrender to despair, and (3) in evasions and attempts to escape.

(1) In politics, attempts at improvement take the form of revolutionary struggles, and the Romantic era is a continuous record of such struggles from the American to the Russian revolution. In economics they caused social reform movements, such as the labor movement and socialism. In graphic arts these attempts expressed themselves in such devastating satire as pervades Daumier's cartoons, and in literature in pamphleteering, propaganda, and art and music criticism. Music, however, unless associated with words, as in the *"Marseillaise"* (see p. 17), can hardly help to overcome dissatisfaction creatively, since it cannot channel feelings into action.

(2) The second reaction, surrender to despair, leads to psychological disturbances of all types. Indeed, insanity has claimed many important Romantic artists, poets, philosophers, and composers. But, whereas individuals may succumb to life's pressures, they do not do so as artists; for as artists they create works of art, i.e. products of well-ordered craftsmanship and purposeful thought, which never reflect defeat but always a victory through mastery and achievement.

(3) The third adjustment, escape from unsatisfactory reality through vicarious satisfaction or relaxation, may be achieved by a flight from (a) the here, (b) the now, and (c) the crushing threat of immediate outside circumstance. Each of these methods of escape from reality provides materials for significant artistic expression.

Cultural Traits of Romanticism

(a) The flight from "the here" leads to distant places, like the countryside or the colorful Orient—in literature to pastoral poetry, travelogues, tales of Indians, of Eskimos, or of inner Africa. With an admixture of escape from the present, the flight from the here goes to the past glories of India (as in the spread of Buddhism in the Occident), the Arabian Nights, the Crusades, or to the future life in heaven. The religious revival, Catholic, Jewish, and Protestant alike, thus was an important facet of the Romantic era (coming after a definite decline of organized religion during the Rococo).

(b) The second kind of goals, those of the flight from "the now," may be directed toward the past or toward the future. The search for the "good old time" or the "golden age" fastens on traditions of family and nation. Nationalism and historicism are therefore two of the strongest traits of the period with a great influence on music. Flight into the future leads to idealism and Utopianism, which can hardly affect music.

(c) The last avenue toward finding vicarious outlets for insufferable surroundings is the flight from the outside to a concentration on the inner adventure of self. It leads to individualism, which during the Romantic era developed into expressionism or extreme emotionalism, into impressionism and general withdrawal, and into psychoanalysis.

Romantic Traits in Music

Each of these three escape mechanisms contributed to the music of the nineteenth century.

(a) The flight to distant places opened the door to picturesque orientalism in opera and ballet, and to the interest in non-European scales and instruments, such as gong, cymbals, triangle, and marimba.

(b) The retreat to the past brought the revival of Gregorian chant and the recovery and spiritual rediscovery of the music of earlier periods in general. It led to the emergence of national schools, delving into, and employing, much material from folklore. It stimulated research into tribal and folk music and interest in folk dances.

The desire to understand the work of art in its historic-social setting also springs from this source.

(c) Individualism expressed itself in music as a search for special effects—sudden contrasts, certain characteristic chords or skips,
highly differentiated orchestration, fragmentariness and surprise
endings, contravention of accepted scales, and so forth. Emotionalism made itself felt especially in erratic and chromatic melodies
and in dissonances, which finally, in our century, led to the revision
of the basic assumptions of Classic and Baroque music, i.e. of the
keys, and of the chords and cadences derived from them (cf. Section J).

Classicism and Romanticism

A word of caution seems necessary here. Classicism and romanticism are the two general attitudes between which the pendulum
of artistic styles swings in a rather complex manner. However, this
pendulum never reaches the extreme of complete realization of
either attitude, for this would spell death to art either in frozen
formalism or in total dissolution. In all works of art and in all periods, therefore, we find both classicist and romanticistic traits.
When we classify a work or a period as classicist and another as
romanticistic, we merely indicate the relative prominence of the
particular traits. The analysis of these traits according to the principles discussed above, and the consequent understanding of their
combination in any particular work of art or period is all the more
valuable to us.

Italian Rococo Opera and Gluck's Reform

It was in the Italian opera of the eighteenth century that the
Rococo style of music found its typical expression. It was characterized by complete simplicity in harmony, rhythm, and orchestration, and absence of polyphony. The melody, however, abounded
in ornamentation intended for, and exemplifying the best tradition
of, *coloratura* singing. Emotionally the music of these operas was
shallow and often slight in artistic significance. The stress was on
external brilliance.

Outstanding and best known among the composers of such operas
—the serious, heroic OPERE SERIE and the slapstick comedies called

OPERE BUFFE—were Alessandro Scarlatti (1660–1725) and his pupil, Giovanni Battista Pergolesi (1710–36). They and their colleagues were active especially at Naples and are therefore known as the "Neapolitan school" of opera composers.[1]

The first great operatic master to find new paths, approaching the Classic style, was the German, Gluck. Like the composers who around 1600 founded opera, Gluck professed to be reviving the Greek drama in all its seriousness and passionate humanity. For his librettos he therefore turned again to Greek myths. As had been true of the Greek tragedy, music and dance were once more to be subsidiary to the drama. The action in his operas became nearly continuous, not, as was the tradition in Italian opera, interrupted by the arias, but carried on by them. Instead of the standardized, set arias of Neapolitan opera—the lyric *cavatina,* the lament, the patter song, the heroic aria, the *coloratura* aria, and so forth, each preceded by a long *secco* recitative—Gluck advocated shorter arias, without the many text repetitions (cf. Example 30, p. 52ff) and with close coordination of word and music. The *secco* recitative was dropped as musically unsatisfactory, and the dramatic recitative with orchestral accompaniment returned to prominence.[2] Gluck's "reform" operas thus are genuine music dramas.

The first "reform" opera was *Orfeo ed Euridice,* based on the often used story of the great singer of Greek myth, Orpheus, who lost his beloved wife, Eurydice,[3] but who through his song won her back from the gods of the netherworld, only to lose her again because of his curiosity. Our example is the famous *Recitative* and *Aria* at the climax of this work.

EXAMPLE 50:   CHRISTOPH WILLIBALD GLUCK [1714–87]

Che farò senza Euridice from *"Orfeo ed Euridice,"* Act III (1762)

Orpheus, sung by an alto as was traditional for leading male roles in the *opera seria,*[4] and Eurydice are on their way up from the nether-

---

[1] See Appendix I, p. 401ff, for an explanation of eighteenth-century opera: *opera seria, opera buffa,* ballad opera, and so forth.

[2] Many of these ideas were suggested to Gluck by his ingenious librettist, the Italian, Raniero de Calzabigi (1714–95).

[3] The English spelling of these names is used in the text, the Italian or French only in titles of works. In the translation of the Italian words the spelling "Euridice" indicates the Italian accentuation on the third syllable.

[4] See Appendix I, p. 387f, for an explanation of operatic singing practices.

world. Observing that Orpheus does not look at her during their ascent, and not knowing that he has been so ordered by the gods, Eurydice complains, then insists that he no longer loves her. Orpheus knows that if he does look at her she must die. Nevertheless he succumbs to her pleading.

Recitative:

Eur.:   My love, in truth recall'st thou me?
Or.:   What wailing! Oh, how my heart is rent with deepest pain. My purpose fails me. Frenzy, trembling, 'tis madness! (Turns and looks at her.) O my beloved!
Eur.:   Ah, ye gods, what befalls me? Strength fails me, I perish.
Or.:   Ah me, how have I blundered! How was I goaded by the madness of my love! Dear one, Euridice, Euridice, beloved! Life is departed, in vain do I cry. Ah, thus to grieve! To lose her yet again, and now forever! Rash promise, 'twas fatal; my remorse has no end. No one can help me; there is none to give counsel. There lies before me—ah, cruel vision —prospect of lonely survival, of miserable anguish. Be thou content, vile fate, desperate am I.

Aria:

Without her, whither go, without her, what shall I do,
    whither go without my love?
b   Euridice, Euridice, oh heaven, give answer, give answer!
    Ever faithful I remain, ever faithful, ever faithful I remain.
a   (as above)
c   Euridice, Euridice! Ah, neither comfort nor yet pity
    is now proffered on this Earth here or in heav'n.
a   (as above)

For psychological reasons as well as for the sake of a well-rounded formulation Gluck here repeats text and music as indicated by *a*. (The last *a* is slightly changed at the end.) A noteworthy detail is the exclamatory recitative on the words "Euridice, Euridice," starting sections *b* and *c*. Except for this feature the expression is somewhat restrained, noble. The music has solidity and balance, and eschews prettiness, surprise, and other superficial effects.

The Cadence

• The clear outline of phrases in this *Aria* is characteristic of Rococo and Classic music. This clarity of design is based on the employment of a few cadences that had been standardized early in the Rococo. A cadence (from Latin: *cádere*—fall) is a passage that evokes a feeling that the succession of tones is inevitable, as if they were falling toward a predestined point of partial or complete repose, as the voice does at the end of a sentence. Let us examine how this may be done.

There are several kinds of cadences—melodic, rhythmic, and harmonic—but usually the term refers to the last of these, with which the others tend to coincide. A cadence therefore usually signifies a return to the TONIC HARMONY, i.e. the harmony which is based on the first tone, or step, of the scale,[5] known as the tonic, after tension has been created by departure from it. In a sense, the music of the Classic-Romantic era can be said to have progressed through ever-increasing elaborations of this idea; in other words through ever longer cadences (cf. p. 81f). The focal point of tension was the DOMINANT harmony, which most often preceded the final tonic harmony, the dominant being the fifth step of the scale. Frequently tonic and dominant are therefore spoken of as the two harmonic poles of music.

To acquire a feeling for harmonic cadence sing "My Country 'Tis of Thee". There are two cadences in the stanza, one at "Of thee I sing", and the other at "let freedom ring". Both close with dominant and tonic. In Gluck's *Aria* the same type of cadence is heard at the end of the musical example as well as at the end of sections *a* and *b*. In fact, every phrase in this *Aria* closes with this or a similar cadence. •

---

[5] For further clarification see Appendix I, p. 384f.

Mozart's Operas

Eighteenth-century opera culminated in Mozart. This master combined Gluck's serious, human approach with the Italian *bel-canto* polish. His melodies are highly expressive and yet delightfully smooth. Every phrase is elegantly turned and finished, but without hindrance to a free flow of ideas, The melodic material is distinctively individual, not, as in the works of lesser contemporaries, commonplace; and this material Mozart expands and varies with consummate skill. Simple as the accompaniments sound, they are subtly differentiated and often involve contrapuntal finesses indicating that the strict homophony of the Rococo is a thing of the past.

These qualities are well illustrated in the following examples from one of Mozart's finest works, *The Marriage of Figaro.* Here as well as in his *Don Giovanni* (1787) Mozart fused comic and serious opera.[6] There are many dramatic and lyric situations in these works, and the stereotyped figures of the usual slapstick comedy are humanized and appear as warm-hearted persons, each with his particular foibles and problems. Complete lightheartedness, true seriousness, emotional intensity, dramatic conflict, and sudden surprise are here mingled with delicacy and humane wisdom. This integration is to a large degree due to the brilliance of Lorenzo da Ponte's (1749–1838)[7] librettos, but it is essentially the music that elevates the good entertainment of the comedy to a broader human plane.

EXAMPLE 51:   WOLFGANG AMADEUS MOZART [1756–91]

From "*Le nozze di Figaro*" (The Marriage of Figaro, 1786)

(a) *La vendetta* (Act I, No. 4)

The opera is based on a highly successful comedy, written by Beaumarchais as a sequel to his play "The Barber of Seville" (cf. Example 30, p. 52ff). Dr. Bartolo, once the guardian of Rosina whom he wanted to

---

[6] I.e. *opera buffa* and *opera seria;* see Appendix I, p. 401f.

[7] This poet, who wrote several other librettos for Mozart, spent his last thirty-three years in the United States, partly as an impresario and partly as a professor of Italian at Columbia University.

marry, has through Figaro's tricks lost her to Count Almaviva (the Lindoro of whom she sings in Example 30). Now Bartolo swears vengeance: He, in turn, believes himself able to make Figaro, the former barber and now the count's valet, lose his bride, Susanna, by forcing him to marry an old woman, the doctor's former mistress. Later, however, to his confusion she turns out to be Figaro's mother and he himself, Figaro's father. Bartolo, a bass, is almost purely comic and here sings a typical comedy aria, characterized by fast tempo and quick, funny chatter (in sections *b* and *b*[1])[8]:

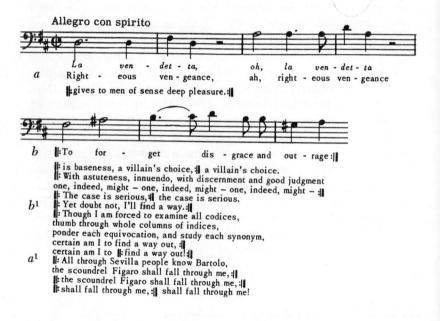

b[1]

(b) *Voi che sapete* (Act II, No. 11)

This is one of the few arias in this opera that describe states of mind and in no other way contribute to the action. Such arias occur frequently in operas down to our time. Cherubino is a boy of about sixteen, his role sung, in conformity with operatic tradition, by a soprano. He is at a stage where he makes love to every woman in sight—here especially to the countess, the former Rosina. The words furnish a splendid example of the new, humanized approach and a surprisingly fine psychological study of adolescence.

---

[8] Such superscribed figures indicate variants.

Andante con moto

a   *Voi   che sa - pe - te   che   co - sa è a - mor*
       You   who so   well know   what   true love   is,

‖: ladies, please tell me, am I in love? :‖

*a*¹   My inmost feelings let me reveal,
       strangely they move me, what can they mean?
       I feel a yearning, teasing desire,
       sometimes delightful, sometimes pure pain.

*a*²   Now I am freezing, then blazing fire,
       then in an instant cold as before.
       Something entices from far away,
       grasp it I cannot, know not its name.

b   I sigh and   cry   out   with no in - tent,

       I weep and tremble all unaware.
       I have no peace by day or by night,
       yet I find joy in suffering so.

a   You who so well know what true love is,
          ‖: ladies, please tell me, am I in love, :‖
       ladies, please tell me, am I in love?

(c) *Aprite presto* (Act II, No. 14)

Here we have a comic duet, yet one that highlights a rather dramatic situation: Cherubino has locked himself in the countess's room. The count, suspicious, departs for tools to open the door. Meanwhile Cherubino, aided by Susanna, Figaro's bride and the countess's chambermaid, escapes. This is a most delightful, realistic little piece. The fast, excited chatter can hardly be understood in whatever language it is sung.

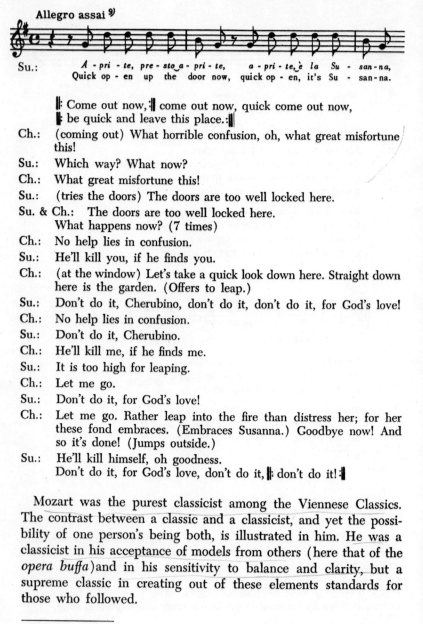

Allegro assai [9]

Su.: *A - pri - te, pre - sto a - pri - te,   a - pri - te, è la Su - san-na,*
      Quick op - en up the door now, quick op - en, it's Su - san - na.

‖: Come out now, ‖ come out now, quick come out now,
‖ be quick and leave this place. :‖

Ch.: (coming out) What horrible confusion, oh, what great misfortune this!

Su.: Which way? What now?

Ch.: What great misfortune this!

Su.: (tries the doors) The doors are too well locked here.

Su. & Ch.: The doors are too well locked here.
            What happens now? (7 times)

Ch.: No help lies in confusion.

Su.: He'll kill you, if he finds you.

Ch.: (at the window) Let's take a quick look down here. Straight down here is the garden. (Offers to leap.)

Su.: Don't do it, Cherubino, don't do it, don't do it, for God's love!

Ch.: No help lies in confusion.

Su.: Don't do it, Cherubino.

Ch.: He'll kill me, if he finds me.

Su.: It is too high for leaping.

Ch.: Let me go.

Su.: Don't do it, for God's love!

Ch.: Let me go. Rather leap into the fire than distress her; for her these fond embraces. (Embraces Susanna.) Goodbye now! And so it's done! (Jumps outside.)

Su.: He'll kill himself, oh goodness.
      Don't do it, for God's love, don't do it, ‖: don't do it! :‖

Mozart was the purest classicist among the Viennese Classics. The contrast between a classic and a classicist, and yet the possibility of one person's being both, is illustrated in him. He was a classicist in his acceptance of models from others (here that of the *opera buffa*) and in his sensitivity to balance and clarity, but a supreme classic in creating out of these elements standards for those who followed.

---

[9] Very fast.

Grand Opera

We shall continue below to trace the line of opera in Germany, which led from Gluck through Mozart and onward; but first we turn to a second line of evolution. Gluck's most important later works were created for France, where a long train of composers followed the path he had indicated. Within a generation or two, however, Gluck's humanistic ideals were forgotten and only his emphasis on drama remained as an influence. The operas of that period, with plots so devised as to afford the greatest possibilities for stage display, exciting clashes, sensational fires, shooting, battling armies, and the like, are called GRAND OPERAS.

Grand opera constitutes a species created for the *nouveaux riches* of the Industrial Revolution, an audience rather coarse in taste. This type of opera was triumphant throughout Europe and America between 1830 and 1850, and its high-priest was Meyerbeer. The term "grand opera," in the United States used too generally by many as synonymous with "opera," therefore has properly a much narrower connotation. The error is due to the accident that in this country grand opera was the first, and for a long time the only kind of serious opera to be widely known.

The Romantic traits in works of this type were limited to special orchestral effects and to spectacular historical or oriental librettos and costumes. In the following example, for instance, the libretto is both historical and oriental. While the most characteristic music of grand opera occurs in powerful ensemble scenes, the *Aria* here chosen throws some light on other aspects of the species. These are a somewhat sentimental though not overly dramatic melody, still following the tradition of noble restraint set by Lully (cf. p. 118); sustained tones of high pitch and other technical challenges to exhibit vocal technic (often much *coloratura*); and the general brevity and, we may say, infrequency of such lyric moments.

EXAMPLE 52:   GIACOMO MEYERBEER [1792–1864]

> *Pays merveilleux* (or *O paradis*) from *"L'Africaine"*
> (The African Woman), also known as "Vasco da
> Gama", Act IV (1860)

Vasco da Gama, the Portuguese navigator (1469?–1524), has just accomplished his voyage of discovery around Africa and looks with admiration on India lying before him:

Recitative:

O thou, wondrous land, garden heaven-blest,
temple radiant, all hail!

Aria:

| O | pa - ra - dis | sor - ti | de | l'on - de, |
| O | par - a - dise | from o - | cean | ris - ing, |

sky so blue, sky so pure, thou beguil'st my gaze.
Thou shalt be mine, world newly beheld,
thou shalt be my gift, on my native land bestowed.
Ah, ours these enrapturing pastures!
Ah, ours this new Eden on Earth!
Ah, the priceless charm, ah, wondrous wealth, all hail!
Newly beheld, world truly mine, yield thou to me,
yield thou to me, to me, O lovely land!
Newly beheld, world truly mine, yield thou to me,
yield thou to me, to me, to me—to me!

Romantic Opera and Wagnerian Music Drama

In Germany Wagner's art evolved from the opera of Gluck by way of the works of Mozart and Carl Maria Weber (1786–1826), who took great pride in being a cousin of Mozart's wife. Whereas in France it was Gluck's emphasis on drama that had the most lasting effect, the Germans stressed the human, emotional side of his ideas and employed music for a searching psychological commentary on the text. In addition, they favored nationalistic and mythological materials, such as folk tales, German sagas, and specific German locale, costume, and dances. The action finally became a symbolic projection of events with deep spiritual significance. The result is known as ROMANTIC OPERA, which culminated in the WAGNERIAN MUSIC DRAMA.

Rich orchestration, large, expressive skips in the melody, a continuous, broad flow of music rather than clearly punctuated phrasing, strong tension that seldom abates, a new harmonic style full of chromaticism—these are all traits of Wagnerian music drama. Other traits include the extensive development of short motifs and the equality of interest between the voices and the orchestra. The traditional relative positions of voices and orchestra—the voices leading and the orchestra accompanying—are here disregarded, the vocal line tending to become only one of the many significant parts of the whole ensemble. There are, therefore, few real arias in these operas, both for the reason just stated and because of Wagner's concept of the music drama as continuous action, prohibitive of any closed, self-sufficient sub-units such as arias, duets, or choruses.

The Leitmotiv

Wagner wrote not only the music but also the librettos for his music dramas, a practice in which many composers have since followed. Like Monteverdi and Gluck before him, he thought he was recreating the Greek tragedy, although instead of Greek mythology he stressed Germanic and Celtic sagas. To revitalize the close relationship between text and music, typical of Greek drama, he made extensive use of symbolic motifs, i.e. motifs that represent persons, ideas, things, or actions. These motifs are intended to clarify the psychological background of the action by presenting the relevant ideas that are not always expressed by the text, a notion related to our contemporary idea of a "stream of consciousness." The main motif of the next selection, for example, is that of "death as the perfect fulfillment of love" or "love-death"—a typically Romantic, pessimistic notion—which is heard prominently throughout the opera whenever this idea is stated or implied (see musical example below). Such a motif is called a LEITMOTIV (plural: *leitmotive*) or LEADING MOTIF. Though the term was specifically created to apply to Wagner's music, the technic had been employed for a long time by such composers as Monteverdi, Gluck, Mozart, and Weber. Wagner, however, used it most prominently and most consistently; and under his influence others came to employ it more extensively.

EXAMPLE 53: RICHARD WAGNER [1813–83]

Isolde's Love-Death from "Tristan and Isolde," Act III (1859)

In *Tristan and Isolde* Romantic music reached its climax. For fifty years this work exerted a powerful influence on musical style, an influence which has not yet completely disappeared. It affected libretto, ideology, melodic style, harmony, texture, and orchestration alike. Isolde's song occurs at the end of this great tragedy of love, taken from Arthurian legend. Addressed to Tristan, who has just died in her arms, it is an interesting variant of the Baroque lament (cf. Example 47, p. 116f and Example 49, p. 119f):

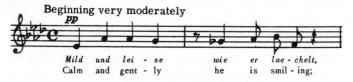

Beginning very moderately

Mild und lei - se   wie   er   lae - chelt,
Calm and gent - ly   he   is   smil - ing;

now his eye he sweetly opens—
    see, o comrades, see ye not?
How he, shining ever brighter,
    steeped in starlight, rises high:
        See ye not?
How his heart with courage swells,
    full and pure his spirit bestirs!
From his lips, how soft and sweet
    comes his gentle breath to me!
        Comrades, see! Feel and see ye not?
Hears none else the tender music
    which so soft and full of magic,
        yearning, happy, all things telling,
            calm and peaceful from him swelling,
                sinketh in me, and sweeps upward,
                    sweetly sounding rings around me?
Flowing clearer, growing nearer,
    are these waves of balmy breezes?
        Are they clouds of wonderful perfumes?
How they billow, rush around me!
    Shall I breathe them, shall I listen?
Shall I sip them, dive within them
    sweet in perfumes all dissolving?
In the billowing wave, in the echoing call,
    in the world's driving, infinite breath
        I'm drowning, and sinking,
            knowing naught—highest bliss! (Dies.)

Though Wagner's operas aroused wide admiration and had a great influence on operatic composition ever since, they were not accepted universally. Above all the composers of southern Europe—the majority of Italians and Frenchmen—opposed his deep pessimism, his intense emotionality, and his mystic symbolism. His influence among them was by no means negligible, but they developed several important types of opera independently.

Lyric Opera and Operetta

French composers after the mid-century, when the vogue of grand opera subsided, became eclectic. They borrowed ideas from both the Romantic opera and the Wagnerian music drama, but they chiefly adapted to the framework of the OPÉRA COMIQUE, the light, lyric French opera of the late eighteenth century, the new realism of the Italians, advanced by Verdi (see below). With their sober clarity they created out of this combination several highly successful operas, such as Gounod's *Faust* (1859) and Bizet's *Carmen* (1875). These are of a type that has been called LYRIC OPERA.

Perhaps the outstanding achievements of the French composers lay, however, in finding a counterbalance to both the grand opera and the Wagnerian music drama: the OPERETTA, whose driving genius was Jacques Offenbach (1819–80). Evolved like the lyric opera from the *opéra comique,* this sparkling, often satirical genre became popular over all Europe in such works as Offenbach's *Orphée en enfer* (1858), which again used the Orpheus story, but as a parody of the hollowness of the court of Napoleon III. The genre was taken up among others by Johann Strauss (1825–99) in Vienna (cf. Example 17, p. 25f; this *Waltz* is composed of excerpts from an operetta) and by Arthur Sullivan (1842–1900) in London.

Verdi and Realism

The serious counterbalance to Wagner's music drama was furnished by Verdi in Italy. His "realistic" opera rejects both Romantic symbolism and the stereotypes of the lingering Neapolitan opera. It eschews mere display in favor of truthful presentation of human actions and conflicts, while idealism is excluded or treated as unimportant. In the last decade of the century this realism became, in the hands of other composers, cruder, more sensational, somewhat like the earlier grand opera. In this form it is known as VERISMO, which to this day remains an important influence on operatic composition.[10]

Among the first worldwide successes of Verdi was *La Traviata*, the first opera to be based on a contemporary event—a sensational news story, as it were. When this opera had its première, its heroine, one of the famous ladies of the Parisian *demi-monde*, had been dead for only five years. Her associates, her lover, and her other patrons were all living. In fact, Alexandre Dumas (the younger, 1824–95), who wrote the play upon which the opera is based, had been among the lady's admirers. In using this libretto Verdi became the founder of realistic opera. As a matter of fact, he also used other types of librettos, but with a sure instinct he turned each one into a realistic human drama.[11]

The following example is one of the most moving scenes in operatic literature, which has inspired many imitations. It is another modern equivalent of the Baroque lament—an aria of remembrance, nostalgia, and regret, sung just before the heroine dies.

EXAMPLE 54:   GIUSEPPE VERDI [1813–1901]

Addio del passato from *"La Traviata"*, Act III (1853)

Violetta—*la traviata*, i.e. the lost one—is reading a letter from her lover's father, who had made her give up her only real love, his son, because of her reputation. The reading of the letter is done in a speaking, not a singing voice, to the accompaniment of the love motif (a leading motif) in a subdued, tearful version:

---

[10] Operatic realism and *verismo* affected the librettos rather than the music. They were the offshoots of the literary naturalism of Flaubert (1821–80) and Zola (1840–1902).

[11] This man-centered and realistic attitude is reflected in Verdi's non-musical endeavors as one of the outstanding fighters for national freedom and democracy, and as a pioneer in the fields of farm improvement and soil conservation.

Such accompanied speaking occurs occasionally in operas at very dramatic moments, and is known technically as MELODRAMA. There are entire works conceived in this fashion, although it is a rather difficult solution of the problem of dramatic presentation. The term does not imply the colloquial meaning of "sensational action."

After this *Melodrama* a *Recitative* leads to an *Aria*, which has two identical musical stanzas of the phrase pattern a-b-a^1-c.

Melodrama:

"You have kept your promise. The duel took place. The baron was wounded but is improving. Alfred is on foreign soil. Your sacrifice I have myself revealed to him. He will return to you for your pardon. I shall soon see you. Hasten to recover. You have deserved a better future. George Germont."—Too late now!

Recitative:

I'm waiting, I'm waiting, no one comes, 'tis idle!
(Looks at herself in the mirror.)
How this illness has changed me!
But the doctor bids me wait, bids me be hopeful.
Ah, mortal illness! He must know it is hopeless.

Aria:

the comfort, support of my spirit has left me,
the comfort, support . . .

a¹   Ah, smile at this lost one and grant her this last prayer,
     O hearken, grant her pardon, O Heaven, accept her!
c   Ah, the end, the end is here, yes, the end, the end is here.

a   All pleasures and all sorrows will shortly have their ending;
     the tomb is for all mortals the body's final mansion.
b   No weeping, no flowers will be on my tomb stone;
     no cross with my name will proclaim where I molder;
     no flower, no cross . . .
a¹   (same as before)
c   (same as before)

Folk Opera

The latest important trend in opera has been toward national or FOLK OPERA. This type is characterized by subjects portraying the life of the common people; it involves folk customs and costumes, folk dances, and genuine or recreated folksongs. Almost all nations have contributed to this trend, but the most successful, internationally, have been the Slavic peoples. We have already studied an excerpt from Smetana's *The Bartered Bride* (see p. 27f). A few years after this masterly comedy had been completed (1866) Musorgsky created his masterwork, *Boris Godunov,* a highly original opera, interweaving all the main trends, with national elements predominating. This predominance is shown in the last two selections of the following example, whereas the first is given as an example of stark, realistic drama, anticipating *verismo.*

EXAMPLE 55: MODESTE MUSORGSKY [1839–81]
            from "Boris Godunov" (1874)

The opera is based on a historical drama by Alexander Pushkin (1799–1837). Boris, Czar of Russia 1598–1605, had allegedly become the sovereign by having Dmitri, the young heir to the throne, killed. There arose a pretender claiming to be Dmitri, and during the subsequent excitement Boris died. (The historical Boris seems to have been innocent.)

(a) *Clock Scene* (end of Act II)

At this point Boris, in order to reassure himself that the young prince is definitely dead, has his executioner recount to him the murder scene.

Then he dismisses him. Deeply disturbed, the Czar succumbs to hallucinations:

a   Oh, give me space, air, I can hardly breathe!
           In waves of racking pain my blood throbs through my
                    brain, my temples, unrelenting.
           How cruelly, remorse, how fiercely thou dost plague me!

b   If thou know'st but once, but once a single lapse,
           the slightest act that hints dishonor,
               the soul is scorched,
                   the heart shrinks under torture.
           I suffer, fear, and tremble,
              and hard remorse pounds like a sledge—
                 no surcease!—pounds out curses.
           My throat is parchéd, I stifle!
             My mind's a whirl, my head spins.
           Behold—the child covered with blood all o'er!
           There! Behold! Who stands back there? There, it moved!

a^1 Approaching me, he grows . . . comes nearer . . .
            He groans and weeps, oh!
           Go! Go! Begone! The crime was not my deed.
           Go! Go, my child! Not I . . . not I . . . they, all the people
               willed it, child.

a^2 Lord in heav'n! Thou canst not desire the sinner's death.
           Oh spare the spent soul, save Thou the guilty Czar Boris!

This is one of the most realistic scenes in all opera. In the continuous, recitative-like utterance, the lack of repetition, and the use of symbolic motifs, it mingles music drama and realism. And yet three of the four sections of this *Aria* are closely related. The chromatic motif that is heard in the first section:

is the parent of the main motif of the third section, a^1:

from which, in turn, that of the last one, a^2, derives:

The second section, *b*, introduces, as the tone symbol for the chiming clock, a variant of the main motif of the opera, heard earlier in the

Coronation Scene (see below):

The style of the music justifies Musorgsky's being called the godfather of "modern" music—the music of the twentieth century.

(b) *Prologue:* Scene I

Folk opera emphasizes mass scenes and folk melodies. This *Scene* is typical. It unfolds before a monastery near Moscow where Boris waits, appearing reluctant to accept the crown after the murder of the prince. The people have been commandeered to crowd around for purposes of an ovation; intermittently they are bullied by the police, sing folk hymns, and break into quarrels, being first told that Boris steadfastly refuses the crown only to hear from the monks later that God has persuaded him to accept.

Our example includes the brief orchestral prelude and the beginning of the *Scene*. The prelude consists of a short folk tune, authentically Slavic in flavor:

with three repetitions, each increasing in fullness of setting. Then, as the tune is varied briefly, the curtain rises and reveals the milling crowd. With a new, vigorous motif:

the police constable steps forward to bully the people in a recitative:

> "What is this?—Are ye turned to wooden idols?—Quickly—on your knees!—Listen (threatens with his cudgel)—be quick!—What a crew of Satan's spawning!"

As they fall on their knees, the people break into a folk hymn, which is later heard once more—simple and simply accompanied, but building impressively up to the final cries of supplication:

Moderato

Why dost thou a - ban - don us thus, O fa - ther?

Ah, unto whom dost Thou leave Thy people, O father?
If Thou desert us, poor orphans, we shall be helpless.
Ah, we entreat Thee to hear our cries, give heed to our weeping!
Heed our burning tears! Mercy, mercy, mercy, master and father!

O fa - ther! O pro - tec - tor!

Thou, our guar - dian, mer - - cy!

(c) *Coronation Scene* (Prologue, Scene II)

In this famous *Scene* the display of grand opera and the music of folk opera are fused. The simple, yet impressive main motif—two chords and their varied repetitions (see above the motif of *b* in the *Clock Scene*) —creates a singularly exciting and festive atmosphere:

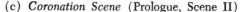

Soon the tones of church bells mingle with it as the curtain rises on the cathedral square and the coronation procession. After two brief phrases of solo and choir—"Long life and health to the Czar"—a folk hymn presents the second idea, which combines with the first in a stirring climax:

Allegro moderato

To the sun in all splen - dor ris - en be glo - ry, glo - ry!
Sing the glory of the Czar Boris in Russia, glory!

Musorgsky belonged to a group of composers, known as "The Five" or the "Mighty Five," who busied themselves constantly with collecting and recreating Russian folksongs; for their contention was that Russian music must be based on indigenous material, and its purpose must be the creation of a genuine Slavic idiom. Folk opera was therefore one of their favorite media.

Twentieth-Century Opera

Later the folk opera was adopted by English and American composers, among them Ralph Vaughan-Williams, Benjamin Britten,
and George Gershwin whose *Porgy and Bess* (1935) is probably
the most famous. Recently this trend has sought further nourish-
ment from folk ballads and has turned to shorter works, suited to
amateur and college performances.

Since the time of Wagner, Verdi, and Musorgsky the style of
opera has changed only insofar as musical style in general has
changed. Many excellent works have been added to the repertory,
especially by Giacomo Puccini (1856–1924) in Italy and by Richard
Strauss (1864–1949) in Germany, but they can all be classified as
various combinations of music drama, folk opera, and *verismo*. A
few works have continued the magnificence of grand opera, and
a few others have kept alive the spirit of *opera buffa*.

The operetta, or rather its offshoot, the MUSICAL COMEDY, has, of
course, remained a great favorite. Such names as Victor Herbert
(1859–1924), Franz Lehár (1870–1950), Oscar Straus (1870–1954),
and Richard Rodgers (b. 1902) have achieved very wide popularity. However, these composers pay for their swift momentary popularity with the prospect of early oblivion, though they have made
a large contribution to the musical life of our society.

Motion-Picture Music

The most important twentieth-century addition to musico-dramatic types has been motion-picture music. Due to its secondary
role as background music it has not as yet brought forth significant
new departures. But film music includes many excellent scores by
good composers, many of which, like those for ballets (cf. Section
H), have been arranged for concert performance and so have
enriched the orchestral repertory.

Summary

Tears and laughter, love and hatred, deep symbolism and shallow triviality, compassion and scorn, the grand court and the poor
hovel, crude realism and fairy tale, hero and clown—all are found
in opera. The history of this art of arts chronicles glory and scan-

dals, the amassing and dissipation of vast fortunes, and the rise and fall of great names. It is a record of artistic fulfillment and backstage intrigue, of triumph and disappointment, of genius and mediocrity. There were periods in which one or another of the manifold arts that fuse in opera was stressed—drama (by Monteverdi, by Gluck, and by the school of *verismo*); singing (in Neapolitan opera); staging (in grand opera); drama and singing (by Verdi); staging and ballet (by Lully); orchestral music and drama (by Wagner)—or a balance was struck among all the arts (by Mozart). Those that have come in close contact with this fascinating art sense its exciting possibilities, and few are able to escape its magic spell.

CONCEPTS AND TOPICS DISCUSSED IN THIS SECTION

SECTION G

PIANO SUITE AND SONG CYCLE

Piano Suites

The gap left in instrumental music by the lapse of the Baroque dance suite was successively filled by the Classic *divertimento* (cf. p. 344), by the Romantic piano suite, and, most recently, by the ballet suite (cf. Section H). The inspiration for the piano suite came from the dance. Schumann initiated the type with several ingenious chains of piano pieces conceived as ballroom impressions, such as *Carnaval* which we shall consider next. Once this new type of suite was established, he composed several such works, some of them descriptive, others consisting of various titbits without visual connotations. Because these highly imaginative suites are bound together by the repetition or sometimes the reminiscence of melodic material, they are, in a sense, cyclic in construction (cf. p. 72f).

Small pieces like those forming such cycles exemplify an important facet of the Romantic spirit. The Romantic, especially when introspective, was inclined to indulge the brief, lyric moment, the sudden inspiration that is soon exhausted. We have already met examples of this trend in Mendelssohn's *Songs Without Words,* Chopin's *Preludes,* and *Songs* of Schubert, Schumann, Brahms, and Wolf, all discussed in Part I. (On the other hand, Romanticism also expresses itself in very large works, such as Wagner's music dramas. This dual tendency only confirms our previous statement that romantic expression runs to extremes; cf. p. 127.)

EXAMPLE 56:   ROBERT SCHUMANN [1810–56]

Carnaval, op. 9 (1835)

This cycle of character pieces deserves many attentive hearings. It is one of the outstanding examples of THEME TRANSFORMATION and of VARIATION. Following an age-old game of deriving melodies from words by way of the letter names of the musical tones,[1] Schumann extracted the two subjects of this work, (a) and (b), from the name of the Bohemian town Asch, home of his early love, Ernestine von Fricken. (In German the notes A-flat, E-flat, and B are called respectively *As, Es,*

---

[1] This musical game goes back to the fifteenth century and is technically known as *soggetto cavato delle parole* (Italian—subject carved from words).

and *H*.) The anagram of this name, Scha, happens to contain all the musical letters in the name, Schumann. Thus (a) reads: *A-(e)S-C-H;* and (b): *AS-C-H;* both are used in two ways, namely:

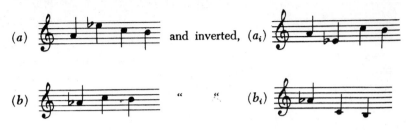

In the various pieces of the cycle these subjects appear altered in rhythm, tempo, expression, and continuation, and so transformed as to characterize the various masks in a carnival crowd. Further material is added at only a few strategic points. The twenty sections of the work, each with its own title, are thus like episodes in a movie sequence wherein the camera picks out the various characters:

No. 1, *Preamble* (introduction, employing various materials not related to the subjects): A description of the swirling carnival crowds.

No. 2, *Pierrot—(a)*: A mask with mysterious gestures—mystery symbolized by slow tempo and softness, gestures by sudden *fortes:* (In the musical examples the subjects are indicated by brackets and, where their notes do not follow one another immediately, by circling of notes.)

No. 3, *Arlequin—(a)*: A gracefully skipping mask—portrayed by wide skips, fast tempo, and *staccato:*

No. 4, *Valse noble*—(*a*): The first general dance, rather passionate:

No. 5, *Eusebius*—(*a*): The mask of the romantic dreamer—described by a soft, smooth, and fanciful melody and *legato*:

No. 6, *Florestan*—(*a*), (quotation): The mask of the romantic idealist and reformer, Eusebius's friend and partner in discussion—characterized by erratic skips and passionate tempo changes:

Schumann here quotes from an earlier cycle of his, *Papillons, op.* 2, to indicate that he means himself by this mask. At the height of the debate Florestan is interrupted by:

No. 7, *Coquette*—(*aᵢ*): A coquettish mask, skipping irresponsibly about and making strange gestures—indicated by heavy accents:

No. 8, *Réplique* (continuation): Reply of Florestan to the coquette—graceful, more dignified, taking up, in turn, (*b*) and the coquette's melody.

No. 9, *Papillons*—(*a*): A group of fast, graceful butterfly masks:

---

² A little majestic.

No. 10, *Lettres dansantes*—(*b*): A group of masks, each representing one letter of the name "Asch," pass dancing before us in rapid *staccato*:

No. 11, *Chiarina* (Clara)—(*b*): A mask—supposedly of the girl later to become Schumann's wife—characterized by passionate, urgent music:

No. 12, *Chopin* (interlude): The mask of the great composer, Schumann's friend—described by a smooth, poetic melody in perfect *legato*, not derived from the subjects.

No. 13, *Estrella*—(b_i): The mask of a female circus rider, supposedly Ernestine von Fricken—loud, passionate, extravagant in her capers:

No. 14, *Reconnaissance*—(*b*): Recognition of friends—a tender, soft, smooth melody:

No. 15, *Pantaleon and Colombine*—(b_i): A pair of very different masks; the flighty Colombine is portrayed by fast-skipping *staccato* passages, which return after the section devoted to Pantaleon:

---

[3] With passion.

No. 16, *Valse Allemande—Paganini*—(b_i): The second general dance, whose trio, not derived from the subjects, represents the mask of the great violinist in all his virtuosity:

Molto vivace

No. 17, *Aveu*—(b): Avowal of love, the fitting emotional climax of the revelry—tender but passionate:

Passionato

No. 18, *Promenade*—(b_i): Arm in arm the lovers stroll away, the music indicating an impassioned dialogue:

Comodo 4)

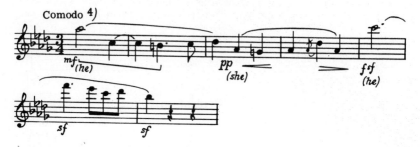

No. 19, *Pause* (introduction): To a portion of the music of No. 1 the revelers step back to rest and to free a passage for:

No. 20, the grand finale of the carnival; it begins with the *March of the League of David against the Philistines*—(b):

Non allegro

---

4 Leisurely.

The League of David was an imaginary group, Schumann's invention, of progressives, i.e. Romantics, who opposed the conservative "Philistines", i.e. the classicists. The League included Eusebius and Florestan as the two outstanding characters. New quotations from *Papillons, op. 2,* take up an old German song, called "Grandfather Song," here signifying the Philistines:

This alternates twice with the material of No. 1, rounding off the cycle appropriately with references to all major materials contained in it.

Several Russian composers later wrote descriptive suites. One of the best of these is the series of character pieces for piano, called *Pictures from an Exhibition,* by Musorgsky. Vivid characterization, striking invention, much humor, and imagination have made this work a perennial favorite, and have inspired several composers to orchestrate it. Ravel's version is unquestionably the most successful.

EXAMPLE 57: MODESTE MUSORGSKY [1839–81]

From "Pictures from an Exhibition" (1874)

The composer selected ten pictures from a memorial exhibition of paintings by his friend, Viktor Hartmann (1834–73), and translated them into spirited music. An introductory section, called *Promenade,* represents the composer as he strolled through the exhibition hall. Its music reappears in one of the "Pictures," *The Catacombs,* where it gives the illusion of movement through those subterranean cemeteries. It is, moreover, heard several times as an interlude, unifying the *Suite* (see below).

(a) No. 4—*Bydlo* (Ox Cart)

The steady, lumbering accompaniment gives a realistic description of the slow-moving ox cart; against it we hear the song of the driver:

Moderato

The vehicle is heard approaching and then receding again to the *a-b-a* of the tune. In the Ravel orchestration this tune is in both *a*-sections played by the bass tuba in one of the rare solos for this instrument.

(b) *Promenade*

This is one of those brief interludes that are all derived from the same motif with its shifting, ambling meter:

(c) No. 5, *Ballet of the Chickens in Their Shells*

The hatching chicks, shown in the painting fancifully dancing in their shells, are portrayed in a fast, elfin scherzo, mostly *piano* and *staccato*, *a*:

It is immediately repeated, followed by a quieter trio in two brief, repeated sections, *b*:

and *c*:

Then the scherzo is heard again without repetition, giving the little piece the arrangement *a-a-b-b-c-c-a*. Appreciated by young and old alike, this charming tone picture, piquant and dissonant, is justly famous for its humor.

Further Types of Romantic Suites

Not all nineteenth-century suites are necessarily descriptive (see comment on Schumann's cycles on p. 150). Often some short pieces, too brief to satisfy by themselves, are joined together in order to create more substantial works. It may be merely contrast that holds the pieces together, or reminiscences and recurrent ideas may unify them and enhance the listener's pleasure. There are, in addition, many suites without any musical unity—suites comprised of various portions of incidental music to a play, and suites that revive the old Baroque dance suite in chains of dances. Like other titles, the term "suite" covers a broad miscellany of musical compositions.

Song Cycles

The song cycle is closely related to the piano suite. Another typical product of the Romantic era, it broadens the significance of the single song by giving it a place within a larger context. There are essentially two types of these cycles: One is narrative, the other contemplative. The latter usually includes few songs, from four to eight, all presenting facets of the same idea but without necessary sequence from one to the next. The other often employs twenty or more songs in a definite sequence to tell a story.

The most famous narrative song cycles are those by Schubert and Schumann, the briefest of which is the following:

EXAMPLE 58:   ROBERT SCHUMANN [1810–56]

Frauenliebe und -leben (Woman's Love and Life),
op. 42 (1840), on poems by Adalbert Chamisso (1781–1838)

Schumann had planned to become a pianist, but through an ill-advised experiment partially paralyzed one of his hands. For ten years thereafter he composed exclusively for the piano. When, at the age of thirty, and after a long courtship, he married the afterwards famous pianist Clara Wieck, the fulfillment of his love made him turn to song composition for an entire year, and later also to other types of music. This *Song Cycle* comes from Schumann's "golden year" in which he composed one hundred and thirty-eight songs. It describes the awakening of a woman's love, her reactions to proposal and engagement, the wedding day, the expectation and birth of the first child, and the death of the husband— truly all that, in the nineteenth century, the title implied. Wild ecstasy, peace in happiness, bottomless despair—these songs express every nuance of emotion.

No. 1

The low, stumbling phrases that open *No. 1* suggest the breathlessness of the girl under the novel experience of love. The music for the two stanzas is identical.

Larghetto

1. Seit ich ihn ge - se - hen, glaub' ich blind zu sein;
   Since on him my glance fell, blind I seem to be;

    wheresoe'er my gaze fall, him alone I see.
    Like a constant daydream floats his image near;
    as the darkness deepens, brighter does my love appear.

2.   Save for him, all lightless, colorless my day.
    Though my sisters beckon, not for me their play;
    lonely in my chamber I weep bitterly.
    Since on him my glance fell, blind I seem to be.

No. 2

In *No. 2* the uncertainty is resolved into the full glow of love, represented by the firmly and rapidly rising melodic motif (*a*) and the heartwarming lyricism of the second line. The seven text stanzas are musically arranged as $A-A-B-A^1-B^1-B^2-A^2$.[5]

Tenderly, lively

(a)

1. Er, der herr - lich - ste von al - len,
   He, most won - der - ful of all men,

oh, so gen - tle, oh, so good!

    Sweet his lip's smile, bright his eye's shine,
    staunch in heart, in thought so shrewd!

---

[5] In this book the following symbols are used: for sections of substantial length, <u>A</u>, <u>B</u>, <u>C</u>, and so forth; for themes, periods, and phrases, <u>*a*</u>, <u>*b*</u>, <u>*c*</u>, and so forth; and for motifs, (<u>*a*</u>), (<u>*b*</u>), (<u>*c*</u>), and so forth.

[6] The sign ∾ indicates a TURN, executed as follows:

2.   Just as yonder in the blue sky
                clear and lordly gleams the star,
             so reigns he within my heaven,
                clear and lordly, lofty, far.

With passion

3.   Speed   thou, speed thou on thy   jour - ney;

            on   thy   rad - iance   let   me   gaze,

             in adoring contemplation,
                tearful, happy pass my days.

4.   Heed thou not my silent bidding,
                consecrate to thy good speed!
             Naught at all of maid so lowly,
                star celestial, hast thou need.

5.   Let the worthiest of women
                win the favor of thy choice;
             to a thousand blessings for her
                will I lend my voice.

6.   Though I weep, I shall rejoice then,
                happiness will then be mine.
             Though my heart break that I lose him,
                break, O heart, and none repine!

7.   He, most wonderful of all men,
                oh, so gentle, oh, so good!
             Sweet his lip's smile, bright his eye's shine,
                staunch in heart, in thought so shrewd,
                oh, so gentle, oh, so good!

No. 3

In *No. 3* the heroine is overwhelmed by happiness. The chords, followed by rests, give a most faithful picture of her state of mind. After the three stanzas A-B-A¹, A is repeated together with its text, followed by a telling coda, much broader than the few measures of piano postlude Schumann usually adds. In this coda the first two lines of the poem are once more sung, as though the girl were completely dazed by her experience. The third stanza reproduces the melody of the first, only on a higher pitch level; at the same time the mode changes from Minor to Major. Both

changes indicate the rapture of the girl. Note also how expressively
Schumann renders the line: "Thine ever shall I be!"

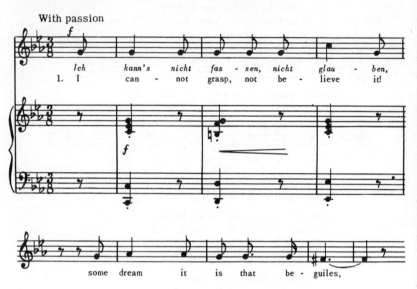

that he should have stooped to raise me—
on me to have lavished his smiles!

Methinks . . . I must yet be dreaming,
such fortune fall unto me!

3.   So dreaming let me then perish,
enfolded in his caress;
taste death in unending rapture,
my tears on the lips that I press.

No. 4

The lyric effusion of *No. 4* is a companion piece to Mozart's *Voi che sapete* (cf. p. 134f). The two attitudes toward the process of growing up reflected by these two pieces deserve close comparison. Here the girl accepts womanhood, a new content of life. Some regret about leaving the innocence of childhood behind and entering a new epoch is beautifully intimated in the chromatic ending of the first phrase (see bracket below), which is almost like a phrase of a folksong. Again the repetition of the first stanza rounds off the song, giving it an *A-B-A-B¹-A* pattern.

1.
Du Ring an mei - nem Fin - ger,
Thou ring up - on my fin - ger,

my dear lit - tle ring of gold,

  devoutly I press my lips on thee,
  devoutly I kiss thee, to my bosom hold.

2.
The dream I dreamed was end - ed,

the won - drous dream of child - hood days;

  I wandered lone and forsaken
  o'er endlessly desolate ways.

3. Thou ring upon my finger,
    as first thou didst make me see,
  so now thou turn'st my glances,
    and life, yes, the infinite showest me.

4. I want to cherish, to love him,
    to live for him entire,
  illumined, enlightened, ‖: transfigured,
    consumed in :‖ his glance of fire.

No. 5

No. 5 is similarly built: A-A^1-A-A^2-A^3. It reflects impatience in its repeated tones, longing in the prominent skips, and busy preparation in the accompaniment.

1. *Helft mir, ihr Schwe - stern, freund - lich mich schmuek - ken,*
   Help me, my sis - ters, please help a - dorn me;

I this day am the hap - py bride.

Quickly then set the crown on my forehead—
bud and blossoming myrtle's pride.

2. Happy, contented, peaceful, enraptured
    used I to lie in my lover's arms.
    Ever he pleaded, heart full of yearning:
    "When, beloved, wilt yield me thy charms?"

3. Help me, sisters, help me to banish
    this, my childish, my foolish fear;
    that without trembling, clear-eyed I greet him,
    fount of joy, whom I hold most dear.

4. When thou, beloved, nearest my presence,
    will then on me thy radiance fall?
    Let me be humble, let me be modest,
    in due obedience come to thy call.

5. Scatter then, sisters, petals and blossoms,
    fling to him rosebuds on either hand;
    yet, my dear sisters, sadly I leave you,
    ‖: joy to seek distant from your band. :‖

No. 6

The utmost happiness, expressed in tears and the shyness of sweet, secret expectancy, pervades *No. 6*. The four stanzas are musically arranged *A-A-B-A*, wherein the *B* is strongly contrasting, even uses another key; and there are significant interludes and postludes.

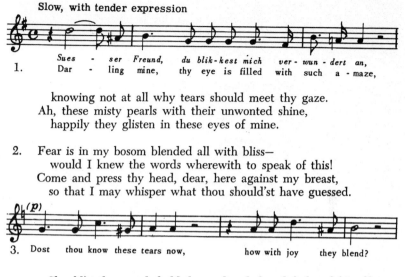

Slow, with tender expression

1. Sues - ser Freund, du blik-kest mich ver - wun - dert an,
   Dar - ling mine, thy eye is filled with such a - maze,

knowing not at all why tears should meet thy gaze.
Ah, these misty pearls with their unwonted shine,
happily they glisten in these eyes of mine.

2. Fear is in my bosom blended all with bliss—
   would I knew the words wherewith to speak of this!
   Come and press thy head, dear, here against my breast,
   so that I may whisper what thou should'st have guessed.

3. Dost thou know these tears now, how with joy they blend?

Should'st thou not behold them—thou beloved, beloved friend?
Rest thou on my heart, dear, list thou to its beat,
so that close and closer I may press thee, sweet!
　　　　　　　　　　Close and closer!

4. Here just at my bedside is the cradle's place;
   precious dream there hiding, waiting my embrace.
   Then will come the morning when no dreams beguile;
   here shall lie thy likeness, and upon me smile!
   　　　　　　　　　　Thy likeness!

No. 7

In *No. 7* the young mother reaches the height of happiness. The
tempo becomes faster and faster, almost getting out of hand. The accompaniment has to be simplified finally to accommodate the speed of the
last stanza. The ecstasy is also expressed by the mere fourfold repetition
with slight changes: *A-A¹-A-A²*, although there are only two text stanzas
and a short ending.

Gay, tender

1. A　An mei - nem Her - zen, an mei - ner Brust,
   　　Here on my heart, ah, here at my breast—

               thou, my delight! Oh, how am I blest!
               All bliss lies in loving; all loving is bliss:
               This is my word, nor speak I amiss.
A¹   My joy I thought beyond all bound;
               true ecstasy I had not found!

2.   Child at her breast, only she knows
               what tenderness with sust'nance flows:
A   Only a mother—only she
               can know what love and bliss can be.
               How with poor man must I condole!
               No joy like this can touch his soul.

A²   O angel, darling, darling child,
               thy gaze is on me—and now hast thou smiled!
               Here on my heart, ah, here at my breast—
               thou, my delight! Oh, how am I blest!

No. 8

No. 8 symbolizes despair and desolation by employment of a low, almost speaking pitch, which but once rises in bitterness to subside again. The two halves of each stanza correspond rhythmically, and in the first also melodically. Few chords accompany this recitative, and in the passage where the higher pitch level is reached (line 2, stanza 2) these chords are reminiscent of the chromaticism in *No. 4*: Another epoch in the woman's life has arrived. The *Cycle* closes with the full repetition of the piano part of the second stanza of *No. 1*.

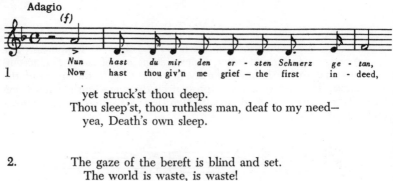

Adagio (f)

1   Nun hast du mir den er - sten Schmerz ge - tan,
    Now hast thou giv'n me grief — the first in - deed,

          yet struck'st thou deep.
          Thou sleep'st, thou ruthless man, deaf to my need—
          yea, Death's own sleep.

2.   The gaze of the bereft is blind and set.
           The world is waste, is waste!
         I've had my love, known joy and fret;
           it leaves a bitter taste.

3.   Myself to inner quietude withdrawn,
                    the veil may fall;
                there thee I hold, and all the joys foregone;
                    thou'rt still my all!

Schumann sought, of course, for effective contrasts in the *Cycle*. Here is a tabular presentation of these contrasts:

No.	Major	Minor	fast	slow	duple	triple	com-pound [7]
	Mode		Tempo		Meter		
1	x			x		x	
2	x		x		x		
3		x	x			x	
4	x			x	x		
5	x		x		x		
6	x			x	x		
7	x		x				x
8		x		x	x		
coda	x			x		x	

At first the situation changes rapidly and therefore contrasts are strong, concerning two items. *Nos. 4-7* form one chain of increasing happiness, and thus only one item changes from song to song (compound and duple meters being related). The last contrasts, however, are again very strong, symbolizing the turn from supreme happiness to death and from the contemplation of death to the reminiscence of first love.

Oriental Color and Pentatonic Scale

Another famous song cycle is Mahler's *The Song of the Earth,* a symphonic (or orchestral) cycle of the contemplative type. The main theme of this beautiful work is the futility of human life, presented in a series of seven old Chinese poems. (The last two of these are joined to form a very long finale, which we omit from detailed consideration.) In order to give the score a faintly oriental color, Mahler based his main motifs throughout on a scale of five tones per octave—a scale that is used by most Far-Eastern peoples and is called a PENTATONIC SCALE (Greek: *pente*—five):

---

[7] See Appendix I, p. 378f, for an explanation of compound and combination meters.

This scale has been employed by many composers since about 1890 for similar purposes, to the point where it has become cliché (hackneyed in technic) for a certain type of light music.

EXAMPLE 59: GUSTAVE MAHLER [1860–1911]

Das Lied von der Erde (The Song of the Earth, 1908)

Copyright 1912, renewed 1939 by Universal Edition A. G. Vienna: Copyright assigned 1952 to Universal Edition (London) Limited.

Mahler was at the beginning of this century one of the leaders of intellectual Europe, one of its most influential and greatest composers, and its most eminent conductor. His deep, romantic pessimism comes alive in this work which invites fruitful comparison with *Isolde's Love-Death* by Wagner (cf. p. 140f), whom Mahler greatly admired. The richness of Wagner's *Aria* contrasts strongly with the resignation and sometimes despairing bitterness of Mahler's music. This is not only Mahler's farewell to life, but the farewell song of the Romantic era itself.

No. 1: *The Drinking Song of the Sorrow of the Earth,*
for tenor; text by Li Po (Li T'ai Po, 701–62)

1. *a*   Here beckons wine in gold-crusted goblets,
    but drink not yet—first listen to my song!
      The song of sorrow uproariously in your souls shall
      re-echo!

   b   For when sorrow comes, lie all waste the gardens of spirit,
    wither and die all pleasure and song.

   c   Dark our life on Earth here, dark is death.

2. *a*   Host of this tavern, your cellar holds a plentiful store of
    bright wine.
    See, I have nothing save this lute.

  c^1 To strike the lute strings and to drain the goblet,
    these are fine things, good things that go together.

   b   One goblet full of wine at the right time
    ‖: holds more worth :‖ than all the empires of this wide
    world.

   c   Dark our life on Earth here, dark is death.

3.   The sky is blue forever,
    and the Earth, too, will stand for eons
    and blossom in spring.
  You now, O man, how long will you live?
    A hundred summers outlast all your pleasure
    'mid all the worthless baubles Earth can offer!

4. *a*   Behold, out there, in moonlight, in the graveyard,
             there squats a form, fantastically wild.
                An ape, see! Listen how his howlings
                   pierce shrilly through the fragrant scent of living!
   c²   Now take the wine, the time has come, O comrades!
             Now drain your golden goblets of wine!
   c   Dark is life on Earth here, dark is death.

   Despite the fact that this is in one sense a song cycle, it is primarily
an instrumental work. The themes therefore are frequently propounded
by the orchestra, while the singer takes a melodically secondary part
(cf. comment on the relationship between voices and orchestra in Wagnerian operas, p. 139). Thus a tumultuous theme, *a*, carried by the
French horn and the violins, opens this *Song:*

It is followed by a quieter section, partly orchestral and partly vocal, *b:*

and a refrain-like ending, *c:*

   With some changes the music of this stanza is repeated to text stanza 2.
This is followed by a section in which the muted trumpet leads, against

---

8 Fast but heavy.

a delicate second melody in the violins. The English horn and the clarinet are prominent also. All motifs in this section, the third text stanza, are derived from *a* and *b*. The music of the last stanza reverts to the beginning, but omits *b*. It touches the utter depth of despair.

No. 2:   *The Lonely One in Autumn*,
for alto; text by Chang-Chi (about 800)

1.
Herbst- ne - bel wal - len   blaeu - lich   ue - berm See;
Dark au - tumn clouds are   roll - ing   o'er the   lake;

the meadows lie begemmed and blanched with hoarfrost,
as if some artist had bespread with jade dust
tenderly flow'ring grasses, silv'ry white.

2.   The sweet perfume of blossoms has quite vanished.
        A cold, raw wind each slender stalk bends earthward.
      The petals of the lotus—golden, faded—
        will soon float idly, on the water strewn.

3.   My heart is weary. Sputtered out the light in my little lantern:
        Heavy are my eyes with sleep.
      I come to you, haven of my comfort.
        Aye, grant me rest; of respite have I need.

4.   Much do I weep, bleakly alone in sorrow;
        the fall here in my heart doth tarry too long.
      Dear Sun of Love—ah, dost thou cease from shining?
        Ah, must my bitter tears flow, and thou not dry them?

   After the shrill, despairing *First Song*, this one speaks of utter desolation, a companion piece to *No. 8* in Example 58. The singer starts as with a sigh, her voice gradually descending from near the upper limit of its range. A creeping violin figure, very softly played with sordines (mutes), runs through the major portion of the piece. To this figure, in the long introduction, a lonely oboe sings a drooping melody in which descending intervals predominate:

(somewhat creeping, tired)

The overall arrangement of the four stanzas is again A-A^1-B-A^2, with B an expansion of A. The last stanza is preceded by an interlude and followed by a postlude, both based on the introduction.

No. 3:   *O Youth,*
for tenor; text by Li Po

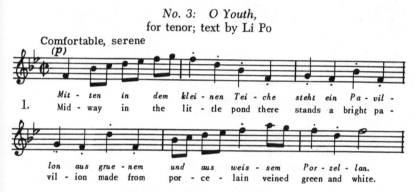

Comfortable, serene
(p)

1. Mit - ten   in   dem   klei - nen   Tei - che   steht   ein   Pa - vil -
    Mid - way   in   the   lit - tle   pond there   stands   a   bright   pa -

lon   aus   grue - nem   und   aus   weis - sem   Por - zel - lan.
vil - ion   made   from   por - ce - lain   veined   green   and   white.

Arching like a tiger's back, the bridge of jade that spans the water leaps to the pavilion yonder.

(p)

2. In   the   ti - ny   house   sit   com - rades,   fine   of   rai - ment —

drink and gossip, ‖: some of them composing verses. :‖
Now their silken sleeves slip back along their arms,
   their silken caps slide down and on their necks ride pertly.
On the quiet, quiet surface of the tiny, tiny water
   it all meets a wondrously reflected image.

3.   Ev'rything stands on its head in the pavilion
       made from porcelain all veined with green and white.

'There the bridge floats like a half-moon, with its arc inverted;
comrades, fine of raiment, drink and gossip.

To the thorough *legato* of the preceding number this one opposes
staccato attack in the short prelude and in the A of the *A-B-A* arrangement of the three stanzas; only B is *legato*. A gay spirit of abandon
hovers over this graceful picture of evanescence. Especially in evidence
are the triangle, which lends a chime-like brilliance to this *Song*, and the
piccolo (high flute).

No. 4:   Of Beauty,
for alto; text by Li Po

1.   Jun-ge Maed - chen pfluek-ken   Blu - men,   pfluek - ken
     Pret-ty maid - ens gath - er   flow - ers, gath - er

     Lo - tos - blu - men
     lo - tus - flow - ers   on the sunlit water.

As they sit amid the bushes and bright leaves,
    gath'ring blossoms, gath'ring blossoms in their laps,
        they call to one another gentle mockeries.
    Golden sunlight plays about their figures,
        mirrors them within the shining water.
Sunlight mirrors well their slender bodies,
    adding brightness to their glances,
        as caressingly the light breeze tosses
            the fine fabric of their sleeves about—
                wafts the magic of their fragrance softly through
                the air.

2.   O see, across the water handsome youngsters
            prancing along the bank on fiery stallions,
                gleaming far and wide like rays of sunlight!
                    Under the branches of the greening willows
                    canter proudly the young men.
         The horse of one of them neighs happily and shies and gallops
                forth;

over blossoms, meadows plunge the clatt'ring hoofs and in
    a storm
    they trample down the beaten, bruiséd blossoms.
      Hi, his mane—how it flies in madness; hi how hotly
        steam his nostrils!

3.   Golden sunlight plays about their figures,
      mirrors them within the shining water.
Of the maidens the most beautiful sends
    after him long looks of yearning great;
      and her lofty bearing—is only pretense.
In the sparkle of her sultry glances,
    in the darkness of her burning gaze
      cry out the pain and the agitation of her heart.

The formulation of this *Song* is similar to that of the preceding: A
brief introduction and a longer coda frame an *A-B-A¹* arrangement. The
B is again derived from *A*, yet is strongly contrasting and builds to a
boisterous climax. At the peak, between the first and second portion of
the stanza, the trombones and the bass tuba come forth raucously with
the main subject, *a,* in Minor.

No. 5: The Toper in Spring,
for tenor; text by Li Po

2. *a*   And then, when I can drink no more my gullet warm to keep,
   b   I stagger slowly to my door and sink in wondrous sleep.

3. *a*   What do I hear when waking? Hark! A bird sings in the tree.
   b   I ask him, if the spring is here. It is, it is, as though I dream.

4. *a*   The bird keeps twitt'ring: "Yea! Yea! The spring,
   b   the spring is here—has come in on night's cloud!"
         From deep perceptions I awake.
         The bird, it sings, laughs loud, laughs loud.

5. *b*   I go and fill my glass again and drain it to the lees—
            and sing until the moon makes bright the sky above the trees.

6. *a*   When I can sing a song no more,
   b   when I can sing a song no more, it's sleep again for me.
         Indeed, what do I care for spring? Let me a toper be!

   The one relieving aspect of life is love, according to the Romantic view. Human love is the theme of *No. 4*, and love of nature, the feeling of oneness with creation, is the subject of this *Song*. The stanza here contains two contrasting phrases, the *a* characterized by wind instruments and the *b* by the string group. The singer adds a rather giddy melody, and a piccolo symbolizes the bird in the poem.

No. 6:   The Farewell, for alto

   This is a gigantic Second Part, almost as long as the first *Five Songs* together. It speaks of utter loneliness and disillusionment, and of a desire to leave this world. It has been taken, and probably rightly, as the most personal confession of the composer, who felt somehow that death was nearing.

CONCEPTS AND TOPICS DISCUSSED IN THIS SECTION

SECTION H

BALLET AND BALLET SUITE

Society and Ballet

Today the ballet, as an independent art form as well as a part of moving pictures and musical comedies, is a favorite entertainment. Many a ballet company is able to compete in box-office appeal with the stage play and the cinema. Indeed, the study of ballet dancing is taking a place next to music and painting as fundamental to the education of children.

Although the ballet has been a leading art for thousands of years in the Orient, in the Western world its popularity is comparatively recent. Only in France has it flourished for several centuries, chiefly because the people followed the taste of the court. Elsewhere it existed exclusively through the support of the rich; or it held an obscure place in the shadow of opera—a servant not a sister-art. Not until our century was it widely accepted in Europe and America as independent and comparable to the other major arts.

Court Ballet and Figure Dancing

The ballet emerged in the fifteenth century from the social dancing of the nobility, which was gradually formalized in its movements and group patterns. Ballets were staged between courses of gala dinners and at other special festival or political functions with the aid of professional dancers and with lavish display of costumes, jewelry, and scenery. A dramatic story connected, however loosely, the various dances of these COURT BALLETS (ballets de cour). Choruses and, in subsequent centuries, recitatives set the stage for each ballet scene, also known as an ENTRÉE or TABLEAU.

During the sixteenth and seventeenth centuries kings and courtiers participated in the performances of court ballets. As the outstanding type of large-scale aristocratic entertainment, these ballets became under Lully and Louis XIV a manifestation of French splendor and power. After their presentation at the royal palace they were also performed publicly in Parisian theatres and were generally accepted as a symbol of the French spirit.

Lully for a time collaborated with Molière (1622–73), France's foremost author of comedies. Together they produced musical plays

By courtesy of the Gazette des Beaux Arts, *New York.*

PLATE VII: Bernardo Bellotto, il Canaletto (1720–80), Italian
             engraver and painter—*Le Turc généreux.*

A climactic scene from the ballet-opera *Les Indes galantes* by
Rameau, as staged at Vienna in 1758. (The same story was later
worked into Mozart's opera *The Abduction from the Seraglio.*) The
pasha is in the act of killing the fleeing lovers, but is restrained by
one of his wives. This is an excellent representation of a rococo
stage and orchestra.

with ballets that came very near to being operas and led to a genre called BALLET-OPERA.[1] Indeed, after Molière's death Lully did turn to opera, as we have seen. In doing so he merely shifted his emphasis from display to story. All his operas, like French opera for the next two centuries, continued to include ballets.

Against the backdrop of magnificent display the performers of court ballets exhibited a highly stylized technic of figure dancing. The dancer was admired for perfect control in performing difficult motions or figures, for the apparent ease with which he overcame the impediment of weight. In devising the dance routines, choreographers used chiefly the appeal of symmetric pattern; the dancers might become human bouquets, flowers opening and closing or swaying in the wind, and so forth, or they would be arranged across the stage with geometric regularity. The music in such ballets was mostly secondary—often, indeed, derived from popular dance music of the day.

Dramatic and Classic Ballet

In 1761 Gluck wrote *Don Juan,* the first thoroughly DRAMATIC BALLET, and thereby established a new type. Dramatic ballet reveals its story solely in expressive gesture. Interpretation through gesture and movement—pantomime—replaced the words used in court ballets and ballet-operas, and the role of pattern and figure dancing decreased. Now music assumed primary significance. It was no longer a mere rhythmic-melodic background for dances but the chief emotional interpreter of the action.

The dramatic ballet had only a short vogue. It soon fused with the ballet-opera, and pattern and figure dancing once more reigned supreme in what is known as the CLASSIC BALLET. When it began to use oriental themes and fairy tales in the nineteenth century, this combination was also called the ROMANTIC BALLET, to which, for example, belong the works of Tchaikovsky and Delibes. After a lapse of more than a hundred years, however, the dramatic ballet again assumed importance through the initiative of the Russian Ballet *(Ballet Russe).* Our ballet repertory includes some Romantic works but is mostly devoted to the dramatic type, and court ballets and ballet-operas are only occasionally revived.

---

[1] A splendid example is Rameau's *Les Indes galantes* (1735), available on records. Cf. Pl. VII, facing this page.

Ballet Suites

Ballet music is known to us mostly in concert arrangements, or suites. These have to some extent taken the place formerly occupied in the orchestral repertory by the Baroque dance suite. In the ballet suite the musical materials of the actual ballet are often rearranged. Extended and scattered passages no longer motivated by the action are integrated into units enjoyable as pure music. Close dramatic interpretation of such suites is therefore not always possible or worth while for the listener. Nevertheless he will appreciate the music much more, if, through studying the scenarios of the ballets discussed, he can associate with it the proper narrative and scenic sequence.[2]

Most scenes of Romantic ballets are mood pictures. Musically these are character pieces (cf. p. 44ff), which are open to varied interpretations on the stage. For instance the following example, just such a mood picture, has supported several very different choreographies.

EXAMPLE 60:   PETER ILICH TCHAIKOVSKY [1840–93]

Scene I from "Swan Lake" (1876)

Swan Lake was the first of those great Russian ballets that have given us some of the best music of recent time. Its scenario belongs to the tradition of Romantic fairy-tale ballets favored after 1830, and the music is likewise Romantic.

Our example opens the second of the five acts of the *Ballet*, today often performed as a separate work. The scene is a lonely forest lake. On the shore a chapel is seen; over it, in the guise of an owl, hovers an evil magician. A group of swans, the leader wearing a crown, glide over the surface of the lake. At the shore they are transformed into beautiful maidens.

The melancholy atmosphere of this fairyland is expressed in a beautiful, quiet melody in two repeated periods:

---

[2] See "Bibliography for Scenarios," Appendix II, p. 431.

The melody is first heard on an oboe, a rather high woodwind instrument, whose thin, at times sharp, nasal tone is very expressive. The oboe is often employed to evoke pastoral moods or, as here, melancholy. The underlying excitement of the *Scene* is reflected in the accompaniment: The high stringed instruments play a TREMOLO, produced by moving the bow rapidly back and forth over a string on the same pitch, and the low stringed instruments add *pizzicato* tones; meanwhile the harp plays the harmonies dissolved into swift, glittering *arpeggios*.

In this fashion the long theme establishes the mood. The orchestra then grows fuller. Four French horns together play the repeated first period of the theme and the violins continue with the repeated second period. This the full orchestra spins out a bit, and, with an increase in tempo and volume, moves toward a climax. With several repetitions of the main motif, (*a*), gradually subsiding, the *Scene* closes. By this simple scheme of pure repetition Tchaikovsky assured easy grasp and retention by the listener, and thus achieved popularity.

The Ballet Russe

The most productive period of dramatic ballet actually extends beyond the Classic-Romantic era and reaches into our time. The next two examples stand at the threshold of the contemporary period; the second, indeed, may be taken as the signal of its very start. Both works belong to the most brilliant phase of Russian ballet which began when a group of the Imperial Ballet, led by Serge Diaghilev (1872–1929), established itself in Paris in 1909. With choreographies first by Michel Fokine (1880–1942) and, after 1915, by Léonide Massine (b.1896), the *Ballet Russe* rapidly rose to world fame.

Diaghilev commissioned many leading composers, among them Albeniz, Debussy, Poulenc, Ravel, and Stravinsky, and artists such as Bakst, Dérain, and Picasso to contribute to his ballets. Other ballets he based on music already existing; this is a customary practice, but the music Diaghilev selected (as distinguished from others less ambitious than he) was always carefully culled from the very best, including music by such eighteenth-century masters as Domenico Scarlatti, Pergolesi, and Mozart, and by many nineteenth-century composers—Berlioz, Brahms, Tchaikovsky, Chopin, Rossini, Schumann, to name but a few.

The following example is from one of the outstanding ballets produced by the group:

EXAMPLE 61:   MAURICE RAVEL [1875–1937]

Daybreak from *"Daphnis et Chloé"*, Suite No. 2 (1912)

Permission for reprint granted by Durand et Cie, Paris, France. Copyright owners: Elkan-Vogel Company, Inc., Philadelphia, Pennsylvania.

The murmur of brooks ripples through the beginning of this piece. An ingratiating motif:

rises from the string bass to the 'cello, thence to the viola. The volume gradually increases, the day dawns and grows brighter. Meanwhile violins and flutes, but especially the piccolo, vividly portray the awakening birds. Then a piccolo pipes a fragmentary little tune, as a shepherd wanders across the distant scene. Yet another shepherd passes by, to the accompaniment of a brief tune on a clarinet.

As the string motif becomes more urgent and rises to the violins, a number of shepherds enter. They awaken Daphnis, who has been discovered lying under a tree. Now appears a new, troubled, anxious motif—Daphnis searches for Chloé. Almost immediately the strains alter; accompanied by shepherdesses, and heralded by another expressive melody:

Chloé enters. The brook figuration, which has never stopped, achieves a climax with the brilliant tones of the brass: Full sunlight illuminates the scene as Daphnis and Chloé embrace. Soon thereafter the sounds of oboes signal the opening of the next *tableau*.

No stronger contrast to Ravel's *Daphnis et Chloé* can be imagined than Stravinsky's *Rite of Spring*, also composed for the *Ballet Russe* and premiered only a year later. Ravel's music expresses a general mood of fulfillment in undulating, continuous melodies, rounded, consonant chords, a flowing rhythm, and a smooth-blending orchestration. Ravel's soft, interweaving lines envelop the action with a glittering atmosphere that suggests the shimmer of hundreds of small lights.

Stravinsky, on the other hand, uses clear, incisive melodic motifs, exciting, halting rhythms, dissonant chords, and instrumental contrasts to evoke a primitive mood.[3] Often his music reveals a metallic hardness. His stress on precise delineation at times culminates in the grotesque—in a caricature or a shriek.

The premiere of *The Rite of Spring* in Paris provoked a resounding scandal, for the audience thought the composer wanted to shock and ridicule them. The style of this work, to be sure, breaks decisively with Romanticism; but today it is recognized as a milestone in the history of music, a masterly projection of its time, and a herald of a new era in music—the contemporary era.

EXAMPLE 62:   IGOR STRAVINSKY [b.1882]

From *"Le sacre du printemps"* (The Rite of Spring, 1913)

Copyright 1921 by Boosey and Hawkes Ltd. By permission of the copyright owner, Boosey and Hawkes.

This work demands of the listener that he imagine the setting, the action, and the dancing with which the music was originally associated; otherwise the sound patterns will at times seem disjointed. This is true because Stravinsky, by adhering to the tenets of the realistic school of music dramatists, emphasizes the interdependence of music and dramatic action.

(a) Introduction

The members of some primitive tribe are gathering to greet the spring with dancing. The very first tone—unusually high in the bassoon, which plays the melody—establishes a strange, savage, exciting mood:

---

[3] Cf. Plate IX, p. 193, for an analogy in the representative arts.

When the English horn enters with the second tune:

two bassoons are heard in their more usual role as bass instruments. Now a third instrument, the clarinet, takes the lead in forced, uncouth tones to sustain the mood of primitiveness, an effect further emphasized by constant repetition of short motifs, which is, as we have seen, important in primitive music.

After a brief interruption, the English horn once more becomes dominant, accompanied this time by three flutes. These come briefly to the fore in the ensuing passage which combines the various musical ideas. At the climax the high bassoon reenters with a short reminiscence of the beginning, as it leads into the first tribal dance.

The Woodwinds

• The flute, oboe, clarinet, and bassoon, which figure prominently in this and in the preceding examples are the chief members of the woodwind section. In orchestral scores their parts appear in this order descending from the top of the page (cf. Plate VIII, p. 186). Each instrument has one or more relatives, e.g. the English horn is the cousin of the oboe and the piccolo belongs to the flute family. In the score the parts for related instruments are grouped together. •

(b) Sacrificial Dance (Finale)

A maiden has been chosen as a sacrifice to spring. Her dance becomes ever wilder, more frenzied, until she falls in ecstasy—dead.

An orgy of primitivism, this selection is nevertheless quite different from the Introduction. Using all the resources of the modern symphony orchestra, highly complicated rhythmic shifts, brief, ever-repeated melodic motifs, and sharp, percussive effects (though mostly without the aid of percussion instruments), Stravinsky creates a tremendously exciting Finale.

Crass loudness marks the first section, A, on motif (a):

The second, *B,* contrasts sharply, as, with sinister implication, muffled trumpets and trombones repeatedly intone a short chromatic motif, (*b*), to the accompaniment of soft yet rhythmically incisive, reiterated, dissonant chords:

Three distinct developments of this idea lead to a climax and to the return of *A,* slightly changed.

Then a third section is introduced: *C.* It again employs unchanging chords as a rhythmic background, but here the percussion instruments

assume importance. Meanwhile the horns propound a brief, powerful
motif echoed in violins and clarinets, (c):

After a brief interjection of (a) this section continues: Trumpets and
strings imitate one another on (c); the horns add full chords. A great
climax is attained; then A, completely regrouped, returns and builds to
the most powerful culmination of all. This selection thus falls into the
simple arrangement A-B-A-C-A[1].

The Brass Section

• These are the three brass instruments prominent in this example: (1) The horn, or French horn—full, brilliant, yet noble in
sound, is the alto of the brass section. In the orchestral score its
music is placed at the top of the group, however, because the horn
tone mixes well and is frequently combined with that of the woodwinds, whose parts are printed directly above (cf. Plate VIII, p.
186). (2) The trumpet is the bright and often majestic soprano
of the brass. (3) The trombone is the solemn tenor. The slide
mechanism whereby the player changes tube-length and thus con-
trols pitch distinguishes the trombone from other brass instruments,
which are equipped with valves for this purpose. The bass of the
section is the bass tuba (see Example 57a, p. 155f). •

Impressionism and Expressionism

The styles that characterize the examples by Ravel and Stravinsky have been differentiated by two terms originally describing two nineteenth-century schools of painting that arose in successive generations: IMPRESSIONISM (applied to Ravel's work) and EXPRESSIONISM (applied to Stravinsky's).[4] The contrast may be pointed up by paired terms like detached observation and emotional participation or lyricism and drama. Impressionists such as Manet, Dégas, Monet, and Renoir among painters, Mallarmé and Verlaine among poets, and Debussy and Ravel in music aimed at replacing the dynamism and pathos of the later Romantics by misty atmosphere and subtle sensation. This attitude soon elicited a sharp reaction, known as expressionism, by a group of artists, including Klee and Picasso, by dramatists such as Strindberg, Hauptmann, and O'Neill, and among composers by Schoenberg, Stravinsky, Berg, and others. To the contemplativeness of the impressionists these opposed stark drama, shock, the irrational, the abstruse. Whereas the former beguile the senses, the expressionists shock the spirit out of complacency. In musical composition the contrasts between the two ideologies are clear from the examples given above—consonance versus dissonance, quiet reserve against insistent loudness, and slow tempo against fast.

Folk Ballet

As in opera, there has been a trend toward national coloring in the ballet of our time (cf. p. 144). Among the outstanding American contributions to the FOLK BALLET perhaps Copland's *Billy the Kid* is best known. Here the music is consciously crude, jaunty, sometimes thin, sometimes strident, to create the atmosphere of the American frontier. Even several cowboy tunes are woven into it to give it a realistic flavor. There are effective melodies that can be whistled, and a driving rhythm is sustained over long passages.

---

[4] A composer may well produce expressionistic works at one time and take a different attitude at other times. Such terms as "impressionistic" or "expressionistic" therefore apply to particular works and only secondarily to their authors.

EXAMPLE 63:   AARON COPLAND [b.1900]

Street Scene from "Billy the Kid" (1938)

The action describes the beginning of Billy's career. A brief introduction sets a spirited, rhythmic pace which continues through several short tunes, mostly repeated and interrelated: *a-a-b-a-b1-c-c1*:

All these tunes are carefree, portraying various sauntering groups of girls, women, and cowboys, whose interest soon focuses on some women who perform a lively *Mexican Dance,* known as *jarabe,* which has an interesting limping rhythm:

Then there is a new melody, for two drunks have entered:

Soon they begin to quarrel. The melody is repeated twice, the last time incompletely, as it builds to a climax. Guns are drawn. In the shooting, Billy's mother, who has been an innocent onlooker, is killed. In the next moment Billy stabs the slayer and flees, an outlaw. All this is swiftly sketched in a few final measures of music which, after the sudden climax, subsides, as if stunned, in some plaintive phrases of an oboe.

The Evolution of Ballet

As we reach the most recent phase of ballet, let us once more recapitulate in brief the evolution of this major composite art form. Its history is a commentary on the people who have made and enjoyed it. It began as a courtly entertainment, starting with presentations during Renaissance banquets, and culminating in the sumptuous spectacles presented at the Baroque court of Louis XIV. Late in the seventeenth century, however, the ballet was adopted by the bourgeousie and thereafter followed two courses: In operas, ballets were used as interludes, or *divertissements,* within the action, and they combined with the opera in the genre of ballet-opera; as an independent art, discarding all vocal expression, ballet evolved into the dramatic pantomime of the eighteenth century, into the Classic-Romantic ballet, which reverted to a greater stress on figure dancing, and most recently into the twentieth-century dramatic ballet fostered by the *Ballet Russe* and into the folk ballet. Latest trends seem to be toward expressions of social and moral criticism and the setting-forth of the aspirations of mankind.

Description and Instrumentation

The examples we have discussed show some of the many approaches to the composition of ballet music—the character piece (Examples 60, 62a), set dances (Examples 62b, 63), musical comment on events and actions (Examples 61, 62a, 63), DESCRIPTIVE detail, commonly called TONE PAINTING, such as the brook and the birds in Example 61, and suggestions of locale or national background (Examples 62a, 63). In order that their music convey as much literal meaning as possible, composers exploit, in the ballet perhaps more than anywhere else, the characteristic tone colors of the orchestra. In this section and the one preceding we have therefore begun the study of the instruments and their timbres, a study we shall continue; for the recognition of tone colors is one of the

PLATE VIII: Ralph Vaughan-Williams—Symphony in *E* Minor
(1948), p. 120 of the orchestral score.

great pleasures in hearing music. A page from a modern score is given on the next page to show the complexity of such an organization as a symphony orchestra.[5]

Audience Appeal of Suites

Ballet and other suites are an important part of our concert repertory. In fact, they are among the most popular types of orchestral music. What endears many of them to so many music lovers?

Often the explanation is simply that smaller units and repetitive arrangements are grasped more easily than lengthy, more complicated works. Then again in most suites various non-musical associations give definite meaning to the music. The pleasure is further enhanced in ballet suites by the strong rhythmic sway, inspired by the dance, and by the especially colorful orchestration. As the listener becomes more and more experienced, the unifying elements of contrast and thematic reference open yet other approaches.

Summary

In this part we have considered composite works, i.e. works which musically are neither single pieces nor sufficiently unified throughout to justify their being called organic wholes.[6] Nevertheless the term "cycle" was needed to indicate a certain unity within some works. Even works thoroughly unified had to be included in some categories or the picture would have been incomplete. Instances of thorough unification, through *leitmotiv* technic, are the examples by Wagner, Verdi, and Musorgsky. Another is Mahler's *Song of the Earth* with its motifs all derived from one oriental scale. With this last work we actually anticipated Part IV, where it will again be mentioned for this reason.

The trend that led from distinct units, as in Italian opera of the eighteenth century, to a more continuous, connected whole points to a major difference in attitude between the Rococo and Classic artist on the one hand and the Romantic on the other. The clear-cut

---

[5] See Appendix I, p. 394ff, for an explanation and a list of the instruments of the orchestra, of instrument families, and of transpositions.

[6] Classic-Romantic works of these other types are discussed in Parts I, III, and IV, whose main contents they constitute.

phrase and singable theme similarly gave way to the "continuous melody" of Wagner; and an orchestration in which each instrument carried distinctive melodic material gradually changed to one in which all colors were fused to produce saturated harmonies. Musical texture followed the same trend, as it proceeded from strict homophony, in which melody and accompaniment were given definite duties and prerogatives, distinct tone colors, and narrow limits of pitch range, to ever greater contrapuntal complexity, in which melody and accompaniment were inseparably interwoven.[7] Concurrently the harmonic palette of the composer grew increasingly rich; the diatonic melodies and simple cadences prevailing in the eighteenth century were replaced by chromatic melodies and surprising, ever new chord sequences, such as those of Wagner and Musorgsky.

Related to these trends, yet different from them, was the change from the cool, rationalistic attitude of the Rococo, through the deeply human, serious approach of the Classic era, to the growing intensity and emotionalism of the Romantics. We shall later study the results of this evolution in greater detail; but we have already seen how it led from the expression of pattern and symmetry to that of spiritual drama, and thence to the portrayal of passion, and how it reached its end early in our century in attitudes of withdrawal (impressionism) or despair (expressionism). The optimism of the "age of reason" and the superficiality of the Rococo courtier were replaced by the pessimism of Romantic philosophy and the repressed atmosphere of the Victorian middle class.[8]

CONCEPTS AND TOPICS DISCUSSED IN THIS SECTION

---

[7] Compare in this respect the examples from Gluck and Mozart, pp. 130ff, 133ff, with those from Wagner and Mahler, pp. 140f, 166ff.

[8] See Appendix I, p. 409ff, for a list of Classic-Romantic composers.

Section J

ATTITUDES AND STYLES IN THE "NEW" MUSIC

Appreciating Contemporary Music

The appreciation of works of bygone generations is certainly of great value; the appreciation of contemporary art and music is of even greater value,[1] for such appreciation amounts to a recognition of the atmosphere in which we live, indeed, to self-knowledge. As in other periods so in ours, the outstanding men of letters, artists, and composers create works that lay before us contemporary currents in thought, in government and international relations, and in socio-economic affairs. These exposures are veiled, and yet revealing; veiled in symbolism, but revealing because each successful work is illuminated by an especially penetrating mind. As we in this way gain fresh insights into our own time, we also encounter new solutions of artistic problems and thus find deep significance in contemporary art and music.

The appreciation of the "new" music is, to be sure, harder to achieve than that of earlier music, to which we are accustomed from the days of our childhood. The frequent dissonance of the "new" music, its shrillness and violence, tend to confuse and irritate us. But are these features not a faithful representation of general attitudes in our time—attitudes that manifest themselves in the creation of atom bombs, in the existence of two hostile worlds or more, in social and moral insecurity, in irrational fears, and the like? Many composers of the twentieth century have, indeed, adopted new musical idioms [2] and searched for new ensembles and formulations of music. But it is not usually their music that is confused; rather it is the world picture reflected in it. The composers betray no lack of skill, no childish wilfullness. In fact, they mostly accept formulations of earlier periods and seek new paths in only one or a few elements. But they respond to social, political, and

---

[1] The term "modern music" is avoided in this book because it is often misused for "modern dance music."

[2] The term "style" we shall reserve for the sum total of traits generally present in the works of a particular period, and employ "idiom" for an individual integration of these traits with more special, personal ones.

cultural uncertainty and react with pity, with derision, with revulsion, or with impersonal objectivity, presenting the uncertainty in as well-articulated a form as they can.

Quality of the "New" Music

As in all periods, there are today composers good, mediocre, and bad. Yet we must remember that of the many thousands of works by literally hundreds of composers in any period—for instance in that of the Viennese Classics—only a few works by a mere handful of masters keep their sheen and live on. The proportion of works that survive from an experimental era such as ours (or that around 1600, for example) is still smaller than that surviving from a generation in which tendencies of development have come to a focus—a classic generation. All the more do we need to listen to many new works in order to select the worthiest. We shall therefore change our method of study in this section. Instead of analyzing rather thoroughly a few works, we shall try to gain insight into the various trends, and the many suggested examples will aid in differentiating among these trends.

The quality of a work of art depends on the degree of integration of meaningful materials in a unique way. Technical proficiency, coherence, the creation of expressive motifs, and a degree of originality are demanded of an artist. The type of work which he chooses and the idiom in which he customarily expresses himself, as well as the aspect of the world that inspires him, are quite secondary in this respect, although they may attract much attention to themselves. To state it bluntly: A great artist may use any content, any language, any tonal idiom, or any color scheme whatsoever, and yet create significant works.

The initial rejection of works of art because of the idiom or the subject matter chosen by the artist may merely reflect the audience's inexperience. The discrepancy between the artist's and our own concepts may prove an obstacle to our aesthetic satisfaction, but we should try to overcome this obstacle. His concepts may not be ours, they may even be "wrong" reactions to reality; after all, the artist is not a natural or social scientist nor a philosopher. But neither does his work serve as an objective exposition of thought; it is, rather, a communication of subjective experience from man to man, and to attain aesthetic satisfaction we should try to see with the artist's eyes and hear with his ears.

Contemporary Attitudes

In discussing the "new" music we shall therefore try to understand first the general attitudes of contemporary composers toward their surroundings, and then the technics they have employed to convey their meanings. Neither approach can here be investigated completely. Only the outstanding attitudes and those technics that can be well presented in isolation will be treated. It must be remembered, however, that, whereas discussion may isolate these, reality is more complex. Many composers assume different attitudes and use various technics or combinations thereof at various times of their lives, and "progressive" attitudes often combine with "conservative" technics and *vice versa*.

What we should do about the examples given below, chosen from small pieces and composite works only, is to search for the skill and originality of the exposition and the integration of significant motifs, regardless of the degree of dissonance. If we search for these things, our awareness of the degree of dissonance itself will slowly recede in proportion to our growing grasp of the meaning of particular dissonances in the whole work.

We shall discuss seven attitudes. These fall into two larger classes —conservative extensions of Romantic emotionalism and progressive rejections of such extensions, turning to objectivism and formalism. The "conservative" attitudes include (1) IMPRESSIONISM, (2) EXPRESSIONISM, (3) NEO-MEDIEVALISM and (4) NEO-ROMANTICISM. Another, (5) BARBARISM or NEO-PRIMITIVISM, is ambivalent, having both Romantic and formalistic aspects. The last two attitudes belong to the "progressive" camp: (6) FUTURISM and (7) NEO-CLASSICISM.

Impressionism and Expressionism

Impressionism and expressionism have already been discussed (see pp. 178f, 182f). We therefore limit ourselves here to a few examples that indicate their continued vogue in our day:

Impressionism:

No. 1—Charles T. Griffes (1884–1920): *The White Peacock,*
    No. 1 of "Roman Sketches", *op.* 7
No. 2—Aaron Copland (b.1900): *Quiet City*

Expressionism:

No. 3—Arnold Schoenberg (1874–1951): *The Sick Moon,*
    No. 7 of *"Pierrot Lunaire",* song cycle
No. 4—Alban Berg (1885–1935): *Wozzeck*

Neo-Medievalism

Neo-medievalism is the outgrowth of the historicism of the Romantic era. The revival of Gregorian chant and of medieval choral and ensemble music has inspired many contemporary composers to adopt certain features of these older bodies of music, especially of church music. These features include the use of the scales of medieval music—the CHURCH MODES; [3] a counterpoint without reference to harmonies, known as DISSONANT or LINEAR COUNTERPOINT; ancient instruments or an instrumentation evoking a similar impression; much chorus; and a melodic formulation similar to that of chants. Some good examples are:

No. 5—Ralph Vaughan-Williams (b.1872): *Kyrie* from "Communion Service in *G"*
No. 6—Igor Stravinsky (b.1882): *Mass*
No. 7—Paul Hindemith (b.1895): *Das Marienleben,* song cycle

Neo-Romanticism

Neo-romanticism is the extension of Romantic lyricism. It continues to employ chromaticism and the smooth chords and mellow orchestration of the impressionists, but stresses expressive melody, often derived from folksong (without the exaggerated, over-emphatic intervals of expressionism). Much of the better motion-picture music illustrates this trend. Except for a slight increase in

---

[3] See Appendix I, p. 383f, for an explanation of the Church modes.

By courtesy of Dr. Irving Epstein.

PLATE IX: Jacob Epstein (b.1880), American sculptor—Adam.

This statue symbolizes fertility in the sense of the Old Testament. Compression of form, reduction of the presentation to essentials, omission of all ornamentation, short motifs and utmost tension, and the power and primitive quality that result—all closely parallel the technics employed in musical expressionism and neo-primitivism (cf. p. 179ff).

dissonance, the style of neo-romantic music does not differ from
that of music by later Romantics such as R. Strauss or Debussy.
Here are a few examples:

No. 8 —Charles Ives (1874–1954): *The Housatonic at Stock-
        bridge*
No. 9 —Maurice Ravel (1875–1937): Shéhérazade, song cycle
No. 10—Serge Prokofiev (1891–1953): *Alexander Nevsky,* can-
        tata excerpted from motion-picture music
No. 11—George Gershwin (1898–1937): *Porgy and Bess*
No. 12—Kurt Weill (1900–50): *Street Scene,* folk opera
No. 13—Brian Easdale (b.1909): *Red Shoes,* ballet suite

Barbarism

Barbarism (neo-primitivism) springs from dissatisfaction with traditional expression; and yet, in reverting to the primitive it follows
a Romantic line of reasoning: flight from the here and now. We
have already studied an outstanding example, Stravinsky's *Rite of
Spring* (see p. 179ff), from which the main characteristics of this
attitude have become clear. Emphasis is given to rhythmic energy,
accentuated by harsh discords with percussive or noise effects of a
primitive type rather than to harmonic implications (cf. the *Acholi
Royal Dance,* p. 8f). The rhythms cut across the traditional meters
and have contributed much toward a greater freedom (a Romantic
trait) in rhythmic and melodic materials; [4] on the other hand, they
have tended toward setting up new patterns, toward clear phrasing,
and toward using distinct sections (Classic trends). Further examples are:

No. 14—Béla Bartók (1881–1945): *Allegro barbaro*
No. 15—Ernst Toch (b.1887): *The Chinese Flute,* symphony
        with voices
No. 16—Serge Prokofiev (1891–1953): *Scythian Suite*

Futurism

Futurism is related to barbarism in that it turns away from complex humanity and toward simpler subjects. Its materials are similar
to those of barbarism, but it stresses the noise of the machine. As
one writer propounded the matter, futuristic music "reflects the

---

[4] All this may be seen, translated into terms of sculpture, or of representative
art in general, in Plate IX, facing this page.

masses, the noises of shipyards, railroads, steamboats, battleships, automobiles, and airplanes." [5] This machine music had its heyday in the 1920's and has left its imprint especially on motion-picture music. A few famous examples are the following:

No. 17—Edgar Varèse (b.1885): *Octandre; Ionisation*
No. 18—Serge Prokofiev (1891–1953): *Suggestion diabolique*
No. 19—Artur Honegger (b.1892): *Pacific 231*

Neo-Classicism

The most radical departure from Romanticism, actually its complete denial, is the mark of neo-classicism. This term refers to two not necessarily connected approaches: to a return to pre-Romantic music, mostly Rococo and Baroque, and to a new objectivism in music, expressed by a completely unemotional, purely technical-intellectual attitude. It is especially in works of the second type that the full array of contemporary musical materials has been developed. The examples are divided among the two approaches:

Return to pre-Romanticism:

No. 20—Maurice Ravel (1875–1937): *Le tombeau de Couperin,* suite
No. 21—Ottorino Respighi (1879–1936): *Gli ucelli* (The Birds), suite
No. 22—Igor Stravinsky (b.1882): *Pulcinella,* ballet suite

Objective approach:

No. 23—Béla Bartók (1881–1945): *Suite op. 14, Nos. 2-4*
No. 24—Igor Stravinsky (b.1882): *Orpheus,* ballet suite

Combination of both approaches:

No. 25—Paul Hindemith (b.1895): *Ludus Tonalis,* especially *Fuga No. 1, Interludium No. 4*

Contemporary Technics

As with the attitudes we may divide the new technics into those growing "conservatively" out of Romanticism, employing (1) ATO-NALITY, (2) MICROTONES, (3) FOLKLORISM, and (4) POLYTONALITY;

---

[5] Futurism is therefore also known as BRUITISM, from French: *bruit*—noise. The passage occurs in Francesco Pratella's *Musica Futurista* (1912).

and "progressive" technics, opposed to Romanticism, employing (5) NEW CHORDS and (6) DISSONANT COUNTERPOINT; with a middle position occupied by the use of (7) POLYRHYTHM.

Atonality and the Twelve-Tone Method

Atonality has perhaps attracted most attention, because it seems to deny the very basis of Classic-Romantic music. There are several varieties of atonality which, though they have one principle in common, differ in others. They all agree in the abandonment of a tonal center, a tonic to which all other tones may be referred. This abandonment was the end result of the evolution of Wagnerian chromaticism. Indeed, toward the end of the Romantic era the tonal center had been gradually obscured until it was no longer discernible. It had ceased to be a vital organizing factor in music long before the atonalists abandoned it.

One particular brand of atonality has been foremost in general interest: the TWELVE-TONE METHOD OF COMPOSITION, or twelve-tone system, created by Arnold Schoenberg. His many students all over the world have added much to its fame. Having abandoned tonality as an organizing principle, Schoenberg, in order to achieve musical coherence, substituted for it a melodic unit containing all twelve tones of the octave, called a ROW. Whereas the Classic and Romantic composers related their compositions to central tonics—such names as "Symphony in D Major" or "Suite in A Minor" reflect this fact— twelve-tone composers derive all the material in a composition from a basic twelve-tone row, which is therefore ever-present in one form or another.[6] Here are some examples of twelve-tone atonality:

No. 26—Arnold Schoenberg (1874–1951): *Ode to Napoleon*
No. 27—Anton Webern (1883–1945): *Bagatelles*
No. 28—Alban Berg (1885–1935): *Lulu*

Microtones

When the Romantics had nearly exhausted their chromaticism, their desire for clearer expression of emotions led them to explore finer gradations in pitches. The great pianist and composer, Feruccio Busoni (1866–1924), introduced thirds of tones (instead of half-

---

[6] The reader will find examples of twelve-tone rows in Barber's *Piano Sonata*, p. 276ff, especially in the *third movement*.

tones). The Czech composer, Aloys Hába, has written for quarter- and sixth-tones, and Julian Carrillo in Mexico even employs eighths and sixteenths of tones. Such microtones have also been employed by others, but not so systematically as in the following little study, which only serves to illustrate some possible effects:

No. 29—Aloys Hába (b.1893): *Duo in Sixth-Tones* for violins

Folklorism

Folklorism consists in the adaptation of folk traits to art music. This procedure grew out of the Romantic trend toward national coloring. Contemporary composers usually go beyond the adaptation of folk melodies to traditional harmonies; they try to catch the flavor in rhythm, phrasing, and typical accompaniments. Easily the most famous in the field, Bartók did yeoman research in Hungarian, Slovak, and Roumanian folk music. Much of it he incorporated in his music, especially in small pieces for beginning pianists. Spain, South America, and the jazz of North America have similarly affected contemporary music. Here are some examples:

No. 30—Béla Bartók (1881–1945): *Roumanian Dance op. 8a; Suite op. 14, No. 1*

No. 31—Heitor Villa-Lobos (b.1887): *Aria-Cantilena* from "Bachiana Brazileira No. 5"

No. 32—Darius Milhaud (b.1892): *Scaramouche Suite*

No. 33—Aaron Copland (b.1900): *Our Town*, ballet suite

No. 34—Morton Gould (b.1913): *Spirituals for Orchestra*

Polytonality

Like atonality, polytonality grew out of the tendency to disregard the single tonal center. Comparable to cubism in painting, where often several views of an object are superimposed in one plane, here various voices in a piece, singing along simultaneously, are presented in different tonalities. Through the resulting clashes, each voice strongly affirms its individuality. In this respect polytonality is related to dissonant counterpoint (see below). There may be as many as four different tonalities employed at once over long passages. A few examples:

No. 35—Karol Szymanowski (1883–1937): *Mazurka No. 1*

No. 36—Darius Milhaud (b.1892): *Saudades do Brazil*

Polyrhythm and Polymeter

Rhythmic inventiveness languished early in the nineteenth century, as composers found themselves unable to free music from the pronounced favor for regularity of meter in Classic music. Later Romantics tried to revitalize rhythm by creating contrasting counter-rhythms in the accompaniment,[7] but they only succeeded in diminishing the overall rhythmic drive. Neo-medievalism, barbarism, and futurism, however, inspired new approaches. Vigorous polyrhythm, i.e. several well defined rhythms simultaneously in various parts, as we found it in Renaissance polyphony, and POLYMETER, i.e. frequent meter changes or also different accentuation patterns in simultaneously presented parts, came to the fore. Here are a few examples of various types of this technic:

> No. 37—Alexander Scriabin (1872–1915): *Poème op. 32*
> No. 38—Igor Stravinsky (b.1882): *Les Noces,* ballet
> No. 39—see No. 17
> No. 40—Francis Poulenc (b.1899): *Gloria* from "Mass in *G*"

New Chords

The traditional chords of the Classic-Romantic era had been worked to exhaustion by 1900. New types of chords were tried out everywhere. They were constructed of all kinds of intervals, not only of thirds, and led to many new combinations, such as the following:

Thus harmonic materials were greatly expanded. Almost all examples cited above can serve here again, but Stravinsky, Bartók, and Hindemith are perhaps outstanding in the creation of new chords, as for instance in:

---

[7] See an example by Brahms, p. 303.

No. 41—Béla Bartók (1881–1945): *Burlesque: A Bit Drunk*
No. 42—see No. 6
No. 43—Paul Hindemith (b.1895): *Ludus Tonalis*, especially
   Fuga No. 5, Praeludium, Interludia 2, 6, 8, and *Post-
   ludium*

Dissonant Counterpoint

Finally, dissonant counterpoint is the result of combining the idea
of real polyphony in several voices (such as that of Palestrina or
Bach) with that of persistent dissonance. Whereas Renaissance and
Baroque polyphony relied on smoothly blending intervals and
used dissonances only to emphasize the basic consonances, much
music of our contemporaries employs dissonance without interruption. Because of the resulting clashes, the voices resist blending and
remain individually distinct (cf. Example 96, p. 365). Most examples previously cited under the headings atonality, polytonality, and
new chords might serve here again, but the following compositions
are especially interesting in this context:

No. 44—Arnold Schoenberg (1874–1951): *Serenade for Septet
   and Baritone Voice*
No. 45—Paul Hindemith (b.1895): *Ludus Tonalis*, especially
   Fugae 1, 2, and 3

Viewing the Future

What we have reviewed briefly in this section is an absorbing
array of contemporary attitudes and technics, which combine into
a still greater number of idioms.[8] We therefore easily understand
the cries of some conservatives that music—and for that matter all
the arts, yes, even our entire civilization—is approaching an igno-
minious end; for they interpret the variety of contemporary approaches as the frantic struggling of a dying art. Yet such outcries
have resounded frequently in past periods and were each time
belied by what followed.[9]

History provides a much sounder interpretation of these events.
What has happened after intervals of uncertainty and experimenta-

---

[8] For detailed discussions of contemporary works see Example 14, p. 21f;
Example 33, p. 55f; Examples 62-63, p. 179ff; Example 82, p. 276ff; Example
87, p. 306ff; Example 92, p. 335ff; Example 96, p. 365ff.

[9] Cf. Nicolas Slonimsky's *Lexicon of Musical Invective: Critical Assaults on
Composers since Beethoven's Time,* New York, Coleman-Ross, 1953.

tion that have followed the demise of a period and a style? Invariably, after two or more generations, a generation of "classic" masters has arisen to create a new standard style through its great works. And signs are multiplying that this is the present course of events, that we may look forward to a generation of new masters—possibly still within this century.

The New International Style

As in previous periods, the initial experimentation has cleared the way for a moderately assertive style of music that is being widely accepted. Even the radical modernists of the 1920's have become conservative, quietly assured. The music composed around 1950 is much simpler in counterpoint, harmony, rhythm, and orchestration than that composed two or three decades earlier. The violent rejection of the tenets of the Classic-Romantic era is yielding to a partial acceptance of its ideas and the integration of those ideas with the new style. Similar trends may be observed also in the other arts and in literature.

Summary

To sum up: Today s music is as vigorous and intensely interesting as any music ever was. It demands more of the listener than older music, but those who put forth the somewhat greater effort necessary will reap abundant gratification. New attitudes, new technics, and new integrations of those already existing have led to novel solutions of artistic problems. There are in this music beauty, excitement, gaiety, deep seriousness, passion, bitterness—in other words, all ingredients that lend themselves to artistic creation and aesthetic pleasure.[10]

CONCEPTS AND TOPICS DISCUSSED IN THIS SECTION

atonality—p. 196

barbarism (neo-primitivism)—p. 194

contemporary period—p. 189f

dissonant counterpoint—pp. 192, 199

folklorism—p. 197

futurism—p. 194f

microtones—p. 196f

neo-classicism—p. 195

neo-medievalism—p. 192

neo-romanticism—p. 192f

new chords—p. 198f

polyrhythm, polymeter—p. 198

polytonality—p. 197

twelve-tone composition—p. 196

---

[10] See Appendix I, p. 411f, for a list of contemporary composers.

PART **III**
LARGE SINGLE PIECES

VI ADDITIVE FORMS

SECTION A

POTPOURRI AND FANTASY

Small Piece and Large Piece

When man achieves a goal, he generally moves on to another, even bigger task. Thus, in the history of music as well as in the career of the individual composer, the small piece often becomes a stepping stone toward larger works. One may almost maintain that a composer reaches maturity only when he takes this step. He may write short pieces by a process of quasi-improvisation, for it is relatively easy to give coherence to them. To create a large work successfully, however, requires concentrated, clear thought, disciplined labor, and spiritual dedication of a rare order. Once the composer has labored so intensely over works of real magnitude, he will usually bring all his fervor and controlled skill to bear on short pieces as well.

Both duration and complexity of organization determine the difference between small and large pieces. Each section of a small piece consists of one or a few phrases or periods; contrasts among these sections are as a rule not strong, one often being evolved from the material of another. (Good examples are the *Songs* from Schumann's *A Woman's Love and Life,* p. 157ff.) The overall pattern of large pieces may be as simple as that of small ones, but each section equals a small piece in length and organization, and the contrasts between sections are usually pronounced. The result is, of course, greater complexity, which forces the composer to concentrate on significant materials, unifying devices, and overall organization, so that the piece may be clear and satisfying to the listener.

Large Pieces as Series of Small Ones

We have already considered a few examples of organization on a large scale. Bach's *D-Minor Toccata* (p. 57f), for instance, is certainly a large work, yet its overall organization is simple: $A-B-A^1$, as toccata sections precede and follow the fugue. Similarly Rossini's *Una voce poco fà* (p. 52ff) presents a combination of two internally patterned and strongly contrasting small pieces, one slow and one fast. The *Finale* from Stravinsky's *Rite of Spring* (p. 180ff) is organized on a still larger scale. It consists of three different sections, arranged in the simple pattern $A-B-A-C-A^1$. In fact, in overall pattern the large piece is often made simpler than the small one in order to assure easier comprehension by the listener.

Additive and Repetitive Form

The composer may employ two methods of organization in both small and large pieces: ADDITIVE or REPETITIVE structure or form.[1] In additive structures different sections follow one another without any repetitions except for those of motifs or phrases that organize the sections internally. In repetitive structures sectional repetition is used to help achieve organization. Certain periods have favored one type or the other, but both are important in the music performed today.

---

[1] The term "form" will be used here as synonymous with "structure" or pattern of organization. It is often loosely employed to label what we have called "musical types" or "species," such as opera or ballet, which do not necessarily possess overall musical structure.

Serial Organization and Potpourri

The simplest organization is the series of loosely connected small units, as exemplified by Palestrina's *Mass* (p. 75f), in which each major portion is composed additively. Here the contrasts in texture among the various sections do contribute to a sense of organization, but the chief unifying factors are the liturgical text and the *cantus firmus,* neither of which creates musical pattern. On the other hand, instrumental compositions lack the binding agent of a text and therefore require a firmer musical organization, one that, especially in large works, involves repetition.

Nevertheless, large pieces of additive form, not supported by a text or an implied narration or description, do exist. They are written to afford enjoyment of the separate tunes involved. These tunes are often presented in the form of complete small pieces, but they may appear only as casually linked phrases. Such works are known as POTPOURRIS or MEDLEYS, though they may appear under various titles (cf. Poulenc's *Toccata,* p. 55f). Sometimes composers will employ the principle of contrast to relate the sections of potpourris to each other; more often they will try to achieve some symmetry by repeating one of the tunes somewhere in the course of the potpourri or by reminiscences in a coda (cf. the Strauss *Waltz,* p. 25f); but these devices do not alter the episodic character of the music.

The Potpourri Overture

Medleys of melodies from popular operas or ballets are still in vogue. They are heard on juke boxes and over the radio, and are performed as dinner music. The vogue arose in the second quarter of the nineteenth century, and is reflected in the hundreds of arrangements by Liszt, who used them to show off his pianistic virtuosity.[2] During the same period it became fashionable for composers of grand opera to preface their works with an orchestral "curtain-raiser" containing the principal tunes of the opera. This anticipation of the melodies, together with their repetition later in the work, helped assure popularity for them and thus for the

---

[2] A famous example is his *Rigoletto Paraphrase,* based on themes from Verdi's opera *Rigoletto.*

opera. Such POTPOURRI OVERTURES were afterwards written for other types of opera as well, and they are still favored in musical comedies. The following is one of the best:

EXAMPLE 64:   GEORGES BIZET [1837–75]

Overture to Carmen (1875)

The music of the *Overture* includes three highlights of the *Opera:* (1) March and Children's Chorus from Act IV, formulated *a-a-b-a:*

(2) The Toréador song, heard in Act II and again in Act IV:

and, after the repetition of *a*, (3) the fate motif, heard frequently throughout the *Opera* and associated with its heroine, Carmen:

From section to section there are abrupt changes in rhythm, tone production, volume, tempo, and key, which add to the zest of this fine *Overture.*

---

[3] Fast and cheerful.

We may here observe the two fundamental ways in which small pieces can be formulated. The first and second sections of the *Carmen Overture* are organized repetitively, whereas the last evolves continuously from one motif, without clear cadences or phrases. This difference in construction provides the composer with a further opportunity for contrasting sections in potpourris. Mozart used this opportunity in the next example:

EXAMPLE 65: WOLFGANG AMADEUS MOZART [1756–91]

Fantasy in C Minor, K.475 [4] (1784)

Mozart composed this *Fantasy* as a separate work, but he published it together with one of his *Piano Sonatas,* K.457, indicating that the *Fantasy* might be played as a prelude to the *Sonata.* The title "fantasy" or "fantasia," it should be added, like the title "overture," heads pieces of very diverse structures, which are by no means always of the potpourri type (cf. Example 42, p. 101f).

The *C-Minor Fantasy* opens with an intense slow section of the continuous kind, *A:*

This is followed by a song-like section, formulated *a-a-b-b,* with the end of *b* taking up part of *a,* a section also slow but lyrical, *B:*

A sudden change to a fast tempo returns us to the tense mood of the beginning, *C:*

---

[4] As no *opus* numbers are available for Mozart's works, his bibliographer, Ludwig Köchel (1800–77), compiled a chronological catalog of the master's works for this purpose. Hence Mozart's compositions are cited by K or Köchel numbers in place of the usual *opus* numbers.

Then the mood again becomes lyric, *D:*

After a CADENZA, a flourish resembling improvisation, a second song-like section is heard, organized like the first and also slow but with different music, *E:*

Similarly, corresponding to *C* but with new melodic material, another fast, turbulent portion intervenes, *F:*

Più allegro [5]

which once more subsides into a lyric mood, like that of *D, G:*

(Più allegro)

A changed recapitulation of *A* concludes the work.

The last section presents the only melodic repetition in the *Fantasy*. Nevertheless the formulation of the work is completely satisfying, for in mood and tempo sections *B, C,* and *D* are related to those designated *E, F,* and *G,* forming the pattern *A-B-C-D-E-F-G-A*[1]. The variety, moreover, and the well-planned alternations in moods, tempos, and technics among the sections contribute greatly toward the total effect.

Other pieces organized as potpourris may be entitled ballade, elegy, legend, prelude, rhapsody, and so forth, but none of these titles necessarily implies additive form. Even in potpourris, in fact, most great composers will follow some such ideas as give cohesion to our last example, namely contrasts and correspondences other than melodic.

CONCEPTS AND TOPICS DISCUSSED IN THIS SECTION

additive form—p. 204f   potpourri—p. 205
cadenza—p. 208   potpourri overture—p. 205f
large and small piece—p. 203f

---

[5] Faster.

SECTION B

VARIATIONS

Variation Form

Whereas the plan of potpourris and fantasies may be likened to that of a rambling story, or to series of stories such as *The Arabian Nights,* the organization termed VARIATION FORM resembles the arabesque, the repeated pattern of oriental rugs and tapestry.

Variation is one of the basic and simplest principles of expanding a design—graphic, musical, or otherwise; yet, however primitive, if well handled, variation always remains effective. Melodies, let alone entire compositions, cannot be constructed without it. As ubiquitous as it is, this device also has a more formal application: that of setting up a theme and then using it as the framework within which, in a series of distinct sections, certain changes produce new meaning. This is variation form. The theme may be taken from a work previously composed, often by another composer. Its quality influences the value of the entire set of variations, but sometimes an inferior theme is kept alive by the wealth of ideas with which a great composer has surrounded it.

These ideas are derived from the theme by modifying it significantly with respect to one or several of the elements of music: rhythm, melody, harmony, counterpoint, instrumentation, expression, and form. We may therefore speak of rhythmic, melodic, harmonic, contrapuntal, tone-color, character, and structural variations, depending on which element is primarily affected by the modification; and, in addition, there are many combined types of variation. In fact, few variations follow a single method throughout. The above classification is useful chiefly for providing general statements regarding certain practices of composition rather than precise descriptions of all types of variation.

Contrapuntal Variations: Basso ostinato and Passacaglia

We have already studied some examples of variation form. Bach's *Crucifixus* (p. 83f) and *Dido's Lament* by Purcell (p. 119f) represent one important type of formal variations. Both are based on melodic-rhythmic subjects which are repeated in the bass without interruption and with only slight changes, if any. Such a repeated

bass subject is called a BASSO OSTINATO (Italian—persistent bass).
The variations consist in the addition of ever new melodic lines to
the *basso ostinato*. This type of CONTRAPUNTAL VARIATIONS, i.e. variations in which the chief concern is the invention of new voices
within a given framework, is known as PASSACAGLIA or CHACONNE.
Although originated in the Renaissance, it was most favored during
the Baroque era, and it still fascinates contemporary composers.[1]

The Finale of Variation Sets

The two examples just mentioned are parts of larger works. They
are therefore not concerned with a problem present in independent
sets of variations. In such sets, as one variation follows another,
the last variation must be given special emphasis to furnish a sufficient climax. Therefore composers may conclude variation sets
with (a) a finale in the form of a free spinning-out or development
of the theme, which with its length and power crowns the work;
(b) a fugue whose subject is derived from the variation theme or,
if new, is in the course of the fugue combined with such a subject;
(c) a repetition of the theme in its original form or in the form of
a chorale; or (d) a *passacaglia* (in sets other than *passacaglias*)
whose theme is derived from that of the variations. In the following *Passacaglia* by Bach a majestic fugue on a subject derived from
the *basso ostinato* forms a magnificent conclusion.

EXAMPLE 66: JOHANN SEBASTIAN BACH [1685–1750]

Passacaglia and Fugue in C Minor for organ

Passacaglia

The subject of Bach's mighty *Passacaglia*, (S):

is followed by *twenty variations*. The first ten and the last five present
the subject in the full, low tones of the pedals, whereas *variations 11-15*

---

[1] See an interesting example by Barber in Example 82, *third movement*,
p. 279. The terms *passacaglia* and *chaconne* are used here interchangeably,
because musically there is no difference between the two types which, coming
from different origins, fused completely. Nevertheless it should be noted that
many writers make a distinction between them.

have it in the manuals and partly in voices other than the bass. These
five *variations*, together with *variation 10*, form a kind of middle section,
soft on the whole and distinguished by the absence of the pedals through
most of it. This organization enabled Bach to reach two climaxes, one in
variation 9 and the other at the end, each after a continuous and carefully planned increase of activity. The beginnings of *variations 1, 11,*
and *16 follow:*

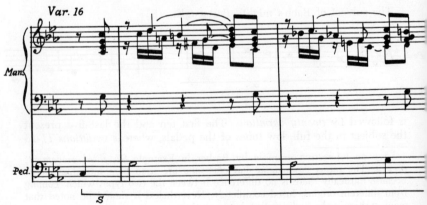

Fugue

Like many fugues for organ the one concluding this work is on a grand scale. All the music of its four voices is derived from three ideas, which are constantly in evidence and give coherence and continuity to the *Fugue:* (1) the majestic subject, consisting of the first four measures of the *Passacaglia* subject and indicated by *a* in the examples, characterized by long note values; (2) an *obbligato* [2] *counterpoint* or *countersubject,* (*b*), one measure in length and characterized by tone repetition, in moderately short note values; and (3) a second countersubject, (*c*), a figuration only one beat long, but expandable and in short note values. Because of the marked rhythmic differences among the three ideas it is rather easy to follow their various uses, separately and in combination:

The *Fugue* is laid out in three sections. In the first the subject is heard five times, one entrance following rather closely after another (A, S, B, T, A). The second section, virtually for only three voices throughout and emphasizing major keys, has three well-spaced entrances of *a* (T, A, B), with the pedals reentering in the last one after a long silence. In the third section, which returns to Minor, the four entrances (A, S, B, S) are

---

[2] The term *"obbligato"* refers to a significant, unchanging secondary element in a composition: an *obbligato* counterpoint, an *obbligato* (solo) instrument (see, e.g. the *obbligato* violin and oboe in *Nos. 3* and *6* of Bach's *Cantata,* pp. 88f, and 90), an *obbligato* rhythm (cf. Example 68, p. 218f).

yet more widely separated, and after the final, glorious entrance the music broadens into a long, powerful coda.

Melodic Variations: Figural and Character Variations

Two examples of a second category of variations, namely MELODIC VARIATIONS, have already been discussed: Paganini's *Caprice No. 24* (p. 51) and Liszt's *La Campanella* (p. 55). Here a complete theme in two or three periods is established and then melodically altered. Tempo, meter, or harmony—either singly or in any combination—may also be involved in the change, but primary interest attaches to the refashioned melody. Such melodic variations were especially in vogue up to the middle of the nineteenth century; today they are comparatively rare.

Two sub-types of melodic variations, not always completely distinguishable, are FIGURAL and CHARACTER VARIATIONS. Figural variations are well exemplified by Liszt's *La Campanella,* in which each variation uses a new figuration motif applied to the entire melody or to large portions of it, while the other elements of the theme, especially the phrase structure [3] and the sequence of harmonies remain unaltered. In character variations the changes primarily affect rhythm, meter, and expression; the original melody may even be entirely abandoned, for, with harmony and phrase structure retained, such variations are still heard as derived from the theme. By means of the new rhythm, supported by changes in meter and expression—volume, tempo, and tone production—certain ideas or notions may be symbolized: persons or animals, moods, and activities (including those discussed under the functional types, e.g. dancing or marching). Although long known previously, character variations were neglected in the latter part of the eighteenth century until revived by Beethoven. The following is one of his earliest variation works so conceived in part.

---

[3] By phrase structure we mean the pattern of phrases in the theme, or its form, which we have previously indicated by *a-b-a, a-a-b-a, a-b-c-a,* and so forth, as well as the length of each phrase in numbers of measures, and often the kinds of cadences used.

EXAMPLE 67:   LUDWIG VAN BEETHOVEN [1770–1827]

Variations in F Major, op. 34 (1802), for piano

Theme

The *Theme* of this short set of *Six Variations* and *Coda* (finale) is simple, slow, song-like. The listener should play it several times before listening to the *Variations* so as to fix its pattern in his mind, an *a-b-a* form consisting of an eight-measure period, *a,* in which measures 1-4 and 5-8 correspond, a middle section of six measures, *b,* and the repetition of *a:*

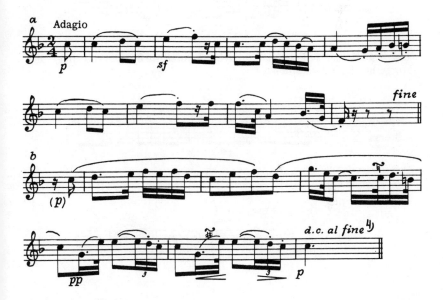

This design is present in all *six Variations.* In addition, the melodic outline, though in altered form, is always retained. To clarify in each *Variation* the deviations from the *Theme,* the melody notes are circled in the examples below.

Variations

The *Six Variations* respectively suggest:

---

⁴ *D.c. al fine or da capo al fine:* Italian—(play) from the beginning to (where it says) the end.

(1) the style of the violin virtuoso (this is also a figural variation):

(2) the sound of hunting horns:

(3) a particular style of piano playing favored in Beethoven's time (another figural variation):

(4) a minuet:

(5) a march:

---

[5] Not too fast.

(6) a style of piano playing used especially in the final sections of large
    Classic works, such as sonatas or concertos:

In *Variations 2-6* the last two periods of the *Theme* are repeated,
establishing the pattern *a-b-a-b-a,* and in *Variation 5* the first period is
also repeated: *a-a-b-a-b-a;* besides, an interlude of a few measures links
this *Variation* to the last. The ensuing *Coda* consists of (a) a short expansion of *Variation 6,* ending in a little cadenza, and (b) a complete
seventh variation in a slow tempo, figural in type, ending in another
cadenza and a few further measures reminiscent of the *Theme* that serve
to confirm the cadence.

In this work each of the first *five Variations* is written in a new key
different from that of the *Theme. Variation 5,* moreover, is also in Minor,
whereas Major prevails elsewhere, and thus also presents a HARMONIC
VARIATION, here restricted to a simple change of mode. (Since it is in a
remote key, the above-mentioned transition to *Variation 6,* which resumes
the original key, is needed.) Such a change in mode in the next to the
last variation is quite usual in Classic variation works, but the change
of key in all the *Variations* is unique. As in suites, the tonic is normally
retained throughout a variation set.

Tone-Color Variations

In variations any element of music may be changed. As long as a
sufficient number of important elements can be identified, the
theme will be recognized in its new guise. We have seen examples
of melodic, rhythmic, harmonic, and contrapuntal variations, i.e.
changes of these elements. In most of them changes of expression
were involved; variations without such changes are, indeed, hard
to imagine. The remaining elements that may be varied are tone
color and phrase structure. The former is involved in most orchestral variations, but is only rarely employed as the sole or the
major factor. Among several entire sets of TONE-COLOR VARIATIONS
the following, composed as a ballet, is the most famous:

EXAMPLE 68:   MAURICE RAVEL [1875–1937]

Bolero (1928)

Permission for reprint granted by Durand et Cie, Paris, France. Copyright owners: Elkan-Vogel Company, Inc., Philadelphia, Pennsylvania, agents.

Theme

Four measures of introduction establish the *obbligato* rhythm of the accompaniment (or rhythmic *ostinato*):

Then, above it, the *Theme* enters. It has two long periods, *a* and *b*, each of sixteen measures followed by two measures asserting only the rhythm:

Variations

The two periods alternate as follows: *a-a-b-b—a-a-b-b—a-a-b-b—a-a-b-b—a-b.* They remain unaltered, except that in each but the last of the eighteen periods the instrumentation of both melody and accompaniment is changed. In the last few measures of the brief coda a sudden shift to another tonality achieves an effective conclusion.

---

[6] Very moderately.

The following instruments are heard playing the melody by turns:

1. flute;—2. clarinet;—3. bassoon;—4. high clarinet;
5. *oboe d'amore* (mezzo-soprano oboe in *A*);
6. muted trumpet and flute, in octaves;—7. tenor saxophone;
8. sopranino saxophone;
9. French horn, celesta, and two piccolos, in triads;
10. oboes and clarinets, in fifths and octaves;—11. trombone;
12. tenor saxophone, flutes, oboes, and clarinets, in triads;
13. violins, flutes, oboes, and clarinets, in octaves;
14. violins, flutes, oboes, clarinets, and tenor saxophones, in triads;
15. violins, flutes, piccolo, English horn, and trumpet, in octaves;
16. violins, violas, 'cellos, soprano saxophone, trombone, flutes, oboes, and clarinets, in triads;
17-18. violins, trumpet, soprano and tenor saxophones, flutes, and later trombone, in triads.

Structural or Free Variations

The last major element that may be changed is form or phrase structure. This is such an essential change that it sets up a new overall classification of FREE VARIATIONS as opposed to all others we have discussed, which under all changes retain the form of the theme and are in this respect called STRICT VARIATIONS. In free variations the only major elements retained from the theme are the melodic motifs and, more rarely, a few characteristic harmonic or rhythmic motifs. These materials are spun out in new ways in each variation, chiefly by development of motifs and theme transformation. The technic of free variation is therefore well suited for character variations and is often used with definite pictorial or narrative connotations. Moreover, while sets of strict variations, with the exception of *passacaglias,* are usually composed discontinuously—that is, with pauses between variations—free variations lend themselves better to continuous composition.

Although Baroque composers knew free variations, they, like the character variations, fell into disuse among the Classics. Thereafter, beginning with Beethoven, free variations appear only sporadically until the last quarter of the nineteenth century. Since then they have again assumed a conspicuous place. One of the early examples, probably the earliest complete set so conceived in the Classic-

Romantic era, is Schumann's *Carnaval* (see p. 150ff). Only few earlier examples can be cited, notably by Beethoven, and these occur mostly within larger works, such as symphonies, providing change of pace in sets of otherwise strict variations. A beautiful set of free variations will be discussed in Part IV (p. 327ff).[7]

Summary

Let us briefly restate the principal ideas of this discussion. Variation is one of the most important means of formulating music. Though involved in almost all music, variation may be the sole principle of organization. In this case the concluding section is usually not a variation proper but a piece organized along new lines—a fugue, a *passacaglia,* a free finale, or a restatement of the theme. A set of variations may well become a portion of a more comprehensive work; [8] then the conclusion becomes less of a problem. The charm of formal variations springs from the freshness and novelty of the guises in which the composer reveals the theme, and this charm is considerably enhanced by an understanding of the elements of music whose manipulation brings about the new guise.

CONCEPTS AND TOPICS DISCUSSED IN THIS SECTION

basso ostinato—p. 210f

character variations—p. 214ff

elements of music—p. 210

figural variations—p. 214

finale of variations—p. 211

obbligato—p. 213

passacaglia (chaconne)—p. 211f

strict and free variations—p. 219f

tone-color variations—p. 217ff

---

[7] See Appendix I, p. 406f, for a tabular explanation of variation types.

[8] See Example 38, p. 83f; Example 49, p. 119f; Example 80, *2nd movement,* p. 270; Example 82, *3rd movement,* p. 274; Example 84, *4th movement,* p. 294f; Example 87, *4th movement,* p. 310f; Example 89, *3rd movement,* p. 325f; Example 94, *4th movement,* p. 351f.

Section C
THE SYMPHONIC FORM

Music and Verbal Meaning

The fact that art music lacks the precise meaning of words has often been regarded as a shortcoming. We are educated to admire verbal clarity—clear ideas and clear expression. The lack of such clarity is felt by realistically minded people to curtail the value of their musical experience. They therefore try to attach verbal or pictorial meanings to the music they hear or compose.[1]

Since these meanings are based on individual associations and vary from person to person, composers who desire to convey definite ideas to the listener often give him a PROGRAM that he may follow, i.e. a written narration or description. In the music they represent non-musical associations in three general ways: (1) through PICTORIAL means—the imitation of various visual and aural impressions, not connected with art music; (2) through SYMBOLIZA-TION of characters and emotions; and (3) through combining pictorialism and symbolization to suggest action or narration.

Music that employs the first of these technics, i.e. pictorialism, to evoke such aural impressions as thunder or the wash of waves, we usually call descriptive (cf. below, Example 69, *D*); when it evokes visual impressions in us, we often speak of tone painting (cf. Example 61, p. 178 for both). The second and third technics, on the other hand, call forth the desired ideas by more remote associations. Certain details of expression (dynamics, tempo, and tone production), combined with certain rhythms and types of melodies are conventionally accepted in any particular period as symbols of character traits or emotions; good examples are the "sigh" motif with which Bach's *Crucifixus* starts (p. 84) or the symbolizations of "exalted" and "plain" in the *Aria* from Handel's

---

[1] Almost all people experience non-musical associations when listening to music. In this respect psychologists speak of extra-subjective listeners, those who have sensory, muscular feelings, such as pressure, stroking, falling, or flying; of associative listeners, to whom music suggests colors, images, scents, tastes, or thoughts; and of intra-subjective listeners, who find revealed in music character traits or moods—heroism, melancholy, playfulness, rage, sadness, mysticism, and so forth. Though such non-musical associations can never be entirely suppressed, the primary values of music do not lie in them. See comment on the functions of art music on p. 39f.

Messiah (p. 93). Changes in such motifs—variations, new contexts —may be used to suggest or be interpreted as symbolizing action.

Compositions in which these various technics are conspicuously displayed are known as programmatic. Music may well gain from such literary or pictorial associations, but the very best program, whether pictorial, expressive, or narrative, avails little unless the music is independently excellent.

Pictorial Music Ancient and Medieval

Program music, though commonly thought of as a nineteenth-century development, existed as early as 586 B.C.E., when, at the Greek national festival known as the Pythian games, Sakadas, a virtuoso on the *aulos* (a double oboe similar to our bagpipe), performed a piece entitled "The Contest Between Apollo and the Dragon." This was what we should call today a suite in five sections: Prelude, First Onset, Contest, Triumph of Apollo, and Death of the Dragon.

Imitative music flourished also during the Middle Ages. When, in the thirteenth century, people in the West first discovered a taste for polyphonic music outside the Church, they created, among other things, musical pieces incorporating street cries of Paris. The sounds of bird song, hunting horns, and baying dogs entered music in the next century, and in the sixteenth the clash of battle as well as the melodic expression of such ideas as "ascent" and "descent," "glory," "tears," "creeping," and "leaping" became staple ingredients of madrigals and motets (cf. Example 35, p. 66f).

Baroque Expression of Emotions

With the rise of opera and oratorio in the Baroque the characterization of emotions, ideas, and scenes acquired special importance for composers. The same composers, when writing for instruments, naturally sought an expressiveness in them approaching that of human voices singing and interpreting a text. Now a new problem arose: How could music, without the help of words, symbolize emotions and characters? Many volumes which greatly influenced Baroque music were written on this subject.

Most program music composed before 1800 was static. Composers would abstract a salient feature of the situation or character to be portrayed, invent a motif or theme that might pictorialize this one feature, and then proceed to build the entire piece around this characteristic idea according to the methods then prevailing. Such character pieces were frequently joined in suites (see Appendix I, p. 403).

Program Music Among Classics and Romantics: Narration

The Viennese Classics at the end of the eighteenth century, with their marked preference for clear distinction and delimitation of elements, abandoned program music and the fusion of music with non-musical ideas almost completely. This combination, however, continued in favor elsewhere and naturally flourished in the Romantic climate that favored the continuity and the amalgamation of elements and culminated in the Wagnerian music drama.

Early in the nineteenth century the vogue for opera and the increased brilliance and flexibility of instruments furnished the inspiration for a new approach. The Romantic composer was not content to portray the general character of moods and emotions, statically, like the Baroque musician; instead he sought to present changes of moods and emotions suggesting narration. To achieve this purpose his first step was to transfer to instrumental music the melodic and rhythmic motifs used in vocal music for interpreting words. As a second step he imitated sounds, such as would arouse pictorial ideas associated with various emotional states—sounds of church bells, of hunting horns, or of galloping horses.

When, in the mid-eighteenth century, Rousseau raised his cry "Back to nature!" the field of possible pictorial imitations was greatly expanded to include the description of weather conditions, pastoral scenes (shepherds' pipes), and noises of nature. More recently, with the growth of industry, the noises of the factory, the airplane, the steam engine, hydro-electric dams, and the city street have become additional colors in the palette of the musical pictorialist. Thus the domain of program music encompasses all human ideas, ideals, emotions, actions, and surroundings. This granted, we may see in program music a sort of sociological record, analogous to the folk ballad at another level of culture.

By applying to a central theme the combination of expressive motifs and pictorialism the Romantic composer took the third and final step toward achieving the illusion of action on the part of a central character or of narration about him. Thus the Romantics went beyond the character piece and the descriptive suite to the portrayal of action.

The Tone Poem

This purpose was served by three new species: the CONCERT OVERTURE (cf. Beethoven's *Egmont Overture*, p. 250ff), the PROGRAM SYMPHONY (cf. Berlioz's *Fantastic Symphony*, p. 353ff), and, as the most successful and most novel, the TONE POEM or, when written for orchestra, SYMPHONIC POEM, created by Liszt out of a combination of the other two. Perhaps the most immediate influence that led Liszt to his formulation of the new type was one of the major piano works of his day: Schumann's *Carnaval* (cf. p. 150ff); for it is the character variation based on theme transformation that gives Liszt's *Symphonic Poems* the required musical continuity, as they follow, verse for verse or scene for scene, a poem or a story.[2] But Liszt sensed that despite all cyclic devices the impact of a program suite, with its rests after all sections, still could not equal that of a single large piece. For the latter makes possible greater developmental intricacies and larger climaxes after longer preparations. Thus, by combining the ideas of a single large work (taken from the overture), of narrative content (from the program symphony), and of theme transformation, Liszt arrived at the concept of the symphonic poem.

Liszt not only created the symphonic poem but also gave the type its fitting name. A literary passage, a scene, or an idea fired his imagination and was transformed into a series of musico-poetic sections, equivalent to lyric reflections of a poet. The result was a series of character pieces, which Liszt unified thematically as well as structurally.

---

[2] Though commonly employed, character variation and theme transformation are not always involved in later tone poems. The very fact that such works obey the dictates of non-musical ideas makes it impossible for all of them to follow the same structure. Hence their forms range all the way from the potpourri and the variation set to the repetitive forms to be discussed in Sections D and E.

Our first example is one of the earliest of Liszt's *thirteen Symphonic Poems:*

EXAMPLE 69: FRANZ LISZT [1811–86]

Les Préludes (1854)

Les Préludes is based on the fifteenth of Alphonse de Lamartine's (1790–1869) *Méditations poétiques* of 1819:

A: What else is our life but a series of preludes to that unknown song whose first solemn note Death intones?

B: Love forms the enchanted dawn of all existence;

C: but where is the destiny in which the first delights of happiness have not been interrupted by some storm whose fatal gust destroyed its fair illusions, whose fatal lightning consumed its altar?

D: And where is the cruelly wounded soul which, emerging from one of these tempests, does not seek to rest its memories in the sweet calm of the countryside?

E: Nevertheless, man hardly resigns himself for long to the taste of the beneficent quiet which first charmed him at the bosom of nature; and when "the trumpet sounds the alarm" he rushes to his perilous post, whatever the battle that calls him to the colors, in order to retrieve in combat the full consciousness of self and the full possession of his powers.

This quotation Liszt divides into five thoughts, as shown above, each expressed in a separate section of music, to which in conclusion a reminiscence of the "solemn note (of) Death" is added.

Section *A* introduces the main theme, at first as a groping "prelude":

then as a "solemn note (of) Death," brilliantly set forth:

and finally in a soft, lyric version—the "unknown song":

The first three tones of this theme, marked by brackets in all examples, are its nucleus, which reappears in the second theme, "love," introduced in section *B*:

This theme is fully presented twice and then subsides in partial repetitions (cf. Tchaikovsky's *Swan Lake,* p. 176f).

Section *B* halts on a suggestion, in flutes and clarinets, of the first theme, which ominously opens *C*. This section develops into a raging storm—a famous instance of descriptive music; at its height a fanfare, a new variant of the first theme, gives dramatic expression to the "lightning (that) consumed (the) altar":

As the storm subsides, a horn initiates the pastoral section *D*, which is subtly related to *a* in a secondary figure:

The second half of this scene is given to the "memories" of love: a broad expansion of *b* combined with the motifs of the pastorale.

The tempo quickens; a new version of *a* announces itself, as though emerging from the love theme, when "the trumpet sounds the alarm," leading into section *E*, a bellicose march. This starts with an easily recognized transformation of the main theme:

The second theme soon follows, now in march meter as well:

This section thus acts as a recapitulation of sections *A* and *B,* giving the work of a well rounded organization: $\frac{I \quad II \quad I}{A\text{-}B\text{-}C\text{-}D\text{-}E}$. With a reminiscence of the second portion of *A* Liszt gives the work an effective and powerful conclusion.

How does Liszt characterize each of the thoughts of Lamartine's *"Méditation"*? Chiefly through ingenious handling of rhythm, meter, tempo, volume, and manner of tone production. The sinister mood of the beginning, for example, is the result of slow tempo, rather even note values, lack of metric accents, low volume, and *legato* playing. The feeling of the solemnity of death is evoked by the same slow tempo and even note values, combined with steady meter, loudness, and *staccato* playing; the one short tone near the beginning contributes much toward a feeling of strength. The love motif is lyrical, being both *legato* and soft; moreover, its uneven rhythm of long and short tones suggests emotional fluctuation.

The storm, of course, is described by rushing chromatic passages, imitating wind, and by loudness. Regularly stressed beats, duple meter, firm, loud *staccato* playing, and the sound of the brasses contribute to the effect of the march. On the other hand, the mood of the pastorale is created by slow tempo, the cradlesong meter of 6/8, and prevailing softness (cf. Corelli's *Pastorale,* p. 29).

Narrative and Contemplative Tone Poems

Toward the end of the century there emerged two essentially different kinds of symphonic poems—narrative and contemplative, the one suggesting action and motion, the other meditation and mood. The narrative tone poem is dynamic. The listener is not merely an onlooker standing still in contemplation of a scene or story. As if participating in the action, he follows it through characteristic changes of tempo, violent fluctuations of volume, marked rhythmic and melodic activity. Narrative tone poems, by trying to establish in our mind associations between the music and actions, create intellectual responses primarily and emotional responses only secondarily. Liszt's *Tone Poems* lean toward this type, but its master was Richard Strauss, one of whose *Symphonic Poems* will be discussed in the next section (p. 240ff).

The contemplative type is but an expanded character piece, like the example from Tchaikovsky's *Swan Lake* (p. 176f). Whether symphonic or for piano only, it reflects the detached attitude of the mere onlooker, who dispassionately takes in the impression made by a scene. This type is therefore generally subdued in volume and moderate in tempo and avoids marked rhythm and other devices that normally symbolize strength and active participation. In other words, it is impressionistic in tendency if not always in technic; it elicits primarily emotional reactions rather than intellectual-associative ones.

Debussy as Tone Poet

The master of the contemplative tone poem was Debussy. Unlike Musorgsky, who turned actual pictures into small music dramas (see Example 57, p. 155f), Debussy in the following example began with a narrative poem, which he converted into a tone picture. He had the best intentions of composing a narrative symphonic suite on the imaginative text of Stephane Mallarmé (1842–98), "*L'après-midi d'un faune,*" but when he came to the end of the prelude to the projected suite, he found that the mood of the scene had been so perfectly expressed that further elaboration would be anticlimactic or even redundant. Thus the *Prelude to The Afternoon of a Faun* has remained an independent symphonic piece.

EXAMPLE 70:   CLAUDE DEBUSSY [1862–1918]

Prélude à L'après-midi d'un faune (1894)

Permission for reprint granted by Durand et Cie, Paris, France. Copyright owners: Elkan-Vogel Company, Inc., Philadelphia, Pennsylvania.

This is a summary of Mallarmé's poem:

> A faun, a simple, sensuous, passionate being, wakens in the forest and tries to recall the events of the previous afternoon. He cannot remember; his impressions become hazy, and as the sun grows warm he curls up and goes back to sleep.

With this composition Debussy became the virtual founder of musical impressionism (cf. pp. 178f, 182f) and a recognized leader in music. The melodic line, however, is still well sustained here, in a Romantic rather than impressionistic manner. As in other pieces of this type—pieces that follow no prescribed action—the formulation is conventional: *A-B-A.* The flute, prominent in *A,* is commonly associated with fauns, pastoral spirits of ancient Greece.

The languid, chromatic main theme, exploiting the low register of the flute, is intoned four times:

These four periods, grouped two and two, form section *A.* Section *B* introduces a number of small motifs, some of them derived from *A.* They emerge and vanish, are taken up again and abandoned, like the drowsy thoughts of the faun. Finally a very lyric strain appears, first in the woodwinds, then in the strings, marking the climax:

When it is heard a third time, echoing in the violins, it leads back to the modified restatement of *A* with its four periods.

Summary

In this chapter on additive forms we have examined the three general types of such an organization and their essential characteristics, namely (1) the potpourri and fantasy, a series of different sections: A-B-C-D- . . . ; (2) the variation form, similar to the potpourri but tied together by the theme: A-A^1-A^2-A^3- . . . ; and (3) the symphonic poem, which has no specific form since it must follow the program, being similar in this respect to compositions with a text, such as madrigals, motets, or through-composed songs. We now turn to repetitive forms.

CONCEPTS AND TOPICS DISCUSSED IN THIS SECTION

VII REPETITIVE FORMS

SONG AND RONDO FORMS

Repetitive Forms and Their Aesthetic Functions

Three essentially different types of repetitive form have evolved. Of these, the simple repetition of one section with or without variation, i.e. stanzaic and variation forms, has already been discussed, for it stands midway between additive and repetitive forms (see Examples 11-12, p. 14ff; Example 58, p. 157ff; and Section B, p. 210ff). The most complicated type, based on interaction among several sections, we shall examine in Section E. Here we shall discuss repetitive forms resulting from the ordered sequence of two or more contrasting sections.

We have already stated that purely additive form in which ideas follow each other without any repetition is unsatisfactory in art; for without repetition of some sort organization does not exist, and art implies organization. Therefore, in additive forms, motifs or phrases are repeated or varied immediately. In repetitive forms, on the other hand, the stress is on the repetition of large sections.

[231]

In their craving for balance and symmetry the Classic composers relied heavily on the use of repetitive forms. Sectional repetitions helped them to solve two important problems in the composition of large works: (1) the creation of unity in a work by means of symmetry, and (2) the creation of points of repose for the listener— repeated material is easy to grasp. Standardized repetitive patterns, moreover, enable the listener to anticipate the general course of the music. Such regularity is particularly important to classicists, but it is important in all art. In fact, in their large works most Romantics followed the standards set by the Classics; and since our musical life is dominated by works of the Classic-Romantic era, repetitive forms occupy the foreground of our attention.

We have already had occasion to study many works of repetitive formulation. Having had the aural experiences, we shall study in this section the terms usually employed in speaking of the various forms and thereby we shall bring into focus many remarks previously made regarding individual examples. The large number of references to material previously covered may aid the reader in gathering his varied aural experiences into a systematic framework of reference. A rehearing of examples studied earlier and referred to in this section will be very helpful in illustrating the forms discussed. The listener should note how repetition, alternation, and contrast contribute to the unity of works in repetitive forms.

Two-Part [1] and Three-Part Song Forms

Before discussing repetitive forms in large pieces we shall briefly consider their simpler manifestations in small pieces. The fundamental issue in the creation of repetitive patterns in both types is the disposition of two separate and different sections, whether large or small. In songs and other small pieces these sections comprise but one or a few phrases, and the forms that result from their various dispositions are appropriately called SONG FORMS. Juxtaposition and alternation of the two sections yield two basic types, namely the TWO-PART FORM: *a-b* and the THREE-PART FORM: *a-b-a*, as shown in the following examples:

---

[1] The hyphenated word "-part" here signifies "section," not a voice part. This usage is common in discussions of musical form. Otherwise the words "portion" or "section" and "part" will be used as before.

Johannes Brahms (1833–97): *Wiegenlied* (Lullaby)

O Logie o'Buchan (Scottish Folksong)

Usually the *b*-section differs at least in part from *a* with respect to harmonization, and the difference may also affect melody, rhythm, expression, texture, and instrumentation. On the other hand, *b* may be derived from, or involve portions of, the material of *a*. The two forms, moreover, rarely occur with the regularity shown in the above songs. One or the other section is likely to be lengthened or shortened, for example, and the second *a* of the three-part form may be somewhat changed.

Examples of Two-Part and Binary Forms

Though *b* is usually related to *a*, a two-part form is, of course, additive rather than repetitive. A two-part song form is therefore rarely stated but once; it may function as a song stanza that is repeated as a whole (cf. Schubert's *Ständchen*, p. 41 and Brahms's *Lullaby* immediately above), or one or both sections may be immediately repeated to produce such patterns as *a-a-b* (cf. the chorales on pp. 36 and 91 and the melody of *Dido's Lament* by Purcell, p. 119f), *a-b-b* (cf. the second portion of Rossini's *Aria*, p. 52ff), and *a-a-b-b* (cf. Lully's *Aria*, p. 118). Some of the examples cited show that the basic two-part form—and this is equally true of the three-part form—may be further enlarged by introducing a *c*-section (or a *d, e*, and so forth).

When used in pieces of larger scope, two-part patterns are called BINARY FORMS. They occur, e.g. in the dances of Bach's *Suites* (cf. p. 108ff), where the two sections are usually related, but also in such composite works based on the principle of contrast of texture or tempo as a prelude and fugue (cf. p. 103ff) or Rossini's *Aria* (p. 52ff; cf. also Example 73, p. 238f).

Examples of Three-Part and Ternary Forms

In three-part forms repetition after contrast is basic. Besides simple *a-b-a* forms (cf. Musorgsky's *Bydlo*, p. 155f) there exist many formulations that combine the idea of immediate repetition with that of alternation, for example *a-a-b-a* (cf. Schumann's *Träumerei*, p. 45) and ‖: *a* :‖-*b-a* :‖, the form of many dances and marches.

The same structures, when occurring in large pieces, are called TERNARY FORMS, and they, too, frequently involve immediate repetitions. Some of these have already been observed in our discussions: A-B-A was the structure of *Nos. 3* and *4* of Mahler's *The Song of the Earth* (p. 169ff), of Corelli's *Pastorale* (p. 29), and of Debussy's *Afternoon of a Faun* (p. 229f). A-A-B-A was found in *No. 6* of *A Woman's Love and Life* (p. 162f) and in *Nos. 1* and *2* of *The Song of the Earth* (p. 166ff). A standardized formulation resembling A-A-B-B-A is that of marches, dances, and scherzos with trios, in which the main portion, in two repeated sections, is followed by the trio, likewise in two repeated sections, and is then heard again without sectional repetitions. This is sometimes called ALTERNATIVO FORM (cf. Example 6, p. 9f, and the Gavottes from Examples 45 and 46, pp. 109, 113).

The French Rondo

With the discussion of the ternary forms we have approached the RONDO FORMS; for the principle of the rondo is alternation of different sections. In fact, ternary form is sometimes called the simplest category of rondos. But it is more typical for the rondo that one section be heard at least three times, for it is related to such social songs as "John Brown's Body," in which a constant refrain or burden, sung by the entire assembly, is repeated after each of the differing solo stanzas, sung by one person after another in the round. In art music the resulting pattern: *a-b-a-c-a-d-a-e-* . . . *-a* is called PRIMITIVE RONDO. In it each section, though variable in length, is only one period. The *a* section is appropriately called the RITORNELLO (returning section), and the others are known as COUPLETS (originally used for couple dances as opposed to group dances during the *ritornelli*). Of course, whereas in songs the text of the couplets changes but not usually the tune, in instrumental pieces it must be the music that changes.

The primitive rondo is found in many compositions of the court harpsichordists of the French Baroque and Rococo: Hence it is also called FRENCH RONDO. Such French compositions were then called not only *"rondeau"* but also *"passecaille"* and *"chaconne."* The last two appellations (here not carrying the meaning they had in Section B, p. 211) were at the time employed for ballet *entrées* with solo and group dances (the couplets and *ritornelli* respectively) as well as for instrumental pieces of a similar formulation. Such are the following two pieces by the greatest of these French keyboard masters or clavecinistes, as they were called after the French name for harpsichord, *clavecin*.

EXAMPLE 71:   FRANÇOIS COUPERIN [1668–1733]

Passecaille or *Chaconne-Rondeau, La favorite*

In both pieces we note the many ornaments characteristic of the Rococo. The *Passecaille* has eight couplets, the *Chaconne* only five, but they are longer than those of the former. In each piece the *ritornello* consists of two identical four-measure phrases:

Passecaille

Chaconne

Large Rondos

Large rondos came into extensive use during the Classic era. They differ from small or primitive rondos by virtue of the fact that in them each section contains several periods and is comparable in length and organization to a small piece. This considerable length of the sections, now called *ritornelli* and EPISODES (rather than couplets), sets a practical limit to their number. Otherwise the essential feature remains the initial statement of a *ritornello* and its return after each of at least two episodes. These episodes may be similar, i.e. derived from the same material, or they may be different. If different, one of the episodes may well be heard twice. Thus there are several possible patterns, such as *A-B-A-B-A, A-B-A-C-A, A-B-A-C-A-B-A*. At times even three different episodes are introduced, but then, obviously, the composition becomes very long.

We have already had occasion to observe some of these rondo patterns. *Nos. 4* and *5* of *A Woman's Love and Life* (p. 161f) both have the stanzaic arrangement *A-B-A-B-A*, which is modified to *A-A-B-A-B-B-A* in *No. 2* of this *Cycle* (p. 158f) to accommodate seven stanzas. Rather free *a-b-a-c-a* arrangements on a small scale organize Debussy's *Minstrels* (p. 46f), Gershwin's *Prelude No. 3* (p. 21f), and the *Aria* from Gluck's *Orfeo* (p. 130ff). Such pieces as these last three may be called short French rondos or RONDO-SONG FORMS to differentiate them from the large-scale rondos, such as the *Finale* from Stravinsky's *The Rite of Spring* (p. 180ff) which follows the same plan.

Value and Limitations of the Study of Forms

The reader may wish to return to these pieces to inspect their rondo patterns. But, however interesting the study of patterns, other sources of pleasure in music must not be forgotten. Thus, although the *ritornelli* may be literal replicas of each other, they are more often related to each other as variations or as developmental expansions. Their lengths may differ vastly, from a mere reminiscence to a long development. Where *ritornelli* are rather similar, one of the episodes may be melodically derived from them as a new formulation of the material. One should also observe the degree of contrast in rhythm, tempo, texture, tone production, and orchestration between the *ritornelli* and the episodes and among the episodes themselves.

These details are far more significant than the formal pattern, yet without understanding the intended design, the listener will never enjoy these details; they will tend to confuse him rather than to satisfy him aesthetically. The importance of knowing and recognizing musical forms is similar to that of being able to follow the plot of a story. To understand musical forms is to understand what order the composer desired to establish and by what means he achieved his purpose.

In addition to the examples of rondo form mentioned above, there will be further opportunities to observe rondo forms in subsequent sections. Nevertheless several independent rondos are briefly analyzed here.

EXAMPLE 72:   MAURICE RAVEL [1875–1937]

Pavane for a Dead Princess (1899)

Rondo form, A-B-A-C-A, is here combined with variations: The second and the third *ritornelli* are tone-color variations of the first. In addition, of the two periods in each episode the second elaborates the first.

EXAMPLE 73:   CAMILLE SAINT-SAËNS [1835–1921]

Introduction and Rondo Capriccioso (1870)

Saint-Saëns wrote this very effective and elaborate concert number for the celebrated Spanish violin virtuoso, Pablo de Sarasate (1844–1904). The slow *Introduction* is cast in two-part song form, *a-a-b-b:*

---
2 Slow and melancholy.

A brief transition or BRIDGE then leads to the *Rondo,* of the form
A-B-A-C-A-B-A-coda. Two fine melodic bridges are employed between
various sections of this *Rondo,* and the coda likewise presents new material. Thus the composition is very rich in melodies. Its detailed scheme is
as follows (br = bridge):

Introd. —   A   —   B   — A — br[1] —   C   — br[2] —
a-a-b-b — c-c-c[1] — d-d-d[1] — c-c — e-e — f-f-f[1] —   g —

A — br[1] —   B   — br[2] —   A   — coda
c-c — e-h — d-d —   g   — c-c —   i

Till Eulenspiegels lustige Streiche
(Till Eulenspiegel's Merry Pranks, 1895)

The story on which this *Symphonic Poem* is based goes back to a book of tales about a mischievous fourteenth-century character. Strauss selected five of the tales and depicted them by sparkling music in rondo form: A-B-A-C-A-coda.[4]

A: After a few introductory measures—"Once upon a time":

—we hear two long themes, "Till the Man," *b*, and "Till the Prankster," *a¹*:

In a variation of *a¹*, Till crashes through the earthenware displayed by the market women—the crash of the shattering pottery is realistically illustrated—and then, as the music subsides, he takes cover.

B: A folkish tune indicates Till's adventure as a mock-priest:

---

[4] All descriptive details offered in this analysis are based on the composer's own notations.

But at the end of the mockery Till shudders at a premonition of death:

A: Till plays the cavalier, falls in love, is rejected, and furiously swears vengeance on all mankind. The two themes, *b* and *a*¹, are combined in this section, varied, and developed. The progress of the action is realistically represented as the music moves from lyricism to urgency and then to a climactic outbreak featuring a variant of *a:*

C: A very dry passage portrays Till in disputation with the "Philistine" professors:

He mocks them with foolish questions and finally with a big grimace—the beginning of *a*¹ in *fortissimo.* Another folkish tune emerges as he walks away whistling:

The beginning, *e*, and this tune, *f*, are new in this section, but otherwise the Till themes are much in evidence.

After a brief passage of recollection, built around an ingratiating combination of *b* and *a*:

A returns. Once more the two themes are heard successively; the second is shortened to permit greater length for their combined expansion. This expansion begins with a chorale-like version of *b* in the brass:

implying Till's decision to throw care to the wind and to challenge everybody.

There is a great climax, whereafter the coda depicts the trial and hanging of Till. His shudders, *d*, return; loud chords and drum rolls indicate the judges' threefold indictment, interrupted by Till's motif, *a¹*, which gradually changes from nonchalance to an anguished shriek (on the high clarinet). Shuddering, Till scales the scaffold and is hanged (two *fortissimo unisonos* [5]), and dies, *a¹*. A beautiful, quiet *Epilogue, a,* describes Till's burial, which leads to his last prank: He will not lie down in his grave; the coffin slides in and settles upright. Strauss called these last measures "the apotheosis of immortal humor."

Summary

Rondos and ternary forms occur frequently. They provide very satisfying patterns and are relatively easy to comprehend at first hearing. Moreover, the principle of return, as exemplified by the rondo, may well be superimposed on such freely improvisational pieces as toccatas, fantasies, potpourris, and symphonic poems. In such cases it is enough to indicate the idea of return by appropriate changes in tempo, instrumentation, or tonality (cf. Mozart's *C-Minor Fantasy,* p. 207ff, or Bach's *D-Minor Toccata,* p. 57f). Such patterned changes will give coherence to a composition.

---

[5] All instruments playing the same tone (or octaves thereof).

Through their thematic material, tempo, orchestration, and expression, rondos can reflect many emotions and ideas. But in general, whether they are programmatic or not, they tend to be narrative in character rather than dramatic, leisurely and digressive rather than tragic and concentrated. Conflicts are not their normal content: The various sections alternate rather than interact.

The ideas of conflict and drama in instrumental music came to the fore in the Rococo era. The composers then felt a need for a new form that would permit the expression of these ideas. The mere juxtaposition of contrasting sections did not satisfy them; neither did themes completely evolved from one main motif. If drama was to be symbolized, a theme had to be equivalent to a person. Like the complex character of an individual, the theme would have to contain several contrasting motifs; it would, furthermore, have to come to grips with another, comparable "personality" to set up conflict, which is the basis of drama.

These were the thought processes that led to the establishment of the foremost new form of the Classic era: the SONATA-FORM with its complex themes and their dramatic development. We now turn to a study of this form.

CONCEPTS AND TOPICS DISCUSSED IN THIS SECTION

Section E

SONATA-FORM AND OVERTURE

Sonata and Sonata-Form

Before we begin our discussion of sonata-form we must first clarify two similar terms which have become so entrenched in the musician's vocabulary that neither can be easily replaced: sonata and sonata-form.

The term "sonata" (Italian—sounded, referring to the sounding of instruments, as opposed to "cantata"—sung) can be traced to the sixteenth century, when it signified merely an "instrumental composition." Several types of composition so named have flourished since—types that differ widely in form, texture, style, and instrumentation. Some of them are large single pieces (see Example 75 below), others are series of small pieces, i.e. composite works (cf. footnote 1, p. 107), still others contain several large pieces or MOVEMENTS. These last we shall discuss in Part IV.

This section deals not with any of these types of sonatas but with the sonata-form—a rather standardized, repetitive structure that evolved during the eighteenth century. While sonata-form is frequently employed in movements of sonatas, it also serves as the pattern of many compositions that are not so titled, e.g. arias, scherzos, overtures, symphonic poems, and movements of string quartets, concertos, and symphonies. Fast as well as slow pieces may be in sonata-form, and in works with several movements, even when called sonatas, any one, several, or none of the movements may follow this plan. In order to emphasize the distinction between sonata and sonata-form, we shall always hyphenate the latter term.

Early Sonata-Form

From simple beginnings—the binary dances in the Baroque suite and the ternary form—the sonata-form developed into the most complex structure music has yet employed. Its beginnings go back to the second quarter of the eighteenth century, when the idea of ternary form, forcefully represented by the *da-capo* aria of the Neapolitan opera, was tentatively combined with that of the binary dance piece developed from a single motif. This was done by

Domenico Scarlatti,[1] son of the master of Neapolitan opera, Alessandro Scarlatti, and a contemporary of Bach and Handel. His fame rests on some five hundred harpsichord pieces, mostly called *Exercises* or *Sonatas,* which are today usually played on the piano. Our first example is one of them.

EXAMPLE 75: DOMENICO SCARLATTI [1685–1757]

Sonata in D Minor, Allegro, K.[2] 9

As in dances of suites, there are two repeated sections here. Despite this apparent binary arrangement the fomal design has really three divisions, as follows:

1. The first section establishes the main motif in the key of *D* Minor:

In the latter half of this section, marked by a trill motif:

a new key is reached: *F* Major, the RELATIVE MAJOR, i.e. the major key that shares all tones, including sharps and flats, with the basic Minor.[3] (For another instance of relative Majors and Minors serving form see Example 77, p. 250ff).

---

[1] See Plate X, p. 265.

[2] Lacking *opus* numbers, the harpsichord pieces of Domenico Scarlatti are usually cited by the number they bear in the nearly complete edition of Alessandro Longo (1864–1946), this one being L. 413. Recently the approximately chronological numbering of Kirkpatrick (see Appendix II, p. 436) has been adopted instead: K.1-555.

[3] The relative Major has its tonic always on the third step of the relative Minor, and conversely the relative Minor has its tonic on the sixth step of the relative Major. Both keys employ the same notes, i.e. have the same KEY SIGNATURE (see Appendix I, p. 383), and it is to this feature that the term "relative" refers:

2. The second section begins with (*a*) in the new key, proceeds to expand it, and then leads back to the key of the beginning, *D* Minor.

3. The last three quarters of the first section are thereupon recapitulated in this (tonic) key.

The music of this *Sonata* is simple, expressive, at times brilliant. In its rare use of polyphony and its reliance on a single line of melody its style is typically Rococo.

Classic Sonata-Form

From these beginnings the next two generations evolved the Classic sonata-form. It was essentially ternary in design, though it preserved the apparent binary division into two large sections. Of these only the first, the STATEMENT or EXPOSITION, was usually repeated. In it the main materials were introduced, consisting of themes in complete periods, including motifs pointedly contrasted rather than merely strung together as in Domenico Scarlatti's *Sonatas*. As in these, however, this first section typically expressed the main tonality and then proceeded to a second one. The brief expansion at the beginning of the second section, noted in Example 73 immediately above, became an arena of dramatic interaction of the themes from which often issued new melodic units. This portion of the sonata-form was called the DEVELOPMENT SECTION; it would usually start in the second tonality, but also stress other keys. The third section, the RECAPITULATION or RESTATEMENT, would then repeat the materials of the statement in the main tonality, often with substantial changes and sometimes in a different order, and might be followed by an extensive coda.

Among single large pieces this mature sonata-form found its clearest embodiment in the operatic overtures of Gluck, Mozart, and their contemporaries. Perhaps the masterpiece among all these overtures is this:

EXAMPLE 76:   WOLFGANG AMADEUS MOZART [1756–91]

Overture to Don Giovanni (1787)

The *Overture* opens with a slow *Introduction*, the brooding music of which is heard again toward the end of the opera, at the climax of the action. The several motifs of this *Introduction* follow each other as in a fantasy.

Exposition

The fast main portion of the *Overture* is in sonata-form. The main tonality of *D* Major is forcefully presented through a theme that includes several contrasting motifs. This first theme is stated in one period, which is repeated with small variants, and concluded with a rushing cadence:

After a brief rest a second group of motifs appears:

which, after a quieter melody in the woodwinds:

refers back to the first theme (cf. the brackets):

This group leads from the key of the first theme, *D* Major, to the second key, *A* Major, here that of the dominant (i.e. the key whose tonic is a fifth above that of the main key). It does not include complete periods with full cadences like a theme; rather it is marked by motif repetition. Therefore this group is called a bridge. (Though often presenting new material as here, a bridge may also be derived from a theme.)

The new (dominant) key is expressed in its own right by a second theme, in part derived from motifs of the first theme (cf. bracket):

---

4 Very fast.

Some sophisticated imitations enliven this theme.

The exposition concludes with a cadence. Sometimes this is called the third theme, although no new tonality is introduced. It may also be called CODETTA, a term used to denote material that rounds off a section in a large piece or in a movement (whereas a coda ends the entire piece). This cadence also refers to the first theme (cf. bracket):

Development Section and Restatement

By leading still further from the basic tonality the ensuing development section creates tension that only much later relaxes with the return to the main key. Melodically the development works out Theme 2 in new combinations, goes to Theme 1, and returns to Theme 2. An extended cadence reaches a climax from which the violins glide scalewise down to the opening of the recapitulation in the basic tonality. The restatement is nearly literal here, except that now all material is presented in *D* Major. A brief coda recalls Themes 2 and 3.[5]

A diagram will disclose the overall form:

Introduction	—			Exposition		—
		Th. 1	br.	Th. 2	Th. 3	
		A-A^1	B-A^2	$C(A^3)$-C^1	$D(A^4)$-D-A^5	
keys: [6]	*d*	*D*	....	*A*		
	Development Section		— br.	—	Recapitulation	— Coda
	C-$C^2(A^6)$-A-A^7-C		$C^3(A^8)$		(like exposition)	C-A^5
keys:	*A* .... *G g*		*A*		*D*	*D*

---

[5] When the *Opera* follows the *Overture* without pause, the ending differs slightly from that employed in concert performances.

[6] From here on we shall, in diagrams and elsewhere, indicate major keys by capital letters and minor keys by lower-case letters.

Sonata-Form and Tonality; Modulation

In this diagram the top line indicates the general scheme of compositions in sonata-form; however, introductions are not always present, and the sequence of ideas in the restatement may differ from that followed in the exposition. Most Classic works in sonata-form employ the same key scheme as our example: key of tonic (exposition, Th. 1), key of dominant (Th. 2, 3), key of dominant and other keys (development section), key of tonic (recapitulation and coda). When the basic tonality is a Minor, the key of the dominant in this scheme is usually replaced by the key of the relative Major (cf. Examples 75, 77, pp. 245f, 250ff). Frequently, where there is an introduction to a work in Major, it is as here in the tonic Minor (see also Example 77, main body and coda; on tonic Major and Minor see p. 110).

The development or fantasia section of the *Don-Giovanni Overture* is typical: A limited number of motifs is chosen for each subsection, and, starting from the dominant key, each new key introduced moves further away from it—i.e. has fewer and fewer tones in common with it, resulting in an increase of accidentals in the score. These progressions from key to key, indicated by dots in the preceding diagram, are called MODULATIONS. They continue until, at the end of the development section, the key of the dominant is regained, culminating the harmonic tension built up through these modulations.

In Romantic music modulation became a central concern. The use of distant keys grew steadily. So strong was the attraction exerted by the clash between distant keys reached through rapid modulations, that the basic tonality was gradually obscured. This process reached its peak in Wagner's *Tristan and Isolde* (see Examples 53, 78, pp. 140f, 254ff). Thence the road leads to contemporary music with its partial or total abandonment of the tonal concepts of the Classics. These concepts were basic to the Classic sonata-form, though not to that of contemporary composers.

Continuing our discussion of the sonata-form, we turn to a masterwork by Beethoven, an *Overture* composed not for an opera but for a play by Goethe.

EXAMPLE 77:   LUDWIG VAN BEETHOVEN [1770–1827]

Overture to Egmont (1809)

The detailed diagram of the *Egmont Overture* is as follows (a "+" means contrapuntal combination; dashes separate periods or sections of about 8-12 measures):

Introduction:

ab-ab-c+a
key: f Sostenuto ma non troppo [7]

Exposition:
Th. 1:

c¹-a¹-a¹-c¹-a¹-d
key: f

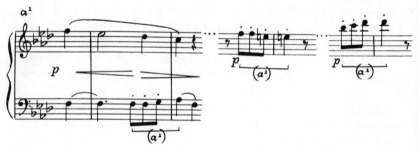

---

[7] Not too sustained.

Th. 2:
ab^1-ae
key: $A\flat$

Th. 3:

fg
key: $A\flat$

Development Section—   Recapitulation   —   Coda 1
c^2-c^2-c^2-c^2c^1-c Th. 1   Th. 2   Th. 3 ag^1-ag^1-a-cadence
keys: $A\flat$ $b\flat$ c f $D\flat$ $D\flat$ $b\flat$ f

Coda 2:

a^2-h-i+a^3-j-k
key: F

Besides introducing both main ideas, the *Introduction* also serves as the vehicle of dramatic exposition. Motif (*a*) indicates Egmont (1522–68), the hero of the play, and (*b*) Klärchen, his beloved, while (*c*) stands for fight for freedom. The main division, in sonata-form, portrays the hero and his fight for the freedom of his people, the Dutch, from Spanish rule. The long, jubilant second coda is taken from the incidental music to the play, a portion called "Victory Symphony," which accom-

---

[8] Fast and spirited.

panies the vision of glory and liberation that comes to Egmont while
he awaits death in his prison cell. It contains several new motifs, and
the change of mode and tempo also marks it as a separate third section.

With this and several similar works Beethoven initiated a practice of
composing independent CONCERT OVERTURES, i.e. large single symphonic
pieces in sonata-form with rather definite programmatic content or associations. A generation afterwards Liszt's *Symphonic Poems* grew in part
out of this idea (cf. *Les Préludes*, p. 225ff). Sonata-form was therefore
one of Liszt's chief approaches toward overall patterning in such works.

Some of his technical approaches are also anticipated in this *Overture*, especially that of theme transformation. Thus, the last motif of the
Introduction, (c), is transformed into a running, rushing figuration before
emerging in a new shape as the rebellious, heroic first theme of the
sonata-form, c^1. Again we may follow (a), as it is transformed into
the second motif of Th. 1, (a^1), where it serves in several variants; afterwards it becomes the second theme, ab^1; transformed into the opening
of the "Victory Symphony," a^2, it once more appears, reshaped, as
the counterpoint in its third section, $i + a^3$.

French and Italian Overtures

The operatic overture has had a career almost as checkered as
that of opera. We have previously met two types of overture—the
French overture of Lully, Handel, and Bach (cf. p. 111) and the
potpourri overture of the nineteenth century (cf. Example 64, p.
206). The French overture left its imprint on the two works we
have just studied, insofar as both have slow introductions. On the
other hand, the inclusion in both of passages from later portions
of the dramatic music points forward to the potpourri overture.

The name "overture" is French, meaning "opening." It was first
associated with Lully's type of operatic introduction, until the
sonata-form overture replaced it in the time of the Classics. After
1700 some *opere serie* and all *opere buffe,* however, opened with
a type of overture called SINFONIA, a creation of Alessandro Scarlatti's and therefore also known as ITALIAN OVERTURE (cf. also p.
84). Here fast sections, set brilliantly for the strings, surrounded
a brief slow interlude, forming a ternary arrangement related to the
contemporary *da-capo* aria (but without melodic reference between the fast sections). The *sinfonia* gave not only a name to its
descendant, the symphony, but also affected its structure: Fast-
slow-fast is still the usual sequence of tempos in the movements
of a symphony.

Classic and Romantic Overtures

In the last quarter of the eighteenth century the Italian overture, like the French, yielded place to the sonata-form overture (see Examples 76, 77 above). The sonata-form is dramatic in itself; in fact, the setting-up of dramatic conflict—through the tension among tonalities, the contrast of themes, and the interaction of motifs— and the resolution thereof is its fundamental idea. As we have seen, this dramatic idea may be further emphasized by the use of material from the opera itself in the overture, thus relating the two to one another.

This procedure led to the creation of the typical overture of Romantic operas, in which the entire material is lifted from the body of the opera and arranged in sonata-form, as for example in Weber's *Overtures*. Thence it was a small step to the creation of the outright potpourri overture of the French grand opera and operetta. In addition, as in the eighteenth century the *sinfonia* had severed its connection with the opera to become an independent concert piece, so the sonata-form overture severed its connection with the opera, and with Beethoven became the independent concert overture. In either case the independent overture led to a new species: in the eighteenth century to the symphony and in the nineteenth to the symphonic poem.

Operatic Preludes

The trend toward integrating the overture with the opera gave rise, after the mid-nineteenth century, to a new type, which Wagner called PRELUDE. The prelude is conceived as a preparation for the action that immediately follows. It may therefore precede any act of an opera and usually employs the motifs or themes of the following scene or scenes. It therefore does not come to a full close, but continues into the action (cf. the *Carmen Overture*, p. 206; but some Classic overtures also lead directly into the action, for example the *Don-Giovanni Overture*, Example 76, above). Preludes may be as short as a few measures, thus practically eliminating the overture; but even when long, they tend toward simple formulation (cf. Debussy's *Prelude to The Afternoon of a Faun*, p. 229f).

Perhaps the most famous of all operatic preludes is the following, by the creator of this type:

EXAMPLE 78:   RICHARD WAGNER [1813–83]

Prelude to Tristan and Isolde (1859)[9]

Wagner here weaves a number of short motifs—all of them leading motifs in the opera (cf. p. 139)—into the dark tapestry, a picture of unrequited longing. They all seem to develop from the same source—emotionally from yearning, technically from chromaticism; and they are often closely related in melodic contour.

The *Prelude* has a simple structure of four stanza-like sections (S), each containing several sub-units.[10]

S.1 starts with the "main theme," a group of three interwoven motifs. Barely audible, as though emerging from vast depths of yearning solitude, the 'cello introduces motif (*a*) with its large upward skip and chromatic descent. Motif (*a*) is continued by the ascending chromatic motif (*b*) in the oboe, which is embedded in the harmonic motif (*b¹*)— an ingenious sequence of two chords that appears whenever (*b*) is heard but also elsewhere:

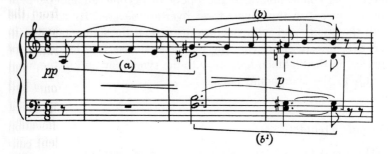

There is a rest before each of the two complete and several partial repetitions of this triple motif, which rise in pitch and intensity toward a climax. This constitutes the first two units of S.1. A new, more active motif:

---

[9] With Wagner's own consent this *Prelude* was coupled for concert performance with the end of the opera that it foreshadows: *Isolde's Love Death* (cf. p. 140f).

[10] The term "unit" is here used instead of "period," because Wagner avoids cadences, which are of primary importance in the establishment of periods and phrases.

starts the third unit, which concludes with yet another (double) motif:

The next unit again reveals two motifs:

and

Then a half-unit on (c) concludes S.1.

S.2 starts almost like S.1—motif repetition, rests, and final climax all reappear in the first unit, but all with a new motif:

employed above the chordal motif (b^1). The two units that follow correspond to those concluding S.1, though the last one is a full unit.

They prepare S.3, which brings the climax with a new motif:

characterized by the upward sweep of the violins. This new motif is coupled with $(b)+(b^1)$. Like the final units of the other sections from which it is derived, the second unit suddenly subsides, ushering in S.4.

This acts as a partial recapitulation of S.1, containing one and one-half units that correspond to the first and last units of S.1. In a brief coda the pervasive feeling of hopeless yearning is wholly confirmed with two subdued repetitions of $(a)+(b)$. A few measures in the low strings represent a bridge to the first scene of the opera, or, in the concert version, to the *Love Death*. It is interesting to note how the stanzas successively decrease in length—an evidence of Wagner's psychological insight: A span of time appears to us shorter the further in the past it has been experienced. Thus four and one-half units of S.1 are well balanced by three units in S.2, two in S.3, and only one and one-half in S.4. Being heard last, S.4 affects us most despite its brevity.

Continuity in the *Prelude* is achieved through the repeated employment of the various motifs as well as through their relations; for (a), (b), and (e), and likewise (c) and (e), are related melodically, and (c), (e), (g), and (h) are related rhythmically. In fact, except for (a), all close with the same rhythm.

Overtures in the Recent Past

The prelude is the latest type of overture. In its lack of standardization it harks back to the very earliest overtures—the curtain raisers in the operas of Monteverdi and his successors. In its dramatic intent, not to speak of its texture, it is, however, a characteristic child of the Classic-Romantic era. Many operas composed after Wagner's death have abandoned overtures altogether, as the curtain rises for the first scene with the first few measures of the music. Only as an independent concert piece has the overture continued to be important.

Summary: Large and Small Forms

Reviewing the discussions of Part III, we discover that essentially there are four ways in which large pieces have been structurally organized: (1) in linked but otherwise disparate sections as in potpourri and fantasy (or, we may add, in motet and madrigal); (2) in chains of variations or stanzas; (3) in ternary and rondo forms, in which the repetitive element gives pattern to several different sections; and (4) in sonata-form, in which separate units interact or react upon each other and some of the materials are developed. Any of these forms may be used to unify works made coherent primarily by a non-musical program, such as tone poems and character pieces (or, we may add, by a text, such as songs or sections of operas). There are, moreover, numerous combinations among these principles of organization.

Small pieces, which were discussed in Parts I and II, are structurally similar to large pieces, but they are chiefly created from a single melodic-rhythmic, contrapuntal, or harmonic idea. The two basic organizations that have been found satisfactory for them are (1) the repetitive arrangements of the various song forms, found in songs since the time of the twelfth-century troubadours and in innumerable piano pieces of the nineteenth and twentieth centuries; and (2) additive or continuous development, embracing, on the one hand, the fugue and, on the other, those polyphonic and improvisational "forms" in which no structure is involved but rather a texture only. Works of these types may also assume large forms by incorporating aspects of the rondo (cf. Bach's *D-Minor Toccata,* p. 57f, or his large *Fugues,* pp. 102f, 105f), or of the variation form (cf. Liszt's *La Campanella,* p. 54).

A combination of these two types of organization of small pieces, that is, repetitive and developmental, led to a somewhat larger piece of binary form with two repeated sections (A-A^1), as found in the longer dances of Baroque suites or in Domenico Scarlatti's *Sonatas.* On a large scale the binary form also includes combinations of two contrasting pieces, such as the prelude and fugue and vocal and instrumental pieces with a slow introduction and a fast main portion (cf. Rossini's *Una voce poco fà,* p. 52ff).

Forms and Titles

Again a word of caution: The title of a composition does not always inform us about its construction. There are fantasies in binary, rondo, and sonata-form. Symphonic poems may involve variation, rondo, ternary, and sonata-form. Overtures are found in song, polyphonic, potpourri, ternary, rondo, and sonata-form. Songs also may involve almost any structure. Musical composition is a living art; every one of its products is an individual combination of ingredients. Structure is but one of these and need not be reflected in the title.

Therefore it is doubly important to become aware of the organization of a piece of music. Only in this way can the composer's intentions become fully clear. Let the reader consider again four outstanding programmatic compositions studied in this part—Beethoven's *Egmont Overture,* Liszt's *Les Préludes,* R. Strauss's *Till Eulenspiegel,* and Debussy's *Afternoon of a Faun*—and he will be convinced of the significance the recognition of form has with respect to the appreciation of these works.

CONCEPTS AND TOPICS DISCUSSED IN THIS SECTION

VIII SOLOISTIC TYPES

SECTION A

THE SONATA

Organization on the Largest Scale

We now turn to what is perhaps the most important subject of
our studies—the consideration of musical coherence on the largest
scale. In works consisting of large pieces or movements, such as
sonatas, quartets, concertos, and symphonies, the composer generally tries to weld the units into an organic whole. Often coherence
manifests itself surreptitiously, as an outgrowth of an organic creative process; at other times the composer openly turns to cyclic
devices, that is, reminiscence and thematic reference. We shall call
such works as are characterized by several cohering movements
COMPLEX ORGANIC WORKS.

Let us pause for a moment and compare these with what we
have called composite works. There each unit is musically independent: The linking of several small pieces does not necessarily
create musical coherence among them. In a Baroque suite, for
instance, the dances follow each other rather haphazardly, and the

[261]

ordering principle is established by the necessity of avoiding bore-
dom; hence the employment of contrasts of tempo and rhythm.
Units of composite works, such as suites, song cycles, motets, operas,
oratorios, and ballets, may be omitted or replaced by others, and
they may be performed singly. What coherence there is in such
works is more often literary than musical.[1]

The successful complex organic work represents the acme of instrumental composition. It demands from the composer a high degree of clarity of purpose, of concentration, and of sustaining power.
Were these lacking, listeners would be unable to discover the
coherence without which the work is heard as merely composite;
they would therefore judge the movements to be too long, and
become bored. In order to achieve coherence on the largest scale
great composers—like Mozart or Beethoven—often carry ideas in
their heads for years while working them out and assigning to
them their places in a work. In this way they mentally perfect entire complex works before committing them to paper. This part
will guide the music lover toward a recognition of coherence in
the complex works analyzed below, and it is hoped that it will help
him to perceive such coherence in other similar works.

The Early Sonata

In the past two centuries the sonata has been the outstanding
type of complex work for solo instruments. As we already know,
the term "sonata" has not always signified a complex work (one divided into several movements) nor soloistic performance. Throughout the Baroque era this term was often applied to single pieces—
for instance Domenico Scarlatti's (cf. p. 245f). Variation sets, potpourris, toccatas, fugues, all were sometimes so named. They were
composed for solo instruments such as violins, lutes, flutes, harpsi-
chords, and organs, as well as for ensembles of these.

The sonata in our sense of the word developed from instrumental versions of French CHANSONS (the French counterparts to
the Italian madrigals), favored in sixteenth-century Italy. Such an

---

[1] Needless to say, in a living art such a classification is not strict. Some
essentially composite works, for example Schumann's *Carnaval* (p. 150ff) or
Wagner's *Tristan and Isolde* (pp. 140f, 254ff), have musical coherence (cf.
p. 186). On the other hand, certain symphonic suites, such as Debussy's
La Mer, are series of disconnected large pieces.

instrumental *chanson* was called CANZONA (plural *canzone*) or *can-zon* (plural *canzoni*). Like its vocal model it had many contrasting sections, some of which might be developed from the same material. Early in the seventeenth century these sections began to be expanded and became pieces of some length, such as complete dances, fugues, instrumental arias, and preludes. They became what we call movements, separate units, each with a well defined subject and with a definite beginning, middle, and close.

Sonata da Camera and da Chiesa; the Trio Sonata

Like the dances in suites, the various movements followed each other largely according to the needs of contrast in tempo, rhythm, and mood. In fact, of the two types of composition evolved (about the mid-seventeenth century) from such beginnings one was virtually a suite and contained mostly dance pieces. It was enjoyed as after-dinner chamber music and called SONATA DA CAMERA (Italian: *camera*—chamber). The other type included movements of a more serious character and was played both in the home and—instead of motets and cantatas—in church. It was therefore known as SONATA DA CHIESA (Italian: *chiesa*—church).

These chamber and church sonatas were usually played by ensembles of three to four instruments, namely (a) one or two violins, oboes, flutes, or recorders (more ancient and simpler cousins of the flute), (b) a 'cello or a bassoon, and (c) a harpsichord or an organ. The soprano instrument or instruments would either play in virtuoso fashion or present a simple duet, imitating vocal arias and duets, while the keyboard instrument, reinforced by the 'cello or bassoon, would play the *basso continuo* or thoroughbass, that continuous bass line typical of Baroque music (cf. p. 88f). In addition, the player of the keyboard instrument would use his right hand to improvise harmonies, often indicated by figures added to the notes of the *basso continuo*, while the players of the soprano instruments, especially in slow movements, were supposed to improvise ornaments.

Around 1700 the two types tended to merge, and sonatas began to include both dance and non-dance movements. Those for two soprano instruments and *basso continuo*—composed in three melodic lines—were then called TRIO SONATAS, though they were played by four musicians, as 'cello and harpsichord doubled on the thoroughbass, while the sonata for one solo instrument and *basso continuo* was called simply sonata. Telemann furnishes us with a cheerful example of a trio sonata of the *sonata-da-chiesa* type: [2]

EXAMPLE 79:   GEORG PHILIPP TELEMANN [1681–1767]

Trio Sonata in E Major

Movement 1: Soave [3]

In the trio sonata of the church-sonata type the arrangement in four movements with the tempo sequence slow-fast-slow-fast was after 1700 an accepted standard. The *First Movement* of this *Sonata* is typical: firm yet lyrical, somewhat reminiscent of the beginning of a French overture (cf. p. 111).

Movement 2: Presto

The *Second Movement* opens, according to custom, with a nod in the direction of the fugue. The first violin plays the entire subject, which the second violin then answers. Little echoes give pretty effects; they are stereotypes of the age, to which the fashionable Telemann—in his time rated the greatest German musician, by far outranking Bach—deferred readily. Otherwise the typical, steady Baroque drive and a running *perpetuum mobile* characterize this *Movement*, whose melodic substance derives continuously from the subject.

Movement 3: Andante

The *Third Movement* is more serious. The many descending, chromatic lines communicate a mood of lamentation, and several pedal points add to the impression of passivity. This is a movement in which Baroque violinists would have improvised ornaments upon the long tones in the music. Such improvisation was definitely implied and demanded. Today, however, since we are no longer sure of the kind of improvisation implied, we play such movements as they are actually written.

---

[2] An example of the *sonata da camera* has already been given in Bach's *'Cello Suite*, p. 108ff; for the only difference between such a sonata and a suite lies in the instrumentation: When written for harpsichord or orchestra the work was called a suite or overture; when written for members of the violin family or for a small ensemble it was called a sonata.

[3] Suave, sweet.

PLATE X: Anonymous print—Satire on the castrato Caffarelli
(1703–83).

Several famous composers are here shown playing accompaniment to the singer's cat, and the text implies that Caffarelli disturbs
the harmony of the music. The players, all renowned virtuosi on
the particular instruments, are: 1. Domenico Scarlatti (1685–1757)
at the two-manual harpsichord (cf. Appendix I, p. 389); 2. Giuseppe
Tartini (1692–1770) and 4. Pietro Locatelli (1693–1764) as violinists; 3. Giuseppe San Martini or Sammartini (1693?–1770?), playing the oboe; and 5. Salvatore Lanzetti (1710?–1780?) with a 'cello
held upside down. This is a typical chamber ensemble of the mid-
eighteenth century.

Movement 4: Scherzando [4]

A cheerful, driving finale, again with echo passages, concludes the *Sonata,* a refreshingly simple and graceful composition.

Except for the prevailing grand style and the unity of key, such trio sonatas can hardly be called organic. They still stand near to their potpourri origin. The concept of inner coherence of an entire complex work crystallized but slowly during the second half of the eighteenth century.

The Classic Sonata

With their preference for a single melodic line Rococo composers retained the sonata proper but dropped the trio sonata. The melodic bass of the Baroque yielded to a harmonic accompaniment. The sonata for a solo instrument with a specific and completely written-out accompaniment became the favorite type in this field. Meanwhile the piano was invented; with its substantial and variable volume it gradually vanquished the harpsichord, and the 'cello was no longer needed to sustain bass tones. Thus the sonata ensemble shrank to two instruments: the violin, preferably, and the piano— or even to the piano alone.

The formulation of the sonata likewise underwent great changes. The Baroque sonata had taken from the suite the idea of uniform tonality throughout, except that the slow third movement might stand in the relative or tonic Major or Minor of the prevailing key. The Classic sonata went further afield. It used contrasting keys in the middle movements in order to set up greater tension, and thereafter to reaffirm the main tonality the more strongly; for the bond of tonality is very important, indeed fundamental in Classic music (see p. 249). The outer movements (the first and the last) are always in the same key. (But in a work that starts in Minor the finale may be in the tonic Major.)

The key that is established in the first movement becomes the point of reference for everything in the whole work: It interrelates passages through its closeness to certain keys, or it becomes the center of tension as the music strays to distant keys.[5] Reappearance

---

[4] Joking, gay.
[5] On distance between keys see p. 249.

of keys in the music is often more important than melodic reference. It takes much experience for the listener to become aware of these things. In subsequent discussions we shall therefore refer to tonal relations only when they are easy to discern.

In their sonatas Haydn, Mozart, and Beethoven abandoned the Baroque practice of presenting only one emotion throughout each movement, a practice reflected in a form evolving continuously from a single subject, in a steady tempo, rhythm, and volume. Instead, continual emotional fluctuation and dramatic contrast became the rule. Consequently the polyphonic types of fugue and chorale setting were replaced with the repetitive structures of rondo and sonata-form. Similarly the slow, introductory first movement of the trio sonata was dropped; on the other hand, a remnant of the suite, the minuet, was sometimes included, usually as a middle movement.

Beethoven's Sonatas

In general, Classic composers exercised greater individual freedom in the construction of their sonatas than Baroque composers, for they conceived them more and more as organic wholes. Thus Beethoven replaced the polite minuet with a faster, more excited movement, the scherzo, which preserved the *alternativo* form of its predecessor but reflected the rebellious spirit of the French Revolution. The opening movement in his *Sonatas,* though usually fast and vigorous and in sonata-form, is sometimes a set of variations and sometimes a lyric composition. The slow middle movement is generally lyrical and in song form, but it, too, is found in a great variety of formulations, including even sonata-form. The finale, in many sonatas by Haydn and Mozart a rather nonchalant rondo, often becomes with Beethoven a surging climax in sonata-form.

It was in music for the piano that Beethoven gave his imagination the freest range.[6] Of his large instrumental works the greatest number are for the piano—his *Thirty-Two Sonatas.* The descriptive title of the one we are about to discuss, "*Appassionata,*" originally given to the work by a publisher, indicates its organic concept—a definite, pervasive idea. The continuity is also emphasized by a smooth

---

[6] See Appendix I, p. 390, for a discussion of the place of the piano in music and of piano virtuosi.

transition from the *Second* to the *Third Movement*. In so well unified a work it would be impossible to replace a movement without danger of violating the spirit of the whole.

EXAMPLE 80:   LUDWIG VAN BEETHOVEN [1770–1827]

Sonata No. 23, in F Minor, "Appassionata," op. 57 (1806)

Beethoven's power, his proverbial unruliness, his romanticism, and his extraordinary concentration all mark this great work. The demoniac *First Movement* vibrates between seemingly incongruous contrasts of haste and repose, quite in keeping with the general concept of the work to which the title draws attention. The *Second Movement* is lyrical, almost brooding. In its variations it gradually achieves a certain agitation, but then reaffirms its first mood. With the briefest of transitions there follows immediately the dramatic, rushing, brilliant *Finale.*

Movement 1: Allegro assai — più allegro [7]

The length of many of Beethoven's movements in sonata-form results from long bridges, extended development, and important codas. His themes are compact units which, like all three themes in this *Movement,* usually end in a well defined cadence. The first theme is given a mysterious statement in *pianissimo:*

It is briefly heard again in full strength, opening a bridge of great originality:

---

[7] Very fast—faster.

The lyric second theme:

dissolves in trills, and a soft, scale-like passage leads to the stormy third theme, which recaptures the mood of the beginning:

Criss-crossing from one hand to the other, *a* opens the development section in an interesting sequence of modulations. In two further subsections *b* is thoroughly reformulated, and finally *c*. Then a motif from *a* leads back to the recapitulation, which is built for some time above reiterated bass tones, but is otherwise fairly regular. The long coda includes a second development of *a* and one of *c*. This last demands an even faster tempo (*più allegro*) and once more stresses the emotional contrasts which abound throughout, before it closes with the mysterious mood of the beginning.

Movement 2: Andante con moto [8]

The serene, expressive theme of the *Second Movement:*

is in two repeated periods. It is followed by four variations, increasing in rhythmic activity but otherwise strict. The first merely shifts the left hand by half a beat, so that it limps after the right in syncopation. The next two variations are simple, figural. Their simplicity forms an effective contrast to the outer movements, and yet there is suppressed restlessness in them. The fourth variation is based on tone color, exploiting high and low pitches alternately; it also functions as a recapitulation of the theme. The transitional chord on which it pauses is vehemently taken up, as the *Finale* begins.

Movement 3: Allegro ma non troppo [9] — *Presto*

Starting as a murmur, the long first theme of the *Finale* is characterized by a running figuration, *f*, and a short motif suggesting the call of horns, (*g*), which is soon added:

The second theme has the simple melody in the left hand, while the rhythmic activity is upheld by a trill-like motif in the right:

---

[8] Fairly slow but moving.
[9] Not too fast.

After a few measures taken from *f*, hammering right-hand chords conclude the exposition of this sonata-form.

The development section is built around the first theme, but it also
introduces a new, syncopating idea:

The texture dissolves completely, and passages descend into the lowest
region of the keyboard as the recapitulation starts. Beethoven apparently felt that, because of its speed, the *Movement* was not long enough
to counterbalance the *First;* he therefore not only demanded the repetition of the development section together with the recapitulation, but, as
in the *First Movement,* added a coda in faster tempo (*presto*).

This coda is remarkable, for it starts with a new, chordal theme in two
repeated periods:

Its effect is electric: It snatches us from the expectation of a continuance
of the toccata-like figuration and plunges us into a wholly novel situation.
The apparent inconsistency once more affirms the general concept of
the work, which clearly communicates itself to us even without a discussion of the technical details that indicate the coherence of the *Three
Movements.*

Among sonatas those for violin and piano rank second in number
only to those for piano alone.[10] As we have seen, in their single

_____

[10] See Appendix I, pp. 392, 393f, for discussions of the emergence of the
violin family and of virtuosi on these instruments.

pieces, large and small, the Romantic composers went their own ways; in complex works, however, they followed mostly Beethoven in formulation, technical approach, and dramatic idea. One of the Romantics who succeeded in both small pieces and complex works was Brahms, and the foregoing remark well applies to him. Among his *Sonatas* for violin, clarinet (or viola), 'cello, and piano the following is probably pre-eminent:

EXAMPLE 81:   JOHANNES BRAHMS [1833–97]

Sonata No. 3 for Violin and Piano, in D Minor, op. 108 (1888)

Movement 1: Allegro

Like the Beethoven *Sonata* just discussed, this one opens with, as it were, subterranean rumblings. But the lyric element in Brahms asserts itself immediately with a winged, melodic theme in the violin:

The first impression is one of greater rhythmic complexity and length than is found in the corresponding opening by Beethoven. Yet many details recall the older master: several contrasting motifs; a forceful restatement (in the piano) of the beginning, and thereafter new, important bridge material:

a lyric second theme (first stated by the piano, then by the violin), which contrasts with the excited first theme:

then the relaxation at the end of the brief closing theme or codetta:

In addition, the very artful weaving-in of motifs from the bridge into *c* as well as into *d* (where the two-tone motif from the bridge is echoed in violin and piano) brings to mind Beethoven's *Egmont Overture* (cf. p. 250ff).

A deeply stirring pedal point is reiterated throughout the development section of this sonata-form, which varies *a* only. In the recapitulation, which reviews all the material of the exposition, *b* is expanded; *d* builds up and ushers in a coda of Beethovenian dimensions, consisting of a complete restatement of *a*, mostly in Major, and a partial restatement of the development section, built on a pedal point on the tonic that expresses relaxation rather than tension, as it did at its previous appearance on the dominant. The end is serene, preparing us for the lyric *Second Movement*.

The mere fact that here two instruments are involved gives the composer ample opportunity for change of color. Restating a melody now becomes an adventure rather than a routine procedure. The interplay of piano and violin as it occurs in *d*, the combination of the two instruments as in the two development sections, and their opposition as at the opening, give new scope to the composer and to the listener.

Movement 2: Adagio

The *Slow Movement* is a simple song in two stanzas. A quiet melody of the violin, *e*, combines with a piano motif, (*f*), characterized by tone repetition, which pervades the entire *Movement*:

Accompanied by the same motif, a second idea is intimated rather than stated by double stops (chords) in the violin:

It completes the stanza, which is then repeated with some changes in *g*. We may also describe the form of this *Movement* as follows: an exposition of two themes and a recapitulation in which the second theme, which was first heard in the dominant key, returns to the tonic key—in other words, a sonata-form without a development section. Such a structure is called a SONATINA-FORM.

Movement 3: Un poco presto e con sentimento [11]

The idyllic mood evoked by this song is further emphasized by the *Third Movement,* a light, evanescent, graceful intermezzo. The tempo superscription itself is significant. The form of this *Movement* is ternary: A-A-A^1-A^2-A-*coda*. The main idea is related to (f):

Vigorous chords highlight the developmental middle section, A^1-A^1_1, whereas the coda is like a rippling of water or the dancing of elves vanishing in the dawn.

Movement 4: Presto agitato

Agitation marks the *Finale.* Having just been transformed into *h,* (f) becomes here, stripped of the tone repetition, the powerful start of the main theme of a sonata-form:

---

[11] Slightly fast and with feeling.

It reappears in the bridge in which the violin and the two hands of the pianist play imitatively:

A climax is reached, and then we hear a quiet second theme, suggesting a chorale:

An imaginative piano passage, in hushed, running octaves, opens and closes the expansive third theme:

and then a restatement of *i* concludes the exposition.

Subdued chords start the development section, suggesting apprehension. A quiet, rocking version of *i* is tentatively advanced. Gradually the music takes on a more courageous tone, and with the help of continuous syncopation a great climax is attained. There Brahms begins to expand the second, rushing motif of the first theme, (i^1), together with a new syncopation.

Having been so amply treated, *i* is omitted at the beginning of the recapitulation, which enters, in direct continuation of the development section, with *j*. Then *k, l,* and *i* are regularly reviewed and the whole culminates in a brief coda full of surprises.

Meaning of Sonatas

It is apparent that such sonatas present a sequence of emotions—a drama, one might say, without material facts or actions. Their essential unity is shown by the continuity of movements in Beethoven's work, by the relationships among movements in both *Sonatas,* through use of motifs by Brahms and through employment of similar tempo sequences by Beethoven (the two fast codas), and finally by the correspondence between the outer movements in tonality and mood. Sonatas are highly serious works. Their craftsmanship, length, and internal unity make us realize the greatness of the composers who conceived and executed them. For without serious purpose, sustained effort, clear vision, and perfect technic, composers could not have achieved such works.[12]

Whereas the formal arrangement of sonatas differs widely, seriousness and intensity have remained their dominant characteristics. A clear instance is provided by one of the best sonatas of recent time, the work of an American composer:

EXAMPLE 82:   SAMUEL BARBER [b.1910]

Piano Sonata op. 26 (in E-flat Minor, 1950)

Copyright 1950 by G. Schirmer, Inc. Reprinted here by permission.

Here is a highly imaginative, vigorous, and brilliant piece of piano music. Its lines, distinctive both rhythmically and melodically, can be easily followed throughout even by those unaccustomed to the sound of contemporary music. The forms are simple, clear, and concise, yet imbued with unceasing energy and emotional drive.

Movement 1: Allegro energico

The main theme of the *First Movement* is stated in a full period:

---

[12] A word of caution: Although as artists they have given of themselves to their work, as men they may not care to give of themselves. They may even arrogate to themselves special privileges as geniuses, and be asocial and even highly unethical in the political, social, or economic sense.

It is easily remembered by the chromaticism and incisive rhythm of its main motif, (a). A bridge then sets forth a second important motif, chromaticism in contrary motion, in two versions, (b) and (c):

The music grows quiet and discloses a lyric second theme with an accompaniment that makes prominent use of a twelve-tone row, i.e. an idea containing all twelve tones of our music,[13] (d)+(e):

Chromatic figuration above this row leads to another bridge which introduces motif (f) of the codetta theme:

---

[13] For the background of the twelve-tone row see p. 196.

Into the latter the chromatic triplet of (c) and other motifs are worked, especially one that has already been heard in the course of the second theme:

The development section of this sonata-form starts by expanding the first theme. It establishes chromaticism in contrary motion, whether converging or diverging, as a main material of the work. A second sub-section creates a *quasi-basso ostinato* from (f) and varies (g) above and below it. Then an *ostinato* figure in the soprano, also derived from (f), leads to the recapitulation.

Grim determination has thus far pervaded the music, and this mood continues to the end. With bridges and codetta abbreviated, the recapitulation ends in a stirring coda. At first the latter takes up the second sub-section of the development section in the main tonality. Then a *basso ostinato* of two chords derived from (b), which is coupled with (c) and another, lightning-like twelve-tone row, crowns the *Movement*.

Movement 2: *Allegro vivace e leggiero* [14]

A lithe, frolicking little *Scherzo* relieves the terrific tension. Its main idea:

is related to (a). It is presented twice, woven into rippling figurations, and is then transferred to the bass. In a most attractive, light fashion the twelve-tone method continues in evidence.

We are treated to a comic touch in a little *Trio* with a waltz-like accompaniment, but with unexpected changes of meter:

---

[14] Fast, vivacious, and light.

The *Trio* is heard twice, and is then expanded into a bridge. When the *Scherzo* returns, the two first presentations of *h* are separated by a development of *h* and a varied statement of *h* in a new key. Afterwards *h* is, as at first, heard in the bass. A little coda of greatest delicacy closes the *Movement,* which seems to evaporate into thin air.

Movement 3: Adagio mesto [15]

The *Slow Movement* is almost everywhere based on a twelve-tone row:

This subject is repeated in the manner of a *chaconne* throughout with only a few interruptions. It is presented in several variants but most prominently as it is heard alone at the beginning. To this harmonization there is added an improvisatory melody reminiscent of chant,[16] in which the repeated tones of (*f*) assume new importance (cf. bracket):

From *k* flows a theme that also closes this ternary *Movement.* The central portion is divided into two developmental sections, each announced by *j* as heard at the start. Much is made here of a chromatic version of *k* and of tone repetitions, which lead to a powerful climax before the restatement. Serious and sad in mood, this *Movement* may well be called a dirge. And we recall that the *basso ostinato* was also a staple feature of Baroque laments (cf. p. 120).

---

[15] Slow and sad.

[16] This is an instance of neo-medievalism; cf. p. 192.

Movement 4: Fuga: Allegro con spirito

The brilliant *Finale* returns to both the mood and the key of the *First Movement*. Except for one passage of exquisite lyricism, an unrelenting drive pervades this difficult piece, a *Fugue* with the character of a toccata.

The *Movement* starts with an orthodox fugue exposition. Alto, bass, soprano, and tenor by turns present the subject, the two portions of which, *l* and *m*, are thereafter used separately:

The episode, like those that follow, employs motif (*n*), which was previously heard as the counterpoint to the answer (the second entrance of the subject) and is related to (*a*), especially when inverted.

The second section takes *l* through the paces, including some imitations in *stretto*.[17] The ensuing episode employs (*n*) as shown above, but also augmented to notes twice and even four times as long. It ends in a powerful sweep downward across the keyboard.

Above pedal points the third section opens softly with *m*¹. Soon *l* is added, augmented to notes of double length, first with its original melodic line, then also inverted; and this combination continues for some time. When (*n*) reappears, opening the third episode, powerful chords lead to another great climax with *m* in thundering octaves. But after a few measures the music subsides in a beautiful, lyric expansion of (*n*) above a pedal point.

---

[17] For a discussion of fugal devices see p. 104f.

The fourth section begins like a prelude. Against various figurations derived from *m* and *l*, *l* is heard several times until it emerges in fourfold augmentation. The following episode is a restatement of the second episode. Its last portion is built on a thundering pedal point and ends in cascades of a glittering cadenza.

The last section uses *l* in double augmentation, and by way of *stretto* imitation makes it grow into full chords. The *Movement* closes with a brilliant, toccata-like coda, in which *l* makes a last augmented appearance in triumphant octaves.

Musical Style and Emotional Response

The sequence of emotions through the various movements and sections provides Classic-Romantic and contemporary sonatas with an important unifying factor. Though it is hardly possible to prove how and why a particular emotional sequence achieves aesthetic "truth," our direct response, or "intuition," tells us that it satisfies. However, our emotional response depends on sufficient familiarity with the musical style in which the work is conceived. We possess this familiarity with respect to Classic-Romantic music, because we have grown up with it. Recent works of some originality, though, run the risk of being rejected merely on the ground of their novelty. Yet significant works can be created in any style. Hence it devolves on us to familiarize ourselves with the styles of contemporary music before we judge contemporary works favorably or otherwise (cf. Part II, Section J).

Summary

The four *Sonatas* presented in this section appear to be so different that the use of the same title for all hardly seems appropriate. Yet there are several quite definite characteristics common to all four—and these characteristics apply to a large majority of such works since 1700: They are organically conceived (though in trio sonatas the bond is still weak); earnest with respect to symbolized emotions (i.e. concentrating on a clear presentation of the idea content); wrought with the finest craftsmanship available; and played by one or a few soloists (since the Classic era rarely by more than two).

The late-Baroque sonata is, in addition, characterized by tonal unity, fugal technic in some movements, a melody with an active bass part in others, and a *basso continuo*. The only exceptions are SOLO SONATAS, i.e. sonatas for single, usually stringed instruments (cf. Bach's *'Cello Suite*, p. 108ff). The Classic-Romantic sonata, in turn, is also characterized by tonal unity, but with greater deviations in the middle movements, and by the use of the sonata-form. The contemporary sonata likewise, while differing in style, usually exhibits tonal unity and sonata-form, but it may involve some Baroque types, such as *passacaglia*, fugue, chorale setting, and dances. It often turns to cyclic devices, about which more will be said in the following sections.

IX ENSEMBLE WORKS

Section B

CHAMBER MUSIC

The Term "Chamber Music"

All music that is primarily intended for the intimacy of the home may be called chamber music: Small piano pieces, songs, madrigals, trio sonatas, and Classic sonatas are all part of chamber music in this broad sense. Yet during the nineteenth century this term came to mean specifically works belonging to the Classic-sonata type that were written for instrumental ensembles of from three to five players. Such works for more than five players are rather rare and are usually intended for concert performance only. Thus, within this narrowed definition, the field of chamber music includes neither vocal works nor trio sonatas. These and other types of Baroque chamber music were abandoned when the Classic types arose.

The String Quartet

The works we shall discuss here are commonly called trios, quartets, and quintets, depending on the number of performers. The standard ensemble, considered most satisfactory by the Classics and accepted ever since, is the string quartet:[1] two violins, a viola,

---

[1] The term "string quartet" denotes a certain ensemble of musicians as well as a type of composition for such an ensemble.

and a 'cello. At first works for this type of ensemble, which emerged around 1750, were played for entertainment by amateurs. As they grew in difficulty, professional organizations began to arrange public quartet concerts. The first such professional string quartet was founded in 1804. It was headed by Beethoven's friend, the violinist Ignaz Schuppanzigh (1776–1830). After a few years it was engaged by Count Andreas Kyrillovitch Rasoumovsky, Russian ambassador at Vienna, as his private musical organization, and thus became known as the Rasoumovsky Quartet.[2]

Haydn's Style

By the mid-eighteenth century, when the quartet ensemble emerged, the Classic sonata also was taking shape. The combination of the new type and the new ensemble in the works of the first great Classic composer of instrumental music, Joseph Haydn, set the standard for all chamber music since. Between 1755 and 1803 this master created over seventy string quartets, many of them among the best works of the type. With one set of six quartets, known as the *Maiden Quartets, op. 33,* he became, in 1781, the creator of the mature Classic style. In the preface to this *opus* Haydn recounts how, after long labors, he finally overcame the unsatisfactory flatness of Rococo music: He reintroduced some polyphony by deriving his accompaniments from thematic material, especially in the development sections of movements in sonata-form.

From small, happy works, written to give pleasure to aristocratic amateurs, Haydn's *Quartets* evolved into large works of art, sincere, genial, full of finesse, and embodying the typical style of Classic music. Unencumbered flow, steadiness of meter, and well differentiated tempos give his music a feeling of optimism and well-being that we associate with the Classics. Despite its general briskness. Haydn's music often glows with a warm lyricism. At times it suggests deep sadness and dramatic crisis, but never to extremes, for classicists value measure and restraint. Haydn never becomes sharp, satirical, edgy, desperate, or raucously hilarious.

---

[2] See Appendix I, p. 393, for further information on the string-quartet ensemble.

By courtesy of the Photo Archive of the Austrian National Library.

PLATE XI: Ferdinand Schmutzer (1870–1928), Austrian etcher— The Joachim Quartet.

This famous ensemble arranged itself on the stage as follows: Left front we see the leader and first violinist, Joachim, then counterclockwise the second violin, the viola, and the 'cello. Today the order usually is: left front—first violin, left rear—second violin, right front—viola, right rear—'cello.

EXAMPLE 83:   JOSEPH HAYDN [1732–1809]

String Quartet No. 73, in D Major, op. 76, 5 (1797)

Every *Movement* of this *Quartet* evidences Haydn's individuality. In
the *First Movement* he builds a sonata-form around a single theme. To
the *Slow Movement,* on the other hand, where one might expect something simpler, he gives a complete sonata-form; further surprise is provided by his use of the main theme as the bass of the second. The
tempo of the *Minuet* is unusually brisk. In the *Finale* Haydn again interrelates the two themes of the sonata-form—they are usually contrasted—
both by a brief melodic motif and by a reiterated chordal accompaniment.

It seems no mere coincidence, either, that each of the *first two Movements* starts with the same prominent interval. Indeed, the *Minuet* employs the same chief motif as the *Second Movement,* and thereby gives
the interval added prominence. Similarly the *First, Second,* and *Fourth
Movements* are linked by harmonic ties.

Movement 1: Allegretto—Allegro

A long, song-like theme in three and one-half periods, *a-a-½b-a,* opens
the work lyrically:

After a full cadence the lyric mood and the mode change. In a more
serious vein and in Minor, the development section consists of three
periods, all derived from continuations of the first measure of the theme,
(*a¹*). Each starts in a single instrument: At the beginning, the 'cello
takes the lead while the other instruments add new motifs. The second
period is divided between the violins and ends with a rapidly descending
staccato scale. The last period exhibits imitations of (*a¹*) as well as of
this scale motif.

The recapitulation is shortened. A coda or second development section
ensues, faster (*allegro*) and fuller than the previous one, and in the bright
main tonality.

Especially noteworthy is the pervasive, delicate polyphony. The material for each instrument is significant, not mere accompaniment, though
the main melody is chiefly given to the first violin. In the development
section there is much imitative interplay as well as DOUBLE and MULTIPLE
COUNTERPOINT, i.e. simultaneous employment of two or more melodies
and their repetition with their relative positions changed—the former
bass line reappears in the soprano, and so forth. For example, at the

beginnings of the first and second periods respectively we hear the following:

and

In the first passage the main motif is in the 'cello, and the first violin adds a new motif above it; in the second the position of the motifs is reversed: The second violin sings (a^1) and the viola intones the new motif below it. This device, along with many others, reappears in the coda.

Movement 2: Largo cantabile e mesto [5]

The *Second Movement* evokes a feeling of sadness even though the music is written in a major key—a refutation of the popular notion that only minor keys possess such power. The first theme:

---

[3] These are the usual abbreviations: vl = violin, vla = viola, vc = violoncello.
[4] The viola part is ordinarily written in a different clef (cf. Appendix I, p. 379f), but for the convenience of the reader we notate it in the usual clefs.
[5] Slow, singing, and sad.

a single period, is characterized by a triadic motif (b^1). The bridge anticipates the brief violin motif (c), against which in the second theme the lower instruments play (b^1):

In the development section, b is shifted from key to key; at the same time it is cut to two measures in the viola, and finally to one in the 'cello. The recapitulation is regular, but the second theme is shortened; it leads to a coda (taken from the bridge) which sustains the wonderfully warm, slightly brooding lyricism that prevails in this *Movement*.

Movement 3: Menuetto–Trio, Allegro

Gaiety and vigor mark the *Minuet*, which has the usual *alternativo* form: two repeated sections each for the *Minuet* and the *Trio*, concluded by the *Minuet* without repetitions. As mentioned before, the *Minuet* theme is related to b and thereby also to a (see the brackets in the examples):

The first section of the *Trio*, on the other hand, with the fast ornamental figures (turns) in the violin, refers to the bridge of the *Slow Movement*, and the long scalewise descent at its end seems to point back to the end of the recapitulation of that *Movement*. Through most of the *Trio*, however, the 'cello is prominent:

Movement 4: Presto

The simplest imaginable beginning in the *Finale* unfolds into a marvel of rhythmic-melodic activity. The backbone of the *Movement* is the re-iterated interval of a fifth, which enters after the chords of the begining:

Around this reiteration the first violin and 'cello answer one another with a playful phrase; then the game is repeated, but expanded more broadly, modulating to the key of the second theme. In this bridge the basic fifth is combined with a second fifth with wonderful effect:

The second theme is derived from the first, and the fifths also appear at the end of both its periods:

Runs, an unexpected rest, and a charmingly melodized cadence close this exposition.

A hesitating passage opens the development section. Suddenly it slips into a distant key in which the game around the fifths is resumed in a more serious mood. Toward the end of the brief development the bridge phrase reappears and with it—twice—the twofold fifths of *g*.

The beginning of the recapitulation is somewhat veiled by a figuration that runs through the chords of *f*. For the remainder of the first theme a lengthened version of the bridge is substituted, but the second theme is stated simply as at first. In its unassuming gaiety it is absolutely disarming. To underscore this mood, Haydn, so to speak, cracks a joke: Quite unexpectedly, after the virtual conclusion of the work, he returns to the chords that opened the *Finale*.

Haydn and Mozart

Despite classicist balance, the zestful spirit of Haydn, revealed alike in the quiet loveliness of the *Opening Movement,* the deep human emotion of the *Second,* the robust vigor of the *Third,* and the playful frolicking in the *Finale,* has hardly ever been more forcefully expressed elsewhere in music. But with his friend, Mozart—whom Haydn himself acclaimed as the greatest of all composers—classicist refinement and restraint prevail to an even greater degree. A full generation younger than Haydn, Mozart enthusiastically adopted the style that the older man had created with his *Maiden Quartets* of 1781 (cf. p. 284), and within the last decade of his brief life-span of thirty-five years he rapidly produced one model work after another. These works set a standard that Haydn himself, after the younger master's death in 1791, adopted in such works as the one discussed above. The compositions of Mozart's last decade have ever since been regarded as the purest representatives of a golden age in music.

Special Ensembles

One of these "perfect" works is the *Clarinet Quintet.* The basic string quartet is here enriched by the color of the woodwind. Works of this kind are commonly referred to by the additional instrument, the strings being taken for granted. Thus we speak of this work as a clarinet quintet, of others similarly as horn, piano, viola, 'cello, or harp quintets. Piano, flute, or oboe quartets are works in which these instruments are added to the Classic string trio: a violin, a viola, and a 'cello. And a piano trio is a work for piano, violin, and 'cello.

In all such works the added instrument may be treated as that of a virtuoso soloist, accompanied by the others, or as part of the ensemble. The former manner is typical of Romantic, especially late-Romantic works, the latter, as in Mozart's *Clarinet Quintet*, of Classic. The clarinet here weaves in and out of the string ensemble, shares the lead with the first violin, but rarely displays virtuoso style. Nevertheless, because of the greater weight given to color and to exchange of leading melodies, the texture in this work is simpler than that in Haydn's *Quartet* above—it is more in the manner of accompanied melody. As in sonatas, moreover, the fact that a further tone color is available invites greater length.

EXAMPLE 84: WOLFGANG AMADEUS MOZART [1756–91]

Clarinet Quintet in A Major, K.581 (1789)

Classic chamber music, more than sonatas, accepted a standard sequence of movements: a fast first movement, a slow second, a minuet or scherzo in third place (but sometimes changing place with the slow movement), and a fast finale in rondo or sonata-form. In the present *Quintet* Mozart chose to deviate slightly from this standard: The *last two Movements* are a *Minuet* with *two Trios* and a *Theme with Variations*. Yet Mozart hardly ever stresses surprise, and he scorns abruptness. His melodies are smooth, with few rests; in contradistinction to Haydn's almost strictly diatonic lines, they include some chromaticism. The last may be observed especially in the *First Trio*, at the end of the *Second Movement*, and in *variations 3* and *4* of the *Finale*.

Movement 1: Allegro

A lyric theme opens the work:

Its two periods are followed by a long and very melodic bridge which includes periods for the clarinet (ending with a fine example of chromaticism), the 'cello and violin, and again the clarinet (with imitations by the violin). The second theme also is lyrical:

but, whereas the first theme was marked by somewhat sustained tones, this melody flows along evenly in shorter tones. After it reaches a climactic trill, a brief third theme:

and a reminiscence of *a* complete the exposition of the sonata-form.

The exposition is repeated. Then a chromatic passage on the clarinet introduces a thorough expansion of *a*, especially of its last two measures. The regular recapitulation seems the only appropriate ending of this *Movement* of angelic balance.

Movement 2: Larghetto

The *Second Movement* is also predominantly lyrical. It is built like a *da-capo* aria, which is not surprising considering how Mozart's inspiration was fired by the opera (cf. Example 51, p. 133ff). The clarinet sings a long melody that is never allowed to pause until its end:

This is followed by a duet between violin and clarinet; the texture thins out to the employment of but three instruments, and in a slow descent a second cadence is achieved.

The middle section of the *Movement* introduces a beautiful SEQUENCE, i.e. a phrase in which the same motif is, without other changes, repeated on various pitch levels that follow each other in a definite order of descending or ascending intervals (cf. the end of Lassus's *Iubilate Deo*, p. 70f, and the bridge from the *Don-Giovanni Overture*, p. 247):

Another ingratiating phrase follows, played by the violin and repeated by the clarinet. Then, with the aid of *e*, the music returns to the key of the first section, which is completely reviewed. A chromatically descending coda rounds out this lovely song.

Movement 3: Menuetto—Trio I, II

The *Minuet* and its *two Trios* are full of dextrous grace. They each have two repeated sections, but are otherwise differently constituted. The Minuet:

which is heard three times, before, between, and after the *Trios,* is shortest. A lilting, especially attractive cross rhythm occurs at the beginning of its second section. The ingratiating *Trio I:*

is written for strings only, whereas *Trio II* presents the clarinet in the lead:

Here the clarinet shows its rustic origin in a yodeling melody, for this piece is a *ländler*—a slow, Alpine cousin of the waltz—rather than a minuet. However rustic, this *Trio* has Mozart's usual dignity and balance.

Movement 4: Allegretto—Adagio—Allegro

The two repeated periods of the variation *theme* enter with the polish and politeness of a cavalier:

The *variations* are strict, but they exhibit various approaches:

Variation 1 preserves the *theme* almost intact; only a new line for the clarinet is added—the first virtuoso passage, displaying large leaps. This is a combination of contrapuntal and tone-color variation.

Variation 2 introduces a new rhythm in the accompaniment and, omitting the melody of the *theme,* gives a new melody to the violin.

Variation 3 changes to Minor, while a completely new contrapuntal texture is woven around the skeleton outline of the *theme.*

Variation 4 returns to the idea of *variation 1;* the *theme* is completely presented, but a new, figural voice is added, divided between clarinet and violin.

Variation 5 corresponds to *variation 2,* but changes tempo. This slow *variation (adagio)* is followed by a fast coda *(allegro),* which states the first phrase of the *theme* and then expands it. Two chromatic phrases have a telling effect: The serenity of the work becomes genial humor.

Mozart's Style

Despite the restraint and dignity of this music, there is a peculiar and endearing warmth about it—it is alive. It sings from first tone to last. It communicates the ideals of balance, clarity, and order. As he assigns the parts to the various instruments, Mozart is not merely interested in clever detail as we observed it in Haydn, although he is its absolute master also. We sense that he has some-how gone beyond intellectual pleasure in mere sophistication and has captured a new, significant simplicity. He presents us with social, conversational music. The instruments do not merely talk at each other, but to each other—they communicate. Mozart's music is almost like a conversation of friends, serene though enthusiastic, wise but warm, individualistic yet co-operative. The range of emotions is wide, but their vehemence is stilled. Here is the rarely attained golden mean in music.

The Viennese Classics

Quite different is the temper of the *Seventeen String Quartets* of Beethoven. This lover of nature, who was energetic, indulged in emotional outbursts, and was given to dramatizing his experiences, was influenced more by Haydn than by Mozart. On his first visit to Vienna in 1787 he had asked Mozart to take him as pupil. But, recalled to his home in Bonn by the death of his mother, Beethoven was unable to return to the capital until 1792, after Mozart's death. For some time then he studied with Haydn. The temperaments of the two men were too different, however, for these studies to be fruitful. Haydn, who loved sophistication and an easy-going, whim-sical approach; Mozart, for whom sophistication was only a means of attaining balance; and Beethoven, whose strength lay in concen-tration and dramatic expression—these constitute the great trio of the Viennese Classics, the suns that were surrounded by dozens of excellent satellite composers, planets soon to be ignored only because of the prodigious brilliance of the three giants.

The differences in temperament among these three masters becomes clear in their three works included in this and the preceding section. A fourth quality—lyricism—soon was in full bloom. For in the shadow of Beethoven there matured in Vienna the great master of song: Franz Schubert, who, although a full generation younger than his greatly admired hero, survived him by only one year and some months. With his *Fifteen String Quartets* and other works Schubert ranks among the greatest composers of chamber music. None of the works demonstrates his wonderful lyric bent better than the following, in which the majority of themes are stated in complete song forms:

EXAMPLE 85:   FRANZ SCHUBERT [1797–1828]

Quartet in A Minor, op. 29 (1824)

Because of his penchant for the voice, Schubert's style resembles Mozart's, whose entire output reflects the influence of the *bel canto*, more than Haydn's or Beethoven's. Schubert's chief strength lies in his tunefulness. He loves to sing. Even his large works should be approached in a spirit of relaxed enjoyment of melody. Although dramatic tension, sophistication, and surprises are present, they are not primary considerations. Schubert rather delights in colorful harmony and is fascinated by interesting clashes between successive harmonies from distant keys.

Movement 1: Allegro ma non troppo [6]

The *First Movement* starts in the mood of a ballad. A long, song-like first theme:

rises above a repetitive, ballad-like accompaniment; then it suddenly brightens as it changes to Major. In the bridge that follows a trill motif and an undulating figure are prominent:

---

[6] Not too fast.

After a brief pause another lyric idea, resembling a folksong, is presented in Major:

Enlivened by some imitative interplay and later by some surprising harmonic shifts, it concludes the exposition of the sonata-form, which, as in Classic works, may be repeated.

The brief development section is built around *a* and offers further harmonic delights. In three distinct subsections—(1) *a* in a new key, (2) a CANON, or passage of strict imitation, for 'cello and violin, based on *a*,[7] and (3) a lively derivation of *a* in *staccato*—a fine climax is attained. Then two phrases, both marked by many surprising harmonic shifts, lead back to the main tonality and the regular recapitulation. A brief coda derived from *a* closes the *Movement* with the expression of assurance.

Movement 2: Andante

Another song in two repeated periods opens the *Second Movement*:

---

[7] Canon is defined as STRICT IMITATION, i.e. imitation in which the intervals of a melody presented by one voice are exactly duplicated in another voice at the same or another pitch level, starting at a different time while the first presentation is still in progress. Such an imitating voice—and there may be three or more voices in a canon—may use any of the fugal devices explained on p. 104f in its presentation. Canons may be complete compositions or, as here, sections of larger works. A special type of canon is the ROUND in which all voices use the original melody on the same pitch and may repeat it while the others continue their presentations. The fugue, the motet, and similar contrapuntal types rely chiefly on FREE IMITATION, i.e. imitation in which the melody of one voice is only approximated in another voice. In such compositions imitation is usually brief and is abandoned and resumed at will. The distance of the imitative voice from the "leader" may also vary.

Schubert liked this particular melody so much that he used it in two
other works. The second theme is equally lyrical:

It enters after a quiet bridge and ends in a brief figure for the first violin
alone. After the lovely closing idea:

another bridge, full of harmonic color, leads to the modified recapitulation of this sonatina-form. A flowing figuration accompanies *d*, now played
without repetitions. Its second period is then shifted to a new key and
a brief expansion leads to the climax of the *Movement*, which ebbs away
as *e* reenters. Elements of both themes combine after *f* in a short, repose-
ful coda.

Movement 3: Menuetto—Trio, Allegretto

The mood of quiet happiness persists in the *Minuet:*

As in the preceding examples, it is first played with repetitions of its
two sections and repeated without them after the similarly constructed
Trio. The motif that opens the second section of the *Minuet:*

is much in evidence as the music shifts to distant keys and it is also used to conclude both sections. The infectious dance rhythm of this piece gives way to the yodel of a *ländler* in the *Trio:*

Movement 4: Allegro moderato

Whereas the *first three Movements* oscillate between Minor and Major, this one finally settles on Major to express a mood of nearly cloudless happiness. The first theme is a playful song in two repeated sections:

Motif (i^2) is treated imitatively in a long bridge that ends in an extended flourish of the first violin alone. The second theme:

is like a puckish little dance. It consists of two repeated periods, both repetitions being shifted by an octave. A brief bridge brings back (i^2) and combines it with the rhythm of *j*. Then, representing the third theme, a *pizzicato* bass and a new, fast idea in the first violin are added to this combination:

---

[8] The early trill sign 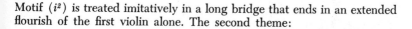 (cf. p. 101, footnote 2) in the nineteenth century indicates a new ornament, the INVERTED MORDENT ∿ (cf. p. 101, footnote 1).

A full close, a brief bridge motif:

and the recapitulation of this sonatina-form begins—regular except that
k combined with (i^1) is inserted after the first theme, and in the second
theme the repetitions are omitted. After the third theme (l) introduces
a little coda, which features chiefly (i^1) and (l) and brings the lovely
work to a sprightly close.

The naive joy in song, shown by Schubert in this and many
other works, gives him a special place in our hearts and in our
music. He was among the few masters who added to the basic
attitudes that musical Romanticism inherited from Beethoven.
Dramatic development of motifs is not of prime importance to
Schubert. His development sections are given rather to the exploita-
tion of harmonic colors; they are brief or even entirely omitted,
as in the *Finale* discussed above.

Chamber Music with Piano

As the piano became the central instrument in the Classic era,
it was only natural for it to be introduced into chamber music.
All Classic composers wrote piano trios. Mozart and Beethoven
composed piano quartets also, and later composers wrote piano
quintets. In all these the problem was how to treat the piano in
relation to the strings,[9] which might be submerged by its powerful
tone.

In piano trios the two stringed instruments (usually a violin and
a 'cello) can hardly compete with the keyboard instrument in volume. Hence the piano usually alternates between playing solos

---

[9] In ordinary usage the terms "strings" and "stringed instruments" refer
only to the violin family, or bowed strings, but not to the piano, whose strings
are struck, nor to the harp, guitar, mandoline, and other instruments whose
strings are plucked.

accompanied by the two strings and furnishing accompaniments to their solo passages. In piano quartets (which include a viola also) and quintets (which add a second violin) the greater sonority of the combined strings adds two further possibilities: The strings can assume the lead without piano support, or together they may act like an orchestra, either providing a background for the piano or competing with it. In the latter case they may exchange similar passages with the piano or oppose it with their own material. All these possibilities are illustrated in the following piano quartet, one of the best possible examples:

EXAMPLE 86: JOHANNES BRAHMS [1833–97]

Piano Quartet No. 1, in G Minor, op. 25 (1862)

Movement 1: Allegro

In the *First Movement* Brahms's lyricism impels him to continue singing and expanding his three themes until a development section becomes superfluous. Thus a mammoth sonatina-form unfolds. The first idea is tersely stated in a period that comes to a full close:

It begins with Brahms's favorite interval, the sixth, and this interval is employed also in chordal fashion throughout the second period:

(This difference in interval employment is technically known as "melodic" and "harmonic" intervals respectively.) The *a* is then vigorously expanded, giving the first theme an *a-b-a* form.

A brief bridge leads from a climactic *fortissimo* to the lyric mood of the second theme, which again begins with a sixth. It consists of three periods, all derived from one idea:

Stated by the 'cello and repeated by the piano, it, too, is expanded with rumbling figurations resembling those that gave the previous expansion vigor. The broadly singing third theme enters with two new ideas:

A hesitant codetta, derived from *a*, is all that separates this rich exposition from the restatement. The changes in the latter become clear from the following diagram, in which a^3 represents a developmental section and a^4 a short coda:

	Th. 1	Th. 2	Th. 3		
Exposition:	a-b-a^1	$- c$-c-$c^1 -$	d-e	$- a^2$	$-$

	Th. 1	Th. 2	Th. 3		
Recapitulation:	a-b-a^3-b-a^1	$- c^1 -$	d-e	$- a^2$	$- a^4$

Movement 2: Intermezzo: Allegro ma non troppo—Trio: Animato

The delicate *Intermezzo* is in striking contrast to the full-blooded, lyric *First Movement*. Throughout it the violin plays with a sordine (mute), and whenever it is heard a hush seems to fall over all the strings. An extraordinary quality, like stealthy effervescence, emanates from this music.

Above the repeated tones of the 'cello, the violin and viola intone the first theme in sixths:

and the piano, first silent, repeats it. The second theme:

is similarly stated twice. It discloses another of Brahms's predilections: the division of the beat variously into two or three equal note values, to create the lilt of polyrhythm.[10] Thereafter both themes are repeated with slight changes, the first in echo fashion, the piano and the strings answering each other. Finally the cadence of *f* is expanded into an effective coda.

The ensuing *Trio* with its rippling figurations in the piano and a winged melody in the strings:

h

is full of vibrant urgency. As usual, it has two repeated sections. In the repetition of the first, melody and figurations exchange instruments; in the repetition of the second, on the other hand, the key changes. Then *h* returns and leads to a literal repetition of the *Intermezzo*, concluded by a brief coda recalling the *Trio*.

---

[10] On polyrhythm see p. 198.

Movement 3: *Andante con moto—Animato*

The *Third Movement* is in an individually conceived ternary form. After the long, quiet, lyric first section:

piano *arpeggios* indicate the beginning of a development section; the latter is interrupted by a repeated, fast middle section, exciting and march-like in briskness and buoyancy but in triple meter:

The development section is then resumed and concluded. It is followed by a complete restatement of the first section, and the *Movement* ends with a quiet coda.

Movement 4: *Rondo alla Zingarese:* [11] *Presto*

The vigorous pace of the middle section of the *Third Movement* carries over into the *Finale,* one of the loveliest and liveliest expressions of optimism in music. The rhythm given to the left hand of the pianist suggests the use of the tambourine in Hungarian Gypsy music. Other typical ingredients of this music, which Brahms loved, are (1) the syncopated chords and the inverted mordent (cf. p. 299, footnote 8) in the first tune, (2) the SNAP RHYTHM (♪♪.) in the second episode, (3) the cadenza in the third, and (4) the large number of melodies used.

This rondo has three episodes, and accordingly three returns of the *ritornello,* which are cleverly varied:

$$A \quad - \quad B \quad - \quad A \quad - \quad C \quad - \quad A \quad - \quad D \quad - \quad A$$
$$k\text{-}l\text{-}k \quad - \quad m \quad - \quad k \quad - \quad n\text{-}o \quad - \quad l \quad - \quad dev. \quad - \quad k$$

The only irregularity is introduced by *D* whose first portion, a development of *B* and *C,* precedes the third *A;* its main portion (following the

---

[11] Rondo in Gypsy style.

third *A*) is a long cadenza in Gypsy fashion. The five main ideas are:

Throughout this work all instruments are skillfully used. Ensemble effects (as, for example, at the beginnings of *k* and *n* in the *Finale*) alternate with the opposition of strings and piano (as in the body of *k* and *m* and in the developmental sections of *D* based on *m*). The piano accompanies the strings, plays solos (e.g. in the cadenza), or is accompanied by the strings (e.g. in the middle section of the *Third Movement*). There are few occasions when one of the three stringed instruments plays an extended solo; such solos would unduly lengthen the work, and are more apt to occur in piano trios.

In general, Brahms was interested in creating unity in his complex works less through melodic or rhythmic relationships than through the sequences of tonalities and moods. This attitude perhaps stems from his marked deference to the Classic composers, in whose works melodic independence of movements is typical; for completeness of sections and clear divisions between them are Classic ideals.[12] By contrast, incompleteness and interrelationship,

---

[12] Nevertheless we have seen that even Classics such as Haydn occasionally arrived at a more overt unity than that afforded by bonds of tonality and the sequence of moods (cf. Example 83, p. 286ff). For an example of melodic interrelationships in Brahms's music see Example 81, p. 272ff.

or the pointing beyond the immediate unit, are Romantic characteristics. Thus we have seen that Beethoven (who was a Romantic in this respect) worked definitely on the interrelationship of sections and movements, as in the *Egmont Overture* or in the *Sonata Appassionata* (cf. pp. 250ff, 268ff).

Cyclic Organization

It was César Franck who first made full use of cyclic devices by deriving the thematic material of later movements from motifs of the preceding ones, in such a way that all movements seem to flow from a few basic ideas. This procedure, which had been suggested by earlier masters, has been called "cyclic form," indicating that it affects the entire "cycle" of three or more movements of a complex work. Consequently it does not imply any particular form or structure. In our discussions this basic approach of Franck and his numerous pupils in France and elsewhere will therefore be called CYCLIC ORGANIZATION rather than "cyclic form."

In addition to complete cyclic organization, many composers, among them Tchaikovsky, Dvořák, Mahler, and Sibelius, have used this organization partially—for example, the finale of a complex work might involve material from the opening movement, or other movements might be so linked. A superb example of complete cyclic organization follows:

EXAMPLE 87:   ERNEST BLOCH [b.1880]

String Quartet No. 2 (1945)

Copyright 1947 by Boosey and Hawkes Ltd. By permission of the copyright owner, Boosey and Hawkes.

This masterpiece is by one of the outstanding contemporary composers. We often hear of the Jewish spirit of some of Bloch's best music, but he has also created works expressive of the American spirit and still others which transcend nationality. This work belongs to the last type.

Swiss by birth and French by musical training, Bloch seems, here as elsewhere, to hark back to Franck's example with respect to cyclic organization. Bloch's musical style, however, is all his own. He creates highly intense, often religiously inspired, typically Romantic music. Technically his Romanticism is reflected in this *Quartet* by the recitative-like, expressive melody and the quasi-improvisational approach, both especially marked in the *First* and *Third Movements*. The flavor of religious chant and sometimes of primitive savagery are also Romantic characteristics.[13] Bloch's fundmental method of presenting his material consists of continuous expansion. A considerable number of motifs are combined in ever new ways, altered in rhythm and tempo, and given new expression.

Movement 1: Moderato

A long violin solo starts the work, like a solitary soul in anxious prayer. The initial motif:

is very important. Not only does it occur as a whole, but the four prominent tones marked by x, (*b*), will later reveal their significance as a separate motif. Gradually the other instruments are added. When they have all been introduced, the music comes to a quiet cadence; and a codetta, chiefly in octaves, closes this first section of a free ternary form.

A sharp rhythm, stressed by the conspicuous use of fifths or complete triads rather than single tones, creates a barbaric, somewhat threatening background against which the prayer-like melody of the first section soars to great intensity. Then this rhythm disappears, and a quieting third section, corresponding to the first, rounds off the *Movement*. The codetta vanishes in a murmur in the lowest range. With a reminiscence of the rhythmic chords and of (*a*) the prayer concludes, somewhat uncertainly.

Movement 2: Presto—Moderato—Meno mosso [14]

The Second Movement is a *Scherzo* with *two Trios*. Its first "theme" starts with the second main idea of the *Quartet*:

Other important motifs are rapidly added. Of these, one in parallel fifths is especially prominent:

---

[13] Cf. the discussions of neo-medievalism and barbarism on pp. 192, 193.
[14] Less moving, slower.

The furious mood of the first section ends with an impressive upward sweep. An *arpeggio* figuration surrounds the lyric second "theme," derived from the *Opening Movement*:

This "theme" includes the third cyclic motif of the work, (*e*). Motifs (*c*) and (*d*) then return as a coda to close the *Scherzo*.

In a slower tempo (*moderato*) and played with sordines (mutes) throughout, the *First Trio* enters and, after a tentative beginning, turns to a variant of *e*. In the ensuing repetition of the *Scherzo* (*c*) appears in a new guise:

Note that the triplet figure used in this version is clearly a new, shortened transformation of the same motif, which, in longer note values, also serves as a *basso ostinato* in the codetta.

The *Second Trio* (*meno mosso*) uses a variant of (*b*), both inverted:

and as originally presented:

Like the *First Trio*, it is slower than the *Scherzo*. When the *Scherzo* returns, it starts with (*d*); the lyric second section on *e* is shortened, but a powerful coda is added, consisting of an expansion of (*d*), broadened into full chords and enhanced by passage work.

Movement 3: Andante

The *Third Movement* is a song in three stanzas. Contrasting strongly with the harsh, barbaric tone of the *Scherzo*, which was only slightly subdued by the *two Trios*, it returns to the mood of the *First Movement*, but expresses greater assurance and a quiet lyricism.

In the manner of an introduction, chords, later shown to be related to (*d*), articulate a brooding rhythm, (*d¹*):

followed by a statement in the viola of a new version of (*c*):

There is a cadence, and then the lyric main theme appears:

It is derived from the first three tones of *e*, as heard in the *First Trio*, and thus also from the *Opening Movement*, a connection that is made amply clear in what follows. Before the second stanza of this song motifs from the *first two Movements* are reviewed. Before the third stanza there is another interlude, in which

is especially conspicuous, leading to an extended reminiscence of the opening section of the *First Movement*. Following the third stanza, a postlude once more reviews all ideas except *e¹*.

Movement 4: Allegro molto—Passacaglia: Deciso [15]—
  Fuga—Epilogue: Calmo [16]

A powerful prelude opens the *Finale*. Against an effective background
suggesting the guitar and mandolin, the violin intones (*a*) and another
variant of (*c*), (*c⁴*), and then repeats (*a*). After a conclusion in *unisono*
and a brief rest, the *Passacaglia* subject is stated in decisive octaves. It is
a combination of (*c*) and (*b¹*):

In *variations 1-5* the subject regularly alternates between the violin
and 'cello, as the rhythmic momentum slowly increases. The triplet
motion of *variation 5* provides a codetta for this section. In *variation 6*
violin and 'cello take the subject in canon (cf. p. 000, fn. 7). The 'cello
states the subject in *variations 7–9*, while the rhythmic momentum again
increases. In the last of these the beginning of (*a*) becomes important.
Once more, in *variation 10*, the subject rises to the first violin. In *variation 11* it falls to the second violin, while viola and 'cello play chromatic
passages. The excitement of the prelude then returns, and in *variation 12*,
as the viola intones the subject, the initial tempo is also recaptured.

The ensuing interlude is chiefly a powerful restatement of the prelude, though it starts with (*b¹*). The *Fugue* subject is identical with that
of the *Passacaglia*, except that all notes are equal in value: *c⁶*. It is accompanied by a lively counterpoint throughout. After the regular statement of *c⁶* in all four instruments and a brief episode, the inversion of
c⁶ opens the second section. The third presents the subject three times
in *stretto*. A powerful coda begins with repeated chords. Once more,
with a diminution (in time values) of the subject, the prelude is brought
back as (*a*), (*c⁴*), and (*a*) are again heard, together with the strumming
effects.

Suddenly there is a change: *e¹* initiates a glorious *Epilogue*, broadly
singing at first, but gradually becoming calm and yielding primacy again
to *c⁶*. The rhythmic motif (*d¹*) of the *Third Movement* is stealthily
thrown in, and finally, in the very last measure, we are greeted by (*a*).
The anxiety of the *First Movement*, the roughness of the *Scherzo*, the

---

[15] Decisive, firm.
[16] Calm.

lyricism of the *Slow Movement,* and the assurance of the *Finale* are all transfigured in this peaceful, blissful ending.

Analysis and Listening Experience

The marvel of the craftsmanship that we have analyzed—and further analysis would reveal additional relationships—is not in mere manipulation. All these relations are woven into an expressive texture through which they touch our emotions directly. Nevertheless, after we listen to complicated music for some time, our responsiveness, if merely emotional, gradually becomes blunted. For unless we can supplement our emotions with intellectual data, they will cease to respond, and we shall become bored. An analysis such as we have made can supply these data and thereby make possible the continued enjoyment of a work over long periods of time. Again it is suggested that this and other contemporary works be heard more often than older works, because their style is less easily comprehended at first hearing than that of Classic-Romantic compositions, with which we have been familiar from childhood.

Other Ensembles

This section has presented Classic-Romantic chamber music from a time near its inception to the present. Other types of chamber music, written during the same period or earlier have been discussed elsewhere.[17] But even within our narrowly defined field we have met only a few characteristic examples and a few composers. At least Beethoven, Dvořák, Bartók, and Hindemith must also be mentioned as pre-eminent in this field.[18]

There are many other chamber-music combinations of instruments and voices. The Classics loved the woodwind quintet, which recent composers are again cultivating after a period of neglect during the nineteenth century. Such a quintet consists of flute, oboe, clarinet, horn, and bassoon. In this century song cycles for voice

---

[17] The madrigal in Example 35, p. 66f; the prelude-and-fugue in Example 43, p. 103ff; the *sonata da camera* or chamber suite in Example 45, p. 108ff; harpsichord music in Examples 71, 75, pp. 236, 245f; songs in Examples 11-13, 24-25, 58, pp. 14f, 41f, 157ff; piano pieces in Examples 19, 26-28, 72, pp. 28f, 45ff, 238; and sonatas in Examples 79-81, p. 264ff.

[18] For additional names see the list of "Additional Recordings" in Appendix II, p. 437f.

and string quartet have come into favor. The repertory is further enriched by string quintets, usually including a second viola; string sextets, with an additional viola and 'cello; and string trios, usually consisting of a violin, a viola, and a 'cello. Some less standardized ensembles include wind instruments, guitar, double bass, harp, or percussion instruments.

Special mention should be made of the abundant ensemble literature for duo-pianists, that is, for two players at either one or two pianos. Throughout the Classic-Romantic era four-hand playing (at one piano) was the chief means of enjoying orchestral music at home. True, transcriptions of this kind lack the original flavor, yet they give the essence of the music. By playing them, the music lover may achieve far greater pleasure and become better acquainted with the orchestral literature than by merely listening, even if his own performance is inferior to that heard in concert, on records, or over the radio and television. In addition, there is a substantial literature originally composed for duo-pianists playing on either one or two pianos, as well as some for three and for four players.

Summary: Chamber Music and Orchestral Music

The essential characteristic of a chamber-music ensemble is that each instrument plays an individualized part. Chamber music thus differs from orchestral music, for the latter employs groups or choirs of stringed, woodwind, and brass instruments, which often combine to play the same parts, though the music given to the wind instruments is somewhat more individualized. We speak of orchestral effects in chamber music when, as in Brahms's *Piano Quartet*, the strings as a choir oppose the piano. Whereas orchestral music depends to a great extent on such effects of fullness, chamber music on the whole tends to give each instrument an individual rôle.

In chamber music the composer does not rely on massed power, many colors, and the great variety of shadings possible in an orchestra. His tools are refined craftsmanship, delicate balance, and rich musical texture rather than instrumental fullness. This is why it is often said that one may recognize the master composer especially by his chamber music. It may be added that the well-trained listener likewise finds the greatest challenge and some of his finest enjoyment in listening to chamber music, for here he experiences music in its essence, divested of the peripheral effects, which in orchestral music are so impressive.

Organic Aspects

A few words should be said about the organic aspect of the works discussed. Evidently there is no fixed formula here. The spiritual unity of a work may be produced with or without the aid of cyclic devices. Movements may have any structure, from potpourri, fugue, and variations to song-forms, binary, *alternativo,* rondo, sonatina-, and sonata-form. The tempo sequence, rather standardized in Classic works, is in later compositions quite free. Tonal unity, also, is in recent works not thought to be as necessary as it was during the Classic era. In Bloch's *Quartet* there are many passages in which it is hard to hear any particular tone as the tonal center, yet this is no detriment to the music.

Let us repeat: The chief factor in organic unity is the symbolization of a series of emotions that can be understood as an ordered sequence rather than as an haphazard collection. Thus, among the works analyzed in this section, Haydn's and Brahms's are optimistic and full of zest. Of the two, Haydn's is more restrained and genial, as classicist music would be, whereas Brahms's is more expansive, warm, and impetuous in typical Romantic fashion. Mozart's *Quintet* reflects serenity and a quiet, sunny unearthiness. Lyric introspection, serene and rarely clouded, is the prevailing quality of Schubert's *Quartet*. The Mozartian detachment is gone, as is Haydn's untroubled enjoyment of life. As a Romantic, Schubert turns more toward the inner self, but without pessimism. In the deeply romantic music of Bloch we find progressive preoccupation with self, and the recognition of suffering. The ever-present yearning to transcend the doubts, the sorrows, and the earthbound character of human destiny lend coherence to his work. Thus the five works we have studied in this section, however different in outlook and style, are all organically unified by their common effort to communicate an emotional attitude.

CONCEPTS AND TOPICS DISCUSSED IN THIS SECTION

X ORCHESTRAL MUSIC

SECTION C

THE CONCERTO

From Sonata to Concerto

During the Baroque era the well-to-do adopted from the aristocracy and the higher clergy the practice of employing chamber music to entertain their guests and friends after dinner. When, after the end of the devastating Thirty Years' War (1648), more peaceful conditions prevailed, and the riches of the new colonial empires began to affect Europe, the magnificence of the entertainments grew. Larger dinner parties required larger ensembles for their entertainment.

In order to satisfy the demand a new type of ensemble was developed from that of the *sonata da camera* and *da chiesa*. The implied harmonies of the figured bass, formerly played by the harpsichord or organ reinforced by a 'cello or bassoon, were now set for an orchestral group of stringed instruments, though the keyboard instrument was retained and continued to be used to improvise chords. Moreover, this orchestra might alternate with the two solo violins rather than merely support them. In solo pas-

[315]

sages of the violins a 'cello was added to provide a bass. This orchestral sonata became known as the CONCERTO GROSSO.

The term is Italian. In that language during the seventeenth century "concerto" meant collaboration and also competition of various elements. It implied the employment of various groups, whether of voices and instruments or of instruments of diverse tone colors. Thus *concerto grosso* came to mean a large group, or orchestra, as opposed to a small group, the solo ensemble or CONCERTINO. The term *concerto grosso* was also used as the title of works that employed two such opposing groups. Another term for the orchestra in these works was RIPIENO (Italian—replenishing or filling-in, i.e. accompanying group).

The Concerto Grosso and Its Composers

The *concerto grosso* was one of three related types of orchestral music that emerged in the latter part of the seventeenth century. The other two were sonatas for orchestra alone, either without or with only a few solo passages, and works in which a single instrument opposed the orchestra. These types were known respectively as CONCERTO (today "orchestral concerto") and as SOLO CONCERTO. The first of these led to the *sinfonia* and thence to the symphony; the other became the leading type of concerto in the Classic-Romantic era.

In the Baroque the most favored type of concerto was the *concerto grosso*. The *concertino* and the *ripieno* provided between them strong contrasts of volume, just as the paintings of the period provided contrasts among large areas of color; and the lush brilliance of the string ensemble paralleled the warm, full colors of Baroque paintings. When large groups of strings were assembled for special outdoor performances, the bass was reinforced by bassoons and the violins by oboes. Indoors the *concerto grosso* required only two instruments to each part, and the soloists would also join in the *ripieno* when not playing solos.

One movement from such a work has already been studied: Corelli's *Pastorale* (p. 29). Corelli was virtually the creator of the *concerto grosso* about 1680. All the great eighteenth-century violinists took it up and developed it. The most famous composers of *concerti grossi* were Vivaldi in Italy, Bach in Germany, and Handel in England.[1]

Handel composed many *concerti grossi,* some of which are known as *Organ Concertos* and *Oboe Concertos.* The following example is one of a set of *Twelve Grand Concertos,* all characterized by a broad sweep and brilliance that suited their function as entr'actes in the performances of the master's oratorios. Handel's creative power and facility are attested to by the fact that all twelve were written within one month, incredible as this may seem.

EXAMPLE 88:   GEORGE FREDERICK HANDEL [1685–1759]

Concerto Grosso No. 9, in F Major (1739)

Movement 1: Largo

The slow *Opening Movement* is a brief introduction, completely chordal and without a melodic subject.

Movement 2: Allegro

The fiery *Second Movement* has two sections which alternate three times in rondo form: *A-B-A-B-A-B-A.* The *ritornello, A,* is for the *ripieno,* but provides brief, attractive echo effects for the *concertino.* It presents two ideas, one march-like:

the other cascading in leaps and runs:

---

[1] See Appendix I, p. 400f, for remarks on the evolution of the *concerto grosso.*

The episode, *B,* is a virtuoso figuration for the first solo violin:

Its last repetition, however, is played by the orchestra; hence the concluding *ritornello* is shortened, limited to *a.*

Movement 3: Larghetto

A lovely aria in *A-B-B* form and in the relative Minor of the main key follows:

In the first portion whole phrases are exchanged between *ripieno* and *concertino,* whereas the interchange of brief snatches marks *B,* which is melodically derived from *A.* The *Movement* ends as if something more were to come—with what is called a HALF CADENCE. Such a connection of two movements is quite frequent in the Baroque era.

Movement 4: Allegro

The *Fourth Movement* is for orchestra alone. Brilliant and fast, it starts as a fugue in three parts:

Punctuated by a rest, the subject falls into two distinct elements, which after the regular exposition are separately expanded with much spirit.

Movement 5: Minuet

Handel then adds two dances to this complete *sonata da chiesa*. The *Minuet*, for *ripieno* only:

is a little unusual; the first two periods of the ‖: *a* :‖: *b*-*c*:‖ structure are in the tonic Minor of the main key, which surprisingly returns in the last period.

Movement 6: Gigue

In the *Gigue* each of the two repeated sections opens with a brief passage for the two solo violins:

Otherwise the *Gigue*, too, is orchestral.

Here, as in Telemann's *Trio Sonata* (p. 264f), we can hardly speak of organic unity. The use of *F* Major and its relative and tonic Minors unites *all Movements;* but otherwise contrast—in tempo, mode, meter, instrumentation, and texture—is the only principle of their sequence:

Movements:	I	II	III	IV	V	VI
tempo (s = slow, f = fast):	s	f	s	f	s	f
mode and key:	F	F	d	F	f	F
meter:	3/4	4/4	6/8	4/4	3/8	12/8
medium (r = *ripieno*, c = *concertino*):	r	c+r	c+r	r	r	c+r
texture (h = homophonic, p = polyphonic):	h	h	h	p	h	p

There is, to be sure, a pervasive spirit of optimism and grandeur in this music, but these are general marks of the style. Handel here abstains from representing rage, heroics, ridicule, or lamentation—the various moods of opera so familiar to him. In Baroque instrumental music the expression of violent emotions was not favored, nor would it have suited the occasions for which Handel intended these *Concertos*.

Early Solo Concerto

In the programs of our time the solo concerto is much more conspicuous than the *concerto grosso*. Shortly before 1700 the first concertos for one violin and orchestra were composed, soon followed by concertos for 'cello and for other solo instruments. Giuseppe Torelli (1658–1709) was among the first to turn to the violin concerto. He adopted the new three-movement plan with the standard tempo sequence fast–slow–fast, which was coming into vogue with Alessandro Scarlatti's *sinfonia* (cf. p. 252). Almost all solo concertos thereafter kept this arrangement.

Vivaldi was the most brilliant of early concerto composers. His concertos are in part for stringed instruments and in part for woodwinds, especially the oboe. The first composer of keyboard concertos was Bach, whose harpsichord concertos are mostly adaptations of string concertos by Vivaldi and other Italian violinists. Handel followed with organ concertos, one of which may also be played as a harp concerto; other composers of the period wrote concertos for trumpet. To these, Rococo composers added concertos for clarinet, for horn, and for bassoon as well as for instruments now obsolete.

The problem in such works is to invent good music which permits the soloist to demonstrate his skill, but with variety enough to maintain the interest of the audience. The most successful solo instruments are therefore the most flexible: the violin, the 'cello, and the piano. Nineteenth-century composers wrote their concertos almost exclusively for these instruments.

The Classic Concerto

Mozart, virtually the first composer of piano concertos, was both the most prolific and the greatest composer in this medium. His concertos, of course, followed Classic rather than Baroque concepts in form and style. The string orchestra was succeeded by a symphonic orchestra, containing, in addition to the strings, timpani and a maximum of two instruments in each of the following categories: flute, oboe, clarinet, bassoon, horn, and trumpet. The wind instruments were treated either soloistically or as a choir opposing the string choir. In the concerto the piano represented a third choir, which might either contrast or blend with the orchestral groups.

The first movement of a Classic concerto has a modified sonata-form, which we may call CONCERTO-FORM. Whereas in a Classic sonata or string quartet the exposition of the sonata-form is repeated, here the orchestra or TUTTI (Italian—all)—the terms *ripieno* and *concerto grosso* are not applied to Classic works—first discloses some of the material (*tutti* exposition), and thereafter the soloist enters to exhibit all or most of it (solo exposition). The development section and recapitulation are about equally shared by orchestra and solo instrument, except for the cadenza.

In earlier concertos and in *concerti grossi* the soloists were expected to improvise, especially in slow movements, to give flesh and blood to the mere skeleton contained in the score. The composer of Classic concertos, on the other hand, wrote everything out meticulously, but set aside definite places for cadenzas without accompaniment by the orchestra. The elaborate main cadenza occurs near the end of the first movement; others may or may not be provided for in the other movements. In these cadenzas the soloist showed his ability not only as instrumentalist but also as composer, for he was expected to play his own expansion of the themes of the movement. Today most virtuosi prefer to play cadenzas written by others, either the composer or former executants. During the past hundred or more years improvisation in art music has been largely neglected, except by certain organists. It still lives in the jazz, however, and may be revived in art music at some future time.

Until Mozart, the first movement of a concerto was treated as the most important section. Its length was usually equal to, or even greater than, that of the other two movements combined. Moreover, no special forms emerged for any but the first movement. With the following work by Mozart a second design took a place alongside the first: The first and last movements are of similar length and import, though in this work the *Finale* is in variation form and therefore not equally dramatic.

EXAMPLE 89:   WOLFGANG AMADEUS MOZART [1756–91]

Piano Concerto in C Minor, No. 20 (or No. 24 [2]), K.491 (1786)

This is the most ambitious of Mozart's *Concertos,* both in length and in fullness of orchestration, and perhaps the greatest. It is one of the two out of his twenty-three *Piano Concertos,* which are in minor keys. As always with the Classics, the Minor indicates great seriousness, drama, perhaps tragedy. Mozart, who was just finishing his *The Marriage of Figaro,* the comic opera we have already discussed, evidently expressed in this *Concerto* his more sombre emotions. Such outstanding works as this probably have suggested the possible affinity between minor mode and sombre mood. This notion, though neither natural nor universal (cf. the *Second Movement* of Haydn's *Quartet,* p. 287f), nevertheless has been widely accepted.

Movement 1: Allegro

Of the six main ideas of the *Opening Movement, a* and *b* constitute the first theme, *c* and *d* the second, and *e* and *f* the third, the latter two themes providing lyric relief for the dramatic first:

Theme 1

---

[2] Only recently has it been discovered that Mozart's four earliest *Piano Concertos* are adaptations from music that others had composed for the piano alone. They are works of his apprenticeship and are no longer counted among his *Concertos.*

Theme 2

Theme 3

The *tutti* exposition states only part of the first theme and the third: *a-a-e-a-f.* The solo exposition starts with a new idea, *b,* as is quite frequent in Classic concertos; *a, c, a¹,* a long solo passage deriving virtuoso figurations from *a,* and *d* follow, but the third theme is omitted and instead there appears, after another developmental passage based on *a,* a new, smoothly flowing, lyric idea:

Whereas the *tutti* exposition remained entirely in the key of C Minor, the second theme (in the solo exposition), *g,* and part of the development section are, according to the principles of sonata-form, set forth in the relative Major, namely E-flat. In this key the *tutti,* as is usual, starts the development section playing *a,* followed by *b* on the piano and by a thorough expansion of *a,* which modulates vigorously until it reaches the climactic dominant. All the while, much scope is given to brilliant passage playing on the piano.

The recapitulation, starting, again as usual, with a brief *tutti*, reviews all three themes: *a-d-c-a¹-e-a*. Reaching a climax, the music then breaks off on a chord that creates an air of expectancy,[3] and gives the soloist an opportunity for his cadenza. Afterwards the third theme is resumed with *f*, and a short coda closes the *Movement*.

The great dramatic tension we feel through most of the *Movement* is beautifully balanced by the lyricism of the second theme. The warmth of parts of the development section, especially where the motifs of the first theme appear in Major, brightens the mood and eases the tension. And again, at the end, when the *arpeggios* of the piano slowly descend above a pedal point, the brief coda has the effect of quieting disturbed waters.

Movement 2: Larghetto

A perfectly delightful, lyric rondo follows, whose limpid quality is reminiscent of the *Clarinet Quintet* (cf. p. 291ff). It takes up both mode and mood of the second theme of the *First Movement*. Quite consistently the device of opposing *tutti* and solo in complete periods is charmingly employed.

This is the form of the *Movement*:

        A — B — A — C — A — coda.
keys: E♭   c   E♭   A♭   E♭

But Mozart is lavish: Both *A* and *B* have three-part form, and the coda also contains two ideas. However, in order to shorten the *Movement*, the second *A* presents only the first period of the theme, and the last *A* the other three. Just a faint reminder of the agitation of the *First Movement* emerges in the first episode—the only portion that returns to C Minor. *A, B,* and *C* begin as follows:

---

[3] For an explanation of this chord see Appendix I, p. 385.

Movement 3: Allegretto

In this work Mozart did not follow the custom of casting the finale in the tonic Major of the first movement. *C* Major appears only once, in *variation 6;* and in *variation 4* the A-flat Major of the second episode of the *Second Movement* is recalled. Otherwise *C* Minor is retained throughout. There is much chromaticism, especially in *variations 1, 5,* and *8,* and in the coda; yet the *Movement* is neither perturbed nor given to dramatic contrasts. It rather maintains a grave dignity that at times relaxes into a smile.

Each period of the theme, which is in two-part form, is repeated:

This repetitive design is continued through the first *six variations.* In *variation 1* it is indicated, as in the theme, by repetition signs, but in *variations 2-6* sheer repetition is replaced by similar modification of either period, thus actually turning these five *variations* into ten. Most of the *variations* are simple and figural; *variations 2, 3, 4,* and *6* also employ the opposition of *tutti* and solo between periods and their repetitions. Nevertheless, *variation 5,* for piano only, presents the first and third periods in form of chromatic polyphonic pieces, and *variation 6,* also somewhat contrapuntal, introduces a new melody.

Variation 7 is like a restatement of the theme. It lacks repetitions and ends in a little bridge. This breaks off to afford another opportunity for a cadenza—a short one to be sure. Then the meter changes, and the tempo becomes twice as fast in *variation 8,* which also omits the repeats. A rousing coda, expanding the motifs into a new, repeated period, brilliantly concludes the *Concerto.*

There are in this work no melodic reminiscences that relate the *Movements* to each other. Two unifying elements are nevertheless present: tonality and the sequence of moods. The former furnishes a particularly strong bond. The sequence of keys throughout the work is: I: *c—Eb—c;* II: *Eb—c—Eb—Ab—Eb;* III: *c—Ab—c—C—c.* This key sequence seems to parallel the sequence of moods: an alternation of dramatic tension (*c*) and lyricism (*Eb*), achieving a measure of cheerfulness (*Ab* and especially *C*) within great seriousness.[4]

Cyclic Organization in Concertos

On the whole, the superb *Concertos* of Beethoven were written within the established framework. In his later concertos, however, the master eliminated the free cadenzas and instead composed passages for the soloist only. He also moved closer to the next step in the evolution of the concerto: greater unity. We saw that the suite of disparate pieces yielded precedence to the program suite, which, in turn, was a root of the symphonic poem. Similarly the sonata became more cyclic in organization, and the definite conclusion of each movement was often dropped for a smooth transition into the next (see Beethoven's *Sonata Appassionata*, p. 268ff). The concerto followed the same trend.

The first to write a complete concerto "in one movement" was the eminent violinist, Ludwig Spohr (1784–1859), and Carl Maria Weber (1786–1826) soon followed. These concertos and many of their successors were conceived in the conventional three or four movements,[5] but were played without break. Liszt went one step further: Theme transformation, applied to such works, led him to write the opening and final movements of such a concerto as the exposition and recapitulation of a gigantic sonata-form, the middle movements or parts of the finale representing the development section. Thus a unified, far-flung plan was created by wedding the sonata or concerto to the sonata-form. Smaller unified concerto numbers also were written profusely, of which Saint-Saëns's *Introduction and Rondo Capriccioso* (p. 238f) is a fine example.

Still another plan was developed to give more evident unity to large works of the concerto type: the variation form. Some con-

---

[4] See Appendix I, p. 386f, for an explanation of "key symbolism."

[5] Whereas symphonies and chamber music are arranged mostly in four movements, sonatas and concertos have preferred a three-movement pattern, without the minuet or scherzo.

certos in variation form, for instance the earliest one, Liszt's *Toten-tanz* (Dance of Death), are not organized in movements, but are genuine variation sets, related to the concerto only by the fact that they provide ample opportunity for a soloist to show his virtuosity against an orchestral background. On the other hand, an excellent example of a concerto in several connected movements, but conceived in variation form throughout, is found in César Franck's *Symphonic Variations.*

The Symphonic Concerto

By combining concerto structure and variation form, Franck achieved an unusual degree of thematic unity as well as musical continuity. In addition to presenting perfect cyclic organization, this work exemplifies the trend toward the "symphonic concerto," which assumed importance in the latter part of the Romantic era. In a symphonic concerto the solo instrument and the orchestra are treated as a unified medium rather than as two opposed media. In such a work the soloist often accompanies either the orchestra or solo passages by its various instruments. He merges in the ensemble, shunning technical display for its own sake. Therefore, neither cadenzas nor *tutti* expositions have a place in symphonic concertos. This trend led to the inclusion of the piano in orchestral works other than concertos, an innovation that Franck pioneered in one of his *Symphonic Poems* a year before he wrote this work.[6]

EXAMPLE 90: CÉSAR FRANCK [1822–90]

Variations Symphoniques (1885)

The *Symphonic Variations* are characteristic of Franck's deeply romantic music. The harmonic beauty, the pervasive air of mystery and foreboding of the beginning, as well as the brooding of the slow middle portion are typical moods. Conversely, romanticism has its brighter moments as attested to by the completely gay *Finale*, which gives a buoyant ending to the work.

This is a set of DOUBLE VARIATIONS, i.e. of variations on two themes. Many of the *variations* are free and combine ingredients of both themes. Nevertheless, the themes are kept separate, though not in regular alternation.

---

[6] For an earlier instance of the use of a piano in the orchestra, for a special effect only, see Berlioz's *Fantastic Symphony*, p. 358.

Movement 1: Poco Allegro [7]

At the very beginning Franck joins the two main motifs in one period, (*a*) rising and *staccato*, and (*b*) falling and *legato*:

There are several echo-like exchanges between the strings with (*a*) and the piano with (*b*) before a climax is attained, marking the end of this prelude. Then theme I, derived from (*a*), is partially stated:

and the piano alone, surging, passionate, quite powerful, introduces theme II, derived from (*b*):

The prelude returns and with it the echoing exchanges; after it reaches another climax, it subsides beautifully in several phrases of the piano. In this fashion Franck achieves a well rounded, functional *First Movement* in ternary form.

---

[7] Somewhat fast.

Movement 2: Allegretto quasi Andante

The *Second Movement* is a scherzo, developed from *a* (theme I). A brief prelude, featuring expressive 'cello phrases, prefaces *variation 1*, for piano alone. This is the first complete statement of theme I, in which the *legato* of (*b*) is combined with the melody of *a*.

Echoing exchanges among strings, piano, and woodwinds mark *variation 2*.

In *variation 3* the strings sing the theme lyrically, while the piano adds a chordal embroidery.

In *variation 4*, the piano, almost entirely by itself, overlays the theme with a delicate web of figurations, increasing in volume until the end.

In the brilliant *variation 5* the original *staccato* returns in an interchange between the full orchestra and the piano. The *variation* is spun out to some length. With repetitions of the first phrase of *a* it abates and leads to a slow section.

Movement 3: Molto più lento [8]

The *Slow Movement* consists of only *two variations*. A most delicate piano figuration runs through the first—*variation 6* of *a*. The 'cellos sing the theme in *legato;* later the woodwinds throw in some soft phrases also.

The other is *variation 1* of *b* (theme II). It is scored only for strings with sordines. The 'cellos once more take the lead against chords of the higher strings, and the piano adds a gossamer of *arpeggios*. After some expansion a rippling passage on the piano reaches a trill—the start of the stirring *Finale*.

Movement 4: Allegro non troppo [9] ·

Here the *staccato* of (*a*) is applied to *b*, which appears for the first time in Major in this *variation—variation 2* of *b*. The low strings present this exhilarating idea:

which functions as the "first theme" of the quasi-sonata-form *Finale*, as fast piano chords furnish the accompaniment.

Variation 3 of *b* gives the piano the lead in firm octaves.

---

[8] Much slower.
[9] Not too fast.

These are dissolved into figuration in *variation 4*. At the climax the full orchestra briefly plays b^1.

The piano returns with full chords in a new, lyric version of *a, variation 7*, while the woodwinds play lightly about it. This *variation* represents the "second theme" of the *Finale:*

The modulatory "development section" begins with a bridge, which suddenly announces b^1 again softly in the basses and in a rapid *crescendo* leads to a very lyric version of *b* in the piano—*variation 5*.

With b^1 played by the flutes and later by the violins against glittering piano passages, the recapitulation of the *Finale* begins—*variation 6* of *b*, corresponding to *variation 2* in the "exposition," the "first theme."

This is followed by *variation 7* of *b*, corresponding to *variation 4*.

Then the figurations of the piano give way to the chords of *variation 8* of *a*, corresponding to *variation 7*, the "second theme." A short, brilliant coda with b^1 imitated between piano and orchestra gives this beautiful work a rousing conclusion.

Briefly then, this is the outline:

$$\begin{array}{cccc}
& I & & \\
\text{prelude} - \text{th. I} - \text{th. II} - \text{postlude} & & \\
(a)-(b) \quad a \quad\quad b \quad\quad (a)-(b) & &
\end{array}$$

I   —   II —   III   —
prelude – th. I – th. II – postlude   var. 1-5   var. 6 – var. 1
$(a)-(b)$ a b $(a)-(b)$ a a b

IV

exposition   —   devel. sec.   —   recapitulation   —   coda
var. 2-4 — var. 7   br. — var. 5   var. 6-7 — var. 8
b^1 a^1 b^1 b b^1 a^1 b^1

Classicist Concertos by Romantics

Not all concertos of the later Romantics were composed in this manner. Many of the best concertos, such as those by Brahms and Tchaikovsky, followed the arrangement of the Classics—three or sometimes four distinct movements. They exhibit romanticism in other ways, as is true of the following, probably the best 'cello concerto of all:

EXAMPLE 91: ANTONIN DVOŘÁK [1841–1904]

'Cello Concerto in B Minor, op. 104 (1895)

Dvořák, one of the greatest Czech composers, was nationalistic in some of his works, using folk dances and the flavor of the folk music of his native country; in others he expressed the spirit of America, where he lived from 1892 to 1895. This work belongs to a third group, in which he transcended nationality and continued Classic traditions both in form and in the use of a purely musical concept. At the same time this work reveals Dvořák as a Romantic and lyricist. Like Schubert, he sings on and dwells on the wealth of his melodies.

Movement 1: Allegro

An orchestral exposition opens the work. In a low register the clarinets announce the exciting main theme:

New motifs are added before the *tutti* restates it. Once more new material appears, and then the clarinets close with the main idea. The lyric second theme:

is played by the horn, then by the clarinet, and is followed by a short closing group.

The solo exposition is similar to the *tutti* exposition, but gives to the 'cello many new variants, among them:

There is also a completely new closing theme, much longer than before. It starts with a woodwind motif:

to which the 'cello adds figurations. Eventually the soloist takes the lead; the excitement grows, and *a*, brilliantly set forth by the *tutti* in Major, closes the exposition with the first climax to this point.

A brief orchestral expansion gives way to a new, lyric version of *a* in the 'cello. Still another melody derived from *a* is heard in the woodwinds against brilliant passages of the 'cello. With increasing animation the figures of the 'cello become double stops, and an octave run leads to the recapitulation. Here the first theme is omitted and the recapitulation begins with a triumphant version of *b*, repeated more lyrically by the 'cello. As in the solo exposition, the full third theme follows and builds to a climax: the forceful restatement of *a*. There is no place here for a cadenza.

Movement 2: *Adagio ma non troppo*

Fullness of life, vigor, and joyful singing are perhaps the best words with which to describe the effect of this beautiful *First Movement*. The mood of the *Second* is blissful contemplation. Again the clarinet intones the first theme:

followed by the 'cello. It also ushers in its second period, which the 'cello spins out to some length, ending with a figure from the closing theme of the *First Movement*:

The second section of the *A-B-B-A* structure starts with a firm *tutti* phrase, which is continued by a singing melody in the 'cello, repeated by flute and oboe:

With *e* the 'cello sets the stage for the restatement of the *B*-section. In the same way it thereafter reintroduces *A*. Now the horns lend their romantic tones to *d,* followed by a cadenza in double stops for the solo instrument. As at first, the clarinets start the second portion of *A,* followed by the 'cello. A long trill makes the transition to the coda: a lyric reminiscence of the *tutti* phrase of *f.* The end comes in a series of HAR-MONICS on the 'cello—delicate high tones produced on stringed instruments by touching the strings lightly rather than firmly pressing them against the fingerboard.

Movement 3: Allegro moderato

The excitement of the *Opening Movement* is recaptured in the *Finale.* Repeated tones of the basses, horn calls, and the full orchestra introduce the first theme:

played by the 'cello and repeated by the violins. Another melody by the 'cello takes its rhythm from a^1. Once more *g* is heard in flutes and oboes, repeated by the violins, and then two more interrelated ideas:

and

are announced by the *tutti* and by the 'cello respectively.

All these riches constitute the *ritornello* of an *A-B-A-C-A* rondo. Once more the clarinet is given prominence in the *B*-section, which consists of a quiet duet between the clarinet and the 'cello:

When the beginning of the duet is repeated, the 'cello emerges with a long, cadenza-like passage in *arpeggios,* runs, and trills, which reintroduces A in reverse: *h, tutti–i,* 'cello–*g,* 'cello and then *tutti.*

Once more the excitement subsides to make room for a beautiful, lyric strain on the 'cello, representing *C:*

It is expanded and then repeated by the strings. Without interruption the *ritornello* follows, represented by *g* only, in a brilliant *tutti* continued by the 'cello. A chorale-like phrase in the brass initiates the coda. Shortly the main theme of the *First Movement, a,* reappears. Another chorale phrase in the brass, and some *tutti* measures on *a* emphasize once more the cyclic conclusion to this rich work.

The vocal quality of the tunes, the pervading lyricism and joyful excitement, as well as melodic relationships unify this *Concerto.* In addition, Dvořák obtains unity in tone color by his frequent conspicuous employment of the woodwinds, the horns, and the violins. The dark accents of trombones and low strings as well as the sharp tones of the trumpets are important only in *tutti* passages. This orchestration gives the music a clean, colorful sound. All these factors contribute to the Romantic character of this work.

The Orchestral Concerto

The next example, Bartók's *Concerto for Orchestra,* is a fine, spirited example of modern orchestral resources, and at the same time an interesting revival of the Baroque concerto. This masterly work, written within three weeks, gives opportunities for solo performance to each orchestral group as well as to individual instruments. It thus harks back, as its name indicates, to the orchestral concerto of the seventeenth century.

EXAMPLE 92: BÉLA BARTÓK [1881–1945]

Concerto for Orchestra (1943)

The work abounds in folk-like melodies and rhythms. It is, on the whole, gay, especially so in its *Second* and *Fourth Movements,* and also in the *Finale,* which is humorous in part. However, this lightness does not detract from Bartók's concentrated craftsmanship.

Movement 1: Andante non troppo—Allegro vivace

The *Introduction* sets forth the main materials of the entire *Concerto.* The very beginning:

announces the fourth as the most important interval, both melodically and as the building material of chords, while (*a*) is a main motif. Mysterious string *tremolos* and flute runs answer this phrase. Then from soft trumpets comes a tune in the folksong manner:

This the strings vary, the tempo quickening and the volume increasing, as we approach the *Allegro.*

Out of the inverted (*a*) grows the first theme of the *First Movement:*

Several phrases of folksong character ensue, until *a*, played in retrograde motion by the trombones:

concludes this theme. A rocking woodwind motif:

is the mainstay of the lyric second theme of the sonata-form.

After a calm close the development section begins with a brilliant expansion of *a¹*. A solo clarinet then plays a quiet variant of it. The high point is a fugue on *a²* for the brass section—a typical *concertino* passage. A flourish of *a¹* closes this exciting portion. In the recapitulation the order of the themes is reversed. In this way the second theme provides lyric contrast for the development section, whereas the final resumption of the first theme provides a lusty conclusion.

Movement 2: *Gioco delle coppie:* [10] *Allegretto scherzando*

The *Second Movement* gives clear expression and a humorous twist to the concerto idea. Besides, it offers an opportunity for studying the effect of the various instruments and intervals. Its over-all ternary plan is as simple as it is clever and amusing:

After an introduction by a solitary side drum there is an opening duet of bassoons in parallel sixths:

This is followed by a charming oboe duet in thirds:

After a brief interruption by *a* in the low strings, two clarinets are heard in parallel sevenths:

They, in turn, are succeeded by two flutes playing in parallel fifths:

Another brief interlude, and two muted trumpets present a comical march in parallel seconds, which is related to *b:*

---

[10] Joke of pairs (of instruments).

These duets are all reviewed in the same order, but enhanced by additional fun, after a short chorale in the brasses:

which is punctuated by the side drum. The *Movement* closes as it began, with the sounds of the side drum.

Movement 3: Elegia: Andante non troppo

The *Elegy* has a haunting prelude, derived from *a*, whose eerie quality is intensified by the sounds of an oboe. After a piccolo phrase concludes this prelude, the main portion begins with the strings playing *b;* a trumpet, supported by full chords of the orchestra, adds a sharp rhythmic motif: ♪♩. ♪♩. . Combined and varied, this is expanded into a long passage, which rises to a climax. The coda recalls the prelude and closes to the quiet strains of (*a*). Finally only the piccolo is heard.

Movement 4: Intermezzo Interrotto: [11] Allegretto

A beautiful little tune, with the characteristic, irregular shifts in meter of Balkan folksongs, constitutes the main idea of the *Fourth Movement:*

The oboe initiates and ends this serenader's tune; the other woodwinds are heard in the middle portion. A second strain follows in the violins—more firmly lyrical, as if the serenader had taken courage:

---

[11] Interrupted Serenade.

Yet the plaintive oboe tune returns. And this is not all, for suddenly we hear a rather common street tune:

Our serenader has been interrupted by an outsider. Consternation seems to grip him. But the street tune rises to even higher, almost boisterous intensity. The two seem to come to blows, and Bartók leaves no doubt who wins: The lyric tune *k* returns, and *j,* including a little cadenza for the flute, closes this delightful *Intermezzo.*

Movement 5: Presto

Great vigor marks the sonata-form *Finale.* The horns announce a motif:

and then a long string toccata gets underway, ending in a polka motif:

(cf. Example 18, p. 27f). The toccata resumes and, after another inter-ruption by the polka motif, reaches a fine peak. Started by the bassoon, a little FUGATO, or fugal passage, on (*m*) marks the beginning of a quiet bridge. With a sudden harmonic shift we are once more propelled into swirling passage work. From this the trumpet rises with a jazzy, bluster-ing second theme:

which is tossed back and forth among several trumpets and horns until the end of the exposition.

The development section starts with an introductory passage for the harp, reminiscent of (a^1). Then the string section, functioning as a *concertino*, plays a *fugato* on *n*. The woodwinds take the lead in the last portion of the development section and establish relations to a^2.

There is a complete ending before the recapitulation starts. First the toccata portion of the first theme with the polka motif is reviewed. After a quiet bridge the tempo quickens again, and bassoons and clarinets intone (*m*). A very effective passage follows, as the second theme appears to be reconstructed from its elements; a great *crescendo* leads to its enunciation by the entire brass section against the toccata background. The work ends with a short, rushing coda, giving the impression of joyful freedom.

Human Circumstances and Artistic Expression

This impressive work deserves many hearings. As we have said before, despite all its jesting it is a serious, carefully considered work, clear in formulation and content, and abounding in fresh musical ideas. It demonstrates the important fact that artists do not always reflect the physical or social events that most concern them at the time of creation. Bartók, kindly, honest, and upright, wrote this work in exile from his beloved native Hungary. He genuinely suffered from this circumstance and from the knowledge of the oppression that was the fate of his country at the time. His health was also failing and he was harassed by financial troubles due to his lack of recognition, which, as often happens, ironically changed to adulation immediately after his death. Nevertheless he had the moral stamina to rally his spirits and to symbolize moods quite contrary to his personal feelings of the moment. The *Elegy* is the only place where a shadow of regret or sadness falls across the *Concerto for Orchestra*.

Answers to the Concerto Problem

As has been indicated, the problem of concerto writing is to secure a good balance between the solo instruments and the orchestra. In almost all cases the need for giving the soloists the most conspicuous position impels the composer to restrain the orchestra whenever it is used for accompaniment. Some Romantic composers tried to avoid this restraint by working toward an integration of the two opposing elements. The result was the "symphonic concerto." But symphonic concertos are feasible only when the solo instrument is the piano, because it can compete with the volume of the orchestra. Even in the most skillfully contrived violin or 'cello concerto the orchestra must be subdued during solo passages. The other solution of the problem is indicated by Bartók's *Concerto:* a return either to the orchestral concerto of the Baroque or to the *concerto grosso;* for an ensemble of instruments may, like the piano, hold its own against the *tutti.*

Summary

The concerto has filled a significant place in the literature of music. The urge to exhibit virtuosity, which we first discussed in Part I, Section G, here finds its best expression in instrumental music. In its provision for solo performance against an orchestra the concerto symbolizes the human drive for self-assertion and self-expression even against opposition.

This is perhaps the key to its popularity. The various trends in concerto composition, may therefore be held to reflect various human situations: the *concerto grosso,* a group of individuals separate from, but in harmony with, society at large; the solo concerto, an individual-facing society; and finally the orchestral and the symphonic concerto, groups or single individuals closely identified or integrated with society. On the other hand, the virtuoso concerto of the Romantic era, which minimized the rôle of the orchestra and emphasized that of the soloist, may reflect the exalted position accorded to heroes and geniuses in certain Romantic circles, coupled with a disdain for the masses of people.

CONCEPTS AND TOPICS DISCUSSED IN THIS SECTION

SECTION D

THE SYMPHONY

Symphony: Acme of Instrumental Music

The symphony arose concurrently with the other types of music used in the Classic era: the Classic sonata, the string quartet, the Classic concerto, and the sonata-form overture. In it music lovers have come to see the acme of instrumental music. The other types may offer music as great as or perhaps greater than symphonies offer, but none has as wide an appeal to concert audiences.

The primacy of the symphony is due, in part at least, to the inherent limitations of the other types of Classic music. Chamber music is originally meant for participating performers rather than for listeners. It is therefore concentrated and subtle, and lacks the appeal of virtuosity as well as of orchestral tone color and dynamics. In the concerto likewise the orchestral volume is usually somewhat subdued in order to permit the soloist to be heard, and the virtuoso's performance occupies the listener's attention to such a degree that all else becomes secondary. For this reason, and also because the composer must make some concessions to virtuosity, the content of concertos is frequently lighter than that of symphonies. Finally, the relatively brief overture cannot attain the weight and grandeur of larger and more complex works.

On the other hand, the symphony need not be sparing in its use of power; yet it may in some passages employ all the subtleties of chamber music, and in others emphasize virtuosity. At its disposal are all structural designs, cyclic organization, and all instrumental effects, as well as all the advantages of picturesque and programmatic content. The one typical requirement of a symphony is that it be broadly conceived, otherwise the employment of a large symphony orchestra could hardly be justified. Indeed, the symphony may be defined as a sonata for orchestra, one whose formal and instrumental resources have been so expanded that it is nearly twice as long as a comparable sonata.

The Orchestra of the Sinfonia and the Classic Symphony

In the early Baroque the term *sinfonia* had a very general meaning and was applied to many kinds of vocal and instrumental music.

It finally was adopted by Alessandro Scarlatti for his operatic overture (cf. p. 252). Having grown independent of opera, this *sinfonia* became the *pièce de résistance* of Rococo concerts. It continued to employ the orchestra of the Italian overture: two sections of violins joining in the melody, 'cellos playing a sparse harmonic support in octaves with double basses, and the violas filling in rather weakly the gap between the two other, larger groups. The harpsichord was a standard feature and played the chords indicated by the figured bass. Brass instruments were totally absent, except in *sinfonie* of a martial character in which they sounded military signals. Woodwinds were optional; one flute, one or two oboes, and a bassoon, when present, would play in unison with the violin and bass parts. The orchestra often included less than twenty musicians, but rarely more than thirty.

After 1750 the composition of symphonies was also cultivated in southern Germany—at Mannheim and Vienna. Beginning as works of four to six minutes, symphonies soon averaged a length of from five to ten minutes. They now employed the sonata-form and other repetitive forms. The facile string passages of the Italian overture disappeared. In time the symphony became a serious, organically conceived work that employed all the resources of the orchestra. Flutes, oboes, bassoons, and the newly-invented clarinets and horns lent greater fullness to the music by playing the harmonic background formerly supplied by the harpsichord. At times these instruments doubled on the string parts, at others they echoed the strings in brief passages. The orchestra now included more stringed instruments, needed to balance the increased strength of the eight to ten wind instruments. It consisted of between twenty and forty players. This was the orchestra of Haydn and Mozart.

Classic Symphonies and Divertimenti

Haydn, though by no means the creator of the symphony, is the earliest master whose symphonies outlasted the period in which they were written. In them, as in his *String Quartets,* he made steady progress toward ever finer artistry. Between 1759 and 1799 he wrote over one hundred *Symphonies,* of which twenty or more are still frequently played. Under his hands the light Rococo work of five to ten minutes grew to a length of nearly twenty minutes.

His younger colleague, Mozart, contributed some fifty *Symphonies* (though the usual numbering runs only to forty-one), over ten of them still in our repertory. Indeed, the six written in his mature years after 1781 all belong to the finest in the field.

The first of these, known as the *Haffner Symphony*, was composed for a family friend of that name and performed on the occasion of his elevation to the nobility. It was therefore originally written in the form that succeeded the Baroque suite for such functions—as a DIVERTIMENTO or SERENADE: The present *four Movements* were preceded by a *March*, also played at the end, and a *second Minuet-and-Trio Movement*, now lost, was placed after the *First Movement.* Such *divertimenti* were composed in large numbers by the Classics, both for orchestra and for various chamber-music ensembles. The purpose easily explains the festive character of this *Symphony.*

EXAMPLE 93:   WOLFGANG AMADEUS MOZART [1756–91]

   Symphony No. 35, in D Major, K.385, "Haffner" (1782)

Movement 1: Allegro con spirito

   A *unisono* of the whole orchestra opens the work, theatrically announcing the main idea:

This together with a soft answer constitutes the first theme of the sonata-form. Immediately *a* opens the bridge in a sophisticated play of imitations and rushing scale passages. The next soft passage reaches the dominant (A Major). While *a* continues, a new, quiet figure is added; but before the second theme proper enters, *a* is once more heard in full force in the bass against a lively idea in the violins. The second theme is a soft duet of the violins above *a* in the viola:

The following bridge again exhibits the contrast of a loud and soft phrase. Several new ideas, which begin with a trill-figure that edges chromatically upwards, give a sparkling conclusion to the whole of the exposition.

The brief development section consists of three periods, soft, loud, and again soft, each treating *a* in a different imitative fashion. In the regular recapitulation the soft passage in the first bridge is omitted; otherwise only a few measures are slightly changed. This simple treatment of the sonata-form is characteristic of *divertimenti;* often, indeed, movements of such works, like overtures to comic operas, are given sonatina-form. This *Movement* is best described as reflecting the spirit of festivity and somewhat pompous dignity.

Movement 2: Andante

The *Slow Movement* is very similar in construction: It opens with a first theme:

in three distinct phrases, the first lyrical, the others increasing in motion. After a brief pause a second theme, light-hearted and characterized by the clock-like repetition of a tone in the accompaniment is introduced:

A short bridge, and the faithful restatement of the themes with but slight changes in the second, which is now heard in the tonic key, follows. Both portions of this ingratiating sonatina-form, which is both lyrical and playful, are repeated.

Movement 3: Menuetto—Trio

The *Minuet* returns to a festive manner and to sudden dynamic contrasts:

All first phrases of the three periods—  —are loud, all second phrases soft. The *Trio* is of identical form, but lyrical throughout.

Movement 4: Presto

The sonata-form *Finale* bubbles over with good spirits. The first theme:

starts softly, but continues vigorously. A brief pause, and the graceful second theme:

h

and a forceful codetta close the exposition. A few quiet measures reintroduce *g*, which modulates so that *h* reappears in Minor. After this simple development section the regular recapitulation follows without break. The coda opens with a questioning phrase:

i

and a chromatic passage; then it reverts to *g* and brings the *Symphony* to a sparkling close.

This work, more than Mozart's other great *Symphonies*, is composed in the optimistic spirit of the "age of reason." It symbolizes the light-heartedness of the Rococo and the ostentatious feudalism of the period in which the composer lived. Depth of feeling and Olympian equanimity, characteristic of his other works, give way to a robust good humor and courtly gallantry similar to the qualities found in many of Haydn's works.

Beethoven's Symphonies

Not long after Mozart's death, at the dawn of the nineteenth century, the Rococo was definitely at an end. Feudalism was dying; revolution and war rocked the world. Instead of an "age of reason" this was an age of emotion, in which man's inner struggles were the center of interest. In this new age Beethoven wrought his *Nine Symphonies*, each a work of major proportions: some idyllic, some ecstatic, and others dramatic in nature. We turn now to one of these masterworks of symphonic literature, incidentally the longest symphony written up to the beginning of the nineteenth century and for twenty years thereafter:

EXAMPLE 94: LUDWIG VAN BEETHOVEN [1770–1827]

Symphony No. 3, in E-flat Major, "Eroica", op. 55 (1803)

Originally Beethoven intended to dedicate this work to Napoleon, the hero of the French Revolution, who, he believed, would give reality to the slogan "liberty, equality, and brotherhood." But when Napoleon assumed the emperor's crown in 1804, Beethoven destroyed the dedicatory page; the hero had become a tyrant. The *Symphony* nevertheless symbolizes the idea of heroism and struggle expressed in its subtitle, an idea which was very dear to the master and which is also the core of the *Egmont Overture* (cf. p. 250ff) and *Sonata Appassionata* (cf. p. 268ff).

Movement 1: Allegro con brio [1]

Like hammer blows two chords of the entire orchestra open the work, whereupon the 'cellos present the main theme of the sonata-form:

The syncopation that leads to the first climax, at the end of this theme, is a special favorite of Beethoven's. A three-tone motif, echoed in woodwinds and violins, is the main material of the second theme:

Beethoven loves strong contrasts, and here within the prevailing soft, lyric mood a sudden loud *unisono* surprises the listener. The interesting motif that starts the ensuing bridge is again turbulent:

By contrast the third theme:

---

[1] Fast and spirited.

starts softly in chords, and builds through *staccato* passages to a climax ending in syncopated chords. A brief codetta, derived from *a*, follows. Starting softly, it soon reaches one more climax, at which *a* reappears. It is through these many climactic *crescendos*, more than through anything else, that Beethoven evokes in us the idea of heroism and struggle.

As is typical of Beethoven's development sections this one is subdivided, each subsection expanding particular motifs. A tremendous tension accumulates in the first two subsections, both derived from *b* and then from *a*+(*c*). Suddenly, then, it relaxes, and a beautiful new theme appears:

It is answered by an heroic call to battle, *a*. Once more *e* is heard, and now the answer from *a* is more conciliatory; but a bass figure of gigantic leaps builds to power again:

The mood of assurance is then reestablished, and through a piquant *tremolo* passage, in which the horn eagerly anticipates the main theme, the tonality of the beginning returns.

The recapitulation is regular, though altered in details. It is followed by a second development section (coda): Above *a* a new violin figuration is created; then *e* and (*f*) are heard again, followed by a long, glorious expansion of *a*, which resoundingly closes the *Movement*.

Firmness, lyricism, strength emanate from this piece. A major problem for Beethoven—how to justify the recapitulation dramatically—is here solved: It represents, so to speak, purified resolution after struggle, and this resolution is reaffirmed by the coda.

Movement 2: Marcia funebre: Adagio assai [2]

A hero, however courageous, meets death. Hence the *Funeral March*. The first theme:

---

[2] Funeral March: Very slow.

is heard in the strings alone, then in the oboe. A new, more hopeful melody in Major emerges in the strings:

h

and alternates twice with *g*. Then, like an assurance of future bliss, the *Trio* enters, with its simple motif:

(*i*)

echoing in the woodwinds.

When the *March* returns, it no longer reflects gloom, but steadfast courage. In place of a development section a *fugato* on a new idea, derived from an inversion of *h*, is inserted (see the brackets in the examples):

h^1

The accompaniment, a firm *staccato*, seems to be related to the *staccato* passages following *d* in the *First Movement*. A brief section of trumpet fanfare and thundering basses introduces a motif related to the gigantic leaps of (*f*), which furnishes the background for *g* as the recapitulation opens, shortened to *g-h-g*. The coda suggests divine assuagement of grief with a new melody, derived from (*i*). Then *g* reappears, but in a process of decomposition, as though wearied by the crushing sorrow.

Movement 3: Scherzo—Trio: Allegro vivace

The *Scherzo* is described best, perhaps, as effervescent. Its puckish theme:

j

is tossed back and forth above a seething string *staccato*. The *Trio* is an attractive horn terzetto—the first such in symphonic literature:

The repetition of the *Scherzo* is exact, except for an attractive brief shift from triple to duple meter and the addition of a brief coda.

Movement 4: Allegro molto—Poco Andante—Presto

The *Symphony* culminates in a *variation Movement* full of wit, gusto, and the joy of living. A short, rushing prelude introduces the enigmatic first theme, *l* (borrowed from Beethoven's earlier *Ballet, The Creatures of Prometheus*), presented by the *unisono* strings in a whispering *pizzicato* throughout, with echoes in the woodwinds and sudden outbursts (see below; in the *Ballet* it apparently described the movements of the first, puppet-like creations of Prometheus).

Variation 1 surrounds this theme with two additional parts.

Variation 2 adds a fourth voice and introduces triplet motion. These two *variations* are written for strings only.

In *variation 3* the woodwinds enter and present the sweeping second theme, *m* (in the *Ballet* portraying the creation of man, with brain and will)—and we discover that the first theme serves as its bass:

A brief interlude leads to *variation 4*, an ironic *fugato* on *l*.

It modulates and ushers in *variation 5*, on *m*, in a new key.

Variation 6, on *l* again, is a free character variation in the style of a march:

Variation 7 starts by expanding both *l* and *m*, but it soon turns to another *fugato* on *l* with passing references to *m*, and finally ends with a free development section that comes to a complete stop.

In a new, slow tempo *(poco andante) m* is given a lyric interpretation in *variation 8*.

Then *m* descends into the basses in the bombastic final *variation 9*. The coda begins in a moderate tempo, in a mood of profound joy. Then, suddenly, the music changes to an almost excessive frolicking in *fortissimo* and *presto*, an expression of Beethoven's basic humanitarian optimism that characterizes many of his triumphant endings (cf. the *Egmont Overture*, p. 250ff).

Although the slight programmatic content ends in the *Second Movement*, there are definite signs that this work was conceived as a whole. The march *variation, No. 6*, in the *Finale* refers back to the *Funeral March*, the *fugato variation, No. 4*, to the development section of that *March*, and *variation 8* to its coda; the gigantic leaps of *f*, prominent in the first two *Movements*, also appear in the others; and there are further melodic, rhythmic, and expressive relationships that unify the work.

One of the chief bonds, however, is tonality. The key of *E*-flat Major, forcefully established as predominant by the two initial chords of the *Symphony*, remains central to the end. Three *Movements* are in *E*-flat, only the *Funeral March* being in the relative key, *C* Minor, but its second idea, *h*, is in *E*-flat. In this way the work is tonally unified. Again, as in Mozart's *C-Minor Concerto* (p. 322ff), the prominent recurrence of keys establishes relationships. This becomes clear, if we compare, for example, the *a* after the first *e* and the *a* at the beginning of the coda in the *First Movement* with the *Trio* in the *Second* and the beginning of *variation 7* in the *Last*, all in *C Major* and all expressing optimism. Similarly we may compare *b* in the second subsection of the development section of the *First Movement* with the start of the coda in the *Funeral March* and with the beginning of the coda in the *Finale*, all prominently displaying *A*-flat Major and expressing joyfulness and lyricism. In the same way, when the *C* Minor of the *Funeral March* reappears in *variation 4* of the *Finale*, the mood of seriousness returns.[3]

---

[3] See Appendix I, p. 386f, for an explanation of "key symbolism."

Berlioz and Orchestration; the Program Symphony

Franz Schubert was the only other early Romantic composer (before about 1830) whose symphonies still live. But they were hardly known during his lifetime and had no immediate influence. The man who, after Beethoven, was the first to open new symphonic paths, whose music was influential in his own time and is still performed in ours, was Hector Berlioz. As a highly imaginative composer, an excellent critic, and the author of an outstanding treatise on orchestration, Berlioz was a commanding figure in the Romantic era. His keen sense for timbres led him to create the new, Romantic orchestra in which all instruments acquired individuality.

With Berlioz tone color assumes thematic importance equivalent with rhythmic, melodic, and harmonic elements. Following his literary inclination, moreover, he developed fully what Beethoven had suggested in the *Egmont Overture*, the *Eroica*, and especially his *Sixth (Pastoral) Symphony*. The result was the program symphony, which became a reality in Berlioz's *Fantastic Symphony*.

EXAMPLE 95:   HECTOR BERLIOZ [1803–69]

Symphonie Phantastique (1830)

"Episode from an Artist's Life, Fantastic Symphony in Five Movements," thus reads the title. The *Five Movements* are held together both by a program and by a *leitmotiv*, the *idée fixe*, as Berlioz calls it. The program was uncertain at first; Berlioz several times changed its wording to have it follow the music more closely. Each *Movement* represents one scene in the "episode"—the jilted artist's unsuccessful attempt at suicide through drugs which, although insufficient to cause death, nevertheless produce a fantastic sequence of dreams. The *leitmotiv* (the first theme of the *First Movement*) represents the beloved, who gives unity to the dreams as does the motif to the *Movements*.

Movement 1: Largo—Allegro agitato e appassionato assai

The *First Movement*—"Reveries, Passions" [4]—relates the feelings of the young man as he falls asleep under the influence of the drugs. A long introduction, slow but with many tempo changes, describes "the uneasy and nervous condition of the young man's mind before his beloved ap-

---

[4] All quotations refer to Berlioz's own program.

peared to him, the alternations of depression and elation without cause."
Many motifs succeed each other, some of them interrelated. Several will
become important later on, especially these two which are heard in the
first few measures:

"Then the beloved appeared and with her came ardent love" heads
the exposition of this *Movement (allegro)* in sonata-form. We hear a long
first theme, whose middle portion derives from (*a*): *a;* its first and last
phrases follow:

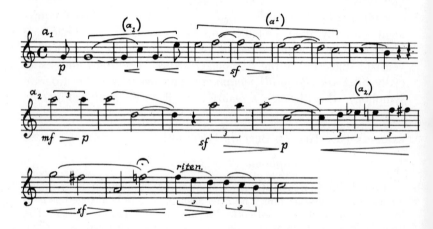

Separated by bridges, two subsidiary ideas follow, the second brought
in as a continuation of (*a₁*):

As in Classic symphonies, this exposition may be repeated. The short development section suggests "anxiety and jealousy." It consists of brief expansions of d, and a chromatic passage derived from (a_2). The last leads to a climax followed by a general rest. But "love reawakens:" After a few preliminary measures the recapitulation starts, expected neither so soon nor in a key different from that of the exposition. The new key shifts the main theme and d, separated by a long bridge, far up into a more brilliant, more urgent pitch range. Only then does c come in, without a bridge but greatly expanded.

And now Berlioz, like Beethoven, writes a coda in the form of a second development section, even longer than the first. A long *crescendo* on $(a_1) + (b)$ leads to a vigorous final statement of a, in which a_2 is replaced by another chromatic phrase. All the elements are then once more reviewed in changing tempos. With an imitation of the sounds of an organ the quiet ending suggests that the would-be suicide has made his peace and has found "consolation in religion."

Movement 2: Waltz: Allegro non troppo

The first dream is that of "A Ball." The strains of harps, which glitter through the prelude and through the entire *Movement*, mark the earliest appearance of this instrument in the symphony orchestra, though it had been used before in opera and ballet. The dream picture becomes clear as the ingratiating *Waltz* enters, consisting of a melody in four periods: *e-f-g-e* (g being marked by tone repetitions):

A brief bridge leads to the *idée fixe*, a, which is heard in its entirety in waltz meter, as, in his dream, the young man sees his beloved among the dancers. Closing the ternary form, a complete restatement of the *Waltz* then ushers in a new motif:

which alternates twice with *g*. As the coda reaches a climax, a_1 in the clarinet suddenly and mysteriously interrupts the tumult, which thereafter concludes with *e*.

Movement 3: Adagio

The second dream is a "Scene in the Country." A pastoral mood is evoked by an introductory duet of English horn and oboe, this being the first use of the English horn in the orchestra since the Baroque. Soon altered motifs from the *First Movement* reappear, and then an extended melody emerges whose form is similar to that of the *Waltz* (*i-i-j-k-i*): "Quiet and peace enter the dreamer's heart, together with hope." Flutes and violins sing *i*:

while *j* is a colorful dialogue between strings and woodwinds. After the cadence *k*, marked by a sharp rhythm,  *i* is heard again in 'cellos and bassoons, while the violins add a rapid figuration.

A climactic *crescendo* reintroduces the *leitmotiv*, (a_1). The bass instruments present it in a furious variant:

while the flutes and oboes reply with it nearly as originally heard: "Painful forebodings grip the young man: 'Should she prove false to him?'" After a great culmination the "forebodings" subside, and the partial restatement of this ternary form begins, as *pizzicato* strings accompany a clarinet melody derived from *i*. The repetition of this melody in the woodwinds is combined with *i* itself in the violins.

In the coda the *idée fixe* re-echoes first in the woodwinds, then in the strings: "Peace and hope are reestablished." Reminiscences of *k* and the English-horn music of the beginning close the *Movement*. Here the English horn is heard against a highly original accompaniment suggesting thunder—four timpani played by two men. This use of two timpanists is another innovation.

Movement 4: Allegretto non troppo

Now the dreamer sees himself, after imagining that he has murdered his beloved, on the "March to the Block." On the whole, Berlioz emphasizes the brass and percussion sections in this *Movement*, as is expected in a march, but he uses them in a very original manner. He even adds two tubas to the orchestra; not only is this the first use of the tuba, but until the end of the century no one else used two tubas.

As the tension mounts, timpani, *pizzicato* double basses and 'cellos, and muted horns paint a gruesome picture. The grim first idea:

is presented twice in the low strings, twice in the high strings, and once more in the basses, to changing accompaniments. It is followed by a powerful march theme, set forth by the full wind choir:

After the repetition of all this material *l* returns, with its single tones ingeniously played by the different instrument choirs—strings, woodwinds, brass, percussion. It is followed by *m*, now with a string accompaniment, and is then heard once more. In the ensuing expansion of *l* an unexpected, fantastic *diminuendo* is especially conspicuous. The expansion leads into the dotted rhythm of *m* and comes to a climax, followed once more by the fantastic diminuendo. Suddenly a few measures of *fortissimo* shatter the quiet, which is immediately re-established as the clarinet intones the *leitmotiv:* "a last thought of love," which is "cut short by the death stroke," the final catastrophe, symbolized by a few brutal chords closing the *Movement*. (We may note the similarity of formulation between this piece and the *Hungarian March*, p. 10f; in both, the march proper is followed by an expansion.)

Movement 5: Larghetto—Allegro

The *Finale*, a "Dream of a Witches' Sabbath," is an ingenious combination of Baroque formulation—prelude, chorale, and fugue—and Romantic program music. It opens with one of the most colorful orchestral passages in the entire literature, in which Berlioz sets another precedent: He divides the two violin choirs into three groups each, and the lower string choirs into two each. These divided strings combine with trombones, piccolo, muted horn, four kettledrums, and a bass drum to produce a tone picture of unsurpassed delicacy, in its way even excelling the colorful instrumentation of the preceding *Movement*.

The prelude describes the dreamer's vision of his own funeral, attended by all kinds of devils and witches, flitting through the air from all directions. Suddenly a clarinet, accompanied only by timpani and bass drum, intones a shrill, burlesque variant of the *idée fixe*, answered by an outburst of the full orchestra: "The beloved arrives and is greeted by howls of the witches as she joins the orgy." Then a piercing E-flat clarinet (another first in this score), soon joined by a piccolo, presents the complete *a*, parodistically varied in rhythm and modified by grace notes. Reaching a raucous climax, *a* is suddenly interrupted by a new motif, (*n*) (see below), as the witches fall in line for their dance.

The witches' dance is delayed, however, by the funeral service, indicated first by "funeral bells," played by orchestral bells and a piano (both first used in this *Symphony*), which interrupt (*n*), and then by the melody of an old Church hymn, the *Dies irae* of the requiem mass (the mass for the dead):

Each of its three lines, of which the first and last are similar, is presented in three versions, namely (1) in long notes (𝅗𝅥.) by bass tubas and bassoons; (2) in shorter notes (𝅘𝅥.) by horns and trombones; and (3) in the sharp rhythm used before for *a* (𝅘𝅥𝅘𝅥𝅮) by woodwinds and *pizzicato* strings. This last version is deliberately blasphemous, suggesting profane mockery of the hymn. Except for a bass line added to version (1) in lines 2 and 3, only the funeral bells accompany this sombre vision.

Now (*n*) returns and the actual "Sabbath Round Dance" starts. From (*n*) springs the subject of a fugue:

The four entrances of the subject, all in *fortissimo*, rise from the bass to the trebles. After a chromatic episode the woodwinds start *n* again, but are interrupted by the complete subject in the basses. The answer, in the violins, is followed by the second episode, which features a soft motif, descending and chromatic, opposed by loud brass chords. Then a new, mysterious version of *n*, pizzicato in the low strings and imitated by the bassoons, leads to a brief allusion to *o*.

The third fugue section is based on a chromatic version of *n*, which rises in four entrances from the 'cellos to the violins. Starting *pianissimo*, this point of imitations and the ensuing expansion gradually return to a tumultuous *fortissimo*. Then all the strings, *unisono*, take up *n* as originally heard. When it is answered by the violins, the wind choir simultaneously intones the slightly lengthened first line of the *Dies irae*. With this interweaving of the sacred and the profane the dance reaches its culmination. A wildly rushing coda, brilliantly orchestrated, concludes the fantastic dream.

Romantic Symphonies

The *Fantastic Symphony* had an immediate influence on Berlioz's friend, Franz Liszt, who later composed both *Symphonic Poems* and the programmatic *Faust* and *Dante Symphonies*. Tchaikovsky, Rimsky-Korsakov, Glière, Richard Strauss, Vaughan-Williams, Bloch, and others have created notable program symphonies. Some composers, indeed, found that, in order to render their meaning explicit, they needed words. Following Beethoven's solution in the *Ninth* (Choral) *Symphony*, they therefore added human voices to the orchestra. An outstanding example is Mahler's *The Song of the Earth* (see p. 166ff). In fact, five of his ten *Symphonies* include voices, either soloists or choir and soloists.

The program symphony and the symphony with voices represent, however, only an interesting trend which expressed itself in comparatively few works. Beethoven's romanticism, as far as it pointed toward programmatic unity, was not readily accepted by all symphonists. Neither did most of the composers named above write program symphonies exclusively. Along with the concerto, the symphony remained in general a classicist type.

Besides Berlioz, the greatest composers of symphonic music during the second quarter of the nineteenth century were Schumann and Mendelssohn. In their hands the symphony gradually accepted a fully dramatic, organic plan. The opening movement was to be the foundation of the structure and the finale its capstone. Such was the concept of the later Romantics—men like Brahms, Franck, d'Indy, Borodin, Tchaikovsky, and especially Bruckner.

Romantic Orchestration

In the nineteenth century, as before, it was the opera orchestra that made the crucial advances in instrumentation; for in connection with the dramatic situation specific timbres and imitations of various sounds are in special demand. Such symphonists as Franck and Bruckner, for example, only follow Wagner's lead in this respect. They rarely indulge in solos, but use the instruments in choirs. They give prominence to the low strings and employ the horns almost without pause. They thus give their orchestra the same rich fullness that we have already noted in connection with Wagner.

Many Romantics, however, used a different kind of orchestration, one that permitted the strings the dominance they enjoyed in Classic music and, in addition, gave prominence to the woodwinds and horns, but as soloists rather than in choirs. We have already met this "coloristic" orchestration in Dvořák's *'Cello Concerto* (p. 331ff).

By courtesy of Louis Carré Gallery, New York.

PLATE XII: Raoul Dufy (1877–1954), French painter—
L'orchestre (1942).

This whimsical impression of an orchestra well conveys the idea of various groups collaborating under a conductor. To the conductor's left are the first violins, behind them the double basses, and to his right the second violins. Confronting him are the 'cellos and, behind the second violins, the violas. The first row of desks across the stage comprises, from left to right, two oboes, three flutes, two clarinets, and a harp; the next row, three bassoons, French horns, and trumpets. Behind the last sit three trombonists and a bass-tuba player. The orchestra is completed by a timpanist, a snare drum to his right, a bass drum to his left, and a cymbal player to his rear.

Development of Orchestration

A comparison of these approaches with those of Mozart and Beethoven on the one hand and of contemporaries such as Bartók (see p. 335ff) and Piston (see below, p. 365ff) on the other discloses further interesting facts. In Mozart's and Beethoven's scores the brass instruments are hardly in evidence except in *tutti*, for in their time they were technically inflexible. The woodwinds, too, were still rather primitive. They served chiefly to relieve the prevailing string color. More recently composers have tended to give equal prominence to all instruments. They are interested in the contrasting sounds of specific instruments rather than in the opposition of different groups. Trombones, trumpets, and percussion instruments add their individual colors, much as they do in Berlioz's music. These composers also appreciate the various members of the woodwind families—piccolo, English horn, high clarinet and bass clarinet, and double bassoon.

As regards orchestration, we may epitomize the changes in the last two centuries as follows: string sound (Italian Rococo); strings and woodwinds (French Rococo); strings and woodwinds reinforced by horns and trumpets (Classics); strings, brass, and individualized woodwinds (Brahms, the Russians, the French Romantics except Franck and his school); rich orchestration, with horns ubiquitous, essentially written for three choirs: strings, woodwinds, and brasses (Wagner, Franck); individualized orchestra, with percussion as a fourth section (composers since 1890, stemming from Berlioz).

During the eighty years after Mozart the average size of orchestras doubled; the addition of new and more powerful wind and percussion instruments also necessitated an increase in the number of stringed instruments, in order to maintain a proper balance of sonorities. There was evident need for better discipline, accuracy, and coordination among the fully developed wind groups and the larger body of strings. This need led to the emergence of the professional conductor and to the division between the fields of conducting and composing.

Social Position of the Composer

In the seventeenth and eighteenth centuries composers were either church music directors or conductors, employed by princes, municipalities, or opera companies in this double capacity. Rarely were they interested solely in conducting, and only a few of them made names for themselves in this field, notably Lully at Paris, about 1665–85, and Johann Stamitz at Mannheim, about 1745–55. At the beginning of the nineteenth century private and municipal orchestras—and therefore conducting positions—disappeared. Similarly, composers were no longer engaged as municipal or feudal servants. Mozart was the first to break away from such employ, and with Beethoven the free-lance composer was definitely established. Thereafter many composers worked on commission, i.e. they delivered works as they were ordered by rich patrons, publishers, or concert managers.

After the mid-century even this partial security came to an end. Perhaps to compensate for the lost financial security, the composer, formerly esteemed as a fine craftsman, now took refuge in the status of "genius," a typical Romantic attitude. The composer-genius composed only when inspired, and then tried to get his music performed. He made a living as a virtuoso or as a teacher of composition, theory, or piano, and less often as a conductor.

The Professional Conductor

These were the circumstances that separated the conductor from the composer. In the first half of the nineteenth century many outstanding conductors were still composers: Weber, who introduced the use of the small baton and experimented with acoustically favorable seating arrangements; Mendelssohn, who brought the Leipzig Gewandhaus (Clothmakers' Hall) Orchestra to world fame; Wagner at the Dresden Opera House; and others. On the other hand, François Habeneck (1781–1849), who made the Paris Conservatory Orchestra the finest group of his time and who first presented Beethoven in France, belongs to the new type of professional conductors.

With the vogue of the gigantic Wagnerian orchestra the professional conductor became a necessity. Wagner's apostles were

the most renowned conductors in the latter third of the century:
Hans von Bülow, Hans Richter, Artur Nikisch, and especially
Gustav Mahler, under whom the Vienna Philharmonic Orchestra
set standards that have since been generally adopted.[5]

Fulfillment of the Romantic Symphony; Twentieth-Century Symphony

The high-water mark of orchestral gigantism was reached with
Mahler's *Symphonies*. Five of each woodwind, eight horns, four
trumpets, four trombones, bass tuba, and often additional brasses
for chorale effects, harp, mandolin, guitar, and up to six percus-
sionists join the strings in his later *Symphonies*. He followed
Beethoven's ideas through to their ultimate conclusions: sonata-
form as the vehicle of drama, voices as the interpreters of a personal philosophy, keys symbolizing definite emotions, a dramatic
plan for the entire work, cyclic organization, and so forth. With
him the evolution of the Romantic symphony, initiated by Beethoven, came to its end.

As was the case among nineteenth-century composers, only the
outstanding composers of the twentieth century have made significant contributions to the symphonic repertory. Ian Sibelius (b.1865)
and Ralph Vaughan-Williams (b.1872) probably stand out among
the older generation. Serge Prokofiev (1891–1953), Artur Honegger
(b.1892), and Dmitri Shostakovich (b.1906), as well as several
American composers, such as Walter Piston (b.1894) and Samuel
Barber (b.1910), have won recognition as leading symphonic
composers since the 1920's. Our last example, Walter Piston's
Symphony No. 2, comes from this group.

The New Style

The style of this *Symphony* approaches what may be called the
emerging international style of our era. This style cannot yet be
clearly defined, but certain ingredients are obviously involved:
dissonant counterpoint; rhythmic freshness, the use of many different chords besides those built in thirds; and a vast expansion of
the ideas of tonality, scale, and cadence. Many eminent composers,

---

[5] See Appendix I, p. 398f, for some information on conducting in the eighteenth and twentieth centuries.

each with his own individual approach, have contributed toward the evolution of this style: Hindemith (Germany), Bartók (Hungary), Honegger and Milhaud (France), Vaughan-Williams and Britten (England), Copland and Barber (U.S.A.), and Stravinsky, Prokofiev, and Shostakovich (Russia) are only a few of them.

EXAMPLE 96: WALTER PISTON [b.1894]

Symphony No. 2 (in A Minor, 1943)

Copyright 1944 by Arrow Music Press, Inc. Used by permission of Arrow Music Press and American Music Center, 250 West 57th Street, New York.

Piston's themes are expressive, broadly flowing tunes, each derived from a single melodic motif or a piquant rhythm. The music, though serious, is fresh and vigorous. Neo-classic in its clarity and simplicity of form and in its emotional restraint, the work nevertheless reaches fine climaxes and has its measure of lyricism and joy. The instrumentation, too, is almost Classic: It employs only three of each woodwind family and gives predominance to the strings. Rich orchestral sound, as an aim in itself, is superseded by clear delineation of the musical content. Also in respect to length (less than half an hour) the *Symphony* is classicist. Today the gigantism of many Romantic symphonies is largely outmoded.

Movement 1: Moderato

The *Symphony* starts with an expansive theme in 'cellos and violas:

It possesses both a characteristic rhythm (the syncopated second main beat in the third measure) and a characteristic mode (*A Minor* with an F-sharp [6]). Gradually other parts enter, until the theme is heard in the high strings and attains a climax. A new, rhythmic bridge motif emerges as the volume abates: (*b*): ⁶₄ ♩. ♪♩ 𝄽 𝄽 |. The attractive woodwind *staccato* and the complicated rhythm of the second theme furnish a strong contrast to *a:*

---

[6] This is the Dorian mode (cf. Appendix I, p. 383f); it shows the influence of neo-medievalism (cf. p. 192).

Oboe and flute take it up in turn and, after a derivative idea is presented in the strings, the entire woodwind choir joins in an effective conclusion of the exposition of this sonata-form.

Motif (*b*) again acts as the bridge to the development section, which begins with an imaginative presentation of *a* in the basses. A second time *a* is heard in canon by horns and trumpet. A sudden *piano* and a string *tremolo* herald the next subsection, in which (*b*) and various rhythmic elements of *a* are expanded to reach a climax borrowed from the end of the first theme.

At the height of the tumult the full string choir with wind support starts the recapitulation. The flute, accompanied quietly by woodwinds, repeats *a*. The bridge, including (*b*), leads to a reorchestrated version of *c*: first brass only, then woodwinds accompanied by brass, and finally, after the strings initiate the derivative idea, the full orchestra. The coda begins like the development section, with *a* in the basses, followed by another canon on *a* in horns and trumpet. The *Movement* concludes with a few solemn phrases of the brass.

Movement 2: Adagio

The *Second Movement* flows from one idea, somewhat like a Baroque composition:

The first two measures of this idea derive from *a;* the third measure, (d^1), is used as the opening of the *Movement* and also as its song-like chief motif.

First the clarinet, then the flute sing the entire melody. A fine *crescendo-*and-*diminuendo* passage, evolved from (d^1), represents the episode of this rondo-like *Movement.* Then *d* returns in the clarinet. Above a second presentation of *d* in the basses the violins introduce a derivative, lively figuration, which is somewhat spun out. A fuller rendition of the *crescendo-*and-*diminuendo* passage on (d^1) leads to a final statement of *d* by the full string choir, and the phrase that opened the *Movement,* (d^1), closes it quietly.

The outline of this *Movement* is therefore as follows:

$$- A - B - \quad A^1 \quad - B^1 - A -$$
(d^1) *d-d* d^1 *d-d+*var. d^1 *d*   (d^1) . This looks like a rondo, but the quickening of the rhythm in A^1 and the disposition of tonalities —the same in both *A*-sections, distant ones elsewhere—give it a symmetric structure, what is sometimes called a BOW FORM: *A-B-C-B-A.* This structure is emphasized by the playing of (d^1) at beginning and end.

Movement 3: Allegro

The *Symphony* has only three *Movements,* similar in this respect also to eighteenth-century precedents. The *Finale,* a rondo of the form *A-B-A-C-A-B-A,* opens with a theme of splendid élan:

As a whole it harks back to passages of the *First Movement,* and the rhythm of the fourth measure, (e^1), gives rise to passages reminiscent of *c.* An interesting brass motif:

closes this section and thereafter recurs frequently. It leads to a second,
march-like idea (*B*-section), marked by an attractive and witty off-beat
accentuation which pays homage to jazz:

Starting softly, *e* and (*e¹*) once more reach a peak and then give way
to a whimsical *staccato* accompaniment in the strings that supports the
third idea (*C*-section). This idea has a new, quiet rhythm that receives
a special character from a conspicuous triplet:

The woodwinds present it, the strings expand it, almost like a chorale,
and then the woodwinds sing it once more.

Piston is a classicist also insofar as he prefers to separate sections
clearly. He does this with figurations that make no reference to the
themes. Each transition in this *Movement* is so treated. The longest
bridge—a *staccato* figuration in the strings, with one choir after another
entering in *fugato* fashion—intervenes at this point. Soon (*e¹*) is added,
and presently the first three sections (*A-B-A*) are completely reviewed
with some changes. The last *A* points insistently to both the interval of a
third and the whimsical rhythm of (*e¹*) as the cyclic links among the
main ideas of all three *Movements*. A brief passage suggesting a chorale,
which is scored for the full orchestra, brilliantly caps the work.

Summary

In its evolution the symphony has described nearly a circle:
from the Classic works of Haydn and Mozart, through the dramatic
and sometimes programmatic symphonies of Beethoven and the
Romantics, to the more restrained, non-programmatic, objective
compositions of our day; from the small orchestra of the Classics,
almost an expanded chamber-music group, through the tone-color
orchestra of gigantic proportions in the Romantic era, to a smaller,
more Classic group today.

The symphony of the nineteenth century is the true counterpart
of social organization during the time. It demands a large, coopera-

tive group of professional specialists who, with disciplined precision, create a fine, integrated piece of artistic work designed for mass consumption. The last trace of the haphazard approach of the amateur is gone. This type of music was written for the mass audiences of an industrial, urban society, not for the enjoyment of a few favored individuals. Whereas chamber music was sociable, and concertos retained a personal note because of the soloist involved, the symphony became the vehicle of mass inspiration, its effect approaching that of religious emotion.

In our time the differences among these types of music have been largely effaced, for phonograph, radio, and television have made song, opera, ballet, mass, instrumental solo, chamber music, concerto, and symphony equally available for private enjoyment in the home. Such lessening of ties between certain functions and certain types of music has occurred several times in the history of music; and "popularization" has been succeeded regularly by a rise of new, distinct types of music and practices of performance to satisfy the new needs. Since the style of contemporary music is nearly crystallized, the creation of these new types and practices may well follow.

CONCEPTS AND TOPICS DISCUSSED IN THIS SECTION

EPILOGUE

The road we have traveled has been full of turns and windings; for during our journey we have tried to touch on the most important of the many complexities of a living art. Let us pause to consider the goals we set out to achieve:

1. The enrichment of our lives through building up for ourselves a well-rounded listening repertory.

2. A modicum of historical information necessary to make us aware of the styles of music that have evolved in the Western world since the middle ages—the styles of the Renaissance, the Baroque, the Classic-Romantic era, and the contemporary period.

3. Some appreciation of the social context of music and of its relationship to the various arts in their evolution.

4. Some understanding of the place of music within composite arts—opera, ballet, song, oratorio, and the like.

5. Discrimination regarding the media of music—voices and instruments, employed singly or in groups.

6. The ability to distinguish musical textures: monophony, polyphony, imitations, homophony.

7. A functional familiarity with the elements of musical composition: rhythm, melody, harmony, counterpoint, expression, instrumentation.

8. An approach to the recognition of musical patterns—additive and repetitive—and their projections in various types of compositions: small and large pieces, composite and complex organic works.

9. Insight into the differences among motif, subject, theme, phrase, period, bridge, melody, recitative, and so forth.

10. A basis for the discernment of cadence, modulation, development, variation, derivation, and the like.

11. A greater responsiveness to aesthetic values—to the inner unifying features in compositions, to the plan of a work and the measure of success in its fulfillment by composer and performer.

With the attainment of these goals—even in small measure—the reader will have made a start toward a fuller life. Further acquaintance with these concepts and further listening will deepen his appreciation so that music will be an integral part of his life—an unfailing source of joy and repose, an inexhaustible reservoir of inspiration.

APPENDICES

APPENDIX I

I. ADDITIONAL TECHNICAL INFORMATION

A. *The Notation of Rhythm and Meter*

Notes and Note Values
(cf. fn. 1, p. 19)

Rhythmic symbols are to music what numerals and letters are to arithmetic and written language. A slow evolution of five hundred years was necessary before the symbols of the NOTATION, or writing, of musical rhythm acquired in the seventeenth century what are approximately their present shapes and meanings.

(cf. fn. 4, p. 7) Since then the beginning and end of each measure are indicated by vertical BARS through the five LINES of the

musical STAFF (plural: staves):

(one measure)

(cf. fn. 1, p. 19) and the various durations of musical tones are symbolized by a series of signs, called NOTES:

𝅝 , a WHOLE-NOTE, implies a tone lasting a certain time;

𝅗𝅥 or 𝅗𝅥 , a HALF-NOTE,   "   "   "   " half that time;

𝅘𝅥 or 𝅘𝅥 , a QUARTER-NOTE,   "   "   "   " one fourth that time;

𝅘𝅥𝅮 or 𝅘𝅥𝅮 , an EIGHTH-NOTE,   "   "   "   " one eighth that time;

𝅘𝅥𝅯 or 𝅘𝅥𝅯 , a SIXTEENTH-NOTE, "   "   "   " one sixteenth that time;

𝅘𝅥𝅰 or 𝅘𝅥𝅰 , a THIRTY-SECOND-NOTE, implies a tone lasting one thirty-second part of that time. The oval of all these notes is called HEAD; the line, STEM; and the added crook or crooks, FLAG(s) or HOOK(s). The last may be straightened out and become cross bars or BEAMS. For example: 𝅘𝅥𝅮 𝅘𝅥𝅮𝅘𝅥𝅮 becomes 𝅘𝅥𝅮𝅘𝅥𝅮𝅘𝅥𝅮

The note values are fixed only relative to each other; they do not represent given durations of time. In one piece the time values of these notes may be: 𝅝 —four seconds, 𝅗𝅥 —two seconds, 𝅘𝅥 —one second, 𝅘𝅥𝅮 —one-half second, and so forth; in another: 𝅝 —three seconds, 𝅗𝅥 —one-and-one-half seconds, and so forth; in yet another: 𝅝 —two seconds, 𝅗𝅥 —one second, and so forth. A series similar to that of the note values contains the following, corresponding symbols for RESTS or silences: ▬ —whole, ▬— half, 𝄽 —quarter, 𝄾 —eighth, 𝄿 —sixteenth, 𝅀 —thirty-second.

Dot and Tie

As is clear from all this, every note and rest value may be divided into only two equal smaller values (or four, eight, and so forth). Wherever a division into three equal subvalues is desired, a DOT is written after the note head or rest as follows:

$$\text{𝅗𝅥} = \text{𝅘𝅥} + \text{𝅘𝅥} \qquad \text{𝅗𝅥.} = \text{𝅘𝅥} + \text{𝅘𝅥} + \text{𝅘𝅥} \ ;$$

in other words, the dotted note is one-and-one-half times as long as the undotted one.

(cf. fn. 2, p. 52) Sometimes also two dots are written after a note to increase its value by three quarters of the original length, for example:

$$\text{𝅗𝅥.} = \text{𝅗𝅥} + \text{𝅘𝅥𝅮} \qquad\qquad \text{𝅗𝅥..} = \text{𝅗𝅥} + \text{𝅘𝅥𝅮} + \text{𝅘𝅥𝅯} \ \text{or} \ \text{𝅗𝅥.} + \text{𝅘𝅥𝅯}$$

(cf. fn. 1, p. 19) Otherwise notes divisible by five, seven, or more odd subvalues can be obtained by TYING two or more notes together with a bow from note head to note head—a TIE:

Rests logically do not require ties. But the continuing of a tone into another measure is also indicated by a tie, for example:

Examples

A few examples will serve to show how rhythmic notation may be applied to some of the examples heard in Chapter I. To permit a comparison between rhythm and meter (cf. p. 19), the metric scheme of the beats is given under each example.

1. *Song of the Volga Boatmen* (Example 4, p. 6)

rhythm

meter

2. Schumann: *Die beiden Grenadiere,* last stanza: *La Marseillaise*
        (Example 12, p. 16)

rhythm

meter

3. Schubert: *Der Erlkönig* (Example 13, p. 17)

rhythm

meter

4. Elgar: *Pomp and Circumstance, No. 1* (Example 8, p. 11)
   a. March:

rhythm

meter

   b. Trio:

rhythm

meter

The Upbeat

In Examples 2 and 3 the first main beat is preceded by an incomplete measure, containing in these instances a single tone. Such incomplete measures are called UPBEATS (avoid the popular equivalent "pick-up!") and they may be longer or shorter than a beat and may comprise several tones.

Time Signatures
(cf. fn. 3, p. 26)

In both waltz and minuet each measure contains three quarter-note values: | ♩ ♩ ♩ | . Such a piece is said to be in three-quarter or in three-four meter, a fact shown at the beginning of the music by a symbol resembling a common fraction:

3 (three beats)
4 (a quarter-note each)

This symbol is called the TIME SIGNATURE. Further triple-meter time signatures are: 3/2, 3/8, 9/8, 9/16. In duple meters the following time signatures are frequent: 2/2, 2/4, 2/8, 4/4, 4/8. (Examples 1 and 2 above are in 4/4; Example 3 is in 2/2; and Example 4 in 2/4.) For 4/4 we often write an old sign, **C** (a semi-circle, not a letter "C"), and for 2/2 the same semi-circle crossed by a vertical bar, **₵** . The latter sign musicians call *alla breve*. (Avoid the popular terms "cut time" for **₵** and "common time" for **C** , which has no special name.)

Compound and Combination Meters
(cf. fn. 5, p. 28)

By tapping the meters of Corelli's *Pastorale* and of "Silent Night" the listener may convince himself that in each there are two main beats per measure. Then he may proceed to tap the sub-beats, and persist until he is able to tap the two main beats with one hand and all six sub-beats with the other. The metric scheme thus is: | ♪♪♪ ♪♪♪ | or 6/8, i.e. twice three eighths. (The sign > above or below a note head indicates an accent.) Actually Corelli combined two such units in each measure, making the meter 12/8, or four times three eighths. Such meters with overall duple meter character, but triple subdivision of each main beat, are called COMPOUND METERS; the more common of these are: 6/4, 6/8, 6/16, 12/8, 12/16. (Some authors, however, speak of duple, triple, and quadruple meters, such as 2/4, 3/4, and 4/4, and call such meters as 6/8, 9/8, and 12/8 compound duple, triple, and quadruple meters.)

We have already considered duple and triple meters; the only remaining type comprises results of added duple and triple units, for example, 5/4 (2 + 3 or 3 + 2) or 7/8 (4 + 3, 3 + 4, or 2 + 3 + 2). Such meters are called COMBINATION METERS. They are comparatively rare, but in recent art music and in Eastern European and non-European folk music they are extensively used.

B. The Notation of Pitch

Staff and Clefs
(cf. fn. 3, p. 33)

The invention of the tone names and the scale was an enormous aid to teaching and transmitting music. Another tremendous step forward was the invention of symbols for the transmission of tunes from generation to generation. Musicians experimented in this field for about two hundred years before a system was perfected by Guido of Arezzo (995?–1050), a French monk cloistered at Arezzo, Italy, who has been credited with establishing for this purpose a musical staff of four lines, still in use for Catholic chants today. For other music the number of lines varied until the seventeenth century, when it was fixed at five.

In front of one or another line of the staff a letter was written: F, C, or (later) G—the name of the note whose head was written around the particular line. Thereby the relative positions of all other notes were also fixed. After many centuries these letters have now assumed the following shapes: F– 𝄢 , C– 𝄡 , and G– 𝄞 . (The heavy lines show where the original letters are hidden in these symbols, and the light lines, the ornaments accrued in their evolution.) They are called CLEFS. The *F*-clef is also known as the BASS CLEF, and the *G*-clef as the TREBLE CLEF. Notes above or below the staff are written on or between short auxiliary or LEDGER (leger) LINES.

Here is a simple picture of how these clefs work and how they correlate with the keyboard. (Our piano, however, extends to one octave below and two octaves above this scale.)

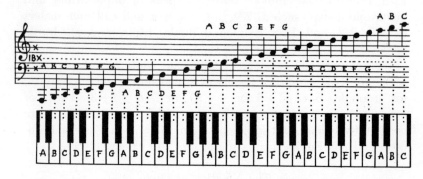

The tone *C* on the dotted line between the staves is appropriately called MIDDLE C. By eliminating the dotted line we arrive at our usual piano GREAT STAFF from which the *C*-clef is eliminated. This clef is still in use, however, for some instruments and voices. It appears on the third line, ⊞, for the viola and for contralto, and on the fourth, ⊞, for the 'cello, bassoon, and tenor, called respectively ALTO and TENOR CLEF. It always indicates middle *C*.

Accidentals
 (cf. fn. 6, p. 37)

Now the question arises how to call and to notate the five tones that correspond to the black keys of the keyboard. The solution adopted is the use of ACCIDENTALS, modifiers by which any tone may be named from its lower or higher neighbor. There are two basic accidentals:

 ♯ , the SHARP, indicates a tone called by the name of its lower neighbor;

 ♭ , the FLAT, indicates a tone called by the name of its higher neighbor.

Thus *C*-sharp: ⊞ , named after its lower neighbor, denotes the tone immediately above *C,* produced by the black key to the right of *C* on the piano; and *D*-flat: ⊞ , named after its higher neighbor, denotes the tone immediately below *D*, produced by the black key to the left of *D* on the piano. Clearly the notes indicate the same key and tone; they are, what is known as, ENHARMONIC tones—identical in sound but not in name and symbol. The reader will observe that we say "*C*-sharp" and "*D*-flat," but that in the notation the accidental precedes the note head. He will note further that accidentals do not necessarily indicate black keys on the piano, as instanced by *E*-sharp or *C*-flat.

In order to cancel any other accidental, a NATURAL, ♮ , is used, for example in the progression *C*-sharp to *C*-natural: .

It has also been found desirable to have accidentals which indicate shifts by a full-tone; thus we speak of a DOUBLE-SHARP, ✗ , for example   (sounding like   ), and of a DOUBLE-FLAT, ♭♭ , for example   (sounding like   ).

We are now able to notate all tones of our music. Indeed, we can do so in various ways; but most usually we employ sharps when the melodic line rises and flats when it descends, as is shown schematically in the chromatic scale (cf. p. 36f). We only have to add one more rule: Any accidental remains in force for its particular note until the next measure bar, unless it is canceled by a natural.

C. Modes, Keys, and Triads

Intervals
 (cf. fn. 2, p. 43)

Why our modes have been called Major and Minor will become clear from the following considerations. We can account for distances between tones in half-tones and whole-tones and their multiples, or in ABSOLUTE INTERVALS (see p. 37). Now we may examine RELATIVE INTERVALS, i.e. intervals as they occur in, or are related to, the modes.

The first of our modes (Major) is represented by the scale *C-D-E-F-G-A-B-(C)*:

The interval *C-C* is, as we know, an octave or eighth, i.e. the interval from the first to the eighth tone of the scale. Similarly *C-E* is a third (from the first to the third tone of the scale), *C-D* a second, and other intervals are fourths, fifths, sixths, and sevenths. All of them may be extended by adding octaves: an octave and a fifth, two octaves and a fifth, and so forth.

The other mode (Minor) is represented by the scale *A-B-C-D-E-F-G-(A)*:

The interval *A-C* is again termed a third, and corresponds to the interval *C-E* in the first mode—the interval from the first to the third tone in the scale. Now a look at the piano will show that the third *C-E* spans four half-tones (or two whole-tones), whereas *A-C* contains only three (one-and-one-half tones). The former is therefore called a MAJOR THIRD and the latter a MINOR THIRD. These intervals, in fact, characterize the two modes, which are therefore called respectively Major and Minor.

Keys

Either mode contains seven tones; and either may be based on any of the twelve tones of the octave as its tonic by shifting the original interval pattern of whole-tones and half-tones with the help of the black-key tones to the desired level. Such shifting of a modal pattern, or of a tune, is called TRANSPOSITION; for example:

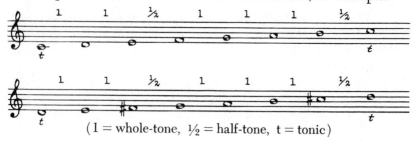

(1 = whole-tone, ½ = half-tone, t = tonic)

As the result of transposition we obtain twelve major and twelve minor keys, named after their tonics, *C* Major, *D* Major, *E*-flat Minor, *B* Minor, and so forth. The *C*-major, *B*-minor, and similar scales are arrangements of all the tones of a key in ladder-like order, made for pedagogical purposes. A scale enables one to inspect the intervals and other relationships in a key with great ease, but it is by no means the only content of the key, nor does it possess musical, i.e. artistic value.

Key Signatures

Each key or tonality employs certain sharps or flats to establish the interval pattern of its mode. These characteristic accidentals are written at the beginning of every staff of a musical piece and are called the KEY SIGNATURE of the particular work. Thus at the beginning of every composition there are three signs: a clef, a key signature, and a time signature; for example: . The key signature must be observed throughout the entire work, or until it is replaced by another key signature; in our example every *F* and *C* that occurs in the piece so headed has to be sharped. (Only pieces in *C* Major and *A* Minor have no accidentals in the key signature.)

The Church Modes
(cf. fn. 3, p. 192)

Many people employ the term "mode" too narrowly as applying only to the Church modes. The following table shows the four chief Church modes in comparison with our two modes. They, also, may be based on any of the twelve tones of the octave as a tonic, and each thus may appear in twelve different keys.

Minor:

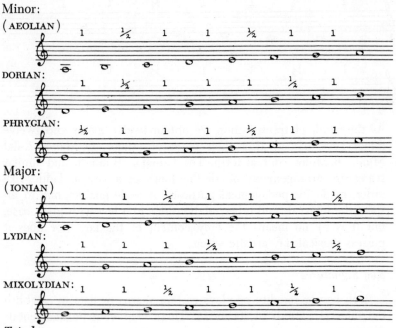

Triads
  (cf. fn. 3, p. 43)

The most usual harmonies, or chords that belong to a key, are TRIADS—three-tone chords built in thirds, such as those comprising the first, third, and fifth tones, or steps or degrees, of a key, whether Major or Minor; or the second, fourth, and sixth; the third, fifth, and seventh; and so forth. The lowest of the three tones, the one above which the two thirds appear, is called the ROOT; and if the root of a triad is the tonic of a key, we speak of a TONIC TRIAD.

The only difference between the tonic triads in Major and **Minor** lies in the chord tone immediately above the root. This tone is a major third above the tonic in Major and a minor third above the tonic in Minor; the respective triads are therefore called MAJOR and MINOR TRIADS. In the above example several further triads are either major (M) or minor (m), while others are neither (x).

It is important to listen carefully to such kinds of chords and to learn to distinguish among them. Perhaps a friend can play them for you on the piano, or you may try to play them yourself. Also compare the kinds of chords found in the first two measures of Brahms's *In the Graveyard* (p. 42) and compare the first three stanzas of Schumann's *The Two Grenadiers* (p. 15ff) to the last one for mode.

Inversions of Triads
  (cf. fn. 3, p. 324)

Triads, e.g. , do not always have their roots as lowest tones (bass). When the third or fifth function as the bass of a triad, musicians speak of "inversion." The first inversion, which has the third in the bass, for example: is also called "six-three" or for short "six-chord" because of the figured-bass symbols that indicate the intervals above the bass tone. Similarly, the second inversion, with the fifth in the bass, for example: is called "six-four-chord." During the Baroque and Classic-Romantic periods the six-four-chord was felt to be a dissonant chord of great tension and suspense and was used in concertos to introduce cadenzas.

Equal Temperament
  (cf. fn. 3, p. 103)

"Well-Tempered" in the title *The Well-Tempered Clavier* (Vol. I, 1722; Vol. II, 1744) refers to TUNING or TEMPERAMENT, terms demanding some explanation. Bach was among the first composers to treat all twelve tones within the octave and all major and minor keys equally in his works. There had been a long struggle to determine a tuning that would permit the satisfactory use of the five tones represented by the black keys of our piano. In Bach's time the solution was finally evolved both theoretically and practically by the establishment of the EQUAL TEMPERAMENT, a tuning in which the interval between any two neighboring tones is exactly the same. Its champion was the great French composer and theorist, Jean Philippe·Rameau (1683–1764).

We value temperament because it gives equal status to all twelve tones of our music: It permits any one of them to become the tonic of a major and a minor key—previously possible only for a few tones. Therefore, whereas formerly a composer could use only a few keys, the intervals of other scales being too far out of tune, now he can avail himself of them all.

Bach did not actually employ Rameau's "equal temperament," but his "good temperament" (cf. the title, *The Well-Tempered Clavier*) was, in effect, the same. It was a tuning which, as an organ builder and as an expert with all kinds of instruments, Bach had found to work. He now set out to prove its usability in this large *opus*.

Keys and Moods
(cf. fn. 3, p. 386)

The general acceptance of equal temperament seems to contradict the following interesting attitude which, for instance, Beethoven follows to create greater unity among the *movements* of the *Eroica*. The expression of the various passages in that work which share the same key is rather similar; as Beethoven himself stated, he connected definite emotional values with the various tonalities. This is a typically Romantic attitude. Moreover, it seems that the particular expressions that Beethoven found to go well with the various keys were accepted as appropriate by later composers. E-flat Major *(Eroica, First movement)*, for instance, has remained the key of heroism, C Minor *(Eroica, Funeral March)* that of tragedy, F Minor *(Appassionata, Egmont Overture,* development section in the *Funeral March* of the *Eroica)* that of conflict.

This KEY SYMBOLISM, as surprising as it is in a system based on equal temperament, is still more so, if we consider that notes in Beethoven's time symbolized tones that were about a half-tone lower than after 1850. For until 1858 no international standard of pitch had ever been agreed on. Even since then pitch has fluctuated, although not so much as before. Three international conferences—at Paris (1858), Vienna (1889), and London (1939)—have had the purpose of inducing all nations to agree on a common standard pitch.

Probably these correlations between keys and moods, like those between modes and expression (see p. 43), reflect the influence of certain outstanding Classic masterworks, such as the *Eroica*, upon the Romantics. Because of the deep impression the work made upon them, they apparently took the often merely coincidental use of a key and a mood for a sign of an intimate and necessary relationship between them.

II. ADDITIONAL INFORMATION ON VOICES AND INSTRUMENTS

A. *Types of Voices*

Operatic Voices
  (cf. fn. 4, p. 130)

In the opera even more than in the cantata and oratorio, human voices have become highly specialized for the various types of characters and music they present. The basic four voice ranges are subdivided, from highest to lowest, in the following way:

sopranos
- *coloratura*—Example 30, p. 52ff
- *soubrette*—Susanna in Example 51c, p. 135f
- lyric—Example 39, p. 85ff; Cherubino in Example 51b, c, p. 134ff; Example 54, p. 142ff; Example 58, p. 157ff
- youthful dramatic or *spinto*—Example 47, p. 116f
- dramatic—Example 53, p. 140f (in a lyric passage)

altos
- mezzo-soprano—Example 41, *No.* 47, p. 97f
- contralto or alto—Example 49, p. 119f; Example 50, p. 130ff; Example 59, p. 166ff

tenors
- oratorio tenor (*coloratura*)—Example 39, p. 85ff; Example 40, p. 92ff
- lyric—Example 59, p. 166ff
- youthful dramatic—Example 52, p. 137f
- dramatic

$$\text{basses} \begin{cases} \text{lyric baritone—Example 48, p. 118} \\ \text{dramatic baritone or bass-baritone} \\ \text{dramatic bass—Example 55a, p. 144ff} \\ \text{lyric bass—Example 39, p. 85ff} \\ \textit{basso buffo} \text{ or } \textit{buffo} \text{ bass—Example 51a, p. 133f} \\ \textit{basso profundo} \text{ or low bass} \end{cases}$$

The Castrati

By assigning the role of Orfeo to an alto, Gluck continued a tradition of the Italian stage. There was an old Church rule that women must not sing in public. Hence boys' voices were employed in religious services and appeared very desirable. Every year, in order to supply voices stronger but of similar quality for the opera, thousands of boys who showed vocal talent were castrated. (This practice was strictly forbidden, but for some the profit was too alluring to resist. Even the Church employed *castrati* from the sixteenth century to the eighteenth.) Though only a few of these boys became good singers, those who did had voices of great power, beauty, flexibility, and very large range. Some *castrati*, stars of heroic roles, achieved places among the richest and most influential musicians of all time. Their voices were favored in Italy, Spain, Germany, and England from about 1620 to 1780, although never to the exclusion of normal male singers. In France this custom never became established. When Gluck introduced *Orfeo* in Paris, he therefore rewrote the title role for a baritone (and furthermore complied with French taste by adding a ballet).

B. Keyboard Instruments

(cf. fn. 5, p. 56)

The harpsichord is a keyboard instrument, much like a piano, but with strings plucked rather than hammered. The organ, on the other hand, produces its sound through pipes, not strings. At home Baroque musicians favored yet another keyboard instrument —the CLAVICHORD. Its tone, however, was too soft for the brilliant toccata.

The Clavichord

The clavichord was developed during the fourteenth century. It is a small, flat box that can be carried around and put on any table. The strings run parallel to the keyboard. When a key is depressed, a small metal plate, the TANGENT, touches a string and produces a very soft but expressive tone, easily variable in volume through finger pressure. The range of the instrument is rather small, between three and four octaves. It dropped out of use around 1790.

The Harpsichord

The harpsichord (see Pl. IV, p. 71; Pl. X, p. 265), which was developed during the fourteenth century also, became the standard instrument for home and concert during the seventeenth and eighteenth centuries, and then, around 1790, yielded place to the piano. In our day its use has been revived, so that old music, composed for this instrument, may be performed more faithfully. However, the harpsichord is best suited for large reception rooms like those in castles. The sound it produces is brilliant but lacks fullness and dies fast, and is inadequate for concert halls except when electrically amplified.

The harpsichord was built in several shapes and sizes. The smallest was called SPINET (Latin: *spina*—thorn), referring to the PRICK or PLECTRUM that plucks the string, usually made of crow quill or of leather. The concert grand, often with two keyboards, was known in Italy as *cembalo* (or *clavicembalo, gravicembalo*), in France as *clavecin,* and in England as *virginal* (Latin: *virga* —prick).

The harpsichord mechanism operates as follows: The depression of a key lifts a JACK with its quill, which latter plucks the string as on a guitar. The range of the instrument is between four and four-and-one-half octaves. Its tone is basically invariable with respect to volume, except that a mechanism of pull-knobs, known as STOPS, can change the quality of sound throughout the range of the keyboard. In general, each stop activates a separate set of jacks, each of which sets plays on a particular set of strings. Up to four such stops or tone-color changes are available on each keyboard.

The Piano

The piano was invented in 1709 by Bartolommeo Cristofori (1655–1731) in Florence, Italy. He named the new instrument *piano-forte* because it could sound either soft or loud, according to the amount of finger pressure applied. Its tone, produced by hammers hitting against strings, blends comfortably with that of any other instrument and is suitable in the home and in the concert hall alike. After some improvements the piano superseded the clavichord and the harpsichord in the 1780's. Since then other important modifications have been made and its range has been increased from about four octaves to seven and one-third.

(cf. fn. 6, p. 267) With Mozart, late in the eighteenth century, the piano became the most important instrument of music. Its brilliance, its full tone, its flexibility which yields all shadings from the light touch of tenderness to the resounding wrath of thunder, from the smoothest *legato* to the shortest *staccato,* made it a universal instrument on which all kinds of music could be easily reproduced. Whereas in the Baroque and the Rococo most composers and conductors had been violinists, those after Mozart were mostly pianists.

The line of piano virtuosi likewise begins with Mozart, who astonished European audiences with his technical skill at the early age of six. It continued with Beethoven, and in the nineteenth century with Chopin, Liszt, Clara Schumann, and Anton Rubinstein, reaching into our century with Feruccio Busoni and Sergei Rachmaninoff, to name only the most eminent, most of them also composers of mark. In our day, although some composers are also fine pianists, as for example Poulenc, on the whole the outstanding virtuosi are not composers. Among the many brilliant pianists of our time probably the best known are Vladimir Horowitz and Artur Rubinstein, neither a composer. As in other fields of activity, in music, too, specialization has practically doomed the universally trained artist.

The Organ
(cf. fn. 5, p. 55)

The organ is the most ancient keyboard instrument. Early reports about it in Europe date from the eighth century, and other peoples knew it almost a thousand years earlier. Today the organ possesses two to five manuals, or keyboards for the hands (Latin: *manus*—hand), and a pedal keyboard for the feet (Latin: *pedes*—feet). The keys control valves which permit wind to produce sound through the sets of pipes that constitute the sound mechanism of the organ. In general each key of a particular keyboard corresponds to a single pipe in each particular set, and the pipes within each set differ in size and pitch to correspond to the keys of any keyboard. Each set of pipes, and there may be hundreds, emits sounds of a particular quality (labeled "violin," "flute," "trumpet," and the like); auxiliary keys or knobs, the STOPS, call into play the sets desired. The choice of stops, or REGISTRATION, often left by the composer to the discretion of the organist, is an important part of the latter's art. The various keyboards, moreover, permit the simultaneous use of different stops for purposes of contrast in tone color and of differentiation of several melodic lines or of melody and accompaniment. The organ has the largest range of any instrument: over eight octaves.

For many centuries the powerful tones of the large organs enriched the religious services, while the lighter-voiced small organs were popular in the home (see Pl. II, p. 65). Around 1600, however, the stringed keyboard instruments replaced the latter and left the organ supreme only in the churches. It is chiefly with them that we associate the organ today.

C. The Violin Family

Lute and Guitar
(cf. fn. 3, p. 68)

The lute and the guitar were the favorite instruments in the Renaissance. The lute, like its small relative, the mandoline, has a curved back derived from the ancestral gourd, whereas the guitar has a flat back. The former, moreover, has strings of gut rather than of metal, as has the guitar, and hence produces a mellower, more refined tone. (See Pl. II, p. 65; Pl. III, p. 69.)

Emergence of the Violin
  (cf. fn. 10, p. 271)

Among instruments of general importance today the violin ranks next to the piano. Out of a combination of folk instruments, variously known as fiddle, *vielle,* or viol, with the lute and guitar, it was developed to nearly its present shape in the last third of the sixteenth century. Slowly its brilliant tone won favor over the flat, noncommittal tone of its cousin, the six-stringed *viola da gamba* (Italian—leg viol). This instrument was built in all sizes, from soprano to bass; the ancestors of the family, of alto size, were played in sitting position supported by the thigh, hence the name. (See Pl. II, p. 65; Pl. IV, p. 69.)

During the time of Monteverdi, about 1615, the violin gained pre-eminence in Italy. (In other countries the violin was not accepted until two or three generations thereafter.) There the finest string instruments were made. The fame of their makers—the families of the Amati, Guarneri, and Stradivari, to name only the most illustrious, all of Cremona[1]—has, if anything, increased. Their violins, violas, and 'cellos have steadily gained in value over the years. Unlike pianos, which deteriorate within decades, these instruments have improved with age; their tone has become mellower, sweeter.

The Violin Family
  (cf. fn. 3, p. 107)

The violin is the soprano of the string family, the viola the alto, the 'cello or violoncello the tenor, and the double bass the bass. Save the last, all have four strings tuned in fifths. The 'cello's four strings are tuned to *C* (next above the lowest *C* on the piano), then in ascending order to *G, D*, and *A*. The strings of the viola are tuned an octave higher than these. The double bass was originally tuned an octave below the 'cello, but today its strings sound *E* (lowest

---

[1] The Amati were: Andrea (1535?–1611); his sons, Antonio and Girolamo; and his grandson, Niccolo (1596–1684); the Guarneri: Andrea (1626?–98), pupil of Niccolo Amati; his sons, Pietro and Giuseppe; and his nephew, Giuseppe del Gesù (1687–1742); the Stradivari: Antonio (1644?–1737), pupil of Niccolo Amati and teacher of Giuseppe Guarneri del Gesù; and his sons, Francesco and Omobono. Their instruments are selling today for an average of $6000, and some for as high as $50,000 and more.

on the piano), A, D, and G. (Many instruments have a fifth string or a mechanical device for lowering the E string to supply the low C. Other names for the double bass are: contra-bass, string bass, and bass viol.) The violin's lower three strings duplicate the viola's higher three, namely G (below the middle C), D, and A, with E as the highest string. The proportionate lengths of the members of the string family are about as 1 (double bass): 2/3 ('cello): 3/8 (viola): 1/3 (violin).

The String Quartet
(cf. fn. 2, p. 284)

The 'cello vanquished the tenor gamba only around 1700, when it was accepted as an instrument adapted to sustain either a *basso continuo* or a solo part, and was frequently combined with one or two violins in ensembles. The viola was at first considered appropriate only for the mediocre violinist. But when during the Rococo preference shifted from a melodic-rhythmic equivalence of bass and soprano to the dominance of the melody accompanied by simple chords, the viola was at once found convenient for supplying the needed middle tones of harmonies, and was therefore added to the ensemble; on the other hand, the harpsichord was dropped as superfluous. Thus around 1750 the string quartet emerged.

Since the formation of the Rasoumovsky String Quartet shortly after 1800 many quartet ensembles have gained fame. Toward the end of the nineteenth century the Joachim (see Pl. XI, p. 285) and the Kneisel Quartets were probably best known. The latter and the Flonzaley Quartet shared pre-eminence early in this century; and during the second quarter of this century perhaps the Busch and the Budapest Quartets were most celebrated.

String Virtuosi
(cf. fn. 10, p. 271)

The Italian violinists of the seventeenth and eighteenth centuries were all distinguished composers. Beginning with Corelli (1653–1713), and continuing with Vivaldi (1678?–1741) and Tartini (1692–1770) (see Pl. X, p. 265) to Paganini (1782–1840), their works belong to our standard repertory. In the nineteenth century the French school of violinists—including men from many

nations who came to study in Paris—replaced the Italian. Perhaps
the best known virtuosi of this school were the Norwegian Ole
Bull (1810–80), the Pole Henri Wieniawski (1835–80), and the
Belgian Eugène Ysaye (1858–1931). Few of the great performers
of this school were important composers, and since later generations do not usually celebrate virtuosi who have not also distinguished themselves in creative works, their names are gradually
fading from memory.

With Joseph Joachim (1831–1904) (see Pl. XI, p. 285), Leopold
Auer (1845–1930), and Karl Flesch (1873–1944) we reach the
teachers of many of our contemporary concert artists. Among these
Jascha Heifetz (b.1901) and Nathan Milstein (b.1904) are probably most widely known. There have been, of course, fine virtuosi
of the viola and 'cello as well, in recent times especially the violist
William Primrose (b.1903) and the cellists Pablo Casals (b.1876)
and Gregor Piatigorsky (b.1903).

D. Wind Instruments, Their Families, and Transpositions

(cf. fn. 5, p. 185)

In looking over the list of instruments on Plate VIII, p. 186, we
see some items that require an explanation, e.g. what does "clarinet
in B-flat" mean? or "trumpet in B-flat?" or "horns in F?" (*Cor anglais*
is French for English horn.)

Transposing Instruments

All woodwind and brass instruments have been built in families,
that is, in various sizes, in order to extend their particular timbres
over a wider range of pitch; for the longer the instrument, the lower
is its range. (See comment on proportionate sizes of stringed instruments, top of p. 393.) To enable a player of a wind instrument to
play all members of its family with equal ease, the following rule
has been observed for centuries: Any particular note will be played
on any instrument of a family in the identical way, i.e. using the
same fingering, hand position, or valves, as the case may be.

Since the instruments of the family differ in length, the pitch of
the tone thus produced differs from instrument to instrument. In
other words, the same notes, appearing in staves serving different

instruments of a family, signify different pitches. We therefore speak of transposing instruments, and indicate the kind of transposition when speaking of them: The clarinet in *B*-flat in Plate VIII, for example, produces the tone *B*-flat when playing the note *C;* so does the trumpet in *B*-flat, whereas the horn in *F* will produce an *F* when playing the note *C.* Even where only one member of a family is still in use, transposition is often conservatively retained.

Instruments of the Orchestra

Our orchestras include most members of the following instrument families:

Family	Type of Mouthpiece	Instrument	written is heard as	Range as written
flutes	hole with sharp edge	piccolo (in high *C*)		
		flute		
oboes	double reed (two reeds tied together)	oboe		
		English horn (in *F*)		
clarinets	single reed	high clarinets in *E*-flat, *D*		
		clarinets in *B*-flat, *A*		
		alto clarinet in *E*-flat		
		bass-clarinet in *B*-flat		
saxophones	single reed	clarino or sopranino in *E*-flat		
		soprano in *B*-flat		
		alto in *E*-flat		

Family	Type of Mouthpiece	Instrument	written is heard as	Range as written
saxo- phones		tenor in *B*-flat		
		baritone in *E*-flat		
		bass in *B*-flat		
bassoons	double reed	bassoon		
		contra- or double-bas- soon (in low *C*)		
horns	funnel	French horn (in *F*)		
trumpets	cup	trumpet in *B*-flat		
Wagner tubas	funnel	tenor tuba in *B*-flat (baritone horn)		
		bass tuba in *F*		
trom- bones	cup	tenor trombone		
		tenor-bass trombone		
tubas or bugles	cup	bass tuba		
drums		timpani (kettle drums)		
		tambourine; small (mil- itary) drum; snare (side) drum; tenor (roll) drum; bass drum		i.p. (indefinite pitch)
wooden plates		xylophone (marimba)		

Family	Playing Mechansim	Instrument	written ♪ is heard as	Range as written
		castanets; rattle; Chinese blocks		i.p.
gourds		maracas, and others		i.p.
metal plates, tubes, bars	keyboard (bars)	celesta (dulcitone, similar but with tuning forks instead of bars)		
	hammers (plates)	*glockenspiel* (bells, carillon)		
	hammers (tubes)	chimes (tubular bells)		
	(plates)	cymbals, gong (tamtam)		i.p.
	(tubes)	triangle		i.p.
harp		harp		
violin		violin		
		viola		
		'cello		
		double-bass (contrabass, string bass)		

Additional brass instruments used mostly in bands are the following, all with cup mouthpieces:

Family	Instrument	written — is heard as	Range as written
cornets	cornet in *B*-flat		
bugles	fluegelhorn in *B*-flat, C		
	baritone in *C*, *B*-flat		
	euphonium		
	helicon (a bass tuba in different shape; also, somewhat altered, sousaphone)		
saxhorns	soprano in *E*-flat, F		
	alto in *B*-flat, C		
	tenor (alto horn) in *E*-flat, F		
	baritone (tenor horn) in *B*-flat, C		

E. Conductors and Orchestras

(cf. fn. 5, p. 364)

Before 1800 the operatic conductor directed by playing the keyboard instrument, and the choral conductor indicated the beats with a large, white paper roll, plainly visible in the twilight of choirlofts. In all cases the direction of the orchestra was in the hands of the concert-master, the first violinist. Only at the Paris Opera, following Lully's custom, the meter was loudly stamped out with a long stick against the floor. All these technics were superseded by the baton during the generation we have called the early Romantics (1803–28).

Since the beginning of this century many great conductors have taken their place beside instrumental and vocal virtuosi: Mahler's disciple, Bruno Walter; Wilhelm Furtwängler, the conductor of the Berlin Philharmonic; Willem Mengelberg, educator of the Amsterdam Concertgebouw (Concert Hall) Orchestra; Pierre Monteux, in France and in the United States; Thomas Beecham in England; Serge Koussevitzky of Boston-Symphony fame; Leopold Stokowski, who gave his best to the Philadelphia Orchestra; and the most famous of them all, Arturo Toscanini, who, after a brilliant career at the Milano Scala (the opera house of Milan, Italy) and at the Metropolitan Opera House in New York, established a model orchestra in the NBC Symphony.

In addition to the orchestras already mentioned, at least the London Philharmonic and the New York Philharmonic must be noted as outstanding. But practically every city of half a million or more inhabitants today has one or several large symphony orchestras. In the United States alone there are several hundred of them, and there are hundreds more elsewhere. It is for such mammoth organizations that most composers of the post-Romantic (about 1893–1912) and the following generation wrote their symphonies.

III. ADDITIONAL INFORMATION ON MUSICAL TYPES

A. Vocal Chamber Music of the Renaissance

(cf. fn. 2, p. 64)

We speak of two kinds of madrigals: the Italian, with an Italian text and sung everywhere during the period in this language; and the English, with an English text and sung only in England. The term "madrigal" seems to have been derived in the fourteenth century from "matricale," meaning "in the mother tongue," i.e. in Italian, not in Latin.

Various nations favored further, similar types of vocal chamber music. The French had their witty CHANSONS; the Spanish turned to guitar-accompanied [1] ROMANCES; the English of Shakespeare's time delighted in lute-accompanied [1] AYRES; and the Germans sang POLYPHONIC LIEDER. A lady or a gentleman not able to participate creditably in such entertainments was considered graceless; social standing depended in large degree upon the ability to write the poetry as well as the music of such pieces.

B. Chorale Settings

(cf. fn. 4, p. 105)

There are several types of chorale settings: (1) a chorale melody with an accompaniment (cf. Example 44, p. 106); (2) the trio setting (cf. Example 39, *No. 4,* p. 89); (3) the fugato setting, actually a chain of short fugues using the various phrases of the hymn tune as subjects; (4) the fantasy on the motifs of the melody; and (5) the CHORALE PARTITA—a simple statement followed by varied repetitions of the entire melody. Some, the CHORALE PRELUDES, are brief because they were meant to be played as introductions to hymns sung by the congregation or the choir; others, the chorale fantasies and partitas, are long, replacing the hymn itself.

C. The Evolution of the Concerto Grosso

(cf. fn. 1, p. 317)

At its birth, the *concerto grosso* used but one important device: contrasting tone colors in brief alternation of *concertino* and *ripieno.* Later came the assignment of different music to the opposing groups, the soloists receiving *bravura* passages to show off their dexterity. Thus arose the practice of giving to each group long passages to play, instead of only a few measures. The last stage of evolution was the allotment of individual melodic ideas, not merely passage work, to each group.

Handel, who met Corelli and learned from him, was somewhat conservative in his *concerti grossi* and used only the first two of these technics. Following Corelli he formulated his *concerti grossi* like trio sonatas, opening with a slow movement, and involving

---

[1] See Appendix I, p. 391, for an explanation of guitar and lute.

both dances and fugal movements. Vivaldi and Bach, on the other hand, liked to start with a fast movement and gave significant new material to the *concertino*. They retained the solo group—which often included woodwind and brass instruments up to a *concertino* of six—through all the movements of a work, whereas Handel might include entirely orchestral movements as well as some that give prominence to one instrument only, in solo-concerto fashion.

D. *Eighteenth-Century Opera*

Opera seria
(cf. fn. 1, p. 130)

Nearly all seventeenth-century operas were serious and tragic. Rarely did comic scenes relieve the heroic tales of love and death. At the beginning of the eighteenth century all comic scenes were, in Italian opera, relegated to interludes between acts. The new serious Italian opera, now called specifically *opera seria*, continued the older tradition in using stereotyped heroic librettos, magnificent stage décor, and large casts; but (1) it was standardized in three acts; (2) the action was carried on almost exclusively in *secco* recitative, while *accompagnato* recitative and *arioso* were minimized; (3) it included many long, elaborate concert arias, often with *coloratura*, which interrupted the action; and (4) it strictly excluded comic scenes.

Opera buffa

The comic scenes, on the other hand, which relieved the monotonous seriousness during the two intermissions and which were therefore known as INTERMEZZI, soon became independent; and in the 1730's they grew into a new operatic type, called OPERA BUFFA. Its two acts were staged simply. The orchestra was small, and so was the number of singers employed. Instead of heroes of myth and romance, the *buffa* brings to the stage people of the middle classes: servants, barbers, lawyers, soldiers, and the like. It is marked by rapid patter songs (cf. Example 51a, c, pp. 133f, 135f) involving much dialect, by slapstick comedy complete with masquerade and mistaken identities (cf. Example 51a, p. 133f), and by many ensembles, especially in the long final scenes, or FINALES, of both acts. A few arias of the *opera-seria* type, such as that cited from Rossini's *The Barber of Seville* (cf. p. 51f), were, however, usually included.

The arias of *opere buffe* and *opere serie* with their many repetitions of words and music (cf. also Example 39, *Nos.* 3 and 6, pp. 88f, 90) represent the climax of *bel canto*. It is mainly because of them that in both *seria* and *buffa* the dramatic action is presented not continuously but in musically independent units—recitatives, arias, duets, choruses, and so forth—permitting the singers to interrupt the story and to step to the footlights to perform their vocal pyrotechnics as if in concert. Therefore especially the *opera seria* is known as the "singers' opera," and both *seria* and *buffa* as "number opera." Other types of opera followed their example and were for a long time characterized by the "number" technic.

The Neapolitan School

The musical mastermind of Italian opera in the eighteenth century was Alessandro Scarlatti (1660–1725). Many students gathered around him at the Spanish court of Naples in southern Italy, and they soon carried the style of NEAPOLITAN OPERA to all countries of Europe, where it remained in high repute throughout the century. In Italy Neapolitan opera, both *seria* and *buffa*, lived on well into the nineteenth century; indeed, it has never been entirely forgotten.

The Rise of Middle-Class Opera

Among the students of Scarlatti was Handel. His about forty *opere serie*, composed mostly for performance in London, belong to the finest examples of *bel canto*. When he turned from opera to oratorio around 1738, signs of the advent of a new era were multiplying. The *opera buffa* was turning to the middle classes and to dialect. The lowest classes—thieves, prostitutes, smugglers, and the like—were being portrayed on the English stage in spoken plays interspersed with many ballads, which were the center of interest. For a hundred years or more these BALLAD OPERAS were the favorite entertainment both in Britain and in North America. Indeed, one of the earliest and the most famous of them, *The Beggar's Opera*, with text by John Gay (1685–1732) and music, partly compiled and partly composed, by John Pepusch (1667–1752), first performed in London in 1728, is still occasionally revived.

A little later, after the mid-century, the oriental and other fairy tales, such as the Arabian Nights or Little Red Riding Hood, were introduced on the French stage in the OPÉRA COMIQUE, and on the German in the SINGSPIEL (song play). In both, spoken text alternated with simple, folk-like songs and occasional arias. The emergence of these operatic types reflects the political and social rise of the middle classes itself.

E. The Suite and Its Dances

Couperin's Suites
(cf. fn. 2, p. 107)

The greatest French composer of suites was François Couperin (1668–1733), called "the Great" to distinguish him from the numerous other musicians in his family through four generations (cf. Example 71, p. 236). As church organist and chamber harpsichordist to Louis XIV and Louis XV, Couperin was the chief figure among French composers of his time in the transition from the massive solidity of the Baroque to the delicacy and finesse of the succeeding Rococo. His suites differ widely in the number and kinds of dances and character pieces they include. Many of the pieces have titles, such as "Lady Auguste," "Lady Majestic," and "Lady Mylord," which grace three of the six dances of one suite. These titles, allusions to various ladies of the court, constitute a social guessing game.

Other famous composers of suites were Purcell and Handel in England, Rameau in France, and Bach in Germany. The last one composed about twenty keyboard suites, called in turn *French Suites, English Suites,* and *Partitas,* as well as three for violin alone, six for 'cello alone, and four for orchestra.

The Dances of the Suite
(cf. fn. 4, p. 108)

The dances most frequently encountered in suites of the later Baroque are almost all French; names of works in the following list indicate where the reader may find such dances as are not discussed in Part II, Section D.

Allemande, slow 4/4

Anglaise, fast 4/4—J. S. Bach: *French Suite No. 3, B* Minor

Bourrée, fast 2/2

Chaconne (Spanish), slow or moderate 3/4—Example 71, p. 236

Corrente (Italian), fast 3/4—Example 45, p. 108 (not a *courante* really)

Courante, moderate 6/4—J. S. Bach: *French Suite No. 1, D* Minor

Gavotte, moderately fast 2/2

Gigue, fast 6/8 or 12/8, sometimes also 4/4

Hornpipe (English), moderate 3/4 or 3/2, sometimes also 4/4—H. Purcell: *Suite No. 7, D* Minor

Loure, moderate 6/4—J. S. Bach: *French Suite No. 5, G* Major

Minuet, moderate 3/4—Example 16, p. 24

Musette (literally "bagpipe"), a *gavotte* with pedal points imitating bagpipes—J. S. Bach: *English Suite No. 3, G* Minor

Passacaglia, same as *chaconne*

Passepied, fast 3/8 or 3/4—J. S. Bach: *English Suite No. 5, E* Major

Polonaise, moderate 3/4—J. S. Bach: *French Suite No. 6, E* Major

Rigaudon, moderate 2/2—H. Purcell: *Suite No. 5, C* Major

Sarabande (Spanish), slow 3/4 or 3/2

Siciliano (Italian), slow 6/8 or 12/8—Example 20, p. 29; H. Purcell: *Suite No. 2, G* Minor

F. A List of Frequently Encountered Dances

(cf. fn. 6, p. 30)

The abbreviations in this list refer to the countries of origin:

Am—United States, En—England, Fr—France, It—Italy, Sp—Spain.

Anglaise (En), cf. *Ecossaise*

Bolero (Sp), since 1780 slow 2/4 or 3/4

Boston (Am), since 1874, moderate 3/4, derived from the waltz

Cancan (Fr), 1830–1870, fast 2/4

Charleston (Am), 1922–1926, fast 2/4, derived from fox trot

Conga (Cuba), since 1930, moderate 2/4

Contre, Contredanse, Country Dance (En), since before 1650, variable tempo and meter

Cotillon, Contredanse française (Fr), since 1723, French variety of *contre*

Csárdás (Hungary), since 1830; first section, "lassu" (cf. lassitude), in slow 2/4; second section, "fris" (cf. fresh), in fast 2/4

Ecossaise, English (En), 1780–1833, fast 2/4, derived from *contre*

Fandango (Sp), before 1600–1800, slow 3/8

Flamenco (Sp, Gypsy), since 1800, slow, variable tempo and meter, derived from the *"cante hondo"* or *"jondo"* (deep, or emotional singing) of Andalusia

Forlana, Furlana (It, Venice), 1600–1900, fast 6/8

Fox trot (Am), since 1912, fast 2/4, but also moderate and slow

Française (Fr), cf. *Cotillon*

Gagliarda, Gaillarde (It, Sp), 1480–1650, moderate 3/4

Galop (Fr), 1850–1900, fast 2/4, derived from the polka

Habañera (Cuba), since before 1800, slow 2/4

Hopak, Gopak (Ukraine), since before 1800, moderate 2/4

Hora (Roumania, Israel), since 1920, moderate 4/4

Jota (Sp, Aragon), since before 1800, fast 3/4

Krakoviak (Poland), since before 1700, moderate 3/4

Ländler (Austria, Styria), since before 1700, moderate 3/4

Malagueña (Sp, Malaga), since before 1800, slow 3/8, derived from the *fandango*

Maxixe (Brazil), since before 1890, moderate 2/4

Mazurka, Mazurek (Poland), since before 1750, moderate 3/4

Minuet, *Menuetto* (Fr), 1650–1790, moderate 3/4

Morris Dance, *Morisco, Moresque* (En, It, Sp), since before 1450, variable tempo and meter

One-step (Am), cf. Turkey trot

Pavane (Sp, It, Fr), 1500–1600, slow 4/4

Polka (Czechoslovakia), 1830–1900, moderate 2/4

Polo (Sp, Andalusia), since before 1850, moderate 3/8
Polonaise (Poland), since before 1650, moderate 3/4
Quadrille (Fr), cf. *cotillon*
Rheinländer (Germany), 1850–1900, moderate 2/4, derived from polka
Rhumba, Rumba (Cuba), since 1930, fast 2/4
Saltarello (It), cf. *tarantella*
Samba (Brazil), since before 1938, moderate 2/4, derived from the *maxixe*
Schottischer (Germany), cf. polka
Seguidilla (Sp, Andalusia), since before 1700, fast 3/4
Slow Fox (Am), since 1920, moderate 2/4
Tango (Argentina), since 1900, slow 2/4, derived from the *habañera*
Tarantella (It, South), since before 1600, fast 6/8 or 12/8
Turkey Trot (Am), 1900–1915, fast 2/4
Two-step (Am), cf. slow fox
Waltz (Germany, South), 1750–1910, fast 3/4

G. Types of Variation

(cf. fn. 7, p. 220)

Variation means change in one or several of a group of musical elements, the others being retained. (Note that variety within unity is a fundamental principle of aesthetics.) The modifications may range from minor additions and subtractions (alterations that leave intact the essentials of the particular element) to the complete replacement of the particular formulation of the element by a new one. Thus we note, in systematic tabulation, the following major types of variation discussed in this volume:

structure	melody	rhythm	expression	harmony	counterpoint	instrumentation	motifs	Type of Variation	Usual Name of Type	Examples studied
O	O	O	O	O	O	X		tone-color		Ex. 68, p. 218f
O	O	O	O	O	X			contrapuntal	passacaglia	Ex. 38, p. 83f; Ex. 49, p. 119f; Ex. 66, p. 211ff
O	C	O	O	O	O			melodic	figural var.	
O	O	O	O	X				harmonic		Ex. 29, p. 51; Ex. 32, p. 55
O	C	X	X		X			rhythmic	character var.	Ex. 67, *Var. 5*, p. 216
O	X	X	X	C		X	O	rhythmic-melodic	character var.	Ex. 94, *4th mvmt*, Var. 6, p. 351f
O	X			C	O	X		contrapuntal		Ex. 84, *4th mvmt*, Var. 2, 5, p. 294f
X	X	X	X	X	X	X	O	structural	free var.	Ex. 90, p. 327ff

(O — element retained)
(X — element replaced)
(C — element partially changed, or changed at times only)

The elements not further indicated in this table may or may not be altered, but they are of secondary importance in the particular types. The various types of variation may also be combined, for example melodic-harmonic, rhythmic-harmonic, melodic-tone-color, contrapuntal-harmonic, and the like. Often, moreover, the method or type of variation differs from one variation to the next in a set or from one group of variations to another.

IV. THE COMPOSERS OF THE VARIOUS PERIODS

A. Renaissance Composers

(cf. fn. 6, p. 76)

Until in recent decades their music was revived, most Renaissance composers were forgotten. Taking into account only the last century of the Renaissance, the following were the most eminent masters, those that also appear most frequently on our concert programs:

Josquin des Prez (or Prés) (1450?–1521), Belgian, but long in Italy and France; virtually the creator of the mature Renaissance style of expressive imitational polyphony.

Aadrian Willaert (1485?–1562), Belgian, but living in Italy; initiator of the sixteenth-century madrigal, of music for two choirs, and of composition for instrumental ensembles.

Giovanni Pierluigi da Palestrina (1525–94), Italian; almost exclusively a church composer, he set the standard of conservative Roman Catholic church music.

Orlandus Lassus (Orlando di Lasso, Roland de Lassus) (1532?–94), Belgian, but living in Italy and Germany; the most universal international composer of his time.

Tomas Luiz de Victoria (Vittoria) (1549–1611), Spanish; exclusively a church composer.

William Byrd (1543–1623), English; the leader among Elizabethan and early Stuart composers, the initiator of the English madrigal, and an outstanding composer of anthems and harpsichord music.

B. Baroque Composers

(cf. fn. 3, p. 121)

Jan Pieterszon Sweelinck (1562–1621), Dutch; famous for motets and *ricercari;* virtually the creator of the fugue.

Claudio Monteverdi (1567–1643), Italian; famous for madrigals; virtually the creator of the opera.

Heinrich Schütz (1585–1672), German; famous for cantatas, oratorios, and passions.

Jean Baptiste Lully (1632–87), French (but of Italian birth); famous for ballets; creator of the French opera and the French overture; sponsor of the modern orchestra and of the minuet.

Arcangelo Corelli (1653–1713), Italian; famous for violin music; creator of the *concerto grosso.*

Henry Purcell (1658–95), English; famous for anthems, operas, harpsichord and violin music.

Alessandro Scarlatti (1660–1725), Italian; famous for cantatas and masses; creator of the style of eighteenth-century opera (Neapolitan opera).

François Couperin (1668–1733), French; famous for harpsichord music.

Antonio Vivaldi (1678?–1741), Italian; famous for concertos, operas, and oratorios.

Johann Sebastian Bach (1685–1750), German; famous for cantatas, passions, chorales, organ and harpsichord fugues and toccatas, suites, concertos, and chorale settings.

George Frederick Handel (Georg Friedrich Händel) (1685–1759), German, but long in England; famous for operas, oratorios, anthems, and concertos.

C. Classic-Romantic Composers

(cf. fn. 8, p. 188)

The following list of the chief composers of the Classic-Romantic era is chronological according to periods rather than birth dates. The periods are indicated for convenient reference, but the dates should be taken only as approximations; for a new period never begins abruptly. Signs of an approaching change always appear before the change is·sufficiently widespread to mark a new period; and after the change many works still continue within the older tradition.

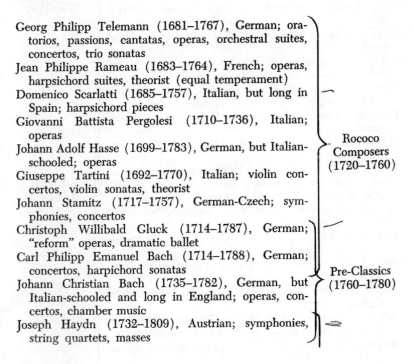

Georg Philipp Telemann (1681–1767), German; oratorios, passions, cantatas, operas, orchestral suites, concertos, trio sonatas

Jean Philippe Rameau (1683–1764), French; operas, harpsichord suites, theorist (equal temperament)

Domenico Scarlatti (1685–1757), Italian, but long in Spain; harpsichord pieces

Giovanni Battista Pergolesi (1710–1736), Italian; operas

Johann Adolf Hasse (1699–1783), German, but Italian-schooled; operas

> Rococo
> Composers
> (1720–1760)

Giuseppe Tartini (1692–1770), Italian; violin concertos, violin sonatas, theorist

Johann Stamitz (1717–1757), German-Czech; symphonies, concertos

Christoph Willibald Gluck (1714–1787), German; "reform" operas, dramatic ballet

Carl Philipp Emanuel Bach (1714–1788), German; concertos, harpichord sonatas

> Pre-Classics
> (1760–1780)

Johann Christian Bach (1735–1782), German, but Italian-schooled and long in England; operas, concertos, chamber music

Joseph Haydn (1732–1809), Austrian; symphonies, string quartets, masses

Ernest Modeste Grétry (1742–1813), French-Belgian; ✓
opéras comiques

Wolfgang Amadeus Mozart (1756–1791), Austrian; ⎫ ✓ Classics
operas, masses, concertos, symphonies, chamber ⎬ (1781–1802)
music

Luigi Cherubini (1760–1842), Italian, but long in ✓
France; operas, masses

Ludwig van Beethoven (1770–1827), German; sym- ⎫
phonies, concertos, overtures, piano sonatas, cham- ⎬ —
ber music ⎭

Carl Maria Weber (1786–1826), German; romantic —
operas, concertos

Franz Schubert (1797–1828), Austrian; songs, cham- ⎫ Early
ber music, symphonies ⎬ Romantics
Niccolo Paganini (1782–1840), Italian; violin and ⎬ (1803–1828)
guitar works ⎭

Gioacchino Rossini (1792–1868), Italian; operas

Gaetano Donizetti (1797–1848), Italian; operas ⎫

Giacomo Meyerbeer (1791–1864), German, but active ⎬
in France; grand operas ⎬ Central

Felix Mendelssohn-Bartholdy (1809–1847), German; ⎬ Romantics
symphonies, overtures, oratorios, Songs Without ⎬ (1829–1848)
Words

Frédéric Chopin (1810–1849), Polish-French; piano — ✓
works

Robert Schumann (1810–1856), German; piano works, — ✓
songs, chamber music, symphonies

Hector Berlioz (1803–1869), French; symphonic pro- — ✓
gram music, Gluckist operas, oratorios

Giuseppe Verdi (1813–1901), Italian; realistic and ⎫ — ✓
grand operas ⎬

Richard Wagner (1813–1883), German; romantic op- — ✓
eras, music dramas

Franz Liszt (1811–1886), Hungarian; piano works, — ✓
symphonic poems, masses, songs ⎬ High

Charles Gounod (1818–1893), French; lyric operas ⎬ Romantics

Jacques Offenbach (1819–1880), German, but active ⎬ (1849–1871)
in France; operettas

Bedřich Smetana (1824–1884), Czech; folk operas, — ✓
symphonic poems

Johann Strauss, son (1825–1899), Austrian; waltzes,
operettas

Anton Bruckner (1824–1896), Austrian; symphonies, ⎫
masses ⎬

Johannes Brahms (1833–1897), German; symphonies, ⎬ — ✓
songs, chamber music, piano works, concertos ⎭

Modeste Musorgsky (1839–1881), Russian; folk operas,
program music, songs

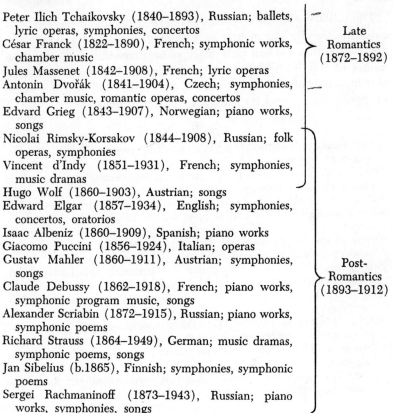

Peter Ilich Tchaikovsky (1840–1893), Russian; ballets, lyric operas, symphonies, concertos

César Franck (1822–1890), French; symphonic works, chamber music

Jules Massenet (1842–1908), French; lyric operas

Antonin Dvořák (1841–1904), Czech; symphonies, chamber music, romantic operas, concertos

Edvard Grieg (1843–1907), Norwegian; piano works, songs

} Late Romantics (1872–1892)

Nicolai Rimsky-Korsakov (1844–1908), Russian; folk operas, symphonies

Vincent d'Indy (1851–1931), French; symphonies, music dramas

Hugo Wolf (1860–1903), Austrian; songs

Edward Elgar (1857–1934), English; symphonies, concertos, oratorios

Isaac Albeniz (1860–1909), Spanish; piano works

Giacomo Puccini (1856–1924), Italian; operas

Gustav Mahler (1860–1911), Austrian; symphonies, songs

Claude Debussy (1862–1918), French; piano works, symphonic program music, songs

Alexander Scriabin (1872–1915), Russian; piano works, symphonic poems

Richard Strauss (1864–1949), German; music dramas, symphonic poems, songs

Jan Sibelius (b.1865), Finnish; symphonies, symphonic poems

Sergei Rachmaninoff (1873–1943), Russian; piano works, symphonies, songs

} Post-Romantics (1893–1912)

D. Contemporary Composers

We discern three generations of composers who have contributed to what we have called contemporary music, the music written since about 1912, namely (1) the "pioneers" of the new era, born before 1890; (2) the "modernists," born between 1890 and 1900 approximately; and (3) the "young" generation, or perhaps better the heirs and consolidators. Of these groups the first, still somewhat attached to the post-Romantic period, experimented with new materials; the second tried to exploit thoroughly the variety of approaches thus established; and the third seems to be at work creating a new, unified style as the basis of the new era. (Usually each period creates new musical species as well, but these tend to emerge after the elements of the new style have been created.)

The following list of composers is very sketchy and merely indicates the trends. The greater or lesser significance of certain composers becomes evident only after some time—therefore only few names of the "young" generation are listed. Let it suffice to say that hundreds of able composers are active today all over the world preparing the ground for the giants of the future.

1.

Ralph Vaughan-Williams (b.1872), English; neo-medievalist; masses, symphonies, operas
Arnold Schoenberg (1874–1951), Austrian; twelve-tone atonalist; piano pieces, chamber music, songs, operas, symphonic works
Maurice Ravel (1875–1937), French; impressionist; ballets, piano works
Manuel de Falla (1876–1949), Spanish; neo-romanticist; ballets, concertos
Ernest Bloch (b.1880), Swiss, but long in America; neo-romanticist; concertos, chamber music
Béla Bartók (1881–1945), Hungarian; neo-barbarist, neo-classicist; concertos, string quartets, piano works, stage works
Igor Stravinsky (b.1882), Russian; neo-barbarist, neo-classicist; ballets, symphonies, oratorios
Karol Szymanowski (1883–1937), Polish; neo-romanticist, polytonalist; piano works, symphonies, concertos, operas, songs
Alban Berg (1885–1935), Austrian; twelve-tone atonalist; operas, chamber music
Heitor Villa-Lobos (b. 1887), Brazilian; neo-romanticist; symphonic works, concertos, chamber music, operas, songs, piano works

2.

Serge Prokofiev (1891–1953), Russian; futurist, neo-romanticist; symphonies, concertos, piano music, operas
Artur Honegger (b.1892), Swiss-French; futurist, neo-romanticist; symphonies, oratorios, symphonic poems, chamber music
Darius Milhaud (b.1892), French; polytonalist, neo-classicist; operas, ballets, chamber music, symphonic works
Paul Hindemith (b.1895), German; neo-classicist; concertos, chamber music, piano works, operas, songs
Aaron Copland (b.1900), American; neo-romanticist; ballets, symphonies

3.

Dmitri Kabalevsky (b.1904), Russian; symphonies, operas, piano works
Dmitri Shostakovich (b.1909), Russian; symphonies, operas, ballets, chamber music
Samuel Barber (b.1910), American; symphonies, chamber music
Benjamin Britten (b.1913), English; operas

APPENDIX II

BIBLIOGRAPHY AND LISTENING MATERIALS IN THE ORDER OF SECTIONS

THE APPROACH

General Reference Works About Musicians and Musical Terms

Apel, Willi, *Harvard Dictionary of Music*. Cambridge, Mass.: Harvard University Press, 1950.

Bacharach, A. L., ed., *The Music Masters*, 4 vols. London: Cassel and Company, Ltd., 1948–54.

Baker's Biographical Dictionary of Musicians, 4th ed. New York: G. Schirmer, Inc., 1940; with supplement, 1949.

Grove's Dictionary of Music and Musicians, 4th ed. London: Macmillan and Company, Ltd., 1954.

Reis, Claire, *Composers in America*, 4th ed. New York: The Macmillan Company, 1947.

Scholes, Percy A., *The Oxford Companion to Music*, 8th ed. London: Oxford University Press, 1950.

Slonimsky, Nicolas, *Music since 1900*, 3rd ed. New York: Coleman-Ross Company, Inc., 1949.

Thompson, Oscar, *The International Cyclopedia of Music and Musicians*, 5th ed., Nicolas Slonimsky, editor. New York: Dodd, Mead and Company, 1949.

Works Discussing Compositions

Baldwin, Lillian, *A Listener's Anthology of Music*. Cleveland: The Kulas Foundation, 1948.

Barlow, H. and S. Morgenstern, *Dictionary of Musical Themes*. New York: Crown Publishers, 1948.

———, *Dictionary of Vocal Themes*. New York: Crown Publishers, 1950.

Biancolli, L. and R. Bagar, *The Concert Companion*. New York: McGraw-Hill Book Company, Inc., 1947.

———, *Victor Book of Operas*. New York: Simon and Schuster, Inc., 1949.

Cobbet's Cyclopedic Survey of Chamber Music. London: Oxford University Press, 1929.

O'Connor, Charles, *Victor Book of Overtures, Tone Poems, and Other Orchestral Works*. New York: Simon and Schuster, Inc., 1950.

———, *Victor Book of Symphonies*. New York: Simon and Schuster, Inc., 1948.

Tovey, Donald F., *Essays in Musical Analysis*. London: Oxford University Press, 1935.

Upton, G. P. and F. Borowski, *The Standard Opera and Concert Guide*. New York: Halcyon House, 1930.

Veinus, Abraham, *Victor Book of Concertos*. New York: Simon and Schuster, Inc., 1948.

PART I, SECTION A

Recordings Used as Examples
(Co. = Columbia; Vi. = Victor)

Examples 1 and 2: Decca, DL 7007 or DU 757, "African Adventure."
Example 3: Folkways, P 417, "Negro Folk Music of Alabama (secular)."
Example 4: Co., 4271-N, Don Cossacks under Serge Jaroff.

Additional Recordings

The finest collection of authentic folk music of all peoples is available on Ethnic Folkways records, both 78 and 33 1/3 RPM; smaller collections are:

Decca, DX 107, "Music of the Orient."
Concert Hall, CHC 57, "Folk Airs of South and Central America."
Lyrichord, LL 4, "American Song Bag."

Examples of art music symbolizing various kinds of work:

Brahms, Johannes: *Lullaby*.
Schubert, Franz: *Gretchen am Spinnrade*.
Villa-Lobos, Heitor: "Song of the Ox-cart Driver," from *Seréstas*.

Recommended Readings

The most easily accessible readings on the origins and functions of music are:

Sachs, Curt, *The History of Musical Instruments*, pp. 25-64. New York: W. W. Norton and Company, Inc., 1940.

——, *The Rise of Music in the Ancient World*, pp. 15-53. New York: W. W. Norton and Company, Inc., 1943.

——, *World History of the Dance*, pp. 3-236, especially pp. 175-217. New York: W. W. Norton and Company, Inc., 1937.

PART I, SECTION B

Recordings Used as Examples

Example 1: Decca, DL 7007 or DU 757, "African Adventure."
Example 2: Decca, DL 5057, "Sousa Marches" (American Legion Band of Hollywood under Joe Colling).

Additional Recordings

"Marches of the World" (London, LPS 30 and 273).

•

Beethoven, Ludwig van: "Turkish March," from *The Ruins of Athens* (Co., 17198-D).
Berlioz, Hector: "*Marche Troyenne*" (Co., 72634-D).
Borodin, Alexander: "Polovtsi March" (Co., 72638-D).
Handel, George F.: "Dead March," from *Saul* (Co., 7340-M).
Mendelssohn, Felix: "Wedding March," from *A Midsummer Night's Dream*.
Meyerbeer, Giacomo: "Coronation March," from *The Prophet* (Co., 71287-D).
Prokofiev, Serge: "March," from *Peter and the Wolf*.
Schubert, Franz: *Marche Militaire No. 1* (Vi., 4314).
Tchaikovsky, Peter I.: *Marche Slave* (Colosseum, 107).
Verdi, Giuseppe: "Triumphal March," from *Aida* (Co., 71401-D).
Wagner, Richard: "Bridal Chorus," from *Lohengrin* (Co., 7271-M; Vi., 49-0298).
——: "Grand March," from *Tannhäuser* (Co., 72635-D; Vi., 7386).
——: "Siegfried's Funeral March," from *Die Götterdämmerung* (Co., ML 54273).

Recommended Readings

Farmer, Henry G., *Memoirs of the Royal Artillery Band*. London: Boosey and Company, Ltd., 1904.

———, *Military Music*. New York: Chanticleer Press, 1950.

———, *The Rise and Development of Military Music*. London: Wm. Reeves, 1912.

White, William C., *A History of Military Music in America*. New York: The Exposition Press, 1944.

•

Barzun, Jacques, *Berlioz and the Romantic Century*. Boston: Little, Brown and Company, 1950.

Dunhill, Thomas F., *Sir Edward Elgar*. London: Blackie and Son, Ltd., 1938.

Elliott, John H., *Berlioz*. London: J. M. Dent and Sons., Ltd., 1938.

Newman, Ernest, *Memoirs of Hector Berlioz*. New York: Tudor Publishing Company, 1935.

Porte, J. F., *Elgar and His Music*. London: Sir Isaac Pitman and Sons, Ltd., 1933.

Reed, Wm. H., *Elgar*. London: J. M. Dent and Sons, Ltd., 1939.

PART I, SECTION C

Recordings Used as Examples

Example 1: Decca, 23591, Burl Ives.

Example 2: Remington, RLP 199-34, Richard Dyer-Bennett; Vi., M 1107, Susan Reed; Vi., M 645, John Charles Thomas.

Additional Recordings

Loewe, Karl: *Ballads*.

———: *Edward* (Vi., 7486).

———: *Prinz Eugen* (Co., DB 837).

Schubert, Franz: *Die junge Nonne*.

Schumann, Robert: *Waldesgespräch*, from *Liederkreis*.

Recommended Readings
(For books on Schumann see under Part II, Section G.)

Lomax, John A., *Adventures of a Ballad Hunter*. New York: The Macmillan Company, 1947.

Northcote, Sidney, *The Ballad in Music*. London: Oxford University Press, 1942.

Scarborough, Dorothy, *A Song Catcher in Southern Mountains.* New York: Columbia University Press, 1937.

Wells, Evelyn K., *The Ballad Tree.* New York: The Ronald Press Company, 1950.

•

Abraham, Gerald, ed., *The Music of Schubert.* New York: W. W. Norton and Company, Inc., 1947.

Flower, Newman, *Franz Schubert,* 2nd ed. New York: Tudor Publishing Company, 1949.

Hutchings, Arthur, *Schubert.* New York: Pellegrini and Cudahy, Inc., 1949.

Newman, Ernest, *Hugo Wolf.* London: Methuen and Company, Ltd., 1907.

Walker, Frank, *Hugo Wolf.* New York: Alfred A Knopf, Inc., 1952.

PART I, SECTION D

Recordings Used as Examples

Example 3: Co., M 376 (Orchestra under Maurice Cauchie).

Additional Recordings

Bartók, Béla: *Roumanian Dances.*
Brahms, Johannes: *Hungarian Dances; Waltzes.*
Chopin, Frédéric: *Waltzes.*
Copland, Aaron: *Blues.*
Dvořák, Antonin: *Slavonic Dances.*
Haydn, Joseph: *Dances.*
Liszt, Franz: *Hungarian Rhapsody No. 2.*
Ravel, Maurice: *Valses nobles et sentimentales.*
Schubert, Franz: *Ländler.*
Smetana, Bedřich: *Bohemian Dances.*
Strauss, Richard: *"Rosenkavalier* Waltzes"; *"Salome's Dance."*
Tchaikovsky, Peter I.: *Waltzes.*

Recommended Readings

Martin, John, *America Dancing.* New York: Dodge Publishing Company, 1936.

——, *Introduction to the Dance.* New York: W. W. Norton and Company, Inc., 1939.

Nettl, Paul, *The Story of Dance Music.* New York: Philosophical Library, 1947.

Porter, Evelyn E. K., *Music through the Dance.* London: B. T. Batsford, Ltd., 1937.

Sharp, Cecil J., *The Dance*. London: Halton and T. Smith, 1924.

Sharp, Evelyn, *Here We Go Round: the Story of the Dance*. New York: William Morrow and Company, 1928.

•

Ewen, David, *The Story of George Gershwin*. New York: Henry Holt and Company, 1949.

Goldberg, Isaac, *George Gershwin, a Study in American Music*. New York: Simon and Schuster, Inc., 1931.

Hedley, Arthur, *Chopin*. London: J. M. Dent and Sons, Ltd., 1949.

Jacob, Heinrich E., *Johann Strauss, Father and Son*. New York: The Greystone Press, 1940.

Levant, Oscar, *A Smattering of Ignorance* (Gershwin). New York: Garden City Publishing Company, Inc., 1942.

Maine, Basil, *Chopin*. New York: A. A. Wyn, Inc., 1949.

Mizwa, Stephen P., *Frédéric Chopin*. New York: The Macmillan Company, 1949.

Suermondt, R. P., *Smetana and Dvořák*. Stockholm: The Continental Book Company A. B., (1950?).

Teetgen, Ada B., *The Waltz Kings of Old Vienna*. London: Herbert Jenkins, Ltd., 1939.

Wierzynski, Casimir, *The Life and Death of Chopin*. New York: Simon and Schuster, Inc., 1949.

PART I, SECTION E

Recordings Used as Examples

Example 1: Folkways, P 408, "Middle East and Palestine."

Example 2: Vi., M 87, vol. 2, "Gregorian Chants" (Monks' Choir of St. Pierre de Solesmes).

Additional Recordings

Bach, Johann S.: *Chorales* (Co., ML 2102).

Gregorian Chants (Co., ML 4394; Vi., DM 177).

Jewish Chants (Folkways, FP 25; Vi., S 48; Vi., S 52; Stinson, 609; Stinson, 614; Disc. 900).

Recommended Readings

Davies, Henry W., *Music and Worship*. New York: The H. W. Gray Company, 1935.

Dickinson, Edward, *Music in the History of the Western Church*. New York: Charles Scribner's Sons, 1902.

Douglas, Winfred, *Church Music in History and Practice*. New York: Charles Scribner's Sons, 1937.

Gradenwitz, Peter, *The Music of Israel*. New York: W. W. Norton and Company, Inc., 1949.

Idelsohn, Abraham Z., *Jewish Music in Its Historical Development*. New York: Henry Holt and Company, 1929.

Lang, Paul H., *Music in Western Civilization*, pp. 37-65, 70-80. New York: W. W. Norton and Company, Inc., 1941.

Robertson, Alec, *Sacred Music*. New York: Chanticleer Press, 1950.

Rothmüller, Arno M., *The Music of the Jews*, H. C. Stevens, transl. New York: Beechhurst Press, 1954.

Smits van Waesberghe, Jos., *Gregorian Chant*. Stockholm: The Continental Book Company A. B. (1947?).

•

Forkel, Johann N., *Johann Sebastian Bach*. New York: Harcourt, Brace, and Howe, 1920.

Mary, E. and S. Grew, *Bach*. New York: Pellegrini and Cudahy, Inc., 1949.

Parry, C. Hubert, *Johann Sebastian Bach*. New York: G. P. Putnam's Sons, 1910.

Spitta, Philipp: *The Life of Bach*. New York: Dover Publications, Inc., 1951.

Terry, Charles S., *Bach, a Biography*. London: Oxford University Press, 1933.

PART I, SECTION F

Recordings Used as Examples

Example 4: Vi., 1326 (Sergei Rachmaninoff).

Additional Recordings

a. Piano

Bach, Johann S.: *Inventions*.
"Béla Bartók Plays Bartók" (Continental, CLP 101).
Chopin, Frédéric: *Nocturnes*.
Debussy, Claude: *Preludes; Children's Corner*.
Fauré, Gabriel: "Piano Music" (London, PLS 246 and 260).
Grieg, Edvard: *Lyric Pieces*.
Mendelssohn, Felix: "Piano Music" (Vi., LM 21).
Schoenberg, Arnold: *Piano Pieces op. 11 and 19* (Dial, 3 and 14).
Schubert, Franz: *Moments musicaux*.
Schumann, Robert: *Fantasiestücke, op. 12*.
Scriabin, Alexander: *Etude No. 11*.

b. Songs

Bartók, Béla: *Hungarian Folksongs, op. 16*.
Brahms, Johannes: *Lieder* (Songs); *Duets; Vier ernste Gesänge*.
Debussy, Claude: *Ariettes oubliées; Cinq poèmes de Charles Baudelaire*.
Dowland, John: *Lute Songs*.
Fauré, Gabriel: *Songs*.
Haydn, Joseph: *Songs* (Allegro, AL 13).
Mozart, Wolfgang A.: *Songs* (Co., ML 4365).
Poulenc, Francis: *Chansons villageoises*.
Purcell, Henry: *Catches and Glees*.
Rachmaninoff, Sergei: *Songs* (Rachmaninoff, RS 2).
Ravel, Maurice: *Shéhérazade; Don Quixote à Dulcinée; Chansons Madecasses*.
Schubert, Franz: *Goethe Songs* (Allegro, AL 27); *Schwanengesang* (Allegro, AL 16); *Lieder* (Songs).
Schumann, Robert: *Songs; Liederkreis* (Vanguard, 411).
Sibelius, Jan: *Songs*.
Wolf, Hugo: *Songs*.

Recommended Readings

(For books on Brahms see under Part IV, Section A; on Debussy, Part III, Section C; on Schubert, Part I, Section C; on Schumann, Part II, Section G.)

Apel, Willi, *Masters of the Keyboard*. Cambridge, Mass.: Harvard University Press, 1947.
Bie, Oscar, *A History of the Pianoforte and Pianoforte Players*. London: J. M. Dent and Company, 1899.
Einstein, Alfred, *Music in the Romantic Era*, pp. 97-100, 183-197. New York: W. W. Norton and Company, Inc., 1947.
Finck, Henry T., *Songs and Song Writers*. New York: Charles Scribner's Sons, 1900.

Geller, James J., *Famous Songs and Their Stories*. New York: Macaulay Company, 1931.

Hutcheson, Ernest, *The Literature of the Piano*. New York: Alfred A. Knopf, Inc., 1948.

Krehbiel, Henry E., *The Pianoforte and Its Music*. New York: Charles Scribner's Sons, 1911.

•

Kaufmann, Schima, *Mendelssohn*. New York: Tudor Publishing Company, 1934.

Stratton, S. S., *Mendelssohn*. London: J. M. Dent and Sons, Ltd., 1934.

Young, Percy M., *Mendelssohn*. London: Dennis Dobson Limited, 1949.

PART I, SECTION G

Recordings Used as Examples

Example 1: Vi., 8828 (Jascha Heifetz).

Example 2: Co., 72131-D (Jennie Tourel); Co., 72519-D (Lili Pons).

Example 3: Vi., DM 1260 (Vladimir Horowitz); Co., M 523 (Egon Petri).

Example 4: Co., 69798-D (Edward Kilenyi); Concert Hall, CHC 10 (Robert Goldsand).

Example 5: Vi., 8996 (Vladimir Horowitz).

Example 6: Vi., 11-0017 (Marcel Dupré).

Additional Recordings

Barber, Samuel: *Excursions* (Co., ML 2174).

Brahms, Johannes: *Rhapsodies, op. 79* (Mercury, MG 10062).

Chopin, Frédéric: *Ballades, Etudes*.

Debussy, Claude: *Estampes; Images*.

Liszt, Franz: "Piano Music" (Co., ML 4084).

Rachmaninoff, Sergei: *Etudes tableaux* (Rachmaninoff, RS 1 and 3).

Schumann, Robert: "Piano Music" (London, LLP 188).

Scriabin, Alexander: "Piano Music" (Allegro, AL 37).

Shostakovich, Dmitri: "Piano Music" (Mercury, MG 10035).

Recommended Readings

(For books on Bach see under Part I, Section E; on Chopin, Part I, Section D.)

Einstein, Alfred: *Music in the Romantic Era*, pp. 202-25. New York: W. W. Norton and Company, Inc., 1947.

•

Day, Lillian: *Paganini of Genoa*. New York: Macaulay Company, 1929.

Edwards, Henry S., *The Life of Rossini*. London: Hurst and Blackett, 1869.

Hill, Ralph, *Liszt*. New York: A. A. Wyn, Inc., 1949.

Newman, Ernest: *The Man Liszt*. New York: Charles Scribner's Sons, 1935.

Pulver, Jeffrey: *Paganini, the Romantic Virtuoso*. London: Herbert Joseph Limited, 1936.

Saussine, Renée de: *Paganini*, Marjorie Laurie, transl. New York: McGraw-Hill Book Company, Inc., 1954.

Toye, Francis, *Rossini*. New York: Alfred A. Knopf, Inc., 1934.

Westerby, Herbert, *Liszt and His Piano Works*. London: William Reeves Bookseller Limited, 1935.

PART II, SECTION A

Recordings Used as Examples

Example 1: Concert Hall, CHC 52, "Madrigals" (David Randolph Singers); Co., M 231, "Columbia History of Music" (St. George's Singers under E. H. Fellowes: repetition of verses 5-8 omitted).

Example 2: Mercury, MG 10063, "Choral Music of the Renaissance" (Roman Vatican Choir under Licinio Refice).

Example 3: Vi., M 212 (Dijon Cathedral Choir under J. Samson).

Additional Recordings

The largest record collection of music composed before 1780 is the *Anthologie Sonore* (Gramophone Shop); others are:

"French and Italian Secular Music of the Renaissance" (Concert Hall, CHC 36).

"French Choral Music" (Allegro, AL 17).

"Gothic and Renaissance Music" (Allegro, AL 14 and 72).

"Lute Music of the Renaissance" (Allegro, AL 6).

"Mediaeval and Renaissance Music" (Vi., M 739).

Single composers are represented by:

William Byrd: *Masses*.

Josquin des Prez ⎱
Orlandus Lassus ⎰ : *Motets* (Concert Hall, CHC 47).

Giovanni Pierluigi da Palestrina: *Masses; Magnificat* (Period, 513).

Recommended Readings

Fellowes, E. H., *The English Madrigal Composers.* London: The Clarendon Press, 1921.

Lang, Paul H., *Music in Western Civilization,* pp. 226-37, 296-303. New York: W. W. Norton and Company, Inc., 1941.

•

Coates, H., *Palestrina.* New York: E. P. Dutton and Company, Inc., 1938.

Gray, C. and P. Heseltine, *Carlo Gesualdo, Prince of Venosa, Musician and Murderer.* London: Kegan Paul, Trench, Trubner and Company, Ltd., 1926.

Pyne, Zoe K., *Giovanni Pierluigi da Palestrina, His Life and Times.* London: John Lane The Bodley Head Limited, 1922.

PART II, SECTION B

Additional Recordings
(including works of the types discussed but written in subsequent periods)

"Baroque Choral Music" (Concert Hall, CHC 44).

"Italian Cantatas" (Allegro, AL 87).

•

Bach, Johann S.: *Arias; Cantatas No. 4 and 21; Christmas Oratorio; Coffee Cantata; Magnificat; Motet No. 1; St. John's Passion.*

Beethoven, Ludwig van: *Mass in C Major; Missa Solemnis.*

Berlioz, Hector: *Requiem Mass.*

Brahms, Johannes: *A German Requiem; Alto Rhapsody.*

Bruckner, Anton: *Te Deum; Mass No. 3, in F Minor.*

Buxtehude, Dietrich: *Cantatas.*

Carissimi, Giacomo: *Jephte.*

Cherubini, Luigi: *Requiem Mass.*

Debussy, Claude: *Le martyre de St. Sébastien; La démoiselle élue.*

Faure, Gabriel: *Requiem Mass.*

Gabrieli, Giovanni: "Processional and Ceremonial Music" (Vi., DM 928).

Handel, George F.: *Israel in Egypt; Judas Maccabaeus; Utrecht Te Deum.*

Haydn, Joseph: *The Creation; Masses; The Seasons.*

Mendelssohn, Felix: *Elijah.*

Mozart, Wolfgang A.: *Coronation Mass; Mass in C Minor; Requiem Mass.*

Pergolesi, Giovanni B.: *Stabat Mater.*

Poulenc, Francis: *Mass in G Major.*

Purcell, Henry: "Choral Music" (Renaissance, X 14).

Rossini, Gioacchino: *Stabat Mater.*
Scarlatti, Alessandro: *Motetto da Requiem.*
Schubert, Franz: *Mass in E-flat Major.*
Schütz, Heinrich: *The Christmas Story; Concerti sacri* and *Symphoniae sacrae; St. John's Passion; The Seven Last Words.*
Stravinsky, Igor: *Mass; Symphony of Psalms.*
Verdi, Giuseppe: *Requiem Mass; Stabat Mater.*
Vivaldi, Antonio: *Gloria Mass.*

Recommended Readings
(For books on Bach see under Part I, Section E.)

Bukofzer, Manfred, *Music in the Baroque Era,* pp. 9-19, 120-8, 291-7, 333-41. New York: W. W. Norton and Company, Inc., 1947.
Lang, Paul H., *Music in Western Civilization,* pp. 314-29, 343-9, 387-98, 430-46, 468-81, 496-504, 522-6. New York: W. W. Norton and Company, Inc., 1941.
Patterson, Annie W., *The Story of Oratorio.* New York: Charles Scribner's Sons, 1915.

•

Dent, E. J., *Handel.* London: Duckworth, 1934.
Flower, Newman, *George Frideric Handel: His Personality and His Times.* New York: Charles Scribner's Sons, 1947.
Myers, Robert M., *Handel's Messiah, a Touchstone of Taste.* New York: The Macmillan Company, 1947.
Shaw, Harold W., *Handel's Messiah, the Story of a Masterpiece.* London: Hinrichsen Edition Limited, 1946.
Young, Percy M., *Handel.* London: J. M. Dent and Sons, Ltd., 1946.

PART II, SECTION C

Additional Recordings

Organ music of various masters (Allegro, AL 36; Renaissance, SX 202).
Harpsichord music of various masters (Allegro, AL 15 and 52; Decca, DL 8019).
Recorder and harpsichord music of various masters (London, LPS 24 and 278).

•

Bach, Johann S.: *Chorale Preludes; Preludes and Fugues* for organ; *Toccatas* for organ and harpsichord.
Brahms, Johannes: *Chorale Preludes.*
Buxtehude, Dietrich: Organ music.

PART II, SECTION D

Additional Recordings

Bach, Johann S.: *English Suites; French Suites; Overtures No. 1, 2,* and *4; Partitas; Sonatas No. 2, 4,* and *6* for solo violin; *Suites No. 1-5* for solo 'cello.

Handel, George F.: *Royal Fireworks Suite; Suites* for harpsichord; *Water Music.*

Purcell, Henry: *Abdelazar Suite; Gordian Knot Suite.*

PART II, SECTION E

Recordings Used as Examples

Example 1: Parlophone, R 1024, "2000 Years of Music" (Maria Peschken).

Example 2: Co., M 578, "French Opera Arias" (Martial Singher).

Example 3: Vi., 17257 (Marian Anderson).

Additional Recordings

EARLY MUSIC DRAMA: Monteverdi, Claudio: *Orfeo.*

TRAGEDIE LYRIQUE: Rameau, Jean P.: *Hippolite et Aricie.*

BALLET-OPERA: Rameau, Jean P.: *Les Indes galantes.*

MASK: Blow, John: *Venus and Adonis.*
Purcell, Henry: *Timon of Athens.*

ENGLISH OPERA: Arne, Thomas: *Thomas and Sally.*
Purcell, Henry: *Dido and Aeneas; The Fairy Queen; King Arthur.*

Recommended Readings

(For further readings and a bibliography of librettos see under Part II, Section F.)

Holland, A. K., *Henry Purcell.* Harmondsworth: Penguin Books, 1948.

Prunières, Henri, *Monteverdi.* New York: E. P. Dutton and Company, Inc., 1926.

Redlich, Hans, *Claudio Monteverdi, Life and Works,* Kathleen Dale, transl. New York: Oxford University Press, 1952.

Schrade, Leo, *Monteverdi, Creator of Modern Music.* New York: W. W. Norton and Company, Inc., 1950.

Westrup, J. A., *Purcell.* London: J. M. Dent and Sons, Ltd., 1937.

PART II, SECTION F

Additional Recordings

OPERA SERIA:

Handel, George F.: *Acis and Galathea.*
Haydn, Joseph: *Orfeo ed Euridice.*
Mozart, Wolfgang A.: *Idomeneo, re di Creta.*

OPERA BUFFA:

Cimarosa, Domenico: *Il matrimonio segreto.*
Donizetti, Gaëtano: *Don Pasquale; L'elisire d'amore.*
Mozart, Wolfgang A.: *Così fan tutte; Don Giovanni; The Impresario.*
Pergolesi, Giovanni B.: *La serva padrona; Il maestro di musica.*[1]
Puccini, Giacomo: *Gianni Schicchi.*
Rossini, Gioacchino: *The Barber of Seville.*
Verdi, Giuseppe: *Falstaff.*
Wolf-Ferrari, Ermanno: *The Secret of Susanna.*

BALLAD OPERA:

Pepusch, John: *The Beggar's Opera.*

OPERA COMIQUE:

Auber, Daniel F.: *Fra Diavolo.*
Donizetti, Gaëtano: *La fille du régiment.*

SINGSPIEL:

Flotow, Friedrich: *Martha.*
Haydn, Joseph: *The Apothecary.*
Lortzing, Albert: *Zar und Zimmermann.*
Mozart, Wolfgang A.: *The Abduction from the Seraglio; Bastien and Bastienne; The Magic Flute.*

GLUCKIST OPERA:

Beethoven, Ludwig van: *Fidelio.*
Gluck, Christoph W.: *Iphigenia in Tauris.*
Spontini, Gasparo: *La Vestale.*

ROMANTIC OPERA:

Wagner, Richard: *The Flying Dutchman; Lohengrin; Tannhäuser.*
Weber, Carl M.: *Euryanthe; Der Freischütz.*

---

[1] As performed today there is no music by Pergolesi contained in this score. It is, what is known as, a PASTICCIO (Italian—salad), i.e. pieced together from numbers by several composers; the two numbers by Pergolesi which were originally included were later replaced by others, but his name, as the most famous one involved, was retained. *Pasticci* were very popular during the mid-eighteenth century.

GRAND OPERA:

Bellini, Vincenzo: *Norma.*
Donizetti, Gaëtano: *Lucia di Lammermoor.*
Goldmark, Karl: *The Queen of Sheba.*
Halévy, Jacques F.: *La Juive.*
Meyerbeer, Giacomo: *Les Huguenots; Le Prophète.*
Puccini, Giacomo: *Turandot.*
Rossini, Gioacchino: *William Tell.*
Saint-Saëns, Camille: *Samson and Delilah.*
Verdi, Giuseppe: *Aida; Don Carlo; Ernani; A Masked Ball; Otello.*

LYRIC OPERA:

Gounod, Charles: *Faust.*
Massenet, Jules: *Manon; Thais.*
Offenbach, Jacques: *The Tales of Hoffmann.*
Tchaikovsky, Peter I.: *Eugen Onegin; The Queen of Spades.*

OPERETTA:

Herbert, Victor: *Naughty Marietta.*
Lehár, Franz: *The Merry Widow.*
Millöcker, Karl: *The Beggar Student.*
Offenbach, Jacques: *La belle Hélène; Orpheus in the Underworld.*
Strauss, Johann: *Die Fledermaus; The Gypsy Baron.*
Sullivan, Arthur S.: *Iolanthe; The Mikado; H.M.S. Pinafore.*
Suppé, Franz: *The Beautiful Galathea.*

WAGNERIAN MUSIC DRAMA:

Debussy, Claude: *Pelleas et Mélisande.*
Strauss, Richard: *Salome; Der Rosenkavalier.*
Wagner, Richard: *Die Meistersinger; Parsifal; Siegfried; Die Walküre.*

REALISTIC OPERA:

Ponchielli, Amilcare: *La Gioconda.*
Puccini, Giacomo: *La Bohème; Madame Butterfly.*
Verdi, Giuseppe: *Rigoletto.*

FOLK OPERA:

Borodin, Alexander: *Prince Igor.*
Dvořák, Antonin: *Rusalka.*
Gershwin, George: *Porgy and Bess.*
Glinka, Michael: *Life for the Czar.*
Smetana, Bedřich: *The Bartered Bride.*
Weill, Kurt: *Down in the Valley; Street Scene.*

VERISMO OPERA:

Berg, Alban: *Lulu; Wozzeck.*
Mascagni, Pietro: *La cavalleria rusticana.*
Menotti, Giancarlo: *The Consul; The Medium.*
Montemezzi, Italo: *L'amore dei tre re.*
Puccini, Giacomo: *Il tabarro; La Tosca.*
Strauss, Richard: *Elektra.*

Bibliography for Librettos

Biancolli, L. and R. Bagar, *The Victor Book of Operas*. New York: Simon and Schuster, Inc., 1949.

Cross, Milton, *Complete Stories of the Great Operas*. New York: Doubleday and Company, Inc., 1949.

Howard, John T., *The World's Great Operas*. New York: Grosset and Dunlap, Publishers, 1948.

Kobbé, Gustav, *The Complete Opera Book*. New York: G. P. Putnam's Sons, 1919.

Krehbiel, Henry E., *A Book of Operas*. New York: The Macmillan Company, 1937.

McSpadden, J. Walker, *Operas and Musical Comedies*. New York: Thomas Y. Crowell, 1946.

Melitz, Leo, *The Opera Goer's Complete Guide*. New York: Garden City Publishers, 1908.

Newman, Ernest, *Stories of the Great Operas*. Philadelphia: The Blakiston Company, 1928.

———, *More Stories of Famous Operas*. New York: Alfred A. Knopf, Inc., 1943.

———, *Seventeen Famous Operas*. New York: Alfred A. Knopf, Inc., 1955.

Sanborn, Pitts, *The Metropolitan Book of Opera*. New York: Simon and Schuster, Inc., 1938.

Upton, G. P. and F. Borowski, *The Standard Opera and Concert Guide*. New York: Halcyon House, 1930.

Recommended Readings

(For books on Mozart see under Part III, Section A; on Wagner, Part III, Section E.)

Bekker, Paul, *The Changing Opera*. New York: W. W. Norton and Company, Inc., 1935.

Brockway, W. and H. Weinstock, *The Opera*. New York: Simon and Schuster, 1941.

Crosten, William L., *French Grand Opera*. New York: King's Crown Press, 1948.

Dent, Edward J., *Opera*. Harmondsworth: Penguin Books, 1949.

Einstein, Alfred, *Music in the Romantic Era*, pp. 3-72, 337-62. New York: W. W. Norton and Company, Inc., 1947.

Graf, Herbert, *The Opera and Its Future in America*. New York: W. W. Norton and Company, Inc., 1941.

Grout, Donald J., *A Short History of Opera*. New York: Columbia University Press, 1947.

Hoover, Kathleen O., *Makers of Opera*. New York: H. H. Bittner and Company, 1948.

Krehbiel, Henry E., *Chapters of Opera*. New York: Henry Holt and Company, 1908.

Lang, Paul H., *Music in Western Civilization*, pp. 618-25, 734-50. New York: W. W. Norton and Company, Inc., 1941.

Bonavia, Feruccio, *Verdi*. London: Oxford University Press, 1930.
Calvocoressi, Michel D., *Musorgsky, the Russian Musical Nationalist*.
London: Kegan Paul, Trench, Trubner and Company, Ltd., 1919.
Cooper, Martin, *Gluck*. New York: Oxford University Press, 1935.
Dieren, Bernard van, *Down among the Dead Men* (Meyerbeer). London: Oxford University Press, 1935.
Einstein, Alfred, *Gluck*. London: J. M. Dent and Sons, Ltd., 1936.
Hussey, Dyneley, *Verdi*. London: J M. Dent and Sons, Ltd., 1940.
Newman, Ernest, *Gluck and the Opera*. London: B. Dobell, 1895.
Riesemann, Oscar, *Moussorgsky*. New York: Tudor Publishing Company, 1935.
Rimsky-Korsakov, Nicolai, *My Musical Life* (Musorgsky). New York: Alfred A. Knopf, Inc., 1942.
Seroff, Victor I., *The Mighty Five* (Musorgsky). New York: Allen, Towne and Heath, Inc., 1948.
Toye, Francis, *Giuseppe Verdi*. New York: Alfred A. Knopf, Inc., 1931.
Werfel, F. and P. Stefan, *Verdi*. New York: L. B. Fischer, 1942.

PART II, SECTION G

Additional Recordings

a. Suites

Bizet, Georges: *L'Arlésienne, No. 2.*
Bloch, Ernest: *Suite for Viola and Piano.*
Debussy, Claude: *Suite Bergamasque.*
Grieg, Edvard: *Peer Gynt, No. 1 and 2; Holberg.*
Milhaud, Darius: *Scaramouche; Suite Provençale.*
Prokofiev, Serge: *Lieutenant Kije; Scythian Suite.*
Ravel, Maurice: *Le tombeau de Couperin.*
Saint-Saëns, Camille: *The Carnival of the Animals.*
Schumann, Robert: *Arabesque; Davidsbündler Tänze; Kreisleriana; Papillons.*
Sibelius, Jan: *Karelia; Tempest* (Vi., DM 446).

b. Song Cycles

Beethoven, Ludwig van: *An die ferne Geliebte.*
Britten, Benjamin: *Serenade for Tenor, Horn, and Strings* (Decca, EDA 7).
Debussy, Claude: *Chansons de Bilitis* (Co., ML 2184).
Fauré, Gabriel: *La bonne chanson.*
Hindemith, Paul: *Das Marienleben* (Lyrichord, LL 6).
Mahler, Gustav: *Kindertotenlieder; Songs of a Wayfarer.*
Musorgsky, Modeste: *Songs and Dances of Death.*

Schubert, Franz: *Die schöne Müllerin; Winterreise.*
Schumann, Robert: *Dichterliebe.*
Williams, Ralph V.: *On Wenlock Edge* (Decca, EDA 67; London, LA 36).

Recommended Readings
(For books on Musorgsky see under Part II, Section F.)

Abraham, Gerald, ed., *Schumann.* New York: Oxford University Press, 1951.
Basch, Victor, *Schumann, a Life of Suffering.* New York: Tudor Publishing Company, 1936.
Bedford, Herbert, *Robert Schumann.* London: Kegan Paul, Trench, Trubner and Company, Ltd., 1925.
Chissell, Joan, *Schumann.* London: J. M. Dent and Sons, Ltd., 1948.
Engel, Gabriel, *Gustav Mahler, Song-Symphonist.* New York: The Bruckner Society of America, Inc., 1932.
Newlin, Dika, *Bruckner, Mahler, Schoenberg.* New York: King's Crown Press, 1947.
Walter, Bruno, *Gustav Mahler.* New York: The Greystone Press, 1941.

PART II, SECTION H
Additional Recordings

Adam, Adolphe: *Giselle.*
Beethoven, Ludwig van: *The Creatures of Prometheus.*
Bernstein, Leonard: *Fancy Free.*
Bliss, Arthur: *Miracle in the Gorbals.*
Borodin, Alexander: "Polovetsian Dances," from *Prince Igor.*
Copland, Aaron: *Appalachian Spring; Rodeo.*
Delibes, Léo: *Coppélia; Sylvia.*
Falla, Manuel de: *El amor brujo; The Three-Cornered Hat.*
Glazounov, Alexander: *The Seasons.*
Gluck, Christoph W.: *Don Juan.*
Gounod, Charles: Ballet from *Faust.*
Hindemith, Paul: *Nobilissima visione.*
Holst, Gustav: *The Planets.*
Milhaud, Darius: *Le boeuf sur le toit.*
Offenbach, Jacques: *Gaité Parisienne.*
Piston, Walter: *The Incredible Flutist* (Vi., M 621).
Prokofiev, Serge: *Cinderella; Romeo and Juliet, No. 2.*
Satie, Eric: *Parade.*
Schubert, Franz: Ballet music to *Rosamunde.*
Stravinsky, Igor: *Apollon Musagète* (Vi., LM 1096); *The Firebird; Orpheus; Petroushka.*
Tchaikovsky, Peter I.: *The Nutcracker; Sleeping Beauty.*
Verdi, Giuseppe: Ballet music from *Aida.*
Walton, William: *Facade.*

Bibliography for Scenarios

Balanchine, George, *Balanchine's Complete Stories of the Great Ballets*. Garden City: Doubleday and Company, Inc., 1954.

Beaumont, Cyril W., *The Complete Book of Ballets*. New York: G. P. Putnam's Sons, 1938.

Goode, Gerald, *The Book of Ballets*. New York: Crown Publishers, 1939.

Lawrence, Robert, *The Victor Book of Ballets and Ballet Music*. New York: Simon and Schuster, Inc., 1950.

Robert, Grace, *The Borzoi Book of Ballets*. New York: Alfred A. Knopf, Inc., 1946.

Recommended Readings
(For books on Ravel see under Part III, Section B.)

Arvey, Verna, *Choreographic Music*. New York: E. P. Dutton and Company, Inc., 1941.

Evans, Edwin, *Music and the Dance*. London: Herbert Jenkins, Ltd., 1948.

Nettl, Paul, *The Story of Dance Music*. New York: Philosophical Library, 1947.

Sachs, Curt, *World History of the Dance*. New York: W. W. Norton and Company, Inc., 1937.

Abraham, Gerald, ed., *The Music of Tchaikovsky*. New York: W. W. Norton and Company, Inc., 1946.

Bowen, C. D. and B. v. Meck, *Beloved Friend* (Tchaikovsky). New York: Dover Publications, Inc., 1946.

Evans, Edwin, *Tchaikovsky*. New York: Pellegrini and Cudahy, Inc., 1949.

Lederman, Minna, ed., *Stravinsky in the Theatre*. New York: Pellegrini and Cudahy, Inc., 1949.

Myers, Rollo H., *Stravinsky*. London: Dennis Dobson Limited, 1949.

Shostakovich, Dmitri, *et al., Russian Symphony, Thoughts about Tchaikovsky*. New York: Philosophical Library, 1947.

Tansman, Alexander, *Igor Stravinsky*. New York: G. P. Putnam's Sons, 1949.

White, Eric W., *Stravinsky*. London: John Lehmann, 1947.

PART II, SECTION J

Recordings Used as Examples

Example 2 and 8: Artist, 100 (Janssen Symphony).

Example 5, 29, and 38: Co., M 361, "Columbia History of Music."

Example 7: Lyrichord, LL 6 (Frances James).

Example 14, 30, and 41: Bartók Recording Studio, BRS 003 (Béla Bartók).

Example 18: Co., ML 4142 (Sigi Weissenberg).
Example 19: Odéon, 170111; Gramophone, W 870.
Example 22: Co., X 36 (Igor Stravinsky).
Example 23: Bartók Recording Studio, BRS 113 (Béla Bartók).
Example 31: Co., 71670-D (Bidu Sayao).
Example 32: Co., 69835-D; Vi., 49-0839.
Example 35: Co., X 189 (Jakob Gimpel).
Example 37: Allegro, AL 37 (Mikhail Sheyne).

Recommended Readings

Bauer, Marion, *Twentieth-Century Music*. New York: G. P. Putnam's Sons, 1933.
Chavez, Carlos, *Toward a New Music: Music and Electricity*. New York: W. W. Norton and Company, Inc., 1937.
Copland, Aaron, *Our New Music*. New York: McGraw-Hill Book Company, Inc., 1941.
Cowell, Henry, *New Musical Resources*. New York: Alfred A. Knopf, Inc., 1930.
Demuth, Norman, *Musical Trends in the 20th Century*. New York: The Macmillan Company, 1952.
Eschman, Karl H., *Changing Forms in Modern Music*. Boston: E. C. Schirmer Music Company, 1945.
Ewen, David, *The Book of Modern Composers*, 2nd ed. New York: Alfred A. Knopf, Inc., 1950.
Křenek, Ernst, *Music Here and Now*. New York: W. W. Norton and Company, Inc., 1939.
Reis, Claire, *Composers in America*, 4th ed. New York: The Macmillan Company, 1947.
Salazar, Adolfo, *Music in Our Time*. New York: W. W. Norton and Company, Inc., 1946.

PART III, SECTION A

Additional Recordings

Enesco, Georges: *Roumanian Rhapsody No. 1.*
Liszt, Franz: *Hungarian Rhapsody No. 2.*
Messiaen, Olivier: *L'ascension.*
Rossini, Gioacchino: *William Tell Overture.*
Suppé, Franz: *Overtures.*
Villa-Lobos, Heitor: *Choros No. 10.*
Wagner, Richard: *Siegfried Idyll.*

Recommended Readings

Biancolli, Louis, ed., *The Mozart Handbook*. Cleveland: The World Publishing Company, 1954.

Blom, Eric, *Mozart*. London: J. M. Dent and Sons, Ltd., 1935.
Cooper, Martin, *Georges Bizet*. New York: Oxford University Press, 1938.
Davenport, Marcia, *Mozart*. New York: Charles Scribner's Sons, 1932.
Dean, Winton, *Bizet*. London: J. M. Dent and Sons, Ltd., 1948.
Einstein, Alfred, *Mozart, His Character, His Work*. New York: Oxford University Press, 1945.
Jahn, Otto, *Life of Mozart*, 3 vols. London: Novello, Ewer and Company, 1882.
Turner, Walter J., *Mozart*. New York: Alfred A. Knopf, Inc., 1938.

PART III, SECTION B

Recordings Used as Examples

Example 2: Remington, 199-17 (Ernst Dohnanyi); Vox, VL 6360 (Leonard Shure).

Additional Recordings

Bach, Johann S.: *Chaconne* from *Violin Sonata No. 4, in D* Minor; *Goldberg Variations*.
Beethoven, Ludwig van: *Variations and Fugue op. 35* (Eroica); *Variations in C Minor; Variations on a Theme by Diabelli*.
Brahms, Johannes: *Variations on a Theme by Handel; Variations on a Theme by Haydn*.
Corelli, Arcangelo: *La folia*.
Delius, Frederick: *Appalachia* (Delius Society, Co., SDX 15-19).
Elgar, Edward: *Enigma Variations*.
d'Indy, Vincent: *Istar Variations*.
Mendelssohn, Felix: *Variations sérieuses*.
Reger, Max: *Variations and Fugue on a Theme by Mozart*.
Schubert, Franz: *Impromptu in B-flat Major*, op. 142, No. 3.
Schumann, Robert: *Andante and Variations in B-flat Major; Symphonic Etudes*.
Williams, Ralph V.: *Fantasia on a Theme by Thomas Tallis*.

Recommended Readings
(For books on Bach see under Part I, Section E.)

Burk, John N., *The Life and Works of Beethoven*. New York: Random House, Inc., 1943.
Demuth, Norman, *Ravel*. London: J. M. Dent and Sons, Ltd., 1947.
Goss, Madeleine, *Bolero, The Life of Maurice Ravel*. New York: Henry Holt and Company, (1940?).
Manuel, Roland, *Maurice Ravel*. London: Dennis Dobson Limited, 1947.

Onnen, Frank, *Maurice Ravel*. Stockholm: The Continental Book Company A. B., (1947?).

Sullivan, J. W. N., *Beethoven, His Spiritual Development*. New York: Alfred A. Knopf, Inc., 1927.

Tovey, Donald F., *Beethoven*. London: Oxford University Press, 1945.

Turner, Walter J., *Beethoven, the Search for Reality*. London: Ernest Benn, Ltd., 1927.

Wellesz, Egon, *Beethoven*. London: Dennis Dobson Limited, 1949.

PART III, SECTION C

Additional Recordings

Albeniz, Isaac: *Iberia*.

Debussy, Claude: *Nocturnes*.

Dukas, Paul: *The Sorcerer's Apprentice*.

Liszt, Franz: *The Battle of the Huns; Ce qu'on entend sur la montagne; Hungaria; Tasso*.

Musorgsky, Modeste: *A Night on Bald Mountain*.

Rachmaninoff, Sergei: *The Isle of the Dead*.

Reger, Max: *Böcklin Suite*.

Respighi, Ottorino: *Fountains of Rome; Pines of Rome; Roman Festivals*.

Saint-Saëns, Camille: *Danse macabre; Omphale's Spinning Wheel*.

Schoenberg, Arnold: *Verklärte Nacht*.

Sibelius, Jan: *En Saga* (Decca, EDA 49); *Lemminkainen's Homeward Journey* (Vi., DM 446 and 750); *Pohjolah's Daughter* (Vi., DM 474); *Tapiola* (Vi., DM 848 and 1311).

Smetana, Bedřich: *My Fatherland* (including *The Moldau*).

Strauss, Richard: *Death and Transfiguration; Don Juan; Don Quixote*.

Tchaikovsky, Peter I.: *Capriccio Italien; Francesca da Rimini; Manfred; Romeo and Juliet*.

Villa-Lobos, Heitor: *Uirapurú*.

Recommended Readings
(For books on Liszt see under Part I, Section G.)

Lang, Paul H., *Music in Western Civilization*, pp. 859-73. New York: W. W. Norton and Company, Inc., 1941.

Niecks, Frederick, *Programme Music*. New York: The H. W. Gray Company, 1907.

•

Dumesnil, Maurice, *Claude Debussy, Master of Dreams*. New York: Ives Washburn, 1940.

Lockspeiser, Edward, *Debussy*. London: J. M. Dent and Sons, Ltd., 1936 (Dennis Dobson Limited, 1949).

Myers, Rollo H., *Debussy*. New York: A. A. Wyn, Inc., 1949.

Thompson, Oscar, *Debussy, Man and Artist.* New York: Dodd, Mead and Company, 1937.

Vallas, Léon, *Claude Debussy.* London: Oxford University Press, 1933.

———, *The Theories of Claude Debussy.* London: Oxford University Press, 1929.

PART III, SECTION D

Recordings Used as Examples

Example 1: Lyrichord, LL 12 (Claude Jean Chiasson, harpsichord).

Example 2: Vox, 610 (Gaby Casadesus); Vi., 12-0066 (E. Robert Schmitz).

Additional Recordings

Chabrier, Emanuel: *Scherzo-Valse* (Co., 71061-D, Robert Casadesus; Allegro, AL 56, Soulima Stravinsky).

Wieniawski, Henri: *Scherzo-Tarantelle* (Vi., 14115, Nathan Milstein; Stradivari, SLP 1003, Arnold Eidus).

Recommended Readings
(For books on Ravel see under Part III, Section B.)

Finck, Henry T., *Richard Strauss.* Boston: Little, Brown and Company, 1917.

Hervey, Arthur, *Giacomo Meyerbeer.* London: J. M. Dent and Sons, Ltd., 1913.

Hervey, Arthur, *Saint-Saëns.* London: John Lane The Bodley Head Limited, 1921.

Huneker, James G., *Mezzotints in Modern Music* (R. Strauss). New York: Charles Scribner's Sons, 1927.

Lyle, Watson, *Camille Saint-Saëns, His Life and Art.* London: Kegan Paul, Trench, Trubner and Company, Ltd., 1923.

Mason, Daniel G., *Contemporary Composers* (R. Strauss). New York: The Macmillan Company, 1918.

Mellers, Wilfrid, *François Couperin and the French Classical Tradition.* New York: Roy Publishers, 1951.

PART III, SECTION E

Recordings Used as Examples

Example 1: Allegro, AL 84 (Soulima Stravinsky, piano); Vi., WDM 1181 (Wanda Landowska, harpsichord).

Additional Recordings

Auber, Daniel F.: *Overtures.*
Beethoven, Ludwig van: *Coriolan Overture; Overture Leonore No. 3.*
Brahms, Johannes: *Academic Festival Overture; Tragic Overture.*
Dvořák, Antonin: *Carnaval Overture.*
Elgar, Edward: *Cockaigne Overture.*
Glinka, Michael: *Overture to Russlan and Ludmilla.*
Gluck, Christoph W.: *Alceste Overture; Iphigenia in Aulis Overture.*
Lalo, Edouard: *Overture to Le roi d'Ys.*
Mendelssohn, Felix: *Fingal's Cave (The Hebrides) Overture; Overture to A Midsummer Night's Dream.*
Rimsky-Korsakov, Nicolai: *Russian Easter Overture.*
Rossini, Gioacchino: *Overtures.*
Schubert, Franz: *Rosamunde Overture.*
Schumann, Robert: *Genofeva Overture; Manfred Overture.*
Tchaikovsky, Peter I.: *Overture 1812.*
Wagner, Richard: *Overture to Tannhäuser; Prelude to Lohengrin; Prelude to Die Meistersinger; Prelude to Parsifal.*
Weber, Carl M.: *Euryanthe Overture; Freischütz Overture; Oberon Overture; Preciosa Overture.*

Recommended Readings
(For books on Beethoven see under Part III, Section B; on Mozart, Part III, Section A.)

Bekker, Paul, *Richard Wagner.* London: J. M. Dent and Sons, Ltd., 1931.
Hadow, William H., *Richard Wagner.* London: Thornton Butterworth, Ltd., 1934.
Kirkpatrick, Ralph, *Domenico Scarlatti.* Princeton: Princeton University Press, 1953.
Newman, Ernest, *Wagner as Man and Artist.* New York: Alfred A. Knopf, Inc., 1924.
———, *The Life of Richard Wagner,* 4 vols. New York: Alfred A. Knopf, Inc., 1933–46.
Sitwell, Sacherevell, *A Background for Domenico Scarlatti.* London: Faber and Faber, Ltd., 1935.
Wellesz, Egon, *Wagner.* London: Dennis Dobson Limited, 1949.

PART IV, SECTION A

Additional Recordings

Bach, Carl P. E.: *Trio Sonatas.*
Bach, Johann S.: *Trio Sonatas* for organ; *Trio Sonata in C Minor.*
Bartók, Béla: *Sonata for Two Pianos and Percussion.*
Beethoven, Ludwig van: *Piano Sonatas No. 7, 8, 14, 17, 21, and 32; Violin Sonata No. 5; 'Cello Sonata No. 3.*

Brahms, Johannes: *Clarinet Sonatas; 'Cello Sonatas; Violin Sonatas No. 1 and 2.*

Chopin, Frédéric: *Piano Sonata No. 2,* in B-flat Minor.

Corelli, Arcangelo: *Violin Sonatas.*

Debussy, Claude: *Violin Sonata; 'Cello Sonata.*

Franck, César: *Violin Sonata.*

Handel, George F.: *Flute Sonatas; Violin Sonatas.*

Ives, Charles: *Concord Sonata.*

Kabalevsky, Dmitri: *Piano Sonata No. 3.*

Liszt, Franz: *Piano Sonata in B Minor.*

Mozart, Wolfgang A.: *Piano Sonatas; Violin Sonatas.*

Prokofiev, Serge: *Piano Sonatas; Violin Sonatas.*

Purcell, Henry: *Trio Sonatas.*

Ravel, Maurice: *Sonatine for Piano.*

Schubert, Franz: *Arpeggione Sonata; Violin Sonatas; Fantasy in C Major,* "Wanderer"; *Piano Sonatas op. 42 and 143.*

Schumann, Robert: *Fantasy in C Major; Piano Sonata in G Minor.*

Scriabin, Alexander: *Piano Sonatas.*

Tartini, Giuseppe: *Violin Sonatas.*

Vivaldi, Antonio: *'Cello Sonatas.*

Recommended Readings

(For books on Beethoven see under Part III, Section B.)

Anderson, W. R., *Brahms.* London: Dennis Dobson Limited, 1949.

Balfoart, Dirk J., *Antonius Stradivarius.* Stockholm: The Continental Book Company A. B., 1947.

Fuller-Maitland, John A., *Brahms.* London: Methuen and Company, Ltd., 1911.

Geiringer, Karl, *Brahms,* 2nd ed. New York: Oxford University Press, 1947.

Hill, W. Henry, *Antonio Stradivari, His Life and Work.* London: William E. Hill and Sons, 1902.

Latham, Peter, *Brahms.* London: J. M. Dent and Sons, Ltd., 1948.

Murdoch, William, *Brahms.* London: Rich and Cowan, 1933.

PART IV, SECTION B

Additional Recordings

Bartók, Béla: *String Quartets No. 1-6.*

Beethoven, Ludwig van: *String Quartets No. 7, 11,* and *14; Grand Septet; Serenade in D Major, op. 25.*

Bloch, Ernest: *String Quartet No. 3.*

Borodin, Alexander: *Quartet No. 1.*

Brahms, Johannes: *Clarinet Quintet; Clarinet Trio; Horn Trio; Piano Quartet in C Minor; Piano Quintet; Piano Trio in B Major.*

Chausson, Ernest: *Concerto for Violin, Piano, and String Quartet.*
Debussy, Claude: *String Quartet.*
Dvořák, Antonin: *String Quartet No. 6; Piano Quintet; Piano Trio op. 90, "Dumky."*
Fauré, Gabriel: *Piano Quartet in C Minor.*
Haydn, Joseph: *String Quartets op. 54, No. 2; 64, No. 5; 76, No. 2-4; and 77, No. 1.*
Hindemith, Paul: *String Quartets No. 1 and 2; Kleine Kammermusik, op. 24, No. 2* (woodwind quartet).
Mendelssohn, Felix: *Octet; Piano Trio in D Minor.*
Milhaud, Darius: *String Quartets No. 14 and 15.*
Mozart, Wolfgang A.: *Divertimento in E-flat Major; Oboe Quartet; String Quartets in D Minor, G Major, E-flat Major, B-flat Major, and C Major; String Quintets in C Major and G Minor.*
Ravel, Maurice: *Introduction and Allegro for Harp and Sextet; String Quartet; Piano Trio.*
Schoenberg, Arnold: *String Quartets No. 1-4; Serenade for Baritone and Septet; Verklärte Nacht* (string sextet).
Schubert, Franz: *Quartet Movement in C Minor; String Quartets in D Minor and G Major; String Quintet; Octet; Quintet in A Major* ("The Trout").
Schumann, Robert: *Piano Quartet; Piano Quintet.*
Shostakovich, Dmitri: *Piano Trio in E Minor.*
Sibelius, Jan: *String Quartet in D Minor.*
Villa-Lobos, Heitor: *String Quartet No. 6.*
Walton, William: *String Quartet in A Minor.*
Wolf, Hugo: *Italian Serenade* (string quartet).

Recommended Readings
(For books on Brahms see under Part IV, Section A; on Mozart, Part III, Section A; on Schubert, Part I, Section C.)

Kilburn, Nicholas, *Chamber Music and Its Masters.* New York: Charles Scribner's Sons, 1932.
King, Alexander H., *Chamber Music.* New York: Chanticleer Press, 1948.
Ulrich, Homer, *Chamber Music.* New York: Columbia University Press, 1948.

•

Brenet, Michel, *Haydn.* London: Oxford University Press, 1926.
Ewen, David, *Haydn, a Good Life.* New York: Henry Holt and Company, 1946.
Geiringer, Karl, *Haydn.* New York: W. W. Norton and Company, Inc., 1946.
Hughes, Rosemary, *Haydn.* London: J. M. Dent and Sons, Ltd., 1950.
Jacob, Heinrich E., *Joseph Haydn.* New York: Rinehart and Company, Inc., 1950.

PART IV, SECTION C

Additional Recordings

Bach, Carl P. E.: *Harpsichord Concerto in D Minor*.

Bach, J. Christian: *Sinfonia Concertante* (Bach, BG 504).

Bach, Johann S.: *Six Brandenburg Concertos; Violin Concertos; Concerto for Two Violins; Harpsichord Concerto in D Minor*.

Bartók, Béla: *Piano Concertos No. 2 and 3; Violin Concerto*.

Beethoven, Ludwig van: *Piano Concertos No. 3-5; Violin Concerto*.

Berg, Alban: *Violin Concerto*.

Berlioz, Hector: *Harold in Italy* (viola concerto).

Bloch, Ernest: *Schelomo* ('cello concerto); *Concerto Grosso No. 1; Violin Concerto* (Co., M 380).

Brahms, Johannes: *Double Concerto; Piano Concertos; Violin Concerto*.

Bruch, Max: *Violin Concerto No. 1*.

Chausson, Ernest: *Poème* (violin concerto).

Chopin, Frédéric: *Piano Concertos*.

Cimarosa, Domenico: *Oboe Concerto*.

Corelli, Arcangelo: *Concerti grossi*.

Couperin, François: *Concert dans le goût theatral; Concerts royaux*.

Dohnanyi, Ernst: *Variations on a Nursery Tune* (piano concerto).

Elgar, Edward: *'Cello Concerto; Violin Concerto*.

Falla, Manuel de: *Concerto for Harpsichord; Nights in the Gardens of Spain* (piano concerto).

Fauré, Gabriel: *Ballade for Piano and Orchestra*.

Françaix, Jean: *Concertino* for Piano and Orchestra.

Gershwin, George: *Piano Concerto*.

Glazounov, Alexander: *Violin Concerto; Saxophone Concerto*.

Goldmark, Karl: *Violin Concerto*.

Grieg, Edvard: *Piano Concerto*.

Haydn, Joseph: *'Cello Concerto; Horn Concerto in D Major; Trumpet Concerto in E-flat Major*.

Hindemith, Paul: *Kammermusik* (concertos for all instruments, including the viola d'amore).

Honegger, Artur: *Concertino for Piano and Orchestra*.

Ibert, Jacques: *Concertino da camera* for Saxophone.

Liszt, Franz: *Piano Concertos; Hungarian Phantasy; Totentanz* (piano concerto).

Loeffler, Charles M.: *A Pagan Poem* (piano concerto).

Mendelssohn, Felix: *Violin Concerto*.

Mozart, Wolfgang A.: *Bassoon Concerto; Horn Concertos No. 2 and 4; Piano Concertos in D Minor, A Major* (K.488), *and C Major* (K.503); *Violin Concertos No. 4 and 5; Flute-Harp Concerto; Clarinet Concerto*.

Prokofiev, Serge: *Piano Concerto No. 3; Violin Concerto No. 2*.

Rachmaninoff, Sergei: *Piano Concertos No. 2* and *3; Rhapsody on a Theme by Paganini.*
Ravel, Maurice: *Piano Concerto; Concerto for the Left Hand.*
Schumann, Robert: *Piano Concerto.*
Sibelius, Jan: *Violin Concerto.*
Tchaikovsky, Peter I.: *Piano Concerto No. 1; Violin Concerto; Rococo Variations* ('cello concerto).
Telemann, Georg P.: *Tafelmusik.*
Vivaldi, Antonio: *Bassoon Concerto* (Concert Hall, CHC 56); *Flute Concertos; Viola d'amore Concerto; Concerti grossi.*
Walton, William: *Viola Concerto; Violin Concerto.*
Williams, Ralph V.: *Oboe Concerto.*

Recommended Readings

(For books on Handel see under Part II, Section B; on Mozart, Part III, Section A.)

Culshaw, John, *The Concerto.* New York: Chanticleer Press, 1949.
Veinus, Abraham, *The Concerto.* New York: Garden City Publishing Company, Inc., 1944.

•

Andriessen, Hendrik, *César Franck.* Stockholm: The Continental Book Company A. B., 1947.
Demuth, Norman, *César Franck.* London: Dennis Dobson Limited, 1949.
Haraszti, Emil, *Béla Bartók, His Life and Works.* Paris: The Lyrebird Press, 1938.
Hoffmeister, Karel, *Antonin Dvořák.* London: John Lane The Bodley Head Limited, 1928.
d'Indy, Vincent, *César Franck.* London: John Lane The Bodley Head Limited, 1909.
Purdy, Claire L., *Antonin Dvořák.* New York: Julian Messner, Inc., 1950.
Robertson, Alec, *Dvořák.* London: J. M. Dent and Sons, Ltd., 1945.
Stefan, Paul, *Anton Dvořák.* New York:.The Greystone Press, 1941.
Stevens, Halsey, *The Life and Music of Béla Bartók.* New York: Oxford University Press, 1953.
Suermondt, R. P., *Smetana and Dvořák.* Stockholm: The Continental Book Company A. B. (1950?).
Vallas, Léon, *César Franck.* New York: Oxford University Press, 1951.

PART IV, SECTION D

Recordings Used as Examples

Example 4: American Recording Society, ARS 1 (Dean Dixon).

Additional Recordings

Bach, Carl P. E.: *Sinfonie.*

Barber, Samuel: *Symphony No. 2.*

Bartók, Béla: *Divertimento for Strings; Music for Strings, Percussion, and Celesta.*

Beethoven, Ludwig van: *Symphonies No. 5, 7,* and *9.*

Borodin, Alexander: *Symphony No. 2.*

Brahms, Johannes: *Symphonies No. 1* and *4.*

Bruckner, Anton: *Symphonies No. 4* and *7.*

Debussy, Claude: *La mer.*

Dvořák, Antonin: *Symphonies No. 4* and *5.*

Franck, César: *Symphony in D Minor.*

Haydn, Joseph: *Symphonies No. 92, 94, 99, 100, 101, 103,* and *104.*

Hindemith, Paul: *Symphony Mathis der Maler; Symphonic Metamorphosis of Themes by Weber; Symphony Harmony of the World.*

d'Indy, Vincent: *Symphony on a French Mountain Air.*

Kabalevsky, Dmitri: *Symphony No. 2.*

Mahler, Gustav: *Symphonies No. 2, 4, 5,* and *8.*

Mendelssohn, Felix: *Symphonies No. 3* (Scotch) and *4* (Italian).

Mozart, Wolfgang A.: *Symphonies No. 38-41.*

Prokofiev, Serge: *Classical Symphony; Symphony No. 5.*

Rimsky-Korsakov, Nicolai: *Sheherazade.*

Roussel, Albert: *Symphony No. 4.*

Schoenberg, Arnold: *Kammersymphonie No. 1.*

Schubert, Franz: *Symphonies No. 8* and *9.*

Schuman, William: *Symphony for Strings.*

Schumann, Robert: *Symphonies No. 1* and *4.*

Sessions, Roger: *Symphony No. 2.*

Shostakovich, Dmitri: *Symphonies No. 1* and *5.*

Sibelius, Jan: *Symphonies No. 1, 2, 4,* and *5.*

Tchaikovsky, Peter I.: *Symphonies No. 4-6.*

Toch, Ernst: *The Chinese Flute.*

Webern, Anton: *Symphony op. 21.*

Williams, Ralph V.: *London Symphony; Symphony No. 6.*

Recommended Readings

(For books on Beethoven see under Part III, Section B; on Berlioz, Part I, Section B; on Mozart, Part III, Section A.)

Ewen, David, *Dictators of the Baton,* 2nd ed. Chicago: Ziff-Davis Publishing Company, 1948.

———, *The Man with the Baton.* New York: Thomas Y. Crowell Company, 1937.

Finn, William J., *The Conductor Raises His Baton.* New York: Harper and Brothers, 1944.

INDEX AND GLOSSARY

For explanations of the following symbols see:

‖ , ‖‖ , ‖ —p. 6

⌢ , ⌣ —p. 36

- —p. 47

> , ＜ , ＞ —p. 48

𝟠 ⁻⁻⁻ , 𝟠 ----- —p. 55

⋎ , ⋀ ,⋀⋀ , tr⋀⋀⋀ —p. 101

A̱, Ḇ, C̱; a̱, ḇ, c̱; (a̱), (ḇ), (c̱)—p. 158

∿ —p. 158

⋀ (19th century)   —p. 299

A

Abduction from the Seraglio, The (Mozart), 174
Absolute intervals, *see* Intervals, absolute
A cappella, 83
Accelerando, 47
Accent, accentuation, 6, 7, 8f
Accidentals, 380f
Accompagnato, see Recitative, *accompagnato*
Adagio, 30
Additive form, *see* Form, additive
Affetto, 153
Africa, 3, 5, 8
Agnus Dei, 73, 75
Air, 110, 111f
Albeniz, Isaac (1860–1909), 22, 177, 411

Alla, 304
Alla breve, 378
Allegretto, 30
Allegro, 30
Alleluya, 33f
Allemande, 108, 404
Alternativo form, *see* Form, *alternativo*
Alto, 68, 97, 119f, 130ff, 168f, 170f
Alto clarinet, 395
Alto clef, 390
Alto oboe, *see* English horn
Amati family (16th-17th centuries), 392
America, Central, 23
America, South, 22f, 197
America, United States, 5f, 21, 23, 133, 183, 197, 399
Analysis, value, 237f, 257f, 311
Andante, 30

F